The Leonine Encyclicals

1878-1902

Pope Leo XIII

The Leonine Encyclicals
Copyright © 2014 Agnus Dei Publishing

ISBN-13: 978-0615984933
ISBN-10: 0615984932

For more information, contact:

Agnus Dei Publishing
1327 N Elm B
McPherson, KS 67460
+1 620-755-8832
info@agnusdeipublishing.com
www.agnusdeipublishing.com

Prayer to St. Michael the Archangel

Leo XIII wrote this prayer in 1886. There are various legends surrounding its origin. One account says that, after offering a Mass, the Pope appeared to be staring at something. He became unwell and retired immediately to his quarters. There he wrote penned the prayer to St. Michael the Archangel in response to his vision of a demonic hoard converging on the Eternal City. Another version tells of a conversation heard by Leo in which Satan claims he is going to destroy the Church. God responds, saying "Do what you will." Whatever the historical accuracy of these accounts, we can say with certainty that the prayer is typical of Leo's mentality. It sets the tone for his entire papacy, which was nothing less than a relentless battle for Truth on behalf of a world which had set aside the teachings of the Church and its pontiffs. May its recitation bring understanding to the reader as he proceeds through the documents that follow.

Sancte Michael Archangele,
defende nos in proelio;
contra nequitiam et insidias diaboli esto
praesidium.
Imperet illi Deus, supplices deprecamur:
tuque, Princeps militiae Caelestis,
satanam aliosque spiritus malignos,
qui ad perditionem animarum
pervagantur in mundo,
divina virtute in infernum detrude.
Amen.

Saint Michael the Archangel,
defend us in battle;
be our protection against the wickedness
and snares of the devil.
May God rebuke him, we humbly pray:
and do thou, O Prince of the heavenly
host,
by the power of God,
thrust into hell Satan and all the evil
spirits
who prowl about the world seeking the
ruin of souls.
Amen

CONTENTS

Publisher's Preface

Vincenzo Gioacchino Raffaele Luigi Pecci was born March 2, 1810, and became Pope Leo XIII on February 20, 1878. His reign was one of the longest in history, during which he produced a total of eighty-six encyclicals—a record approached by no other pope before or since. Out of this immense canon, fifteen have been collected for this volume based on their social impact and doctrinal profundity. They cover subjects such as the proper relationship between church and state, the foundations of political authority, the study of Sacred Scripture, Christian philosophy, and Catholic Social Teaching, including Pope Leo's most famous social encyclical, *Rerum Novarum*. While all papal letters are timely in their own manner, these were chosen because they are, in the opinion of the publisher, most indispensible.

Daniel Schwindt
Editor
Agnus Dei Publishing

I: Inscrutabili Dei Consilio

April 21, 1878

ON THE EVILS OF SOCIETY

When by God's unsearchable design, We, though all unworthy, were raised to the height of apostolic dignity, at once We felt Ourselves moved by an urgent desire and, as it were, necessity, to address you by letter, not merely to express to you Our very deep feeling of love, but further, in accordance with the task entrusted to Us from heaven, to strengthen you who are called to share Our solicitude, that you may help Us to carry on the battle now being waged on behalf of the Church of God and the salvation of souls.

2. For, from the very beginning of Our pontificate, the sad sight has presented itself to Us of the evils by which the human race is oppressed on every side: the widespread subversion of the primary truths on which, as on its foundations, human society is based; the obstinacy of mind that will not brook any authority however lawful; the endless sources of disagreement, whence arrive civil strife, and ruthless war and bloodshed; the contempt of law which molds characters and is the shield of righteousness; the insatiable craving for things perishable, with complete forgetfulness of things eternal, leading up to the desperate madness whereby so many wretched beings, in all directions, scruple not to lay violent hands upon themselves; the reckless mismanagement, waste, and misappropriation of the public funds; the shamelessness of those who, full of treachery, make semblance of being champions of country, of freedom, and every kind of right; in fine, the deadly kind of plague which infects in its inmost recesses, allowing it no respite and foreboding ever fresh disturbances and final disaster.[1]

---

[1] This description of what is usually called a "corrupt government" or

3. Now, the source of these evils lies chiefly, We are convinced, in this, that the holy and venerable authority of the Church, which in God's name rules mankind, upholding and defending all lawful authority, has been despised and set aside. The enemies of public order, being fully aware of this, have thought nothing better suited to destroy the foundations of society than to make an unflagging attack upon the Church of God, to bring her into discredit and odium by spreading infamous calumnies and accusing her of being opposed to genuine progress. They labor to weaken her influence and power by wounds daily inflicted, and to overthrow the authority of the Bishop of Rome, in whom the abiding and unchangeable principles of right and good find their earthly guardian and champion. From these causes have originated laws that shake the structure of the Catholic Church, the enacting whereof we have to deplore in so many lands; hence, too, have floured forth contempt of episcopal authority; the obstacles thrown in the way of the discharge of ecclesiastical duties; the dissolution of religious bodies; and the confiscation of property that was once the support of the Church's ministers and of the poor. Thereby, public institutions, vowed to charity and benevolence, have been withdrawn from the wholesome control of the Church; thence, also, has arisen that unchecked freedom to teach and spread abroad all mischievous principles, while the Church's claim to train and educate youth is in every way outraged and baffled. Such, too, is the purpose of the seizing of the temporal power, conferred many centuries ago by Divine Providence on the Bishop of Rome, that he might without let or hindrance use the authority conferred by Christ for the eternal welfare of the nations.[2]

---

the government of a "corrupt party" is, in fact, the description of what necessarily happens to any government, or ruling party, when it rejects the moral rules taught by the Church. A religious error is the main root of all social and political evils.

[2] An allusion to the capture of the Papal States by the Piedmontese army (1860) and to the usurpation of the temporal power of the Popes by King Victor Emmanuel II, in 1870.

4. We have recalled to your minds, venerable brothers, this deathly mass of ills, not to increase the sorrow naturally caused by this most sad state of things, but because we believe that from its consideration you will most plainly see how serious are the matters claiming our attention as well as devotedness, and with what energy We should work and, more than ever, under the present adverse conditions, protect, so far as in Us lies, the Church of Christ and the honor of the apostolic see - the objects of so many slanders - and assert their claims.

5. It is perfectly clear and evident, venerable brothers, that the very notion of civilization is a fiction of the brain if it rest not on the abiding principles of truth and the unchanging laws of virtue and justice, and if unfeigned love knit not together the wills of men, and gently control the interchange and the character of their mutual service. Now, who would make bold to deny that the Church, by spreading the Gospel throughout the nations, has brought the light of truth amongst people utterly savage and steeped in foul superstition, and has quickened them alike to recognize the Divine Author of nature and duly to respect themselves? Further, who will deny that the Church has done away with the curse of slavery and restored men to the original dignity of their noble nature; and - by uplifting the standard of redemption in all quarters of the globe, by introducing, or shielding under her protection, the sciences and arts, by founding and taking into her keeping excellent charitable institutions which provide relief for ills of every kind - has throughout the world, in private or in public life, civilized the human race, freed it from degradation, and with all care trained it to a way of Living such as befits the dignity and the hopes of man? And if any one of sound mind compare the age in which We live, so hostile to religion and to the Church of Christ, with those happy times when the Church was revered as a mother by the nations, beyond all question he will see that our epoch is rushing wildly along the straight road to destruction; while in those times which most abounded in excellent institutions, peaceful life, wealth, and prosperity the people showed themselves most obedient to the

Church's rule and laws. Therefore, if the many blessings We have mentioned, due to the agency and saving help of the Church, are the true and worthy outcome of civilization, the Church of Christ, far from being alien to or neglectful of progress, has a just claim to all men's praise as its nurse, its mistress, and its mother.

6. Furthermore, that kind of civilization which conflicts with the doctrines and laws of holy Church is nothing but a worthless imitation and meaningless name. Of this those peoples on whom the Gospel light has never shown afford ample proof, since in their mode of life a shadowy semblance only of civilization is discoverable, while its true and solid blessings have never been possessed. Undoubtedly, that cannot by any means be accounted the perfection of civilized life which sets all legitimate authority boldly at defiance; nor can that be regarded as liberty which, shamefully and by the vilest means, spreading false principles, and freely indulging the sensual gratification of lustful desires, claims impunity for all crime and misdemeanor, and thwarts the goodly influence of the worthiest citizens of whatsoever class. Delusive, perverse, and misleading as are these principles, they cannot possibly have any inherent power to perfect the human race and fill it with blessing, for "sin maketh nations miserable."[3] Such principles, as a matter of course, must hurry nations, corrupted in mind and heart, into every kind of infamy, weaken all right order, and thus, sooner or later, bring the standing and peace of the State to the very brink of ruin.

7. Again, if We consider the achievements of the see of Rome, what can be more wicked than to deny how much and how well the Roman bishops have served civilized society at large? For Our predecessors, to provide for the peoples' good, encountered struggles of every kind, endured to the utmost burdensome toils, and never hesitated to expose themselves to most dangerous trials. With eyes fixed on heaven, they neither bowed down their head before the threats of the wicked, nor allowed themselves to

---

[3] Prov. 14:34.

be led by flattery or bribes into unworthy compliance. This apostolic chair it was that gathered and held together the crumbling remains of the old order of things; this was the kindly light by whose help the culture of Christian times shone far and wide; this was an anchor or safety in the fierce storms by which the human race has been convulsed; this was the sacred bond of union that linked together nations distant in region and differing in character; in short, this was a common center from which was sought instruction in faith and religion, no less than guidance and advice for the maintenance of peace and the functions of practical life. In very truth it is the glory of the supreme Pontiffs that they steadfastly set themselves up as a wall and a bulwark to save human society from falling back into its former superstition and barbarism.

8. Would that this healing authority had never been slighted or set aside! Assuredly, neither would the civil power have lost that venerable and sacred glory, the lustrous gift of religion, which alone renders the state of subjection noble and worthy of man; nor would so many revolutions and wars have been fomented to ravage the world with desolation and bloodshed; nor would kingdoms, once so flourishing, but now fallen from the height of prosperity, lie crushed beneath the weight of every kind of calamity. Of this the peoples of the East also furnish an example, who, by breaking the most sweet yoke that bound them to this apostolic see, forfeited the splendor of their former greatness, their renown in science and art, and the dignity of their sway.

9. Of these remarkable benefits, however, which illustrious monuments of all ages prove to have flowed upon every quarter of the world from the apostolic see, this land of Italy has had the most abounding experience. For it has derived advantages from the see of Rome proportionate to the greater nearness of its natural situation. Unquestionably, to the Roman Pontiffs it is that Italy must own herself indebted for the substantial glory and majesty by which she has been preeminent amongst nations. The influence and fatherly care of the Popes have upon many

occasions shielded her from hostile attack and brought her relief and aid, the effect of which is that the Catholic faith has been ever maintained inviolate in the hearts of Italians.

10. These services of Our predecessors, to omit mention of many others, have been witnessed to in a special manner by the records of the times of St. Leo the Great, Alexander III, Innocent III, St. Pius V, Leo X, and other Pontiffs,[4] by whose exertions or protection Italy has escaped unscathed from the utter destruction threatened by barbarians; has kept unimpaired her old faith, and, amid the darkness and defilement of the ruder age, has cultivated and preserved in vigor the luster of science and the splendor of art. To this, furthermore, bears witness Our own fostering city, the home of the Popes, which, under their rule, reaped this special benefit, that it not only was the strong citadel of the faith, but also became the refuge of the liberal arts and the very abode of wisdom winning for itself the admiration and respect of the whole world. As these facts in all their amplitude have been handed down in historical records for the perpetual remembrance of posterity, it is easy to understand that it is only with hostile design and shameless calumny - meant to mislead men - that any one can venture in speech and in writing to accuse the apostolic see of being an obstacle to the civil progress of nations and to the prosperity of Italy.

11. Seeing, therefore, that all the hopes of Italy and of the whole world lie in the power, so beneficent to the common good and profit, wherewith the authority of the apostolic see is endowed, and in the close union which binds all the faithful of Christ to

---

[4] Pope St. Leo I, Leo the Great (440-61), caused Attila, King of the Huns, to retreat without having attacked Rome. Pope Alexander III (1159-81) fought against the German Emperor Friedrick Barbarossa, to whom he opposed the Lombard League. Pope Innocent III (1198-1216) strongly resisted the French King Philip Augustus. St. Pius V was Pope from 1566 to 1572 and during his reign occurred the naval victory over the Turks at Lepanto in 1571. Leo X (John of Medici), Pope from 1513 to 1521, presided over one of the most brilliant epochs in history: the "century of Leo X."

the Roman Pontiff, We recognize that nothing should be nearer Our heart than how to preserve safe and sound the dignity of the Roman see, and to strengthen ever more and more the union of members with the head, of the children with their father.

12. Wherefore, that We may above all things, and in every possible way, maintain the rights and freedom of this holy see, We shall never cease to strive that Our authority may meet with due deference; that obstacles may be removed which hamper the free exercise of Our ministry and that We may be restored to that condition of things in which the design of God's wisdom had long ago placed the Roman Pontiffs. We are moved to demand this restoration, venerable brethren, not by any feeling of ambition or desire of supremacy, but by the nature of Our office and by Our sacred promise confirmed on oath; and further, not only because this sovereignty is essential to protect and preserve the full liberty of the spiritual power, but also because it is an ascertained fact that, when the temporal sovereignty of the apostolic see is in question, the cause of the public good and the well-being of all human society in general are also at stake. Hence, We cannot omit, in the discharge of Our duty, which obliges Us to guard the rights of holy Church, to renew and confirm in every particular by this Our letter those declarations and protests which Pius IX,[5] of sacred memory, Our predecessor, on many and repeated occasions published against the seizing of the civil sovereignty and the infringement of rights belonging to the Catholic Church. At the same time We address ourselves to princes and chief rulers of the nations, and earnestly beseech them in the august name of the Most High God, not to refuse the Church's aid, proffered them in a season of such need, but with united and friendly aims, to join themselves to her as the source of authority and salvation, and to attach themselves to

---

[5] Pope Pius IX (1846-78) proclaimed the dogmas of the Immaculate Conception and of the infallibility of the Popes in all matters related to faith and morals; published the *Syllabus*, or conspectus of modern errors; witnessed the usurpation by Victor Emmanuel II of the temporal power of the Popes, but never acknowledged it.

her more and more in the bonds of hearty love and devotedness.
God grant that-seeing the truth of Our words and considering
within themselves that the teaching of Christ is, as Augustine
used to say, "a great blessing to the State, if obeyed,"[6] and that
their own peace and safety, as well as that of their people, is
bound up with the safety of the Church and the reverence due to
her - they may give their whole thought and care to mitigating
the evils by which the Church and its visible head are harassed,
and so it may at last come to pass that the peoples whom they
govern may enter on the way of justice and peace, and rejoice in
a happy era of prosperity and glory.

13. In the next place, in order that the union of hearts between
their chief Pastor and the whole Catholic flock may daily be
strengthened, We here call upon you, venerable brothers, with
particular earnestness, and strongly urge you to kindle, with
priestly zeal and pastoral care, the fire of the love of religion
among the faithful entrusted to you, that their attachment to this
chair of truth and justice may become closer and firmer, that they
may welcome all its teachings with thorough assent of mind and
will, wholly rejecting such opinion, even when most widely
received, as they know to be contrary to the Church's doctrine.
In this matter, the Roman Pontiffs, Our predecessors, and the
last of all, Pius IX, of sacred memory, especially in the General
Council of the Vatican, have not neglected, so often as there was
need, to condemn widespreading errors and to smite them with
the apostolic condemnation. This they did, keeping before their
eyes the words of St. Paul: "Beware lest any man cheat you by
philosophy and vain deceit, according to the tradition of men,
according to the elements of the world and not according to
Christ."[7] All such censures, We, following in the steps of Our
predecessors, do confirm and renew from this apostolic seat of
truth, whilst We earnestly ask of the Father of lights[8] that all the
faithful, brought to thorough agreement in the like feeling and

---

[6] Letter 138, to Marcellinus, 15 (PL 33, 532).
[7] Col. 2:8.
[8] James 1:17.

the same belief, may think and speak even as Ourselves. It is your duty, venerable brothers, sedulously to strive that the seed of heavenly doctrine be sown broadcast in the field of God, and that the teachings of the Catholic faith may be implanted early in the souls of the faithful, may strike deep root in them, and be kept free from the ruinous blight of error. The more the enemies of religion exert themselves to offer the uninformed, especially the young, such instruction as darkens the mind and corrupts morals, the more actively should we endeavor that not only a suitable and solid method of education may flourish but above all that this education be wholly in harmony with the Catholic faith in its literature and system of training, and chiefly in philosophy, upon which the direction of other sciences in great measure depends.[9] Philosophy seeks not the overthrow of divine revelation, but delights rather to prepare its way, and defend it against assailants, both by example and in written works, as the great Augustine and the Angelic Doctor, with all other teachers of Christian wisdom, have proved to Us.

14. Now, the training of youth most conducive to the defense of true faith and religion and to the preservation of morality must find its beginning from an early stage within the circle of home life; and this family Christian training sadly undermined in these our times, cannot possibly be restored to its due dignity, save by those laws under which it was established in the Church by her Divine Founder Himself. Our Lord Jesus Christ, by raising to the dignity of a sacrament the contract of matrimony, in which He would have His own union with the Church typified, not only made the marriage tie more holy, but, in addition, provided efficacious sources of aid for parents and children alike, so that, by the discharge of their duties one to another, they might with greater ease attain to happiness both in time and in eternity. But when impious laws, setting at naught the sanctity of this great sacrament, put it on the same footing of mere civil contracts, the lamentable result followed, that, outraging the dignity of

---

[9] This point is developed in the encyclical *Aeterni Patris.*

Christian matrimony, citizens made use of legalized concubinage in place of marriage; husband and wife neglected their bounden duty to each other; children refused obedience and reverence to their parents; the bonds of domestic love were loosened; and alas! the worst scandal and of all the most ruinous to public morality, very frequently an unholy passion opened the door to disastrous and fatal separations. These most unhappy and painful consequences, venerable brothers, cannot fail to arouse your zeal and move you constantly and earnestly to warn the faithful committed to your charge to listen with docility to your teaching regarding the holiness of Christian marriage, and to obey laws by which the Church controls the duties of married people and of their offspring.[10]

15. Then, indeed, will that most desirable result come about, that the character and conduct of individuals also will be reformed; for, just as from a rotten stock are produced healthless branches or worthless fruits, so do the ravages of a pestilence which ruins the household spread wide their cruel infection to the hurt and injury of individual citizens. On the other hand, when domestic society is fashioned in the mould of Christian life, each member will gradually grow accustomed to the love of religion and piety, to the abhorrence of false and harmful teaching, to the persuit of virtue, to obedience to elders, and to the restraint of the insatiable seeking after self interest alone, which so spoils and weakens the character of men. To this end it will certainly help not a little to encourage and promote those pious associations which have been established, in our own times especially, with so great profit to the cause of the Catholic religion.

16. Great indeed and beyond the strength of man are these objects of our hopes and prayers, venerable brothers; but, since God has "made the nations of the earth for health,"[11] when He

---

[10] This point is developed in the encyclical *Arcanum*. See also the encyclical letter of Pope Pius XI, *Divini Illius Magistri* (December 31, 1929, *On the Christian Education of Youth*).

[11] Wisd. 1:14: "For he created all things that they might be: and he

founded the Church for the welfare of the peoples, and promised that He will abide with her by His assistance to the end of the world, We firmly trust that, through your endeavors, the human race, taking warning from so many evils and visitations, will submit themselves at length to the Church, and turn for health and prosperity to the infallible guidance of this apostolic see.

17. Meanwhile, venerable brothers, before bringing this letter to a close, We must express Our congratulations on the striking harmony and concord which unites your minds among yourselves and with this apostolic see. This perfect union We regard as not merely an impregnable bulwark against hostile attacks, but also as an auspicious and happy omen, presaging better times for the Church; and, while it yields great relief to Our weakness, it seasonably encourages Us to endure with readiness all labors and all struggles on behalf of God's Church in the arduous task which We have undertaken.

18. Moreover, from the causes of hope and rejoicing which We have made known to you We cannot separate those tokens of love and obedience which you, venerable brethren, in these first days of Our pontificate, have shown Our lowliness, and with you so many of the clergy and the faithful, who by letters sent, by offerings given, by pilgrimages undertaken, and by other works of love, have made it clear that the devotion and charity which they manifested to Our most worthy predecessor still lasts, so strong and steadfast and unchanged as not to slacken toward the person of a successor so much inferior. For these splendid tokens of Catholic piety We humbly confess to the Lord that He is good and gracious, while to you, venerable brothers, and to all Our beloved children from whom We have received them, We publicly, from the bottom of Our heart, avow the grateful feelings of Our soul, cherishing the fullest confidence that, in the present critical state of things and in the difficulties of the times,

---

made the nations of the earth for health: and there is no poison of destruction in them, nor kingdom of hell upon the earth."

this your devotion and love and the devotion and love of the faithful will never fail Us. Nor have We any doubt that these conspicuous examples of filial piety and Christian virtue will be of such avail as to make Our most merciful God, moved by these dutiful deeds, look with favor on His flock and grant the Church peace and victory. But as We are sure that this peace and victory will more quickly and more readily be given Us, if the faithful are unremitting in their prayers and supplications to obtain it, We earnestly exhort you, venerable brothers, to stir up for this end the zeal and ardor of the faithful, taking the Immaculate Queen of Heaven as their intercessor with God, and having recourse as their advocates to St. Joseph, the heavenly patron of the Church, and to Sts. Peter and Paul, the Princes of the Apostles. To the powerful patronage of all these We humbly commit Our lowliness, all ranks of the ecclesiastical hierarchy, and all the flock of Christ our Lord.

19. For the rest, We trust that these days, on which We renew the memory of Jesus Christ, risen from the dead, may be to you, venerable brothers, and to all the fold of God, a source of blessing and salvation and fullness of holy joy, praying our most gracious God that by the blood of the Lamb without spot, which blotted out the handwriting that was against Us, the sins We have committed may be washed away, and the judgment We are suffering for them may mercifully be mitigated.

"The grace of our Lord Jesus Christ, and the Charity of God, and the communication of the Holy Spirit be with you all,"[12] venerable brothers; to each and all of whom, as well as to Our beloved children, the clergy and faithful of your churches, as a pledge of Our special good-will and as an earnest of the protection of heaven, We lovingly impart the apostolic benediction.

---

[12] 2 Cor. 13:13.

Given at St. Peter's, in Rome, on the solemnity of Easter, the twenty-first day of April, 1878, in the first year of our pontificate.

II: Aeterni Patris

August 4, 1879

ON THE RESTORATION OF CHRISTIAN PHILOSOPHY

The only-begotten Son of the Eternal Father, who came on earth to bring salvation and the light of divine wisdom to men, conferred a great and wonderful blessing on the world when, about to ascend again into heaven, He commanded the Apostles to go and teach all nations,[1] and left the Church which He had founded to be the common and supreme teacher of the peoples. For men whom the truth had set free were to be preserved by the truth; nor would the fruits of heavenly doctrines by which salvation comes to men have long remained had not the Lord Christ appointed an unfailing teaching authority to train the minds to faith. And the Church built upon the promises of its own divine Author, whose charity it imitated, so faithfully followed out His commands that its constant aim and chief wish was this: to teach religion and contend forever against errors. To this end assuredly have tended the incessant labors of individual bishops; to this end also the published laws and decrees of councils, and especially the constant watchfulness of the Roman Pontiffs, to whom, as successors of the blessed Peter in the primacy of the Apostles, belongs the right and office of teaching and confirming their brethren in the faith. Since, then, according to the warning of the apostle, the minds of Christ's faithful are apt to be deceived and the integrity of the faith to be corrupted among men by philosophy and vain deceit,[2] the supreme pastors of the Church have always thought it their duty to advance, by every means in their power, science truly so called, and at the same time to provide with special care that all studies should accord with the Catholic faith, especially philosophy, on which a

---

[1] Matt.28:19.
[2] Col. 2:8.

right interpretation of the other sciences in great part depends. Indeed, venerable brethren, on this very subject among others, We briefly admonished you in Our first encyclical letter; but now, both by reason of the gravity of the subject and the condition of the time, we are again compelled to speak to you on the mode of taking up the study of philosophy which shall respond most fitly to the excellence of faith, and at the same time be consonant with the dignity of human science.

2. Whoso turns his attention to the bitter strifes of these days and seeks a reason for the troubles that vex public and private life must come to the conclusion that a fruitful cause of the evils which now afflict, as well as those which threaten, us lies in this: that false conclusions concerning divine and human things, which originated in the schools of philosophy, have now crept into all the orders of the State, and have been accepted by the common consent of the masses. For, since it is in the very nature of man to follow the guide of reason in his actions, if his intellect sins at all his will soon follows; and thus it happens that false opinions, whose seat is in the understanding, influence human actions and pervert them. Whereas, on the other hand, if men be of sound mind and take their stand on true and solid principles, there will result a vast amount of benefits for the public and private good. We do not, indeed, attribute such force and authority to philosophy as to esteem it equal to the task of combating and rooting out all errors; for, when the Christian religion was first constituted, it came upon earth to restore it to its primeval dignity by the admirable light of faith, diffused "not by persuasive words of human wisdom, but in the manifestation of spirit and of power",[3] so also at the present time we look above all things to the powerful help of Almighty God to bring back to a right understanding the minds of man and dispel the darkness of error.[4] But the natural helps with which the grace of the divine wisdom, strongly and sweetly disposing all things, has

---

[3] 1 Cor. 2:4.
[4] See Inscrutabili Dei consilio, 78:113.

supplied the human race are neither to be despised nor neglected, chief among which is evidently the right use of philosophy. For, not in vain did God set the light of reason in the human mind; and so far is the super-added light of faith from extinguishing or lessening the power of the intelligence that it completes it rather, and by adding to its strength renders it capable of greater things.

3. Therefore, Divine Providence itself requires that, in calling back the people to the paths of faith and salvation, advantage should be taken of human science also-an approved and wise practice which history testifies was observed by the most illustrious Fathers of the Church. They, indeed, were wont neither to belittle nor undervalue the part that reason had to play, as is summed up by the great Augustine when he attributes to this science "that by which the most wholesome faith is begotten . . . is nourished, defended, and made strong."[5]

4. In the first place, philosophy, if rightly made use of by the wise, in a certain way tends to smooth and fortify the road to true faith, and to prepare the souls of its disciples for the fit reception of revelation; for which reason it is well called by ancient writers sometimes a steppingstone to the Christian faith,[6] sometimes the prelude and help of Christianity,[7] sometimes the Gospel teacher.[8] And, assuredly, the God of all goodness, in all that pertains to divine things, has not only manifested by the light of faith those truths which human intelligence could not attain of itself, but others, also, not altogether unattainable by reason, that by the help of divine authority they may be made known to all at once and without any admixture of error. Hence it is that certain truths which were either divinely proposed for belief, or were bound by the closest chains to the doctrine of

---

[5] De Trinitate, 14, 1, 3 (PL 42, 1037); quoted by Thomas Aquinas, Summa theologiae, 1, 1, 2.

[6] Clement of Alexandria, Stromata, 1, 16 (PG 8, 795); 7, 3 (PG 9, 426).

[7] Origen, Epistola ad Gregorium (PG 11, 87-91).

[8] Clement of Alexandria, Stromata, 1,5 (PG 8, 718-719).

faith, were discovered by pagan sages with nothing but their
natural reason to guide them, were demonstrated and proved by
becoming arguments. For, as the Apostle says, the invisible
things of Him, from the creation of the world, are clearly seen,
being understood by the things that are made: His eternal power
also and divinity;[9] and the Gentiles who have not the Law show,
nevertheless, the work of the Law written in their hearts.[10] But it
is most fitting to turn these truths, which have been discovered
by the pagan sages even, to the use and purposes of revealed
doctrine, in order to show that both human wisdom and the very
testimony of our adversaries serve to support the Christian faith-
a method which is not of recent introduction, but of established
use, and has often been adopted by the holy Fathers of the
Church. What is more, those venerable men, the witnesses and
guardians of religious traditions, recognize a certain form and
figure of this in the action of the Hebrews, who, when about to
depart out of Egypt, were commanded to take with them the
gold and silver vessels and precious robes of the Egyptians, that
by a change of use the things might be dedicated to the service of
the true God which had formerly been the instruments of
ignoble and superstitious rites. Gregory of NeoCaesarea[11] praises
Origen expressly because, with singular dexterity, as one snatches
weapons from the enemy, he turned to the defense of Christian
wisdom and to the destruction of superstition many arguments
drawn from the writings of the pagans. And both Gregory of
Nazianzen[12] and Gregory of Nyssa[13] praise and commend a like
mode of disputation in Basil the Great; while Jerome[14] especially
commends it in Quadratus, a disciple of the Apostles, in
Aristides, Justin, Irenaeus, and very many others. Augustine says:

---

[9] Rom. 1:20.
[10] Rom. 2:14-15.
[11] Gregory of Neo-Caesarea (also called Gregory Thaumaturgus that is "the miracle worker"), In Origenem oratio panegyrica, 6 (PG 10, 1093A).
[12] Carm., 1, Iamb. 3 (PG 37, 1045A-1047A).
[13] Vita Moysis (PG 44, 359).
[14] Epistola ad Magnum, 4 (PL 22, 667). Quadratus, Justin Irenaeus, are counted among the early Christian apologists, who devoted their works to the defence of Christian truth against the pagans.

"Do we not see Cyprian, that mildest of doctors and most blessed of martyrs, going out of Egypt laden with gold and silver and vestments? And Lactantius, also and Victorinus, Optatus and Hilary? And, not to speak of the living, how many Greeks have done likewise?"[15] But if natural reason first sowed this rich field of doctrine before it was rendered fruitful by the power of Christ, it must assuredly become more prolific after the grace of the Saviour has renewed and added to the native faculties of the human mind. And who does not see that a plain and easy road is opened up to faith by such a method of philosophic study?

5. But the advantage to be derived from such a school of philosophy is not to be confined within these limits. The foolishness of those men who "by these good things that are seen could not understand Him, that is, neither by attending to the works could have acknowledged who was the workman,"[16] is gravely reproved in the words of Divine Wisdom. In the first place, then, this great and noble fruit is gathered from human reason, that it demonstrates that God is; for the greatness of the beauty and of the creature the Creator of them may be seen so as to be known thereby.[17] Again, it shows God to excel in the height of all perfections, especially in infinite wisdom before which nothing lies hidden, and in absolute justice which no depraved affection could possibly shake; and that God, therefore, is not only true but truth itself, which can neither deceive nor be deceived. Whence it clearly follows that human reason finds the fullest faith and authority united in the word of God. In like manner, reason declares that the doctrine of the Gospel has even from its very beginning been made manifest by certain wonderful signs, the established proofs, as it were, of unshaken truth; and that all, therefore, who set faith in the Gospel do not believe rashly as though following cunningly devised fables,[18] but, by a most reasonable consent, subject their intelligence and judgment

---

[15] De doctrina christiana, 1, 2, 40 (PL 34, 63).
[16] Wisd. 13:1.
[17] Wisd. 13:5.
[18] 2 Peter 1:16.

to an authority which is divine. And of no less importance is it that reason most clearly sets forth that the Church instituted by Christ (as laid down in the Vatican Council), on account of its wonderful spread, its marvellous sanctity, and its inexhaustible fecundity in all places, as well as of its Catholic unity and unshaken stability, is in itself a great and perpetual motive of belief and an irrefragable testimony of its own divine mission.[19]

6. Its solid foundations having been thus laid, a perpetual and varied service is further required of philosophy, in order that sacred theology may receive and assume the nature, form, and genius of a true science. For in this, the most noble of studies, it is of the greatest necessity to bind together, as it were, in one body the many and various parts of the heavenly doctrines, that, each being allotted to its own proper place and derived from its own proper principles, the whole may join together in a complete union; in order, in fine, that all and each part may be strengthened by its own and the others' invincible arguments. Nor is that more accurate or fuller knowledge of the things that are believed, and somewhat more lucid understanding, as far as it can go, of the very mysteries of faith which Augustine and the other fathers commended and strove to reach, and which the Vatican Council itself[20] declared to be most fruitful, to be passed over in silence or belittled. Those will certainly more fully and more easily attain that knowledge and understanding who to integrity of life and love of faith join a mind rounded and finished by philosophic studies, as the same Vatican Council teaches that the knowledge of such sacred dogmas ought to be sought as well from analogy of the things that are naturally known as from the connection of those mysteries one with another and with the final end of man.[21]

---

[19] Const. Dogm, de Fid. Cath., c.3.
[20] Const. cit., c.4.
[21] Loc. cit.

7. Lastly, the duty of religiously defending the truths divinely delivered, and of resisting those who dare oppose them, pertains to philosophic pursuits. Wherefore, it is the glory of philosophy to be esteemed as the bulwark of faith and the strong defense of religion. As Clement of Alexandria testifies, the doctrine of the Saviour is indeed perfect in itself and wanteth naught, since it is the power and wisdom of God. And the assistance of the Greek philosophy maketh not the truth more powerful; but, inasmuch as it weakens the contrary arguments of the sophists and repels the veiled attacks against the truth, it has been fitly called the hedge and fence of the vine.[22] For, as the enemies of the Catholic name, when about to attack religion, are in the habit of borrowing their weapons from the arguments of philosophers, so the defenders of sacred science draw many arguments from the store of philosophy which may serve to uphold revealed dogmas. Nor is the triumph of the Christian faith a small one in using human reason to repel powerfully and speedily the attacks of its adversaries by the hostile arms which human reason itself supplied. This species of religious strife St. Jerome, writing to Magnus, notices as having been adopted by the Apostle of the Gentiles himself; Paul, the leader of the Christian army and the invincible orator, battling for the cause of Christ, skillfully turns even a chance inscription into an argument for the faith; for he had learned from the true David to wrest the sword from the hands of the enemy and to cut off the head of the boastful Goliath with his own weapon.[23] Moreover, the Church herself not only urges, but even commands, Christian teachers to seek help from philosophy. For, the fifth Lateran Council, after it had decided that "every assertion contrary to the truth of revealed faith is altogether false, for the reason that it contradicts, however slightly, the truth,"[24] advises teachers of philosophy to pay close attention to the exposition of fallacious arguments; since, as Augustine testifies, "if reason is turned against the

---

[22] Stromata, l, 20 (PG 8, 818).

[23] Epistola ad Magnum, 2 (PL 22, 666).

[24] Bulla Apostolici regiminis.

authority of sacred Scripture, no matter how specious it may seem, it errs in the likeness of truth; for true it cannot be."[25]

8. But in order that philosophy may be bound equal to the gathering of those precious fruits which we have indicated, it behooves it above all things never to turn aside from that path which the Fathers have entered upon from a venerable antiquity, and which the Vatican Council solemnly and authoritatively approved. As it is evident that very many truths of the supernatural order which are far beyond the reach of the keenest intellect must be accepted, human reason, conscious of its own infirmity, dare not affect to itself too great powers, nor deny those truths, nor measure them by its own standard, nor interpret them at will; but receive them, rather, with a full and humble faith, and esteem it the highest honor to be allowed to wait upon heavenly doctrines like a handmaid and attendant, and by God's goodness attain to them in any way whatsoever. But in the case of such doctrines as the human intelligence may perceive, it is equally just that philosophy should make use of its own method, principles, and arguments-not, indeed, in such fashion as to seem rashly to withdraw from the divine authority. But, since it is established that those things which become known by revelation have the force of certain truth, and that those things which war against faith war equally against right reason, the Catholic philosopher will know that he violates at once faith and the laws of reason if he accepts any conclusion which he understands to be opposed to revealed doctrine.

9. We know that there are some who, in their overestimate of the human faculties, maintain that as soon as man's intellect becomes subject to divine authority it falls from its native dignity, and hampered by the yoke of this species of slavery, is much retarded and hindered in its progress toward the supreme truth and excellence. Such an idea is most false and deceptive, and its sole tendency is to induce foolish and ungrateful men wilfully to

---

[25] Epistola 147, ad Marcellinum, 7 (PL 33, 589).

repudiate the most sublime truths, and reject the divine gift of faith, from which the fountains of all good things flow out upon civil society. For the human mind, being confined within certain limits, and those narrow enough, is exposed to many errors and is ignorant of many things; whereas the Christian faith, reposing on the authority of God, is the unfailing mistress of truth, whom whoso followeth he will be neither enmeshed in the snares of error nor tossed hither and thither on the waves of fluctuating opinion. Those, therefore, who to the study of philosophy unite obedience to the Christian faith, are philosophizing in the best possible way; for the splendor of the divine truths, received into the mind, helps the understanding, and not only detracts in nowise from its dignity, but adds greatly to its nobility, keenness, and stability. For surely that is a worthy and most useful exercise of reason when men give their minds to disproving those things which are repugnant to faith and proving the things which conform to faith. In the first case they cut the ground from under the feet of error and expose the viciousness of the arguments on which error rests; while in the second case they make themselves masters of weighty reasons for the sound demonstration of truth and the satisfactory instruction of any reasonable person. Whoever denies that such study and practice tend to add to the resources and expand the faculties of the mind must necessarily and absurdly hold that the mind gains nothing from discriminating between the true and the false. Justly, therefore, does the Vatican Council commemorate in these words the great benefits which faith has conferred upon reason: Faith *frees* and saves reason *from error, and* endows it with*manifold* knowledge.[26] A wise man, therefore, would not accuse faith and look upon it as opposed to reason and natural truths, but would rather offer heartfelt thanks to God, and sincerely rejoice that, in the density of ignorance and in the flood-tide of error, holy faith, like a friendly star, shines down upon his path and points out to him the fair gate of truth beyond all danger of wandering.

---

[26] Const. Dogm. de Fid. Cath., c.4.

10. If, venerable brethren, you open the history of philosophy, you will find all We have just said proved by experience. The philosophers of old who lacked the gift of faith, yet were esteemed so wise, fell into many appalling errors. You know how often among some truths they taught false and incongruous things; what vague and doubtful opinions they held concerning the nature of the Divinity, the first origin of things, the government of the world, the divine knowledge of the future, the cause and principle of evil, the ultimate end of man, the eternal beatitude, concerning virtue and vice, and other matters, a true and certain knowledge of which is most necessary to the human race; while, on the other hand, the early Fathers and Doctors of the Church, who well understood that, according to the divine plan, the restorer of human science is Christ, who is the power and the wisdom of God,[27] and in whom are hid all the treasures of wisdom and knowledge,[28] took up and investigated the books of the ancient philosophers, and compared their teachings with the doctrines of revelation, and, carefully sifting them, they cherished what was true and wise in them and amended or rejected all else. For, as the all-seeing God against the cruelty of tyrants raised up mighty martyrs to the defense of the Church, men prodigal of their great lives, in like manner to false philosophers and heretics He opposed men of great wisdom, to defend, even by the aid of human reason, the treasure of revealed truths. Thus, from the very first ages of the Church, the Catholic doctrine has encountered a multitude of most bitter adversaries, who, deriding the Christian dogmas and institutions, maintained that there were many gods, that the material world never had a beginning or cause, and that the course of events was one of blind and fatal necessity, not regulated by the will of Divine Providence.

11. But the learned men whom We call apologists speedily encountered these teachers of foolish doctrine and, under the

---

[27] 1 Cor. 1:24.
[28] Col. 2:3.

guidance of faith, found arguments in human wisdom also to prove that one God, who stands pre-eminent in every kind of perfection, is to be worshiped; that all things were created from nothing by His omnipotent power; that by His wisdom they flourish and serve each their own special purposes. Among these St. Justin Martyr claims the chief place.

After having tried the most celebrated academies of the Greeks, he saw clearly, as he himself confesses, that he could only draw truths in their fullness from the doctrine of revelation. These he embraced with all the ardor of his soul, purged of calumny, courageously and fully defended before the Roman emperors, and reconciled with them not a few of the sayings of the Greek philosophers.

12. Quadratus, also, and Aristides, Hermias, and Athenagoras stood nobly forth in that time. Nor did Irenaeus, the invincible martyr and Bishop of Lyons, win less glory in the same cause when, forcibly refuting the perverse opinions of the Orientals, the work of the Gnostics, scattered broadcast over the territories of the Roman Empire, he explained (according to Jerome) the origin of each heresy and in what philosophic source it took its rise.[29] But who knows not the disputations of Clement of Alexandria, which the same Jerome thus honorably commemorates: "What is there in them that is not learned, and what that is not of the very heart of philosophy?"[30] He himself, indeed, with marvellous versatility treated of many things of the greatest utility for preparing a history of philosophy, for the exercise of the dialectic art, and for showing the agreement between reason and faith. After him came Origen, who graced the chair of the school of Alexandria, and was most learned in the teachings of the Greeks and Orientals. He published many volumes, involving great labor, which were wonderfully adapted to explain the divine writings and illustrate the sacred dogmas;

---

[29] Epistola ad Magnum, 4 (PL 22, 667).
[30] Loc. cit.

which, though, as they now stand, not altogether free from error, contain nevertheless a wealth of knowledge tending to the growth and advance of natural truths. Tertullian opposes heretics with the authority of the sacred writings; with the philosophers he changes his fence and disputes philosophically; but so learnedly and accurately did he confute them that he made bold to say: "Neither in science nor in schooling are we equals, as you imagine."[31] Arnobius, also, in his works against the pagans, and Lactantius in the divine Institutions especially, with equal eloquence and strength strenuously strive to move men to accept the dogmas and precepts of Catholic wisdom, not by philosophic juggling, after the fashion of the Academicians, but vanquishing them partly by their own arms, and partly by arguments drawn from the mutual contentions of the philosophers.[32] But the writings on the human soul, the divine attributes, and other questions of mighty moment which the great Athanasius and Chrysostom, the prince of orators, have left behind them are, by common consent, so supremely excellent that it seems scarcely anything could be added to their subtlety and fulness. And, not to cover too wide a range, we add to the number of the great men of whom mention has been made the names of Basil the Great and of the two Gregories, who, on going forth from Athens, that home of all learning, thoroughly equipped with all the harness of philosophy, turned the wealth of knowledge which each had gathered up in a course of zealous study to the work of refuting heretics and preparing Christians.

13. But Augustine would seem to have wrested the palm from all. Of a most powerful genius and thoroughly saturated with sacred and profane learning, with the loftiest faith and with equal knowledge, he combated most vigorously all the errors of his age. What topic of philosophy did he not investigate? What region of it did he not diligently explore, either in expounding the loftiest mysteries of the faith to the faithful, or defending

---

[31] Tertullian, Apologet., 46 (PL 1, 573).
[32] Lactantius, Div. Inst., 7, 7 (PL 6, 759).

them against the full onslaught of adversaries, or again when, in demolishing the fables of the Academicians or the Manichaeans, he laid the safe foundations and sure structure of human science, or followed up the reason, origin, and causes of the evils that afflict man? How subtly he reasoned on the angels, the soul, the human mind, the will and free choice, on religion and the life of the blessed, on time and eternity, and even on the very nature of changeable bodies. Afterwards, in the East, John Damascene, treading in the footsteps of Basil and of Gregory of Nazianzen, and in the West, Boethius and Anselm following the doctrines of Augustine, added largely to the patrimony of philosophy.

14. Later on, the doctors of the middle ages, who are called Scholastics, addressed themselves to a great work-that of diligently collecting, and sifting, and storing up, as it were, in one place, for the use and convenience of posterity the rich and fertile harvests of Christian learning scattered abroad in the voluminous works of the holy Fathers. And with regard, venerable brethren, to the origin, drift, and excellence of this scholastic learning, it may be well here to speak more fully in the words of one of the wisest of Our predecessors, Sixtus V: "By the divine favor of Him who alone gives the spirit of science wisdom, and understanding, and who thou ages, as there may be need, enriches His Church with new blessings and strengthens it with safeguards, there was founded by Our fathers, men of eminent wisdom, the scholastic theology, which two glorious doctors in particular angelic St. Thomas and the seraphic St. Bonaventure, illustrious teachers of this faculty, . . .with surpassing genius, by unwearied diligence, and at the cost of long labors and vigils, set in order and beautified, and when skilfuly arranged and clearly explained in a variety of ways, handed down to posterity.

15. "And, indeed, the knowledge and use of so salutary a science, which flows from the fertilizing founts of the sacred writings, the sovereign Pontiffs, the holy Fathers and the councils, must always be of the greatest assistance to the Church, whether with

the view of really and soundly understanding and interpreting the Scriptures, or more safely and to better purpose reading and explaining the Fathers, or for exposing and refuting the various errors and heresies; and in these late days, when those dangerous times described by the Apostle are already upon us, when the blasphemers, the proud, and the seducers go from bad to worse, erring themselves and causing others to err, there is surely a very great need of confirming the dogmas of Catholic faith and confuting heresies."

16. Although these words seem to bear reference solely to Scholastic theology, nevertheless they may plainly be accepted as equally true of philosophy and its praises. For, the noble endowments which make the Scholastic theology so formidable to the enemies of truth-to wit, as the same Pontiff adds, "that ready and close coherence of cause and effect, that order and array as of a disciplined army in battle, those clear definitions and distinctions, that strength of argument and those keen discussions, by which light is distinguished from darkness, the true from the false, expose and strip naked, as it were, the falsehoods of heretics wrapped around by a cloud of subterfuges and fallacies"[33] - those noble and admirable endowments, We say, are only to be found in a right use of that philosophy which the Scholastic teachers have been accustomed carefully and prudently to make use of even in theological disputations. Moreover, since it is the proper and special office of the Scholastic theologians to bind together by the fastest chain human and divine science, surely the theology in which they excelled would not have gained such honor and commendation among men if they had made use of a lame and imperfect or vain philosophy.

17. Among the Scholastic Doctors, the chief and master of all towers Thomas Aquinas, who, as Cajetan observes, because "he most venerated the ancient doctors of the Church, in a certain

---

[33] Bulla Triumphantis, an. 1588.

way seems to have inherited the intellect of all."[34] The doctrines of those illustrious men, like the scattered members of a body, Thomas collected together and cemented, distributed in wonderful order, and so increased with important additions that he is rightly and deservedly esteemed the special bulwark and glory of the Catholic faith. With his spirit at once humble and swift, his memory ready and tenacious, his life spotless throughout, a lover of truth for its own sake, richly endowed with human and divine science, like the sun he heated the world with the warmth of his virtues and filled it with the splendor of his teaching. Philosophy has no part which he did not touch finely at once and thoroughly; on the laws of reasoning, on God and incorporeal substances, on man and other sensible things, on human actions and their principles, he reasoned in such a manner that in him there is wanting neither a full array of questions, nor an apt disposal of the various parts, nor the best method of proceeding, nor soundness of principles or strength of argument, nor clearness and elegance of style, nor a facility for explaining what is abstruse.

18. Moreover, the Angelic Doctor pushed his philosophic inquiry into the reasons and principles of things, which because they are most comprehensive and contain in their bosom, so to say, the seeds of almost infinite truths, were to be unfolded in good time by later masters and with a goodly yield. And as he also used this philosophic method in the refutation of error, he won this title to distinction for himself: that, single-handed, he victoriously combated the errors of former times, and supplied invincible arms to put those to rout which might in after-times spring up. Again, clearly distinguishing, as is fitting, reason from faith, while happily associating the one with the other, he both preserved the rights and had regard for the dignity of each; so much so, indeed, that reason, borne on the wings of Thomas to its human height, can scarcely rise higher, while faith could scarcely expect more or

---

[34] Cajetan's commentary on Sum. theol., IIa-IIae 148, 9. Art. 4; Leonine edit., Vol. 10, p. 174, n.6.

stronger aids from reason than those which she has already obtained through Thomas.

19. For these reasons most learned men, in former ages especially, of the highest repute in theology and philosophy, after mastering with infinite pains the immortal works of Thomas, gave themselves up not so much to be instructed in his angelic wisdom as to be nourished upon it. It is known that nearly all the founders and lawgivers of the religious orders commanded their members to study and religiously adhere to the teachings of St. Thomas, fearful least any of them should swerve even in the slightest degree from the footsteps of so great a man. To say nothing of the family of St. Dominic, which rightly claims this great teacher for its own glory, the statutes of the Benedictines, the Carmelites, the Augustinians, the Society of Jesus, and many others all testify that they are bound by this law.

20. And, here, how pleasantly one's thoughts fly back to those celebrated schools and universities which flourished of old in Europe - to Paris, Salamanca, Alcalá, to Douay, Toulouse, and Louvain, to Padua and Bologna, to Naples and Coimbra, and to many another! All know how the fame of these seats of learning grew with their years, and that their judgment, often asked in matters of grave moment, held great weight everywhere. And we know how in those great homes of human wisdom, as in his own kingdom, Thomas reigned supreme; and that the minds of all, of teachers as well as of taught, rested in wonderful harmony under the shield and authority of the Angelic Doctor.

21. But, furthermore, Our predecessors in the Roman pontificate have celebrated the wisdom of Thomas Aquinas by exceptional tributes of praise and the most ample testimonials. Clement VI in the bull In *Ordine;* Nicholas V in his brief to the friars of the Order of Preachers, 1451; Benedict XIII in the bull *Pretiosus,* and others bear witness that the universal Church borrows lustre from his admirable teaching; while St. Pius V declares in the bull *Mirabilis* that heresies, confounded and convicted by the same

teaching, were dissipated, and the whole world daily freed from fatal errors; others, such as Clement XII in the bull *Verbo Dei*, affirm that most fruitful blessings have spread abroad from his writings over the whole Church, and that he is worthy of the honor which is bestowed on the greatest Doctors of the Church, on Gregory and Ambrose, Augustine and Jerome; while others have not hesitated to propose St. Thomas for the exemplar and master of the universities and great centers of learning whom they may follow with unfaltering feet. On which point the words of Blessed Urban V to the University of Toulouse are worthy of recall: "It is our will, which We hereby enjoin upon you, that ye follow the teaching of Blessed Thomas as the true and Catholic doctrine and that ye labor with all your force to profit by the same."[35] Innocent XII, followed the example of Urban in the case of the University of Louvain, in the letter in the form of a brief addressed to that university on February 6, 1694, and Benedict XIV in the letter in the form of a brief addressed on August 26, 1752, to the Dionysian College in Granada; while to these judgments of great Pontiffs on Thomas Aquinas comes the crowning testimony of Innocent VI: "His teaching above that of others, the canonical writings alone excepted, enjoys such a precision of language, an order of matters, a truth of conclusions, that those who hold to it are never found swerving from the path of truth, and he who dare assail it will always be suspected of error."[36]

22. The ecumenical councils, also, where blossoms the flower of all earthly wisdom, have always been careful to hold Thomas Aquinas in singular honor. In the Councils of Lyons, Vienna, Florence, and the Vatican one might almost say that Thomas took part and presided over the deliberations and decrees of the Fathers, contending against the errors of the Greeks, of heretics and rationalists, with invincible force and with the happiest results. But the chief and special glory of Thomas, one which he

---

[35] Constitutio 5a, data die 3 Aug. 1368, ad Cancell. Univ. Tolos.
[36] Sermo de S. Thoma.

has shared with none of the Catholic Doctors, is that the Fathers of Trent made it part of the order of conclave to lay upon the altar, together with sacred Scripture and the decrees of the supreme Pontiffs, the Summa of Thomas Aquinas, whence to seek counsel, reason, and inspiration.

23. A last triumph was reserved for this incomparable man-namely, to compel the homage, praise, and admiration of even the very enemies of the Catholic name. For it has come to light that there were not lacking among the leaders of heretical sects some who openly declared that, if the teaching of Thomas Aquinas were only taken away, they could easily battle with all Catholic teachers, gain the victory, and abolish the Church.[37] A vain hope, indeed, but no vain testimony.

24. Therefore, venerable brethren, as often as We contemplate the good, the force, and the singular advantages to be derived from his philosophic discipline which Our Fathers so dearly loved. We think it hazardous that its special honor should not always and everywhere remain, especially when it is established that daily experience, and the judgment of the greatest men, and, to crown all, the voice of the Church, have favored the Scholastic philosophy. Moreover, to the old teaching a novel system of philosophy has succeeded here and there, in which We fail to perceive those desirable and wholesome fruits which the Church and civil society itself would prefer. For it pleased the struggling innovators of the sixteenth century to philosophize without any respect for faith, the power of inventing in accordance with his own pleasure and bent being asked and given in turn by each one. Hence, it was natural that systems of philosophy multiplied beyond measure, and conclusions differing and clashing one with another arose about those matters even which are the most important in human knowledge. From a mass of conclusions men often come to wavering and doubt; and who knows not how easily the mind slips from doubt to error? But, as men are

---

[37] Bucer.

apt to follow the lead given them, this new pursuit seems to have caught the souls of certain Catholic philosophers, who, throwing aside the patrimony of ancient wisdom, chose rather to build up a new edifice than to strengthen and complete the old by aid of the new-ill-advisedly, in sooth, and not without detriment to the sciences. For, a multiform system of this kind, which depends on the authority and choice of any professor, has a foundation open to change, and consequently gives us a philosophy not firm, and stable, and robust like that of old, but tottering and feeble. And if, perchance, it sometimes finds itself scarcely equal to sustain the shock of its foes, it should recognize that the cause and the blame lie in itself. In saying this We have no intention of discountenancing the learned and able men who bring their industry and erudition, and, what is more, the wealth of new discoveries, to the service of philosophy; for, of course, We understand that this tends to the development of learning. But one should be very careful lest all or his chief labor be exhausted in these pursuits and in mere erudition. And the same thing is true of sacred theology, which, indeed, may be assisted and illustrated by all kinds of erudition, though it is absolutely necessary to approach it in the grave manner of the Scholastics, in order that, the forces of revelation and reason being united in it, it may continue to be "the invincible bulwark of the faith."[38]

25. With wise forethought, therefore, not a few of the advocates of philosophic studies, when turning their minds recently to the practical reform of philosophy, aimed and aim at restoring the renowned teaching of Thomas Aquinas and winning it back to its ancient beauty.

26. We have learned with great joy that many members of your order, venerable brethren, have taken this plan to heart; and while We earnestly commend their efforts, We exhort them to hold fast to their purpose, and remind each and all of you that Our first and most cherished idea is that you should all furnish to

---

[38] Sixtus V, Bulla Triumphantis.

studious youth a generous and copious supply of those purest
streams of wisdom flowing inexhaustibly from the precious
fountainhead of the Angelic Doctor.

27. Many are the reasons why We are so desirous of this. In the
first place, then, since in the tempest that is on us the Christian
faith is being constantly assailed by the machinations and craft of
a certain false wisdom, all youths, but especially those who are
the growing hope of the Church, should be nourished on the
strong and robust food of doctrine, that so, mighty in strength
and armed at all points, they may become habituated to advance
the cause of religion with force and judgment, "being ready
always, according to the apostolic counsel, to satisfy every one
that asketh you a reason of that hope which is in you,"[39] and that
they may be able to exhort in sound doctrine and to convince the
gainsayers."[40] Many of those who, with minds alienated from the
faith, hate Catholic institutions, claim reason as their sole
mistress and guide. Now, We think that, apart from the
supernatural help of God, nothing is better calculated to heal
those minds and to bring them into favor with the Catholic faith
than the solid doctrine of the Fathers and the Scholastics, who so
clearly and forcibly demonstrate the firm foundations of the
faith, its divine origin, its certain truth, the arguments that sustain
it, the benefits it has conferred on the human race, and its perfect
accord with reason, in a manner to satisfy completely minds
open to persuasion, however unwilling and repugnant.

28. Domestic and civil society even, which, as all see, is exposed
to great danger from this plague of perverse opinions, would
certainly enjoy a far more peaceful and secure existence if a more
wholesome doctrine were taught in the universities and high
schools-one more in conformity with the teaching of the Church,
such as is contained in the works of Thomas Aquinas.

---

[39] 1 Peter 3:15.
[40] Titus 1:9.

29. For, the teachings of Thomas on the true meaning of liberty, which at this time is running into license, on the divine origin of all authority, on laws and their force, on the paternal and just rule of princes, on obedience to the higher powers, on mutual charity one toward another-on all of these and kindred subjects-have very great and invincible force to overturn those principles of the new order which are well known to be dangerous to the peaceful order of things and to public safety. In short, all studies ought to find hope of advancement and promise of assistance in this restoration of philosophic discipline which We have proposed. The arts were wont to draw from philosophy, as from a wise mistress, sound judgment and right method, and from it, also, their spirit, as from the common fount of life. When philosophy stood stainless in honor and wise in judgment, then, as facts and constant experience showed, the liberal arts flourished as never before or since; but, neglected and almost blotted out, they lay prone, since philosophy began to lean to error and join hands with folly. Nor will the physical sciences themselves, which are now in such great repute, and by the renown of so many inventions draw such universal admiration to themselves, suffer detriment, but find very great assistance in the restoration of the ancient philosophy. For, the investigation of facts and the contemplation of nature is not alone sufficient for their profitable exercise and advance; but, when facts have been established, it is necessary to rise and apply ourselves to the study of the nature of corporeal things, to inquire into the laws which govern them and the principles whence their order and varied unity and mutual attraction in diversity arise. To such investigations it is wonderful what force and light and aid the Scholastic philosophy, if judiciously taught, would bring.

30. And here it is well to note that our philosophy can only by the grossest injustice be accused of being opposed to the advance and development of natural science. For, when the Scholastics, following the opinion of the holy Fathers, always held in anthropology that the human intelligence is only led to the knowledge of things without body and matter by things

sensible, they well understood that nothing was of greater use to the philosopher than diligently to search into the mysteries of nature and to be earnest and constant in the study of physical things. And this they confirmed by their own example; for St. Thomas, Blessed Albertus Magnus, and other leaders of the Scholastics were never so wholly rapt in the study of philosophy as not to give large attention to the knowledge of natural things; and, indeed, the number of their sayings and writings on these subjects, which recent professors approve of and admit to harmonize with truth, is by no means small. Moreover, in this very age many illustrious professors of the physical sciences openly testify that between certain and accepted conclusions of modern physics and the philosophic principles of the schools there is no conflict worthy of the name.

31. While, therefore, We hold that every word of wisdom, every useful thing by whomsoever discovered or planned, ought to be received with a willing and grateful mind, We exhort you, venerable brethren, in all earnestness to restore the golden wisdom of St. Thomas, and to spread it far and wide for the defense and beauty of the Catholic faith, for the good of society, and for the advantage of all the sciences. The wisdom of St. Thomas, We say; for if anything is taken up with too great subtlety by the Scholastic doctors, or too carelessly stated-if there be anything that ill agrees with the discoveries of a later age, or, in a word, improbable in whatever way-it does not enter Our mind to propose that for imitation to Our age. Let carefully selected teachers endeavor to implant the doctrine of Thomas Aquinas in the minds of students, and set forth clearly his solidity and excellence over others. Let the universities already founded or to be founded by you illustrate and defend this doctrine, and use it for the refutation of prevailing errors. But, lest the false for the true or the corrupt for the pure be drunk in, be ye watchful that the doctrine of Thomas be drawn from his own fountains, or at least from those rivulets which, derived from the very fount, have thus far flowed, according to the established agreement of learned men, pure and clear; be careful to guard the

minds of youth from those which are said to flow thence, but in reality are gathered from strange and unwholesome streams.

32. But well do We know that vain will be Our efforts unless, venerable brethren, He helps Our common cause who, in the words of divine Scripture, is called the God of all knowledge;[41] by which we are also admonished that "every best gift and every perfect gift is from above, coming down from the Father of lights",[42] and again: "If any of you want wisdom, let him ask of God, who giveth to all men abundantly, and upbraideth not: and it shall be given him."[43]

33. Therefore in this also let us follow the example of the Angelic Doctor, who never gave himself to reading or writing without first begging the blessing of God, who modestly confessed that whatever he knew he had acquired not so much by his own study and labor as by the divine gift; and therefore let us all, in humble and united prayer, beseech God to send forth the spirit of knowledge and of understanding to the children of the Church and open their senses for the understanding of wisdom. And that we may receive fuller fruits of the divine goodness, offer up to God the most efficacious patronage of the Blessed Virgin Mary, who is called the seat of wisdom; having at the same time as advocates St. Joseph, the most chaste spouse of the Virgin, and Peter and Paul, the chiefs of the Apostles, whose truth renewed the earth which had fallen under the impure blight of error, filling it with the light of heavenly wisdom.

34. In fine, relying on the divine assistance and confiding in your pastoral zeal, most lovingly We bestow on all of you, venerable brethren, on all the clergy and the flocks committed to your charge, the apostolic benediction as a pledge of heavenly gifts and a token of Our special esteem.

---

[41] 1 Kings 2:3.
[42] James 1:17.
[43] James 1:5.

The Leonine Encyclicals

Given at St. Peter's, in Rome, the fourth day of August, 1879, the second year of our pontificate.

III: Arcanum Divinae Sapientiae

February 10, 1880

ON CHRISTIAN MARRIAGE

The hidden design of the divine wisdom, which Jesus Christ the Saviour of men came to carry out on earth, had this end in view, that, by Himself and in Himself, He should divinely renew the world, which was sinking, as it were, with length of years into decline. The Apostle Paul summed this up in words of dignity and majesty when he wrote to the Ephesians, thus: "That He might make known unto us the mystery of His will... to re-establish all things in Christ that are in heaven and on earth."[1]

2. In truth, Christ our Lord, setting Himself to fulfill the commandment which His Father had given Him, straightway imparted a new form and fresh beauty to all things, taking away the effects of their time-worn age. For He healed the wounds which the sin of our first father had inflicted on the human race; He brought all men, by nature children of wrath, into favor with God; He led to the light of truth men wearied out by longstanding errors; He renewed to every virtue those who were weakened by lawlessness of every kind; and, giving them again an inheritance of neverending bliss, He added a sure hope that their mortal and perishable bodies should one day be partakers of immortality and of the glory of heaven. In order that these unparalleled benefits might last as long as men should be found on earth, He entrusted to His Church the continuance of His work; and, looking to future times, He commanded her to set in order whatever might have become deranged in human society, and to restore whatever might have fallen into ruin.

---

[1] Eph. 1:9-10.

3. Although the divine renewal we have spoken of chiefly and directly affected men as constituted in the supernatural order of grace, nevertheless some of its precious and salutary fruits were also bestowed abundantly in the order of nature. Hence, not only individual men, but also the whole mass of the human race, have in every respect received no small degree of worthiness. For, so soon as Christian order was once established in the world, it became possible for all men, one by one, to learn what God's fatherly providence is, and to dwell in it habitually, thereby fostering that hope of heavenly help which never confoundeth. From all this outflowed fortitude, self-control, constancy, and the evenness of a peaceful mind, together with many high virtues and noble deeds.

4. Wondrous, indeed, was the extent of dignity, steadfastness, and goodness which thus accrued to the State as well as to the family. The authority of rulers became more just and revered; the obedience of the people more ready and unforced; the union of citizens closer; the rights of dominion more secure. In very truth, the Christian religion thought of and provided for all things which are held to be advantageous in a State; so much so, indeed, that, according to St. Augustine, one cannot see how it could have offered greater help in the matter of living well and happily, had it been instituted for the single object of procuring or increasing those things which contributed to the conveniences or advantages of this mortal life.

5. Still, the purpose We have set before Us is not to recount, in detail, benefits of this kind; Our wish is rather to speak about that family union of which marriage is the beginning and the foundation. The true origin of marriage, venerable brothers, is well known to all. Though revilers of the Christian faith refuse to acknowledge the never-interrupted doctrine of the Church on this subject, and have long striven to destroy the testimony of all nations and of all times, they have nevertheless failed not only to quench the powerful light of truth, but even to lessen it. We record what is to all known, and cannot be doubted by any, that

God, on the sixth day of creation, having made man from the slime of the earth, and having breathed into his face the breath of life, gave him a companion, whom He miraculously took from the side of Adam when he was locked in sleep. God thus, in His most far-reaching foresight, decreed that this husband and wife should be the natural beginning of the human race, from whom it might be propagated and preserved by an unfailing fruitfulness throughout all futurity of time. And this union of man and woman, that it might answer more fittingly to the infinite wise counsels of God, even from the beginning manifested chiefly two most excellent properties - deeply sealed, as it were, and signed upon it-namely, unity and perpetuity. From the Gospel we see clearly that this doctrine was declared and openly confirmed by the divine authority of Jesus Christ. He bore witness to the Jews and to His Apostles that marriage, from its institution, should exist between two only, that is, between one man and one woman; that of two they are made, so to say, one flesh; and that the marriage bond is by the will of God so closely and strongly made fast that no man may dissolve it or render it asunder. "For this cause shall a man leave father and mother, and shall cleave to his wife, and they two shall be in one flesh. Therefore now they are not two, but one flesh. What, therefore, God bath joined together, let no man put asunder."[2]

6. This form of marriage, however, so excellent and so pre-eminent, began to be corrupted by degrees, and to disappear among the heathen; and became even among the Jewish race clouded in a measure and obscured. For in their midst a common custom was gradually introduced, by which it was accounted as lawful for a man to have more than one wife; and eventually when "by reason of the hardness of their heart,"[3] Moses indulgently permitted them to put away their wives, the way was open to divorce.

---

[2] Matt 19:5-6.
[3] Matt.l9:8.

7. But the corruption and change which fell on marriage among the Gentiles seem almost incredible, inasmuch as it was exposed in every land to floods of error and of the most shameful lusts. All nations seem, more or less, to have forgotten the true notion and origin of marriage; and thus everywhere laws were enacted with reference to marriage, prompted to all appearance by State reasons, but not such as nature required. Solemn rites, invented at will of the law-givers, brought about that women should, as might be, bear either the honorable name of wife or the disgraceful name of concubine; and things came to such a pitch that permission to marry, or the refusal of the permission, depended on the will of the heads of the State, whose laws were greatly against equity or even to the highest degree unjust. Moreover, plurality of wives and husbands, as well as divorce, caused the nuptial bond to be relaxed exceedingly. Hence, too, sprang up the greatest confusion as to the mutual rights and duties of husbands and wives, inasmuch as a man assumed right of dominion over his wife, ordering her to go about her business, often without any just cause; while he was himself at liberty "to run headlong with impunity into lust, unbridled and unrestrained, in houses of ill-fame and amongst his female slaves, as if the dignity of the persons sinned with, and not the will of the sinner, made the guilt."[4] When the licentiousness of a husband thus showed itself, nothing could be more piteous than the wife, sunk so low as to be all but reckoned as a means for the gratification of passion, or for the production of offspring. Without any feeling of shame, marriageable girls were bought and sold, like so much merchandise,[5] and power was sometimes given to the father and to the husband to inflict capital punishment on the wife. Of necessity, the offspring of such marriages as these were either reckoned among the stock in trade of the common-wealth or held to be the property of the father of the family;[6] and the

---

[4] Jerome Epist. 77, 3 (PL 22, 691).

[5] Arnobius, Adversus Gentes, 4 (sic, perhaps 1, 64).

[6] Dionysius Halicarnassus, lib. II, chs. 26-27 (see Roman Antiquities, tr. E. Cary, Loeb Classical Library, Harvard University Press, 1948, Vol. I, pp. 386-393).

law permitted him to make and unmake the marriages of his children at his mere will, and even to exercise against them the monstrous power of life and death.

8. So manifold being the vices and so great the ignominies with which marriage was defiled, an alleviation and a remedy were at length bestowed from on high. Jesus Christ, who restored our human dignity and who perfected the Mosaic law, applied early in His ministry no little solicitude to the question of marriage. He ennobled the marriage in Cana of Galilee by His presence, and made it memorable by the first of the miracles which he wrought;[7] and for this reason, even from that day forth, it seemed as if the beginning of new holiness had been conferred on human marriages. Later on He brought back matrimony to the nobility of its primeval origin by condemning the customs of the Jews in their abuse of the plurality of wives and of the power of giving bills of divorce; and still more by commanding most strictly that no one should dare to dissolve that union which God Himself had sanctioned by a bond perpetual. Hence, having set aside the difficulties which were adduced from the law of Moses, He, in character of supreme Lawgiver, decreed as follows concerning husbands and wives, "I say to you, that whosoever shall put away his wife, except it be for fornication, and shall marry another, committeth adultery; and he that shall marry her that is put away committeth adultery."[8]

9. But what was decreed and constituted in respect to marriage by the authority of God has been more fully and more clearly handed down to us, by tradition and the written Word, through the Apostles, those heralds of the laws of God. To the Apostles, indeed, as our masters, are to be referred the doctrines which "our holy Fathers, the Councils, and the Tradition of the Universal Church have always taught,"[9] namely, that Christ our

---

[7] John 2.

[8] Matt. 19:9.

[9] Trid., sess. xxiv, in principio (that is, Council of Trent, Canones et decreta; the text is divided into sessions, chapters, and canons, i.e., decrees).

Lord raised marriage to the dignity of a sacrament; that to husband and wife, guarded and strengthened by the heavenly grace which His merits gained for them, He gave power to attain holiness in the married state; and that, in a wondrous way, making marriage an example of the mystical union between Himself and His Church, He not only perfected that love which is according to nature,[10] but also made the naturally indivisible union of one man with one woman far more perfect through the bond of heavenly love. Paul says to the Ephesians: "Husbands, love your wives, as Christ also loved the Church, and delivered Himself up for it, that He might sanctify it. . . So also ought men to love their wives as their own bodies. . . For no man ever hated his own flesh, but nourisheth and cherisheth it, as also Christ doth the Church; because we are members of His body, of His flesh, and of His bones. For this cause shall a man leave his father and mother, and shall cleave to his wife, and they shall be two in one flesh. This is a great sacrament; but I speak in Christ and in the Church."[11] In like manner from the teaching of the Apostles we learn that the unity of marriage and its perpetual indissolubility, the indispensable conditions of its very origin, must, according to the command of Christ, be holy and inviolable without exception. Paul says again: "To them that are married, not I, but the Lord commandeth that the wife depart not from her husband; and if she depart, that she remain unmarried or be reconciled to her husband."[12] And again: "A woman is bound by the law as long as her husband liveth; but if her husband die, she is at liberty."[13] It is for these reasons that marriage is "a great sacrament";[14] "honorable in all,"[15] holy, pure, and to be reverenced as a type and symbol of most high mysteries.

---

[10] Trid., sess. xxiv, cap. 1, De reformatione matrimonii.

[11] Eph.5:25-32.

[12] 1 Cor. 7:10-11.

[13] 1 Cor. 7:39.

[14] Eph. 5:32.

[15] Heb. 13:4.

10. Furthermore, the Christian perfection and completeness of marriage are not comprised in those points only which have been mentioned. For, first, there has been vouchsafed to the marriage union a higher and nobler purpose than was ever previously given to it. By the command of Christ, it not only looks to the propagation of the human race, but to the bringing forth of children for the Church, "fellow citizens with the saints, and the domestics of God";[16] so that "a people might be born and brought up for the worship and religion of the true God and our Saviour Jesus Christ."[17]

11. Secondly, the mutual duties of husband and wife have been defined, and their several rights accurately established. They are bound, namely, to have such feelings for one another as to cherish always very great mutual love, to be ever faithful to their marriage vow, and to give one another an unfailing and unselfish help. The husband is the chief of the family and the head of the wife. The woman, because she is flesh of his flesh, and bone of his bone, must be subject to her husband and obey him; not, indeed, as a servant, but as a companion, so that her obedience shall be wanting in neither honor nor dignity. Since the husband represents Christ, and since the wife represents the Church, let there always be, both in him who commands and in her who obeys, a heaven-born love guiding both in their respective duties. For "the husband is the head of the wife; as Christ is the head of the Church. . . Therefore, as the Church is subject to Christ, so also let wives be to their husbands in all things."[18]

12. As regards children, they ought to submit to the parents and obey them, and give them honor for conscience' sake; while, on the other hand, parents are bound to give all care and watchful thought to the education of their offspring and their virtuous bringing up: "Fathers,... bring them up" [that is, your children]

---

[16] Eph. 2:19.
[17] Catech. Rom., ch. 8.
[18] Eph.5:23-24.

47

"in the discipline and correction of the Lord."[19] From this we see clearly that the duties of husbands and wives are neither few nor light; although to married people who are good these burdens become not only bearable but agreeable, owing to the strength which they gain through the sacrament.

13. Christ, therefore, having renewed marriage to such and so great excellence, commended and entrusted all the discipline bearing upon these matters to His Church. The Church, always and everywhere, has so used her power with reference to the marriages of Christians that men have seen clearly how it belongs to her as of native right; not being made hers by any human grant, but given divinely to her by the will of her Founder. Her constant and watchful care in guarding marriage, by the preservation of its sanctity, is so well understood as to not need proof. That the judgment of the Council of Jerusalem reprobated licentious and free love,[20] we all know; as also that the incestuous Corinthian was condemned by the authority of blessed Paul.[21] Again, in the very beginning of the Christian Church were repulsed and defeated, with the like unremitting determination, the efforts of many who aimed at the destruction of Christian marriage, such as the Gnostics, Manichaeans, and Montanists; and in our own time Mormons, St. Simonians, phalansterians, and communists.[22]

---

[19] Eph. 6:4.

[20] Acts 15:29.

[21] 1 Cor. 5:5.

[22] Gnostics: common name for several early sects claiming a Christian knowledge (gnosis) higher than faith. Manichaeans: disciples of the Persian Mani (or Manes, c.216-276) who taught that everything goes back to two first principles, light and darkness, or good and evil. Montanises: disciples of Montanus (in Phrygia, last third of the second century), condemned marriage as a sinfulinstitution. Mormons: sect founded in 1830 by Joseph Smith, which favored polygamy. Saint-Simonians: disciples of the French philosopher Saint-Simon (1760-1825) founder of a "new Christianity" based upon science instead of faith. Phalansterians: members of a phalanstery, that is, of a socialist community after the principles of Charles Fourier (1772-1837). Communists: supporters of a regime in which property belongs to the body politic, each member being supposed to work according to his capacity

14. In like manner, moreover, a law of marriage just to all, and the same for all, was enacted by the abolition of the old distinction between slaves and free-born men and women; 'and thus the rights of husbands and wives were made equal: for, as St. Jerome says, "with us that which is unlawful for women is unlawful for men also, and the same restraint is imposed on equal conditions."[23] The self-same rights also were firmly established for reciprocal affection and for the interchange of duties; the dignity of the woman was asserted and assured; and it was forbidden to the man to inflict capital punishment for adultery,[24] or lustfully and shamelessly to violate his plighted faith.

15. It is also a great blessing that the Church has limited, so far as is needful, the power of fathers of families, so that sons and daughters, wishing to marry, are not in any way deprived of their rightful freedom;[25] that, for the purpose of spreading more widely the supernatural love of husbands and wives, she has decreed marriages within certain degrees of consanguinity or affinity to be null and void;[26] that she has taken the greatest pains to safeguard marriage, as much as is possible, from error and violence and deceit;[27] that she has always wished to preserve the holy chasteness of the marriage bed, the security of persons,[28] the honor of husband and wife,[29] and the sanctity of religion.[30]

---

and to receive according to his wants; communism is usually associated with the name of Karl Marx (1818-1893).

[23] Jerome, Epist. 77 (PL 22, 691).

[24] Can. Interfectores and Canon Admonere, quaest. 2 Corpus juris canonici (Leipzig, 1879), Part 1, eols. 1152-1154.

[25] Saus. 30, quaest. 3, cap. 3, De cognac. spirit. (op. cit., Part 1, col. 1101).

[26] Cap. 8, De consang. et affin. (op. cit., Part 2, col. 703); cap 1, De cognac. legali (col. 696).

[27] Cap. 26, De spousal. (op. cit., Part 2, col. 670); cap. 13 (col. 665); cap. 15 (col. 666); cap. 29 (col. 671); De spon salibus et matrimonio et alibi.

[28] Cap. 1, De convers. infid. (op. cit., Part 2, col. 587); cap. 5, 6, De eo qui duxit in marrim. (cols. 688-689).

[29] Cap. 3, 5, 8, De spousal. et matr. (op. cit., Part 2, cols. 661, 663). Trid., sess. xxiv, cap. De reformatione matrimonii.

Lastly, with such foresight of legislation has the Church guarded its divine institution that no one who thinks rightfully of these matters can fail to see how, with regard to marriage, she is the best guardian and defender of the human race; and how, withal, her wisdom has come forth victorious from the lapse of years, from the assaults of men, and from the countless changes of public events.

16. Yet, owing to the efforts of the archenemy of mankind, there are persons who, thanklessly casting away so many other blessings of redemption, despise also or utterly ignore the restoration of marriage to its original perfection. It is a reproach to some of the ancients that they showed themselves the enemies of marriage in many ways; but in our own age, much more pernicious is the sin of those who would fain pervert utterly the nature of marriage, perfect though it is, and complete in all its details and parts. The chief reason why they act in this way is because very many, imbued with the maxims of a false philosophy and corrupted in morals, judge nothing so unbearable as submission and obedience; and strive with all their might to bring about that not only individual men, but families, also-indeed, human society itself-may in haughty pride despise the sovereignty of God.

17. Now, since the family and human society at large spring from marriage, these men will on no account allow matrimony to be the subject of the jurisdiction of the Church. Nay, they endeavor to deprive it of all holiness, and so bring it within the contracted sphere of those rights which, having been instituted by man, are ruled and administered by the civil jurisprudence of the community. Wherefore it necessarily follows that they attribute all power over marriage to civil rulers, and allow none whatever to the Church; and, when the Church exercises any such power, they think that she acts either by favor of the civil authority or to its injury. Now is the time, they say, for the heads of the State to

---

[30] Cap. 7, De divort. (op. cit., Part 2, col. 722).

vindicate their rights unflinchingly, and to do their best to settle all that relates to marriage according as to them seems good.

18. Hence are owing *civil marriages,* commonly so called; 'hence laws are framed which impose impediments to marriage; hence arise judicial sentences affecting the marriage contract, as to whether or not it have been rightly made. Lastly, all power of prescribing and passing judgment in this class of cases is, as we see, of set purpose denied to the Catholic Church, so that no regard is paid either to her divine power or to her prudent laws. Yet, under these, for so many centuries, have the nations lived on whom the light of civilization shone bright with the wisdom of Christ Jesus.

19. Nevertheless, the naturalists,[31] as well as all who profess that they worship above all things the divinity of the State, and strive to disturb whole communities with such wicked doctrines, cannot escape the charge of delusion. Marriage has God for its Author, and was from the very beginning a kind of foreshadowing of the Incarnation of His Son; and therefore there abides in it a something holy and religious; not extraneous, but innate; not derived from men, but implanted by nature. Innocent III, therefore, and Honorius III, our predecessors, affirmed not falsely nor rashly that a sacrament of marriage existed ever amongst the faithful and unbelievers.[32] We call to witness the monuments of antiquity, as also the manners and customs of those people who, being the most civilized, had the greatest knowledge of law and equity. In the minds of all of them it was a fixed and foregone conclusion that, when marriage was thought of, it was thought of as conjoined with religion and holiness. Hence, among those, marriages were commonly celebrated with religious ceremonies, under the authority of pontiffs, and with the ministry of priests. So mighty, even in the

---

[31] Maintain the self-sufficiency of the natural order.

[32] Concerning Innocent III, see Corpus juris canonici, cap. 8, De divort., ed. cit., Part 2, col. 723. Innocent III refers to 1 Cor. 7:13. Concerning Honorius III, see cap. ii, De transact., (op. cit., Part 2 col. 210).

souls ignorant of heavenly doctrine, was the force of nature, of the remembrance of their origin, and of the conscience of the human race. As, then, marriage is holy by its own power, in its own nature, and of itself, it ought not to be regulated and administered by the will of civil rulers, but by the divine authority of the Church, which alone in sacred matters professes the office of teaching.

20. Next, the dignity of the sacrament must be considered, for through addition of the sacrament the marriages of Christians have become far the noblest of all matrimonial unions. But to decree and ordain concerning the sacrament is, by the will of Christ Himself, so much a part of the power and duty of the Church that it is plainly absurd to maintain that even the very smallest fraction of such power has been transferred to the civil ruler.

21. Lastly should be borne in mind the great weight and crucial test of history, by which it is plainly proved that the legislative and judicial authority of which We are speaking has been freely and constantly used by the Church, even in times when some foolishly suppose the head of the State either to have consented to it or connived at it. It would, for instance, be incredible and altogether absurd to assume that Christ our Lord condemned the long-standing practice of polygamy and divorce by authority delegated to Him by the procurator of the province, or the principal ruler of the Jews. And it would be equally extravagant to think that, when the Apostle Paul taught that divorces and incestuous marriages were not lawful, it was because Tiberius, Caligula, and Nero agreed with him or secretly commanded him so to teach. No man in his senses could ever be persuaded that the Church made so many laws about the holiness and indissolubility of marriage,[33] and the marriages of slaves with the free-born,[34] by power received from Roman emperors, most

---

[33] Canones Apostolorum, 16 17, 18, ed. Fr. Lauchert, J. C. B. Mohr (Leipzig, 1896) p. 3.

hostile to the Christian name, whose strongest desire was to destroy by violence and murder the rising Church of Christ. Still less could anyone believe this to be the case, when the law of the Church was sometimes so divergent from the civil law that Ignatius the Martyr,[35] Justin,[36] Athenagoras,[37] and Tertullian[38] publicly denounced as unjust and adulterous certain marriages which had been sanctioned by imperial law.

22. Furthermore, after all power had devolved upon the Christian emperors, the supreme pontiffs and bishops assembled in council persisted with the same independence and consciousness of their right in commanding or forbidding in regard to marriage whatever they judged to be profitable or expedient for the time being, however much it might seem to be at variance with the laws of the State. It is well known that, with respect to the impediments arising from the marriage bond, through vow, disparity of worship, blood relationship, certain forms of crime, and from previously plighted troth, many decrees were issued by the rulers of the Church at the Councils of Granada,[39] Arles,[40] Chalcedon,[41] the second of Milevum,[42] and others, which were often widely different from the decrees sanctioned by the laws of the empire. Furthermore, so far were Christian princes from arrogating any power in the matter of Christian marriage that they on the contrary acknowledged and declared that it belonged exclusively in all its fullness to the Church. In fact, Honorius, the younger Theodosius, and Justinian,[43] also, hesitated not to confess that the only power

---

[34] Philosophumena (Oxford, 1851), i.e., Hippolytus, Refutation of All Heresies, 9, 12 (PG 16 3386D-3387A).

[35] Epistola ad Polycarpum, cap. 5 (PG 5, 723-724).

[36] Apolog. Maj., 15 (PG 6, 349A, B).

[37] Legal. pro Christian., 32, 33 (PG 6, 963-968).

[38] De coron. milit., 13 (PL 2, 116).

[39] De Aguirre, Conc. Hispan., Vol. 1, can. 11.

[40] Harduin, Act. Conch., Vol. 1, can. 11.

[41] Ibid., can. 16.

[42] Ibid., can. 17.

[43] Novel., 137 (Justinianus, Novellae, ed. C. E. Z. Lingenthal, Leipzig,

belonging to them in relation to marriage was that of acting as guardians and defenders of the holy canons. If at any time they enacted anything by their edicts concerning impediments of marriage, they voluntarily explained the reason, affirming that they took it upon themselves so to act, by leave and authority of the Church,[44] whose judgment they were wont to appeal to and reverently to accept in all questions that concerned legitimacy[45] and divorce;[46] as also in all those points which in any way have a necessary connection with the marriage bond.[47] The Council of Trent, therefore, had the clearest right to define that it is in the Church's power "to establish diriment impediments of matrimony,"[48] and that "matrimonial causes pertain to ecclesiastical judges."[49]

23. Let no one, then, be deceived by the distinction which some civil jurists have so strongly insisted upon - the distinction, namely, by virtue of which they sever the matrimonial contract from the sacrament, with intent to hand over the contract to the power and will of the rulers of the State, while reserving questions concerning the sacrament of the Church. A distinction, or rather severance, of this kind cannot be approved; for certain it is that in Christian marriage the contract is inseparable from the sacrament, and that, for this reason, the contract cannot be true and legitimate without being a sacrament as well. For Christ our Lord added to marriage the dignity of a sacrament; but marriage is the contract itself, whenever that contract is lawfully concluded.

1881, Vol. 2, p. 206).

[44] Fejer, Matrim. ex instit. Chris. (Pest, 1835).

[45] Cap. 3, De ord. cogn. (Corpus juris canonici, ed. cit., Part 2, col. 276).

[46] Cap. 3, De divort. (ed. cit., Part 2, col. 720).

[47] Cap. 13, Qui filii sint legit. (ed. cit., Part 2, col. 716).

[48] Trid., sess. xxiv, can. 4.

[49] Ibid., can. 12.

24. Marriage, moreover, is a sacrament, because it is a holy sign which gives grace, showing forth an image of the mystical nuptials of Christ with the Church. But the form and image of these nuptials is shown precisely by the very bond of that most close union in which man and woman are bound together in one; which bond is nothing else but the marriage itself. Hence it is clear that among Christians every true marriage is, in itself and by itself, a sacrament; and that nothing can be further from the truth than to say that the sacrament is a certain added ornament, or outward endowment, which can be separated and torn away from the contract at the caprice of man. Neither, therefore, by reasoning can it be shown, nor by any testimony of history be proved, that power over the marriages of Christians has ever lawfully been handed over to the rulers of the State. If, in this matter, the right of anyone else has ever been violated, no one can truly say that it has been violated by the Church. Would that the teaching of the naturalists, besides being full of falsehood and injustice, were not also the fertile source of much detriment and calamity! But it is easy to see at a glance the greatness of the evil which unhallowed marriages have brought, and ever will bring, on the whole of human society.

25. From the beginning of the world, indeed, it was divinely ordained that things instituted by God and by nature should be proved by us to be the more profitable and salutary the more they remain unchanged in their full integrity. For God, the Maker of all things, well knowing what was good for the institution and preservation of each of His creatures, so ordered them by His will and mind that each might adequately attain the end for which it was made. If the rashness or the wickedness of human agency venture to change or disturb that order of things which has been constituted with fullest foresight, then the designs of infinite wisdom and usefulness begin either to be hurtful or cease to be profitable, partly because through the change undergone they have lost their power of benefiting, and partly because God chooses to inflict punishment on the pride and audacity of man. Now, those who deny that marriage is holy, and who relegate it,

striped of all holiness, among the class of common secular things, uproot thereby the foundations of nature, not only resisting the designs of Providence, but, so far as they can, destroying the order that God has ordained. No one, therefore, should wonder if from such insane and impious attempts there spring up a crop of evils pernicious in the highest degree both to the salvation of souls and to the safety of the commonwealth.

26. If, then, we consider the end of the divine institution of marriage, we shall see very clearly that God intended it to be a most fruitful source of individual benefit and of public welfare, Not only, in strict truth, was marriage instituted for the propagation of the human race, but also that the lives of husbands and wives might be made better and happier. This comes about in many ways: by their lightening each other's burdens through mutual help; by constant and faithful love; by having all their possessions in common; and by the heavenly grace which flows from the sacrament. Marriage also can do much for the good of families, for, so long as it is conformable to nature and in accordance with the counsels of God, it has power to strengthen union of heart in the parents; to secure the holy education of children; to temper the authority of the father by the example of the divine authority; to render children obedient to their parents and servants obedient to their masters. From such marriages as these the State may rightly expect a race of citizens animated by a good spirit and filled with reverence and love for God, recognizing it their duty to obey those who rule justly and lawfully, to love all, and to injure no one.

27. These many and glorious fruits were ever the product of marriage, so long as it retained those gifts of holiness, unity, and indissolubility from which proceeded all its fertile and saving power; nor can anyone doubt but that it would always have brought forth such fruits, at all times and in all places, had it been under the power and guardianship of the Church, the trustworthy preserver and protector of these gifts. But, now, there is a spreading wish to supplant natural and divine law by

human law; and hence has begun a gradual extinction of that most excellent ideal of marriage which nature herself had impressed on the soul of man, and sealed, as it were, with her own seal; nay, more, even in Christian marriages this power, productive of so great good, has been weakened by the sinfulness of man. Of what advantage is it if a state can institute nuptials estranged from the Christian religion, which is the mother of all good, cherishing all sublime virtues, quickening and urging us to everything that is the glory of a lofty and generous soul? When the Christian religion is reflected and repudiated, marriage sinks of necessity into the slavery of man's vicious nature and vile passions, and finds but little protection in the help of natural goodness. A very torrent of evil has flowed from this source, not only into private families, but also into States. For, the salutary fear of God being removed, and there being no longer that refreshment in toil which is nowhere more abounding than in the Christian religion, it very often happens, as indeed is natural, that the mutual services and duties of marriage seem almost unbearable; and thus very many yearn for the loosening of the tie which they believe to be woven by human law and of their own will, whenever incompatibility of temper, or quarrels, or the violation of the marriage vow, or mutual consent, or other reasons induce them to think that it would be well to be set free. Then, if they are hindered by law from carrying out this shameless desire, they contend that the laws are iniquitous, inhuman, and at variance with the rights of free citizens; adding that every effort should be made to repeal such enactments, and to introduce a more humane code sanctioning divorce.

28. Now, however much the legislators of these our days may wish to guard themselves against the impiety of men such as we have been speaking of, they are unable to do so, seeing that they profess to hold and defend the very same principles of jurisprudence; and hence they have to go with times, and render divorce easily obtainable. History itself shows this; for, to pass over other instances, we find that, at the close of the last century, divorces were sanctioned by law in that upheaval or, rather, as it

might be called, conflagration in France, when society was wholly degraded by the abandoning of God. Many at the present time would fain have those laws reenacted, because they wish God and His Church to be altogether exiled and excluded from the midst of human society, madly thinking that in such laws a final remedy must be sought for that moral corruption which is advancing with rapid strides.

29. Truly, it is hardly possible to describe how great are the evils that flow from divorce. Matrimonial contracts are by it made variable; mutual kindness is weakened; deplorable inducements to unfaithfulness are supplied; harm is done to the education and training of children; occasion is afforded for the breaking up of homes; the seeds of dissension are sown among families; the dignity of womanhood is lessened and brought low, and women run the risk of being deserted after having ministered to the pleasures of men. Since, then, nothing has such power to lay waste families and destroy the mainstay of kingdoms as the corruption of morals, it is easily seen that divorces are in the highest degree hostile to the prosperity of families and States, springing as they do from the depraved morals of the people, and, as experience shows us, opening out a way to every kind of evil-doing in public and in private life.

30. Further still, if the matter be duly pondered, we shall clearly see these evils to be the more especially dangerous, because, divorce once being tolerated, there will be no restraint powerful enough to keep it within the bounds marked out or presurmised. Great indeed is the force of example, and even greater still the might of passion. With such incitements it must needs follow that the eagerness for divorce, daily spreading by devious ways, will seize upon the minds of many like a virulent contagious disease, or like a flood of water bursting through every barrier. These are truths that doubtlessly are all clear in themselves, but they will become clearer yet if we call to mind the teachings of experience. So soon as the road to divorce began to be made smooth by law, at once quarrels, jealousies, and judicial

separations largely increased; and such shamelessness of lifefollowed that men who had been in favor of these divorces repented of what they had done, and feared that, if they did not carefully seek a remedy by repealing the law, the State itself might come to ruin. The Romans of old are said to have shrunk with horror from the first example of divorce, but ere long all sense of decency was blunted in their soul; the meager restraint of passion died out, and the marriage vow was so often broken that what some writers have affirmed would seem to be true-namely, women used to reckon years not by the change of consuls, but of their husbands. In like manner, at the beginning, Protestants allowed legalized divorces in certain although but few cases, and yet from the affinity of circumstances of like kind, the number of divorces increased to such extent in Germany, America, and elsewhere that all wise thinkers deplored the boundless corruption of morals, and judged the recklessness of the laws to be simply intolerable.

31. Even in Catholic States the evil existed. For whenever at any time divorce was introduced, the abundance of misery that followed far exceeded all that the framers of the law could have foreseen. In fact, many lent their minds to contrive all kinds of fraud and device, and by accusations of cruelty, violence, and adultery to feign grounds for the dissolution of the matrimonial bond of which they had grown weary; and all this with so great havoc to morals that an amendment of the laws was deemed to be urgently needed.

32. Can anyone, therefore, doubt that laws in favor of divorce would have a result equally baneful and calamitous were they to be passed in these our days? There exists not, indeed, in the projects and enactments of men any power to change the character and tendency with things have received from nature. Those men, therefore, show but little wisdom in the idea they have formed of the well-being of the commonwealth who think that the inherent character of marriage can be perverted with impunity; and who, disregarding the sanctity of religion and of

the sacrament, seem to wish to degrade and dishonor marriage more basely than was done even by heathen laws. Indeed, if they do not change their views, not only private families, but all public society, will have unceasing cause to fear lest they should be miserably driven into that general confusion and overthrow of order which is even now the wicked aim of socialists and communists. Thus we see most clearly how foolish and senseless it is to expect any public good from divorce, when, on the contrary, it tends to the certain destruction of society.

33. It must consequently be acknowledged that the Church has deserved exceedingly well of all nations by her ever watchful care in guarding the sanctity and the indissolubility of marriage. Again, no small amount of gratitude is owing to her for having, during the last hundred years, openly denounced the wicked laws which have grievously offended on this particular subject;[50] as well as for her having branded with anathema the baneful heresy obtaining among Protestants touching divorce and separation;[51] also, for having in many ways condemned the habitual dissolution of marriage among the Greeks;[52] for having declared invalid all marriages contracted upon the understanding that they may be at some future time dissolved;[53] and, lastly, for having, from the earliest times, repudiated the imperial laws which disastrously favored divorce.[54]

---

[50] Pius VI, Epist. ad episc. Lucion., May 20, 1793; Pius VII, encycl. letter, Feb. 17, 1809, and constitution given July 19, 1817; Pius VIII, encycl. letter, May 29, 1829; Gregory XVI, constitution given August 15, 1832; Pius IX, address, Sept. 22, 1852.

[51] Trid., less. xxiv, can. 5 7.

[52] Council of Florence and instructions of Eugene IV to the Armenians Benedict XIV, constitution Etsi Pastoralis, May 6, 1742.

[53] Cap. 7, De condit. appos. (Corpus juru canonici, ed. cit., Part 2, col. 684).

[54] Jerome, Epist. 69, ad Oceanum (PL 22, 657); Ambrose, Lib. 8 in cap. 16 Lucae, n. 5 (PL 15, 1857); Augustine, De nuptiis, 1, 10 11 (PL 44, 420). Fifty years after the publication of Arcanum, Pope Pius XI published his own encyclical Casti Connubii (December 31 1930).

34. As often, indeed, as the supreme pontiffs have resisted the most powerful among rulers, in their threatening demands that divorces carried out by them should be confirmed by the Church, so often must we account them to have been contending for the safety, not only of religion, but also of the human race. For this reason all generations of men will admire the proofs of unbending courage which are to be found in the decrees of Nicholas I against Lothair; of Urban II and Paschal II against Philip I of France; of Celestine III and Innocent III against Alphonsus of Leon and Philip II of France; of Clement VII and Paul III against Henry VIII; and, lastly, of Pius VII, that holy and courageous pontiff, against Napoleon I, when at the height of his prosperity and in the fullness of his power. This being so, all rulers and administrators of the State who are desirous of following the dictates of reason and wisdom, and anxious for the good of their people, ought to make up their minds to keep the holy laws of marriage intact, and to make use of the proffered aid of the Church for securing the safety of morals and the happiness of families, rather than suspect her of hostile intention and falsely and wickedly accuse her of violating the civil law.

35. They should do this the more readily because the Catholic Church, though powerless in any way to abandon the duties of her office or the defence of her authority, still very greatly inclines to kindness and indulgence whenever they are consistent with the safety of her rights and the sanctity of her duties. Wherefore she makes no decrees in relation to marriage without having regard to the state of the body politic and the condition of the general public; and has besides more than once mitigated, as far as possible, the enactments of her own laws when there were just and weighty reasons. Moreover, she is not unaware, and never calls in doubt, that the sacrament of marriage, being instituted for the preservation and increase of the human race, has a necessary relation to circumstances of life which, though connected with marriage, belong to the civil order, and about

which the State rightly makes strict inquiry and justly
promulgates decrees.

36. Yet, no one doubts that Jesus Christ, the Founder of the
Church, willed her sacred power to be distinct from the civil
power, and each power to be free and unshackled in its own
sphere: with this condition, however - a condition good for both,
and of advantage to all men - that union and concord should be
maintained between them; and that on those questions which
are, though in different ways, of common right and authority, the
power to which secular matters have been entrusted should
happily and becomingly depend on the other power which has in
its charge the interests of heaven. In such arrangement and
harmony is found not only the best line of action for each power,
but also the most opportune and efficacious method of helping
men in all that pertains to their life here, and to their hope of
salvation hereafter. For, as We have shown in former encyclical
letters,[55] the intellect of man is greatly ennobled by the Christian
faith, and made better able to shun and banish all error, while
faith borrows in turn no little help from the intellect; and in like
manner, when the civil power is on friendly terms with the
sacred authority of the Church, there accrues to both a great
increase of usefulness. The dignity of the one is exalted, and so
long as religion is its guide it will never rule unjustly; while the
other receives help of protection and defence for the public good
of the faithful.

37. Being moved, therefore, by these considerations, as We have
exhorted rulers at other times, so still more earnestly We exhort
them now, to concord and friendly feeling; and we are the first to
stretch out Our hand to them with fatherly benevolence, and to
offer to them the help of Our supreme authority, a help which is
the more necessary at this time when, in public opinion, the
authority of rulers is wounded and enfeebled. Now that the
minds of so many are inflamed with a reckless spirit of liberty,

---

[55] Aeterni Patris, above, pp. 38-39.

and men are wickedly endeavoring to get rid of every restraint of authority, however legitimate it may be, the public safety demands that both powers should unite their strength to avert the evils which are hanging, not only over the Church, but also over civil society.

38. But, while earnestly exhorting all to a friendly union of will, and beseeching God, the Prince of peace, to infuse a love of concord into all hearts, We cannot, venerable brothers, refrain from urging you more and more to fresh earnestness, and zeal, and watchfulness, though we know that these are already very great. With every effort and with all authority, strive, as much as you are able, to preserve whole and undefiled among the people committed to your charge the doctrine which Christ our Lord taught us; which the Apostles, the interpreters of the will of God, have handed down; and which the Catholic Church has herself scrupulously guarded, and commanded to be believed in all ages by the faithful of Christ.

39. Let special care be taken that the people be well instructed in the precepts of Christian wisdom, so that they may always remember that marriage was not instituted by the will of man, but, from the very beginning, by the authority and command of God; that it does not admit of plurality of wives or husbands; that Christ, the Author of the New Covenant, raised it from a rite of nature to be a sacrament, and gave to His Church legislative and judicial power with regard to the bond of union. On this point the very greatest care must be taken to instruct them, lest their minds should be led into error by the unsound conclusions of adversaries who desire that the Church should be deprived of that power.

40. In like manner, all ought to understand clearly that, if there be any union of a man and a woman among the faithful of Christ which is not a sacrament, such union has not the force and nature of a proper marriage; that, although contracted in accordance with the laws of the State, it cannot be more than a

rite or custom introduced by the civil law. Further, the civil law can deal with and decide those matters alone which in the civil order spring from marriage, and which cannot possibly exist, as is evident, unless there be a true and lawful cause of them, that is to say, the nuptial bond. It is of the greatest consequence to husband and wife that all these things should be known and well understood by them, in order that they may conform to the laws of the State, if there be no objection on the part of the Church; for the Church wishes the effects of marriage to be guarded in all possible ways, and that no harm may come to the children.

41. In the great confusion of opinions, however, which day by day is spreading more and more widely, it should further be known that no power can dissolve the bond of Christian marriage whenever this has been ratified and consummated; and that, of a consequence, those husbands and wives are guilty of a manifest crime who plan, for whatever reason, to be united in a second marriage before the first one has been ended by death. When, indeed, matters have come to such a pitch that it seems impossible for them to live together any longer, then the Church allows them to live apart, and strives at the same time to soften the evils of this separation by such remedies and helps as are suited to their condition; yet she never ceases to endeavor to bring about a reconciliation, and never despairs of doing so. But these are extreme cases; and they would seldom exist if men and women entered into the married state with proper dispositions, not influenced by passion, but entertaining right ideas of the duties of marriage and of its noble purpose; neither would they anticipate their marriage by a series of sins drawing down upon them the wrath of God.

42. To sum up all in a few words, there would be a calm and quiet constancy in marriage if married people would gather strength and life from the virtue of religion alone, which imparts to us resolution and fortitude; for religion would enable them to bear tranquilly and even gladly the trials of their state, such as, for instance, the faults that they discover in one another, the

difference of temper and character, the weight of a mother's cares, the wearing anxiety about the education of children, reverses of fortune, and the sorrows of life.

43. Care also must be taken that they do not easily enter into marriage with those who are not Catholics; for, when minds do not agree as to the observances of religion, it is scarcely possible to hope for agreement in other things. Other reasons also proving that persons should turn with dread from such marriages are chiefly these: that they give occasion to forbidden association and communion in religious matters; endanger the faith of the Catholic partner; are a hindrance to the proper education of the children; and often lead to a mixing up of truth and falsehood, and to the belief that all religions are equally good.

44. Lastly, since We well know that none should be excluded from Our charity, We commend, venerable brothers, to your fidelity and piety those unhappy persons who, carried away by the heat of passion, and being utterly indifferent to their salvation, live wickedly together without the bond of lawful marriage. Let your utmost care be exercised in bringing such persons back to their duty; and, both by your own efforts and by those of good men who will consent to help you, strive by every means that they may see how wrongly they have acted; that they may do penance; and that they may be induced to enter into a lawful marriage according to the Catholic rite.

45. You will at once see, venerable brothers, that the doctrine and precepts in relation to Christian marriage, which We have thought good to communicate to you in this letter, tend no less to the preservation of civil society than to the everlasting salvation of souls. May God grant that, by reason of their gravity and importance, minds may everywhere be found docile and ready to obey them! For this end let us all suppliantly, with humble prayer, implore the help of the Blessed and Immaculate Virgin Mary, that, our hearts being quickened to the obedience of faith, she may show herself our mother and our helper. With

equal earnestness let us ask the princes of the Apostles, Peter and Paul, the destroyers of heresies, the sowers of the seed of truth, to save the human race by their powerful patronage from the deluge of errors that is surging afresh. In the meantime, as an earnest of heavenly gifts, and a testimony of Our special benevolence, We grant to you all, venerable brothers, and to the people confided to your charge, from the depths of Our heart, the apostolic benediction.

Given at St. Peter's in Rome, the tenth day of February, 1880, the third year of Our pontificate.

IV: Diuturnum

June 29, 1881

ON THE ORIGIN OF CIVIL POWER

The long-continued and most bitter war waged against the divine authority of the Church has reached the culmination to which it was tending, the common danger, namely, of human society, and especially of the civil power on which the public safety chiefly reposes. In our own times most particularly this result is apparent. For popular passions now reject, with more boldness than formerly, every restraint of authority. So great is the license on all sides, so frequent are seditious and tumults, that not only is obedience often refused to those who rule states, but a sufficiently safe guarantee of security does not seem to have been left to them.

2. For a long time, indeed, pains have been taken to render rulers the object of contempt and hatred to the multitude. The flames of envy thus excited have at last burst forth, and attempts have been several times made, at very short intervals, on the life of sovereign princes, either by secret plots or by open attacks. The whole of Europe was lately filled with horror at the horrible murder of a most powerful emperor.[1] Whilst the minds of men are still filled with astonishment at the magnitude of the crime, abandoned men do not fear publicly to utter threats and intimidations against other European princes.

3. These perils to commonwealth, which are before Our eyes, fill Us with grave anxiety, when We behold the security of rulers and

---

[1] An allusion to Alexander II (1818-81) Emperor of Russia, a liberally minded sovereign and a great social reformer, who was murdered March 13, 1881, by a group of nihilists, in St. Petersburg.

67

the tranquility of empires, together with the safety of nations, put in peril almost from hour to hour. Nevertheless, the divine power of the Christian religion has given birth to excellent principles of stability and order for the State, while at the same time it has penetrated into the customs and institutions of States. And of this power not the least nor last fruit is a just and wise proportion of mutual rights and duties in both princes and peoples. For in the precepts and example of Christ our Lord there is a wonderful force for restraining in their duty as much those who obey as those who rule; and for keeping between them that agreement which is most according to nature, and that concord of wills, so to speak, from which arises a course of administration tranquil and free from all disturbance. Wherefore, being, by the favor of God, entrusted with the government of the Catholic Church, and made guardian and interpreter of the doctrines of Christ, We judge that it belongs to Our jurisdiction, venerable brethren, publicly to set forth what Catholic truth demands of every one in this sphere of duty; thus making clear also by what way and by what means measures may be taken for the public safety in so critical a state of affairs.

4. Although man, when excited by a certain arrogance and contumacy, has often striven to cast aside the reins of authority, he has never yet been able to arrive at the state of obeying no one. In every association and community of men, necessity itself compels that some should hold pre-eminence, lest society, deprived of a prince or head by which it is ruled should come to dissolution and be prevented from attaining the end for which it was created and instituted. But, if it was not possible that political power should be removed from the midst of states, it is certain that men have used every art to take away its influence and to lessen its majesty, as was especially the case in the sixteenth century, when a fatal novelty of opinions infatuated many. Since that epoch, not only has the multitude striven after a liberty greater than is just, but it has seen fit to fashion the origin and construction of the civil society of men in accordance with its own will.

5. Indeed, very many men of more recent times, walking in the footsteps of those who in a former age assumed to themselves the name of philosophers,[2] say that all power comes from the people; so that those who exercise it in the State do so not as their own, but as delegated to them by the people, and that, by this rule, it can be revoked by the will of the very people by whom it was delegated. But from these, Catholics dissent, who affirm that the right to rule is from God, as from a natural and necessary principle.

6. It is of importance, however, to remark in this place that those who may be placed over the State may in certain cases be chosen by the will and decision of the multitude, without opposition to or impugning of the Catholic doctrine. And by this choice, in truth, the ruler is designated, but the rights of ruling are not thereby conferred. Nor is the authority delegated to him, but the person by whom it is to be exercised is determined upon.

7. There is no question here respecting forms of government, for there is no reason why the Church should not approve of the chief power being held by one man or by more, provided only it be just, and that it tend to the common advantage. Wherefore, so long as justice be respected, the people are not hindered from choosing for themselves that form of government which suits best either their own disposition, or the institutions and customs of their ancestors.[3]

8. But, as regards political power, the Church rightly teaches that it comes from God, for it finds this clearly testified in the sacred Scriptures and in the monuments of antiquity; besides, no other doctrine can be conceived which is more agreeable to reason, or more in accord with the safety of both princes and peoples.

---

[2] The name of Philosophers is usually given to a group of eighteenth-century French writers, especially Voltaire, d'Alembert and Diderot. Their main views are contained in the Encyclopédie (1751-7Z).

[3] See Introduction, p. 13-15.

9. In truth, that the source of human power is in God the books of the Old Testament in very many places clearly establish. "By me kings reign . . . by me princes rule, and the mighty decree justice."[4] And in another place: "Give ear you that rule the people . . . for power is given you of the Lord and strength by the Most High."[5] The same thing is contained in the Book of Ecclesiasticus: "Over every nation he bath set a ruler."[6] These things, however, which they had learned of God, men were little by little untaught through heathen superstition, which even as it has corrupted the true aspect and often the very concept of things, so also it has corrupted the natural form and beauty of the chief power. Afterwards, when the Christian Gospel shed its light, vanity yielded to truth, and that noble and divine principle whence all authority flows began to shine forth. To the Roman governor, ostentatiously pretending that he had the power of releasing and of condemning, our Lord Jesus Christ answered: "Thou shouldst not have any power against me unless it were given thee from above."[7] And St. Augustine, in explaining this passage, says: "Let us learn what He said, which also He taught by His Apostle, that there is no power but from God."[8] The faithful voice of the Apostles, as an echo, repeats the doctrine and precepts of Jesus Christ. The teaching of Paul to the Romans, when subject to the authority of heathen princes, is lofty and full of gravity: "There is not power but from God," from which, as from its cause, he draws this conclusion: "The prince is the minister of God."[9]

10. The Fathers of the Church have taken great care to proclaim and propagate this very doctrine in which they had been instructed. "We do not attribute," says St. Augustine, "the power of giving government and empires to any but the true God."[10]

---

[4] Prov.8:15-16.
[5] Wisd. 6:3-4.
[6] Ecclus. 7:14.
[7] John 19:11.
[8] Tract. 116 in Joan., n. 5 (PL 35, 1942).
[9] Rom.13:1-4.

On the same passage St. John Chrysostom says: "That there are kingdoms, and that some rule, while others are subject, and that none of these things is brought about by accident or rashly . . . is, I say, a work of divine wisdom."[11] The same truth is testified by St. Gregory the Great, saying: "We confess that power is given from above to emperors and kings."[12] Verily the holy doctors have undertaken to illustrate also the same precepts by the natural light of reason in such a way that they must appear to be altogether right and true, even to those who follow reason for their sole guide.

11. And, indeed, nature, or rather God who is the Author of nature, wills that man should live in a civil society; and this is clearly shown both by the faculty of language, the greatest medium of intercourse, and by numerous innate desires of the mind, and the many necessary things, and things of great importance, which men isolated cannot procure, but which they can procure when joined and associated with others. But now, a society can neither exist nor be conceived in which there is no one to govern the wills of individuals, in such a way as to make, as it were, one will out of many, and to impel them rightly and orderly to the common good; therefore, God has willed that in a civil society there should be some to rule the multitude. And this also is a powerful argument, that those by whose authority the State is administered must be able so to compel the citizens to obedience that it is clearly a sin in the latter not to obey. But no man has in himself or of himself the power of constraining the free will of others by fetters of authority of this kind. This power resides solely in God, the Creator and Legislator of all things; and it is necessary that those who exercise it should do it as having received it from God. "There is one lawgiver and judge, who is able to destroy and deliver."[13] And this is clearly seen in every kind of power. That that which resides in priests comes from

[10] De civ., Dei, 5, 21 (PL 41, 167).
[11] In Epist. ad Rom., Homil. 23, n. 1 (PG 60, 615).
[12] In Epist. lib. 11, epist. 61.
[13] James 4:12.

God is so acknowledged that among all nations they are recognized as, and called, the ministers of God. In like manner, the authority of fathers of families preserves a certain impressed image and form of the authority which is in God, "of whom all paternity in heaven and earth is named."[14] But in this way different kinds of authority have between them wonderful resemblances, since, whatever there is of government and authority, its origin is derived from one and the same Creator and Lord of the world, who is God.

12. Those who believe civil society to have risen from the free consent of men, looking for the origin of its authority from the same source, say that each individual has given up something of his right,[15] and that voluntarily every person has put himself into the power of the one man in whose person the whole of those rights has been centered. But it is a great error not to see, what is manifest, that men, as they are not a nomad race, have been created, without their own free will, for a natural community of life. It is plain, moreover, that the pact which they allege is openly a falsehood and a fiction, and that it has no authority to confer on political power such great force, dignity, and firmness as the safety of the State and the common good of the citizens require. Then only will the government have all those ornaments and guarantees, when it is understood to emanate from God as its august and most sacred source.

13. And it is impossible that any should be found not only more true but even more advantageous than this opinion. For the authority of the rulers of a State, if it be a certain communication of divine power, will by that very reason immediately acquire a dignity greater than human - not, indeed, that impious and most absurd dignity sometimes desired by heathen emperors when affecting divine honors, but a true and solid one received by a

---

[14] Eph. 3:15.

[15] An allusion to the doctrine of "Social contract," developed by Jean-Jacques Rousseau (1712-78). According to this doctrine, all political power comes to rulers from the people.

certain divine gift and benefaction. Whence it will behoove citizens to submit themselves and to be obedient to rulers, as to God, not so much through fear of punishment as through respect for their majesty; nor for the sake of pleasing, but through conscience, as doing their duty. And by this means authority will remain far more firmly seated in its place. For the citizens, perceiving the force of this duty, would necessarily avoid dishonesty and contumacy, because they must be persuaded that they who resist State authority resist the divine will; that they who refuse honor to rulers refuse it to God Himself.

14. This doctrine the Apostle Paul particularly inculcated on the Romans; to whom he wrote with so great authority and weight on the reverence to be entertained toward the higher powers, that it seems nothing could be prescribed more weightily: "Let every soul be subject to higher powers, for there is no power but from God, and those that are, are ordained of God. Therefore he that resisteth the power resisteth the ordinance of God, and they that resist purchase to themselves damnation . . . wherefore be subject of necessity, not only for wrath, but also for conscience' sake."[16] And in agreement with this is the celebrated declaration of Peter, the Prince of the Apostles, on the same subject: "Be ye subject, therefore, to every human creature for God's sake; whether it be to the king as excelling, or to governors, as sent by him for the punishment of evildoers, and for the praise of the good, for so is the will of God."[17]

15. The one only reason which men have for not obeying is when anything is demanded of them which is openly repugnant to the natural or the divine law, for it is equally unlawful to command to do anything in which the law of nature or the will of God is violated. If, therefore, it should happen to any one to be compelled to prefer one or the other, viz., to disregard either the commands of God or those of rulers, he must obey Jesus

---

[16] Rom. 13:1-2, 5.
[17] 1 Peter 2:13, 15.

Christ, who commands us to "give to Caesar the things that are Caesar's, and to God the things that are God's,"[18] and must reply courageously after the example of the Apostles: "We ought to obey God rather than men."[19] And yet there is no reason why those who so behave themselves should be accused of refusing obedience; for, if the will of rulers is opposed to the will and the laws of God, they themselves exceed the bounds of their own power and pervert justice; nor can their authority then be valid, which, when there is no justice, is null.

16. But in order that justice may be retained in government it is of the highest importance that those who rule States should understand that political power was not created for the advantage of any private individual; and that the administration of the State must be carried on to the profit of those who have been committed to their care, not to the profit of those to whom it has been committed. Let princes take example from the Most High God, by whom authority is given to them; and, placing before themselves His model in governing the State, let them rule over the people with equity and faithfulness, and let them add to that severity, which is necessary, a paternal charity. On this account they are warned in the oracles of the sacred Scriptures, that they will have themselves some day to render an account to the King of kings and Lord of lords; if they shall fail in their duty, that it will not be possible for them in any way to escape the severity of God: "The Most High will examine your work and search out your thoughts: because being ministers of his kingdom you have not judged rightly. . . Horribly and speedily will he appear to you, for a most severe judgement shall be for them that bear rule. . . For God will not accept any man's person, neither will he stand in awe of any man's greatness; for he made the little and the great, and he hath equally care of all. But a greater punishment is ready for the more mighty."[20]

---

[18] Matt. 22:21.
[19] Acts 5:29.
[20] Wisd. 6:4-6, 8-9. 21.

17. And if these precepts protect the State, all cause or desire for seditions is removed; the honor and security of rulers, the quiet and wellbeing of societies will be secure. The dignity also of the citizen is best provided for; for to them it has been permitted to retain even in obedience that greatness which conduces to the excellence of man. For they understand that, in the judgment of God, there is neither slave nor free man; that there is one Lord of all, rich "to all that call upon Him,"[21] but that they on this account submit to and obey their rulers, because these in a certain sort bring before them the image of God, "whom to serve is to reign."

18. But the Church has always so acted that the Christian form of civil government may not dwell in the minds of men, but that it may be exhibited also in the life and habits of nations. As long as there were at the helm of the States pagan emperors, who were prevented by superstition from rising to that form of imperial government which We have sketched, she studied how to instill into the minds of subjects, immediately on their embracing the Christian institutions, the teaching that they must be desirous of bringing their lives into conformity with them. Therefore, the pastors of souls, after the example of the Apostle Paul, were accustomed to teach the people with the utmost care and diligence "to be subject to princes and powers, to obey at a word,"[22] and to pray God for all men and particularly "for kings and all that are in a high station: for this is good and acceptable in the sight of God our Saviour."[23] And the Christians of old left the most striking proofs of this; for, when they were harassed in a very unjust and cruel way by pagan emperors, they nevertheless at no time omitted to conduct themselves obediently and submissively, so that, in fact, they seemed to vie with each other: those in cruelty, and these in obedience.

---

[21] Rom. 10:12.
[22] Tit. 3:1.
[23] 1 Tim. 2:1-3.

19. This great modesty, this fixed determination to obey, was so well known that it could not be obscured by the calumny and malice of enemies. On this account, those who were going to plead in public before the emperors for any persons bearing the Christian name proved by this argument especially that it was unjust to enact laws against the Christians because they were in the sight of all men exemplary in their bearing according to the laws. Athenagoras thus confidently addresses Marcus Aurelius Antoninus and Lucius Aurelius Commodus, his son: "You allow us, who commit no evil, yea, who demean ourselves the most piously and justly of all toward God and likewise toward your government, to be driven about, plundered and exiled."[24] In like manner, Tertullian openly praises the Christians because they were the best and surest friends of all to the Empire: "The Christian is the enemy of no one, much less of the emperor, whom he knows to be appointed by God, and whom he must, therefore, of necessity love, reverence and honor, and wish to be preserved together with the whole Roman Empire."[25] Nor did he hesitate to affirm that, within the limits of the Empire, the number of enemies was wont to diminish just in proportion as the number of Christians increased.[26] There is also a remarkable testimony to the same point in the Epistle to Diognetus, which confirms the statement that the Christians at that period were not only in the habit of obeying the laws, but in every office they of their own accord did more, and more perfectly, than they were required to do by the laws. "Christians observe these things which have obtained the sanction of the law, and in the character of their lives they even go beyond the law."[27]

20. The case, indeed, was different when they were ordered by the edicts of emperors and the threats of praetors to abandon the Christian faith or in any way fail in their duty. At these times,

---

[24] Legatio pro christianis, 1 (PG 6, 891B-894A).

[25] Apolog., 35.

[26] Apolog., 37 (PL 1, 526A).

[27] Ad Diogn., 10 (A Diognete, ed. H. I. Marrow Paris, 1951, pp. 64-65).

undoubtedly, they preferred to displease men rather than God. Yet, even under these circumstances, they were so far from doing anything seditious or despising the imperial majesty that they took it on themselves only to profess themselves Christians, and declare that they would not in any way alter their faith. But they had no thought of resistance, calmly and joyfully they went to the torture of the rack, in so much that the magnitude of the torments gave place to their magnitude of mind. During the same period the force of Christian principles was observed in like manner in the army. For it was a mark of a Christian soldier to combine the greatest fortitude with the greatest attention to military discipline, and to add to nobility of mind immovable fidelity towards his prince. But, if anything dishonorable was required of him, as, for instance, to break the laws of God, or to turn his sword against innocent disciples of Christ, then, indeed, he refused to execute the orders, yet in such wise that he would rather retire from the army and die for his religion than oppose the public authority by means of sedition and tumult.

21. But afterward, when Christian rulers were at the head of States, the Church insisted much more on testifying and preaching how much sanctity was inherent in the authority of rulers. Hence, when people thought of princedom, the image of a certain sacred majesty would present itself to their minds, by which they would be impelled to greater reverence and love of rulers. And on this account she wisely provides that kings should commence their reign with the celebration of solemn rites; which, in the Old Testament, was appointed by divine authority.[28]

22. But from the time when the civil society of men, raised from the ruins of the Roman Empire, gave hope of its future Christian greatness, the Roman Pontiffs, by the institution of the Holy Empire, consecrated the political power in a wonderful manner. Greatly, indeed, was the authority of rulers ennobled; and it is not to be doubted that what was then instituted would always

---

[28] 1 Kings 9:16; 10:1; 16:13.

have been a very great gain, both to ecclesiastical and civil society, if princes and peoples had ever looked to the same object as the Church. And, indeed, tranquility and a sufficient prosperity lasted so long as there was a friendly agreement between these two powers. If the people were turbulent, the Church was at once the mediator for peace. Recalling all to their duty, she subdued the more lawless passions partly by kindness and partly by authority. So, if, in ruling, princes erred in their government, she went to them and, putting before them the rights, needs, and lawful wants of their people, urged them to equity, mercy, and kindness. Whence it was often brought about that the dangers of civil wars and popular tumults were stayed.

23. On the other hand, the doctrines on political power invented by late writers have already produced great ills amongst men, and it is to be feared that they will cause the very greatest disasters to posterity. For an unwillingness to attribute the right of ruling to God, as its Author, is not less than a willingness to blot out the greatest splendor of political power and to destroy its force. And they who say that this power depends on the will of the people err in opinion first of all; then they place authority on too weak and unstable a foundation. For the popular passions, incited and goaded on by these opinions, will break out more insolently; and, with great harm to the common weal, descend headlong by an easy and smooth road to revolts and to open sedition. In truth, sudden uprisings and the boldest rebellions immediately followed in Germany the so-called Reformation,[29] the authors and leaders of which, by their new doctrines, attacked at the very foundation religious and civil authority; and this with so fearful an outburst of civil war and with such slaughter that there was scarcely any place free from tumult and bloodshed. From this heresy there arose in the last century a false philosophy - a new right as it is called, and a popular authority, together with an unbridled license which many regard as the only true liberty. Hence we have

---

[29] Especially the Peasant Revolt and its repression by the German princes. Luther himself then had to stress the duty of the citizens to obey the civil power (On the Civil Power, 1523).

reached the limit of horrors, to wit, communism, socialism, nihilism, hideous deformities of the civil society of men and almost its ruin. And yet too many attempt to enlarge the scope of these evils, and under the pretext of helping the multitude, already have fanned no small flames of misery. The things we thus mention are neither unknown nor very remote from us.

24. This, indeed, is all the graver because rulers, in the midst of such threatening dangers, have no remedies sufficient to restore discipline and tranquility. They supply themselves with the power of laws, and think to coerce, by the severity of their punishment, those who disturb their governments. They are right to a certain extent, but yet should seriously consider that no power of punishment can be so great that it alone can preserve the State. For fear, as St. Thomas admirably teaches, "is a weak foundation; for those who are subdued by fear would, should an occasion arise in which they might hope for immunity, rise more eagerly against their rulers, in proportion to the previous extent of their restraint through fear." And besides, "from too great fear many fall into despair; and despair drives men to attempt boldly to gain what they desire."[30] That these things are so we see from experience. It is therefore necessary to seek a higher and more reliable reason for obedience, and to say explicitly that legal severity cannot be efficacious unless men are led on by duty, and moved by the salutary fear of God. But this is what religion can best ask of them, religion which by its power enters into the souls and bends the very wills of men causing them not only to render obedience to their rulers, but also to show their affection and good will, which is in every society of men the best guardian of safety.

25. For this reason the Roman Pontiffs are to be regarded as having greatly served the public good, for they have ever endeavored to break the turbulent and restless spirit of innovators, and have often warned men of the danger they are to

---

[30] On the Governance of Rulers, 1, 10.

civil society. In this respect we may worthily recall to mind the declaration of Clement VII to Ferdinand, King of Bohemia and Hungary: "In the cause of faith your own dignity and advantage and that of other rulers is included, since the faith cannot be shaken without your authority being brought down; which has been most clearly shown in several instances." In the same way the supreme forethought and courage of Our predecessors have been shown, especially of Clement XI, Benedict XIV, and Leo XII,[31] who, when in their day the evil of vicious doctrine was more widely spreading and the boldness of the sects was becoming greater, endeavored by their authority to close the door against them. And We Ourselves have several times declared what great dangers are impending, and have pointed out the best ways of warding them off. To princes and other rulers of the State we have offered the protection of religion, and we have exhorted the people to make abundant use of the great benefits which the Church supplies. Our present object is to make rulers understand that this protection, which is stronger than any, is again offered to them; and We earnestly exhort them in our Lord to defend religion, and to consult the interest of their Lord to defend religion, and to consult the interest of their States by giving that liberty to the Church which cannot be taken away without injury and ruin to the commonwealth.

26. The Church of Christ, indeed, cannot be an object of suspicion to rulers, nor of hatred to the people; for it urges rulers to follow justice, and in nothing to decline from their duty; while at the same time it strengthens and in many ways supports their authority. All things that are of a civil nature the Church acknowledges and declares to be under the power and authority of the ruler; and in things whereof for different reasons the decision belongs both to the sacred and to the civil power, the Church wishes that there should be harmony between the two so that injurious contests may be avoided. As to what regards the people, the Church has been established for the salvation of all

---

[31] Clement XI (1700-21); Benedict XIV (1740-58); Leo XII (1823-29).

men and has ever loved them as a mother. For it is the Church which by the exercise of her charity has given gentleness to the minds of men, kindness to their manners, and justice to their laws. Never opposed to honest liberty, the Church has always detested a tyrant's rule. This custom which the Church has ever had of deserving well of mankind is notably expressed by St. Augustine when he says that "the Church teaches kings to study the welfare of their people, and people to submit to their kings, showing what is due to all: and that to all is due charity and to no one injustice."[32]

27. For these reasons, venerable brethren, your work will be most useful and salutary if you employ with us every industry and effort which God has given you in order to avert the dangers and evils of human society. Strive with all possible care to make men understand and show forth in their lives what the Catholic Church teaches on government and the duty of obedience. Let the people be frequently urged by your authority and teaching to fly from the forbidden sects, to abhor all conspiracy, to have nothing to do with sedition, and let them understand that they who for God's sake obey their rulers render a reasonable service and a generous obedience. And as it is God "who gives safety to kings,"[33] and grants to the people "to rest in the beauty of peace and in the tabernacles of confidence and in wealthy repose,"[34] it is to Him that we must pray, beseeching Him to incline all minds to uprightness and truth, to calm angry passions, to restore the long-wished - for tranquility to the world.

28. That we may pray with greater hope, let us take as our intercessors and protectors of our welfare the Virgin Mary, the great Mother of God, the help of Christians, and protector of the human race; St. Joseph, her chaste spouse, in whose patronage the whole Church greatly trusts; and the Princes of the Apostles,

---

[32] De mor. eccl., 1, 30, 53 (PL 32, 1236).
[33] Ps. 152:11.
[34] Isa. 37:18.

The Leonine Encyclicals

Peter and Paul, the guardians and protectors of the Christian name.

Given at St. Peter's in Rome, the twenty-ninth day of June, 1881, the third year of Our pontificate.

V: Humanum Genus

April 20, 1884

ON FREEMASONRY

The race of man, after its miserable fall from God, the Creator and the Giver of heavenly gifts, "through the envy of the devil," separated into two diverse and opposite parts, of which the one steadfastly contends for truth and virtue, the other of those things which are contrary to virtue and to truth. The one is the kingdom of God on earth, namely, the true Church of Jesus Christ; and those who desire from their heart to be united with it, so as to gain salvation, must of necessity serve God and His only-begotten Son with their whole mind and with an entire will. The other is the kingdom of Satan, in whose possession and control are all whosoever follow the fatal example of their leader and of our first parents, those who refuse to obey the divine and eternal law, and who have many aims of their own in contempt of God, and many aims also against God.

2. This twofold kingdom St. Augustine keenly discerned and described after the manner of two cities, contrary in their laws because striving for contrary objects; and with a subtle brevity he expressed the efficient cause of each in these words: "Two loves formed two cities: the love of self, reaching even to contempt of God, an earthly city; and the love of God, reaching to contempt of self, a heavenly one."[1] At every period of time each has been in conflict with the other, with a variety and multiplicity of weapons and of warfare, although not always with equal ardour and assault. At this period, however, the partisans of evil seems to be combining together, and to be struggling with united vehemence, led on or assisted by that strongly organized and

---

[1] De civ. Dei, 14, 28 (PL 41, 436).

widespread association called the Freemasons. No longer making any secret of their purposes, they are now boldly rising up against God Himself. They are planning the destruction of holy Church publicly and openly, and this with the set purpose of utterly despoiling the nations of Christendom, if it were possible, of the blessings obtained for us through Jesus Christ our Saviour. Lamenting these evils, We are constrained by the charity which urges Our heart to cry out often to God: "For lo, Thy enemies have made a noise; and they that hate Thee have lifted up the head. They have taken a malicious counsel against Thy people, and they have consulted against Thy saints. They have said, 'come, and let us destroy them, so that they be not a nation.'"[2]

3. At so urgent a crisis, when so fierce and so pressing an onslaught is made upon the Christian name, it is Our office to point out the danger, to mark who are the adversaries, and to the best of Our power to make head against their plans and devices, that those may not perish whose salvation is committed to Us, and that the kingdom of Jesus Christ entrusted to Our charge may not stand and remain whole, but may be enlarged by an ever-increasing growth throughout the world.

4. The Roman Pontiffs Our predecessors, in their incessant watchfulness over the safety of the Christian people, were prompt in detecting the presence and the purpose of this capital enemy immediately it sprang into the light instead of hiding as a dark conspiracy; and , moreover, they took occasion with true foresight to give, as it were on their guard, and not allow themselves to be caught by the devices and snares laid out to deceive them.

5. The first warning of the danger was given by Clement XII in the year 1738,[3] and his constitution was confirmed and renewed by Benedict XIV[4] Pius VII followed the same path;[5] and Leo

---

[2] Ps. 82:24.
[3] Const. In Eminenti, April 24, 1738.

XII, by his apostolic constitution, *Quo Graviora*,[6] put together the acts and decrees of former Pontiffs on this subject, and ratified and confirmed them forever. In the same sense spoke Pius VIII,[7] Gregory XVI,[8] and, many times over, Pius IX.[9]

6. For as soon as the constitution and the spirit of the masonic sect were clearly discovered by manifest signs of its actions, by the investigation of its causes, by publication of its laws, and of its rites and commentaries, with the addition often of the personal testimony of those who were in the secret, this apostolic see denounced the sect of the Freemasons, and publicly declared its constitution, as contrary to law and right, to be pernicious no less to Christiandom than to the State; and it forbade any one to enter the society, under the penalties which the Church is wont to inflict upon exceptionally guilty persons. The sectaries, indignant at this, thinking to elude or to weaken the force of these decrees, partly by contempt of them, and partly by calumny, accused the sovereign Pontiffs who had passed them either of exceeding the bounds of moderation in their decrees or of decreeing what was not just. This was the manner in which they endeavoured to elude the authority and the weight of the apostolic constitutions of Clement XII and Benedict XIV, as well as of Pius VII and Pius IX.[10] Yet, in the very society itself, there were to be found men who unwillingly acknowledged that the Roman Pontiffs had acted within their right, according to the Catholic doctrine and discipline. The Pontiffs received the same assent, and in strong terms, from many princes and heads of governments, who made it their business either to delate the masonic society to the apostolic see, or of their own accord by

---

[4] Const. Providas, May 18, 1751.

[5] Const. Ecclesiam a Jesu Christo, Sept. 13, 1821.

[6] Const. given March 13, 1825.

[7] Encyc. Traditi, May 21, 1829.

[8] Encyc. Mirari, Augusr 15, 1832.

[9] Encyc. Qui Pluribus, Nov. 9, 1846; address Multiplices inter, Sept. 25, 1865, etc.

[10] Clement XII (1730-40); Benedict XIV (1740-58); Pius VII (1800-23); Pius IX (1846-78).

special enactments to brand it as pernicious, as, for example, in Holland, Austria, Switzerland, Spain, Bavaria, Savoy, and other parts of Italy.

7. But, what is of highest importance, the course of events has demonstrated the prudence of Our predecessors. For their provident and paternal solicitude had not always and every where the result desired; and this, either because of the simulation and cunning of some who were active agents in the mischief, or else of the thoughtless levity of the rest who ought, in their own interest, to have given to the matter their diligent attention. In consequence, the sect of Freemasons grew with a rapidity beyond conception in the course of a century and a half, until it came to be able, by means of fraud or of audacity, to gain such entrance into every rank of the State as to seem to be almost its ruling power. This swift and formidable advance has brought upon the Church, upon the power of princes, upon the public well-being, precisely that grievous harm which Our predecessors had long before foreseen. Such a condition has been reached that henceforth there will be grave reason to fear, not indeed for the Church - for her foundation is much too firm to be overturned by the effort of men - but for those States in which prevails the power, either of the sect of which we are speaking or of other sects not dissimilar which lend themselves to it as disciples and subordinates.

8. For these reasons We no sooner came to the helm of the Church than We clearly saw and felt it to be Our duty to use Our authority to the very utmost against so vast an evil. We have several times already, as occasion served, attacked certain chief points of teaching which showed in a special manner the perverse influence of Masonic opinions. Thus, in Our encyclical letter, *Quod Apostolici Muneris*, We endeavoured to refute the monstrous doctrines of the socialists and communists; afterwards, in another beginning "*Arcanum*," We took pains to defend and explain the true and genuine idea of domestic life, of which marriage is the spring and origin; and again, in that which

begins "*Diuturnum*,"[11] We described the ideal of political government conformed to the principles of Christian wisdom, which is marvellously in harmony, on the one hand, with the natural order of things, and, in the other, with the well-being of both sovereign princes and of nations. It is now Our intention, following the example of Our predecessors, directly to treat of the masonic society itself, of its whole teaching, of its aims, and of its manner of thinking and acting, in order to bring more and more into the light its power for evil, and to do what We can to arrest the contagion of this fatal plague.

9. There are several organized bodies which, though differing in name, in ceremonial, in form and origin, are nevertheless so bound together by community of purpose and by the similarity of their main opinions, as to make in fact one thing with the sect of the Freemasons, which is a kind of center whence they all go forth, and whither they all return. Now, these no longer show a desire to remain concealed; for they hold their meetings in the daylight and before the public eye, and publish their own newspaper organs; and yet, when thoroughly understood, they are found still to retain the nature and the habits of secret societies. There are many things like mysteries which it is the fixed rule to hide with extreme care, not only from strangers, but from very many members, also; such as their secret and final designs, the names of the chief leaders, and certain secret and inner meetings, as well as their decisions, and the ways and means of carrying them out. This is, no doubt, the object of the manifold difference among the members as to right, office, and privilege, of the received distinction of orders and grades, and of that severe discipline which is maintained.

Candidates are generally commanded to promise - nay, with a special oath, to swear - that they will never, to any person, at any time or in any way, make known the members, the passes, or the subjects discussed. Thus, with a fraudulent external appearance,

---

[11] See nos. 79, 81, 84.

and with a style of simulation which is always the same, the Freemasons, like the Manichees of old, strive, as far as possible, to conceal themselves, and to admit no witnesses but their own members. As a convenient manner of concealment, they assume the character of literary men and scholars associated for purposes of learning. They speak of their zeal for a more cultured refinement, and of their love for the poor; and they declare their one wish to be the amelioration of the condition of the masses, and to share with the largest possible number all the benefits of civil life. Were these purposes aimed at in real truth, they are by no means the whole of their object. Moreover, to be enrolled, it is necessary that the candidates promise and undertake to be thenceforward strictly obedient to their leaders and masters with the utmost submission and fidelity, and to be in readiness to do their bidding upon the slightest expression of their will; or, if disobedient, to submit to the direst penalties and death itself. As a fact, if any are judged to have betrayed the doings of the sect or to have resisted commands given, punishment is inflicted on them not infrequently, and with so much audacity and dexterity that the assassin very often escapes the detection and penalty of his crime.

10. But to simulate and wish to lie hid; to bind men like slaves in the very tightest bonds, and without giving any sufficient reason; to make use of men enslaved to the will of another for any arbitrary act ; to arm men's right hands for bloodshed after securing impunity for the crime - all this is an enormity from which nature recoils. Wherefore, reason and truth itself make it plain that the society of which we are speaking is in antagonism with justice and natural uprightness. And this becomes still plainer, inasmuch as other arguments, also, and those very manifest, prove that it is essentially opposed to natural virtue. For, no matter how great may be men's cleverness in concealing and their experience in lying, it is impossible to prevent the effects of any cause from showing, in some way, the intrinsic nature of the cause whence they come. "A good tree cannot produce bad fruit, nor a bad tree produce good fruit."[12] Now, the

masonic sect produces fruits that are pernicious and of the bitterest savour. For, from what We have above most clearly shown, that which is their ultimate purpose forces itself into view - namely, the utter overthrow of that whole religious and political order of the world which the Christian teaching has produced, and the substitution of a new state of things in accordance with their ideas, of which the foundations and laws shall be drawn from mere naturalism.

11. What We have said, and are about to say, must be understood of the sect of the Freemasons taken generically, and in so far as it comprises the associations kindred to it and confederated with it, but not of the individual members of them. There may be persons amongst these, and not a few who, although not free from the guilt of having entangled themselves in such associations, yet are neither themselves partners in their criminal acts nor aware of the ultimate object which they are endeavoring to attain. In the same way, some of the affiliated societies, perhaps, by no means approve of the extreme conclusions which they would, if consistent, embrace as necessarily following from their common principles, did not their very foulness strike them with horror. Some of these, again, are led by circumstances of times and places either to aim at smaller things than the others usually attempt or than they themselves would wish to attempt. They are not, however, for this reason, to be reckoned as alien to the masonic federation; for the masonic federation is to be judged not so much by the things which it has done, or brought to completion, as by the sum of its pronounced opinions.

12. Now, the fundamental doctrine of the naturalists, which they sufficiently make known by their very name, is that human nature and human reason ought in all things to be mistress and guide. Laying this down, they care little for duties to God, or pervert them by erroneous and vague opinions. For they deny that anything has been taught by God; they allow no dogma of

---

[12] Matt. 7:18.

religion or truth which cannot be understood by the human intelligence, nor any teacher who ought to be believed by reason of his authority. And since it is the special and exclusive duty of the Catholic Church fully to set forth in words truths divinely received, to teach, besides other divine helps to salvation, the authority of its office, and to defend the same with perfect purity, it is against the Church that the rage and attack of the enemies are principally directed.

13. In those matters which regard religion let it be seen how the sect of the Freemasons acts, especially where it is more free to act without restraint, and then let any one judge whether in fact it does not wish to carry out the policy of the naturalists. By a long and persevering labor, they endeavor to bring about this result - namely, that the teaching office and authority of the Church may become of no account in the civil State; and for this same reason they declare to the people and contend that Church and State ought to be altogether disunited. By this means they reject from the laws and from the commonwealth the wholesome influence of the Catholic religion; and they consequently imagine that States ought to be constituted without any regard for the laws and precepts of the Church.

14. Nor do they think it enough to disregard the Church - the best of guides - unless they also injure it by their hostility. Indeed, with them it is lawful to attack with impunity the very foundations of the Catholic religion, in speech, in writing, and in teaching; and even the rights of the Church are not spared, and the offices with which it is divinely invested are not safe. The least possible liberty to manage affairs is left to the Church; and this is done by laws not apparently very hostile, but in reality framed and fitted to hinder freedom of action. Moreover, We see exceptional and onerous laws imposed upon the clergy, to the end that they may be continually diminished in number and in necessary means. We see also the remnants of the possessions of the Church fettered by the strictest conditions, and subjected to

the power and arbitrary will of the administrators of the State, and the religious orders rooted up and scattered.

15. But against the apostolic see and the Roman Pontiff the contention of these enemies has been for a long time directed. The Pontiff was first, for specious reasons, thrust out from the bulwark of his liberty and of his right, the civil princedom; soon, he was unjustly driven into a condition which was unbearable because of the difficulties raised on all sides; and now the time has come when the partisans of the sects openly declare, what in secret among themselves they have for a long time plotted, that the sacred power of the Pontiffs must be abolished, and that the papacy itself, founded by divine right, must be utterly destroyed. If other proofs were wanting, this fact would be sufficiently disclosed by the testimony of men well informed, of whom some at other times, and others again recently, have declared it to be true of the Freemasons that they especially desire to assail the Church with irreconcilable hostility, and that they will never rest until they have destroyed whatever the supreme Pontiffs have established for the sake of religion.

16. If those who are admitted as members are not commanded to abjure by any form of words the Catholic doctrines, this omission, so far from being adverse to the designs of the Freemasons, is more useful for their purposes. First, in this way they easily deceive the simple-minded and the heedless, and can induce a far greater number to become members. Again, as all who offer themselves are received whatever may be their form of religion, they thereby teach the great error of this age-that a regard for religion should be held as an indifferent matter, and that all religions are alike. This manner of reasoning is calculated to bring about the ruin of all forms of religion, and especially of the Catholic religion, which, as it is the only one that is true, cannot, without great injustice, be regarded as merely equal to other religions.

17. But the naturalists go much further; for, having, in the highest things, entered upon a wholly erroneous course, they are carried headlong to extremes, either by reason of the weakness of human nature, or because God inflicts upon them the just punishment of their pride. Hence it happens that they no longer consider as certain and permanent those things which are fully understood by the natural light of reason, such as certainly are - the existence of God, the immaterial nature of the human soul, and its immortality. The sect of the Freemasons, by a similar course of error, is exposed to these same dangers; for, although in a general way they may profess the existence of God, they themselves are witnesses that they do not all maintain this truth with the full assent of the mind or with a firm conviction. Neither do they conceal that this question about God is the greatest source and cause of discords among them; in fact, it is certain that a considerable contention about this same subject has existed among them very lately. But, indeed, the sect allows great liberty to its votaries, so that to each side is given the right to defend its own opinion, either that there is a God, or that there is none; and those who obstinately contend that there is no God are as easily initiated as those who contend that God exists, though, like the pantheists, they have false notions concerning Him: all which is nothing else than taking away the reality, while retaining some absurd representation of the divine nature.

18. When this greatest fundamental truth has been overturned or weakened, it follows that those truths, also, which are known by the teaching of nature must begin to fall - namely, that all things were made by the free will of God the Creator; that the world is governed by Providence; that souls do not die; that to this life of men upon the earth there will succeed another and an everlasting life.

19. When these truths are done away with, which are as the principles of nature and important for knowledge and for practical use, it is easy to see what will become of both public and private morality. We say nothing of those more heavenly

virtues, which no one can exercise or even acquire without a special gift and grace of God; of which necessarily no trace can be found in those who reject as unknown the redemption of mankind, the grace of God, the sacraments, and the happiness to be obtained in heaven. We speak now of the duties which have their origin in natural probity. That God is the Creator of the world and its provident Ruler; that the eternal law commands the natural order to be maintained, and forbids that it be disturbed; that the last end of men is a destiny far above human things and beyond this sojourning upon the earth: these are the sources and these the principles of all justice and morality. If these be taken away, as the naturalists and Freemasons desire, there will immediately be no knowledge as to what constitutes justice and injustice, or upon what principle morality is founded. And, in truth, the teaching of morality which alone finds favor with the sect of Freemasons, and in which they contend that youth should be instructed, is that which they call "civil," and "independent," and "free," namely, that which does not contain any religious belief. But, how insufficient such teaching is, how wanting in soundness, and how easily moved by every impulse of passion, is sufficiently proved by its sad fruits, which have already begun to appear. For, wherever, by removing Christian education, this teaching has begun more completely to rule, there goodness and integrity of morals have begun quickly to perish, monstrous and shameful opinions have grown up, and the audacity of evil deeds has risen to a high degree. All this is commonly complained of and deplored; and not a few of those who by no means wish to do so are compelled by abundant evidence to give not infrequently the same testimony.

20. Moreover, human nature was stained by original sin, and is therefore more disposed to vice than to virtue. For a virtuous life it is absolutely necessary to restrain the disorderly movements of the soul, and to make the passions obedient to reason. In this conflict human things must very often be despised, and the greatest labors and hardships must be undergone, in order that reason may always hold its sway. But the naturalists and

Freemasons, having no faith in those things which we have learned by the revelation of God, deny that our first parents sinned, and consequently think that free will is not at all weakened and inclined to evil.[13] On the contrary, exaggerating rather the power and the excellence of nature, and placing therein alone the principle and rule of justice, they cannot even imagine that there is any need at all of a constant struggle and a perfect steadfastness to overcome the violence and rule of our passions.

Wherefore we see that men are publicly tempted by the many allurements of pleasure; that there are journals and pamphlets with neither moderation nor shame; that stage-plays are remarkable for license; that designs for works of art are shamelessly sought in the laws of a so called verism; that the contrivances of a soft and delicate life are most carefully devised; and that all the blandishments of pleasure are diligently sought out by which virtue may be lulled to sleep. Wickedly, also, but at the same time quite consistently, do those act who do away with the expectation of the joys of heaven, and bring down all happiness to the level of mortality, and, as it were, sink it in the earth. Of what We have said the following fact, astonishing not so much in itself as in its open expression, may serve as a confirmation. For, since generally no one is accustomed to obey crafty and clever men so submissively as those whose soul is weakened and broken down by the domination of the passions, there have been in the sect of the Freemasons some who have plainly determined and proposed that, artfully and of set purpose, the multitude should be satiated with a boundless license of vice, as, when this had been done, it would easily come under their power and authority for any acts of daring.

---

[13] Trid., sess. vi, De justif., c. 1. Text of the Council of Trent: "tametsi in eis (sc. Judaeis)liberum arbitrium minime extinctum esset, viribus licet attenuatum et inclinatum".

21. What refers to domestic life in the teaching of the naturalists is almost all contained in the following declarations: that marriage belongs to the genus of commercial contracts, which can rightly be revoked by the will of those who made them, and that the civil rulers of the State have power over the matrimonial bond; that in the education of youth nothing is to be taught in the matter of religion as of certain and fixed opinion; and each one must be left at liberty to follow, when he comes of age, whatever he may prefer. To these things the Freemasons fully assent; and not only assent, but have long endeavoured to make them into a law and institution. For in many countries, and those nominally Catholic, it is enacted that no marriages shall be considered lawful except those contracted by the civil rite; in other places the law permits divorce; and in others every effort is used to make it lawful as soon as may be. Thus, the time is quickly coming when marriages will be turned into another kind of contract - that is into changeable and uncertain unions which fancy may join together, and which the same when changed may disunite.

With the greatest unanimity the sect of the Freemasons also endeavours to take to itself the education of youth. They think that they can easily mold to their opinions that soft and pliant age, and bend it whither they will; and that nothing can be more fitted than this to enable them to bring up the youth of the State after their own plan. Therefore, in the education and instruction of children they allow no share, either of teaching or of discipline, to the ministers of the Church; and in many places they have procured that the education of youth shall be exclusively in the hands of laymen, and that nothing which treats of the most important and most holy duties of men to God shall be introduced into the instructions on morals.

22. Then come their doctrines of politics, in which the naturalists lay down that all men have the same right, and are in every respect of equal and like condition; that each one is naturally free; that no one has the right to command another; that it is an

act of violence to require men to obey any authority other than
that which is obtained from themselves. According to this,
therefore, all things belong to the free people; power is held by
the command or permission of the people, so that, when the
popular will changes, rulers may lawfully be deposed and the
source of all rights and civil duties is either in the multitude or in
the governing authority when this is constituted according to the
latest doctrines. It is held also that the State should be without
God; that in the various forms of religion there is no reason why
one should have precedence of another; and that they are all to
occupy the same place.

23. That these doctrines are equally acceptable to the
Freemasons, and that they would wish to constitute States
according to this example and model, is too well known to
require proof. For some time past they have openly endeavoured
to bring this about with all their strength and resources; and in
this they prepare the way for not a few bolder men who are
hurrying on even to worse things, in their endeavor to obtain
equality and community of all goods by the destruction of every
distinction of rank and property.

24. What, therefore, sect of the Freemasons is, and what course
it pursues, appears sufficiently from the summary We have
briefly given. Their chief dogmas are so greatly and manifestly at
variance with reason that nothing can be more perverse. To wish
to destroy the religion and the Church which God Himself has
established, and whose perpetuity He insures by His protection,
and to bring back after a lapse of eighteen centuries the manners
and customs of the pagans, is signal folly and audacious impiety.
Neither is it less horrible nor more tolerable that they should
repudiate the benefits which Jesus Christ so mercifully obtained,
not only for individuals, but also for the family and for civil
society, benefits which, even according to the judgment and
testimony of enemies of Christianity, are very great. In this
insane and wicked endeavor we may almost see the implacable
hatred and spirit of revenge with which Satan himself is inflamed

against Jesus Christ. - So also the studious endeavour of the Freemasons to destroy the chief foundations of justice and honesty, and to co-operate with those who would wish, as if they were mere animals, to do what they please, tends only to the ignominious and disgraceful ruin of the human race.

The evil, too, is increased by the dangers which threaten both domestic and civil society. As We have elsewhere shown,[14] in marriage, according to the belief of almost every nation, there is something sacred and religious; and the law of God has determined that marriages shall not be dissolved. If they are deprived of their sacred character, and made dissoluble, trouble and confusion in the family will be the result, the wife being deprived of her dignity and the children left without protection as to their interests and well being.-To have in public matters no care for religion, and in the arrangement and administration of civil affairs to have no more regard for God than if He did not exist, is a rashness unknown to the very pagans; for in their heart and soul the notion of a divinity and the need of public religion were so firmly fixed that they would have thought it easier to have city without foundation than a city without God. Human society, indeed for which by nature we are formed, has been constituted by God the Author of nature; and from Him, as from their principle and source, flow in all their strength and permanence the countless benefits with which society abounds. As we are each of us admonished by the very voice of nature to worship God in piety and holiness, as the Giver unto us of life and of all that is good therein, so also and for the same reason, nations and States are bound to worship Him; and therefore it is clear that those who would absolve society from all religious duty act not only unjustly but also with ignorance and folly.

25. As men are by the will of God born for civil union and society, and as the power to rule is so necessary a bond of society that, if it be taken away, society must at once be broken up, it

---

[14] See Arcanum, no. 81.

follows that from Him who is the Author of society has come also the authority to rule; so that whosoever rules, he is the minister of God. Wherefore, as the end and nature of human society so requires, it is right to obey the just commands of lawful authority, as it is right to obey God who ruleth all things; and it is most untrue that the people have it in their power to cast aside their obedience whensoever they please.

26. In like manner, no one doubts that all men are equal one to another, so far as regards their common origin and nature, or the last end which each one has to attain, or the rights and duties which are thence derived. But, as the abilities of all are not equal, as one differs from another in the powers of mind or body, and as there are very many dissimilarities of manner, disposition, and character, it is most repugnant to reason to endeavor to confine all within the same measure, and to extend complete equality to the institutions of civic life. Just as a perfect condition of the body results from the conjunction and composition of its various members, which, though differing in form and purpose, make, by their union and the distribution of each one to its proper place, a combination beautiful to behole, firm in strength, and necessary for use; so, in the commonwealth, there is an almost infinite dissimilarity of men, as parts of the whole. If they are to be all equal, and each is to follow his own will, the State will appear most deformed; but if, with a distinction of degrees of dignity, of pursuits and employments, all aptly conspire for the common good, they will present the image of a State both well constituted and conformable to nature.

27. Now, from the disturbing errors which We have described the greatest dangers to States are to be feared. For, the fear of God and reverence for divine laws being taken away, the authority of rulers despised, sedition permitted and approved, and the popular passions urged on to lawlessness, with no restraint save that of punishment, a change and overthrow of all things will necessarily follow. Yea, this change and overthrow is deliberately planned and put forward by many associations of

communists and socialists; and to their undertakings the sect of Freemasons is not hostile, but greatly favours their designs, and holds in common with them their chief opinions. And if these men do not at once and everywhere endeavour to carry out their extreme views, it is not to be attributed to their teaching and their will, but to the virtue of that divine religion which cannot be destroyed; and also because the sounder part of men, refusing to be enslaved to secret societies, vigorously resist their insane attempts.

28. Would that all men would judge of the tree by its fruit, and would acknowledge the seed and origin of the evils which press upon us, and of the dangers that are impending! We have to deal with a deceitful and crafty enemy, who, gratifying the ears of people and of princes, has ensnared them by smooth speeches and by adulation. Ingratiating themselves with rulers under a pretense of friendship, the Freemasons have endeavoured to make them their allies and powerful helpers for the destruction of the Christian name; and that they might more strongly urge them on, they have, with determined calumny, accused the Church of invidiously contending with rulers in matters that affect their authority and sovereign power. Having, by these artifices, insured their own safety and audacity, they have begun to exercise great weight in the government of States; but nevertheless they are prepared to shake the foundations of empires, to harass the rulers of the State, to accuse, and to cast them out, as often as they appear to govern otherwise than they themselves could have wished. In like manner, they have by flattery deluded the people. Proclaiming with a loud voice liberty and public prosperity, and saying that it was owing to the Church and to sovereigns that the multitude were not drawn out of their unjust servitude and poverty, they have imposed upon the people, and, exciting them by a thirst for novelty, they have urged them to assail both the Church and the civil power. Nevertheless, the expectation of the benefits which was hoped for is greater than the reality; indeed, the common people, more oppressed than they were before, are deprived in their misery of

that solace which, if things had been arranged in a Christian manner, they would have had with ease and in abundance. But, whoever strive against the order which Divine Providence has constituted pay usually the penalty of their pride, and meet with affliction and misery where they rashly hoped to find all things prosperous and in conformity with their desires.

29. The Church, if she directs men to render obedience chiefly and above all to God the sovereign Lord, is wrongly and falsely believed either to be envious of the civil power or to arrogate to herself something of the rights of sovereigns. On the contrary, she teaches that what is rightly due to the civil power must be rendered to it with a conviction and consciousness of duty. In teaching that from God Himself comes the right of ruling, she adds a great dignity to civil authority, and on small help towards obtaining the obedience and good will of the citizens. The friend of peace and sustainer of concord, she embraces all with maternal love, and, intent only upon giving help to mortal man, she teaches that to justice must be joined clemency, equity to authority, and moderation to lawgiving; that no one's right must be violated; that order and public tranquility are to be maintained; and that the poverty of those are in need is, as far as possible, to be relieved by public and private charity. "But for this reason," to use the words of St. Augustine, "men think, or would have it believed, that Christian teaching is not suited to the good of the State; for they wish the State to be founded not on solid virtue, but on the impunity of vice."[15] Knowing these things, both princes and people would act with political wisdom, and according to the needs of general safety, if, instead of joining with Freemasons to destroy the Church, they joined with the Church in repelling their attacks.

30 .Whatever the future may be, in this grave and widespread evil it is Our duty, venerable brethren, to endeavour to find a remedy. And because We know that Our best and firmest hope of a

---

[15] Epistola 137, ad Volusianum, c. v, n. 20 (PL 33 525).

remedy is in the power of that divine religion which the
Freemasons hate in proportion to their fear of it, We think it to
be of chief importance to call that most saving power to Our aid
against the common enemy. Therefore, whatsoever the Roman
Pontiffs Our predecessors have decreed for the purpose of
opposing the undertakings and endeavours of the masonic sect,
and whatsoever they have enacted to enter or withdraw men
from societies of this kind, We ratify and confirm it all by our
apostolic authority: and trusting greatly to the good will of
Christians, We pray and beseech each one, for the sake of his
eternal salvation, to be most conscientiously careful not in the
least to depart from what the apostolic see has commanded in
this matter.

31. We pray and beseech you, venerable brethren, to join your
efforts with Ours, and earnestly to strive for the extirpation of
this foul plague, which is creeping through the veins of the body
politic. You have to defend the glory of God and the salvation of
your neighbour; and with the object of your strife before you,
neither courage nor strength will be wanting. It will be for your
prudence to judge by what means you can best overcome the
difficulties and obstacles you meet with. But, as it befits the
authority of Our office that We Ourselves should point out some
suitable way of proceeding, We wish it to be your rule first of all
to tear away the mask from Freemasonry, and to let it be seen as
it really is; and by sermons and pastoral letters to instruct the
people as to the artifices used by societies of this kind in
seducing men and enticing them into their ranks, and as to the
depravity of their opinions and the wickedness of their acts. As
Our predecessors have many times repeated, let no man think
that he may for any reason whatsoever join the masonic sect, if
he values his Catholic name and his eternal salvation as he ought
to value them. Let no one be deceived by a pretense of honesty.
It may seem to some that Freemasons demand nothing that is
openly contrary to religion and morality; but, as the whole
principle and object of the sect lies in what is vicious and

criminal, to join with these men or in any way to help them cannot be lawful.

32. Further, by assiduous teaching and exhortation, the multitude must be drawn to learn diligently the precepts of religion; for which purpose we earnestly advise that by opportune writings and sermons they be taught the elements of those sacred truths in which Christian philosophy is contained. The result of this will be that the minds of men will be made sound by instruction, and will be protected against many forms of error and inducements to wickedness, especially in the present unbounded freedom of writing and insatiable eagerness for learning.

33. Great, indeed, is the work; but in it the clergy will share your labours, if, through your care, they are fitted for it by learning and a well-turned life. This good and great work requires to be helped also by the industry of those amongst the laity in whom a love of religion and of country is joined to learning and goodness of life. By uniting the efforts of both clergy and laity, strive, venerable brethren, to make men thoroughly know and love the Church; for, the greater their knowledge and love of the Church, the more will they be turned away from clandestine societies.

34. Wherefore, not without cause do We use this occasion to state again what We have stated elsewhere, namely, that the Third Order of St. Francis, whose discipline We a little while ago prudently mitigated,[16] should be studiously promoted and

---

[16] The text here refers to the encyclical letter Auspicato Concessum (Sept. 17, 1882), in which Pope Leo XIII had recently glorified St. Francis of Assisi on the occasion of the seventh centenary of his birch. In this encyclical, the Pope had presented the Third Order of St. Francis as a Christian answer to the social problems of the times. The constitution Misericors Dei Filius (June 23, 1883) expressly recalled that the neglect in which Christian virtues are held is the main cause of the evils that threaten societies. In confirming the rule of the Third Order and adapting it to the needs of modern times, Pope Leo XIII had intended to bring back the largest possible number of souls to the practice of these virtues.

sustained; for the whole object of this Order, as constituted by its founder, is to invite men to an imitation of Jesus Christ, to a love of the Church, and to the observance of all Christian virtues; and therefore it ought to be of great influence in suppressing the contagion of wicked societies. Let, therefore, this holy sodality be strengthened by a daily increase. Amongst the many benefits to be expected from it will be the great benefit of drawing the minds of men to liberty, fraternity, and equality of right; not such as the Freemasons absurdly imagine, but such as Jesus Christ obtained for the human race and St. Francis aspired to: the liberty, We mean, of *sons of God*, through which we may be free from slavery to Satan or to our passions, both of them most wicked masters; the fraternity whose origin is in God, the common Creator and Father of all; the equality which, founded on justice and charity, does not take away all distinctions among men, but, out of the varieties of life, of duties, and of pursuits, forms that union and that harmony which naturally tend to the benefit and dignity of society.

35. In the third place, there is a matter wisely instituted by our forefathers, but in course of time laid aside, which may now be used as a pattern and form of something similar. We mean the associations of guilds of workmen, for the protection, under the guidance of religion, both of their temporal interests and of their morality. If our ancestors, by long use and experience, felt the benefit of these guilds, our age perhaps will feel it the more by reason of the opportunity which they will give of crushing the power of the sects. Those who support themselves by the labour of their hands, besides being, by their very condition, most worthy above all others of charity and consolation, are also especially exposed to the allurements of men whose ways lie in fraud and deceit. Therefore, they ought to be helped with the greatest possible kindness, and to be invited to join associations that are good, lest they be drawn away to others that are evil. For this reason, We greatly wish, for the salvation of the people, that, under the auspices and patronage of the bishops, and at convenient times, these gilds may be generally restored. To Our

great delight, sodalities of this kind and also associations of masters have in many places already been established, having, each class of them, for their object to help the honest workman, to protect and guard his children and family, and to promote in them piety, Christian knowledge, and a moral life. And in this matter We cannot omit mentioning that exemplary society, named after its founder, St. Vincent, which has deserved so well of the lower classes. Its acts and its aims are well known. Its whole object is to give relief to the poor and miserable. This it does with singular prudence and modesty; and the less it wishes to be seen, the better is it fitted for the exercise of Christian charity, and for the relief of suffering.

36. In the fourth place, in order more easily to attain what We wish, to your fidelity and watchfulness We commend in a special manner the young, as being the hope of human society. Devote the greatest part of your care to their instruction; and do not think that any precaution can be great enough in keeping them from masters and schools whence the pestilent breath of the sects is to be feared. Under your guidance, let parents, religious instructors, and priests having the cure of souls use every opportunity, in their Christian teaching, of warning their children and pupils of the infamous nature of these societies, so that they may learn in good time to beware of the various and fraudulent artifices by which their promoters are accustomed to ensnare people. And those who instruct the young in religious knowledge will act wisely if they induce all of them to resolve and to undertake never to bind themselves to any society without the knowledge of their parents, or the advice of their parish priest or director.

37. We well know, however, that our united labors will by no means suffice to pluck up these pernicious seeds from the Lord's field, unless the Heavenly Master of the vineyard shall mercifully help us in our endeavours. We must, therefore, with great and anxious care, implore of Him the help which the greatness of the danger and of the need requires. The sect of the Freemasons

shows itself insolent and proud of its success, and seems as if it would put no bounds to its pertinacity. Its followers, joined together by a wicked compact and by secret counsels, give help one to another, and excite one another to an audacity for evil things. So vehement an attack demands an equal defence-namely, that all good men should form the widest possible association of action and of prayer. We beseech them, therefore, with united hearts, to stand together and unmoved against the advancing force of the sects; and in mourning and supplication to stretch out their hands to God, praying that the Christian name may flourish and prosper, that the Church may enjoy its needed liberty, that those who have gone astray may return to a right mind, that error at length may give place to truth, and vice to virtue. Let us take our helper and intercessor the Virgin Mary, Mother of God, so that she, who from the moment of her conception overcame Satan may show her power over these evil sects, in which is revived the contumacious spirit of the demon, together with his unsubdued perfidy and deceit. Let us beseech Michael, the prince of the heavenly angels, who drove out the infernal foe; and Joseph, the spouse of the most holy Virgin, and heavenly patron of the Catholic Church; and the great Apostles, Peter and Paul, the fathers and victorious champions of the Christian faith. By their patronage, and by perseverance in united prayer, we hope that God will mercifully and opportunely succor the human race, which is encompassed by so many dangers.

38. As a pledge of heavenly gifts and of Our benevolence, We lovingly grant in the Lord, to you, venerable brethren, and to the clergy and all the people committed to your watchful care, Our apostolic benediction.

Given at St. Peter's in Rome, the twentieth day of April, 1884, the sixth year of Our pontificate.

VI: Immortale Dei

November 1, 1885

ON THE CHRISTIAN CONSTITUTION OF STATES

The Catholic Church, that imperishable handiwork of our all-merciful God, has for her immediate and natural purpose the saving of souls and securing our happiness in heaven. Yet, in regard to things temporal, she is the source of benefits as manifold and great as if the chief end of her existence were to ensure the prospering of our earthly life. And, indeed, wherever the Church has set her foot she has straightway changed the face of things, and has attempered the moral tone of the people with a new civilization and with virtues before unknown. All nations which have yielded to her sway have become eminent by their gentleness, their sense of justice, and the glory of their high deeds.

2. And yet a hackneyed reproach of old date is levelled against her, that the Church is opposed to the rightful aims of the civil government, and is wholly unable to afford help in spreading that welfare and progress which justly and naturally are sought after by every well-regulated State. From the very beginning Christians were harassed by slanderous accusations of this nature, and on that account were held up to hatred and execration, for being (so they were called) enemies of the Empire. The Christian religion was moreover commonly charged with being the cause of the calamities that so frequently befell the State, whereas, in very truth, just punishment was being awarded to guilty nations by an avenging God. This odious calumny, with most valid reason, nerved the genius and sharpened the pen of St. Augustine, who, notably in his treatise, The City of God, set forth in so bright a light the worth of Christian wisdom in its relation to the public wealth that he seems not merely to have

pleaded the cause of the Christians of his day, but to have refuted for all future times impeachments so grossly contrary to truth. The wicked proneness, however, to levy like charges and accusations has not been lulled to rest. Many, indeed, are they who have tried to work out a plan of civil society based on doctrines other than those approved by the Catholic Church. Nay, in these latter days a novel conception of law has begun here and there to gain increase and influence, the outcome, as it is maintained, of an age arrived at full stature, and the result of progressive liberty. But, though endeavours of various kinds have been ventured on, it is clear that no better mode has been devised for the building up and ruling the State than that which is the necessary growth of the teachings of the Gospel. We deem it, therefore, of the highest moment, and a strict duty of Our apostolic office, to contrast with the lessons taught by Christ the novel theories now advanced touching the State. By this means We cherish hope that the bright shining of the truth may scatter the mists of error and doubt, so that one and all may see clearly the imperious law of life which they are bound to follow and obey.

3. It is not difficult to determine what would be the form and character of the State were it governed according to the principles of Christian philosophy. Man's natural instinct moves him to live in civil society, for he cannot, if dwelling apart, provide himself with the necessary requirements of life, nor procure the means of developing his mental and moral faculties. Hence, it is divinely ordained that he should lead his life-be it family, or civil-with his fellow men, amongst whom alone his several wants can be adequately supplied. But, as no society can hold together unless some one be over all, directing all to strive earnestly for the common good, every body politic must have a ruling authority, and this authority, no less than society itself, has its source in nature, and has, consequently, God for its Author. Hence, it follows that all public power must proceed from God. For God alone is the true and supreme Lord of the world. Everything, without exception, must be subject to Him, and

must serve him, so that whosoever holds the right to govern holds it from one sole and single source, namely, God, the sovereign Ruler of all. "There is no power but from God."[1]

4. The right to rule is not necessarily, however, bound up with any special mode of government. It may take this or that form, provided only that it be of a nature of the government, rulers must ever bear in mind that God is the paramount ruler of the world, and must set Him before themselves as their exemplar and law in the administration of the State. For, in things visible God has fashioned secondary causes, in which His divine action can in some wise be discerned, leading up to the end to which the course of the world is ever tending. In like manner, in civil society, God has always willed that there should be a ruling authority, and that they who are invested with it should reflect the divine power and providence in some measure over the human race.

5. They, therefore, who rule should rule with evenhanded justice, not as masters, but rather as fathers, for the rule of God over man is most just, and is tempered always with a father's kindness. Government should, moreover, be administered for the well-being of the citizens, because they who govern others possess authority solely for the welfare of the State. Furthermore, the civil power must not be subservient to the advantage of any one individual or of some few persons, inasmuch as it was established for the common good of all. But, if those who are in authority rule unjustly, if they govern overbearingly or arrogantly, and if their measures prove hurtful to the people, they must remember that the Almighty will one day bring them to account, the more strictly in proportion to the sacredness of their office and preeminence of their dignity. "The mighty shall be mightily tormented."[2] Then, truly, will the majesty of the law meet with the dutiful and willing homage of the people, when they are

---

[1] Rom. 13:1.
[2] Wisd. 6:7.

convinced that their rulers hold authority from God, and feel that it is a matter of justice and duty to obey them, and to show them reverence and fealty, united to a love not unlike that which children show their parents. "Let every soul be subject to higher powers."[3] To despise legitimate authority, in whomsoever vested, is unlawful, as a rebellion against the divine will, and whoever resists that, rushes willfully to destruction. "He that resisteth the power resisteth the ordinance of God, and they that resist, purchase to themselves damnation."[4] To cast aside obedience, and by popular violence to incite to revolt, is therefore treason, not against man only, but against God.

6. As a consequence, the State, constituted as it is, is clearly bound to act up to the manifold and weighty duties linking it to God, by the public profession of religion. Nature and reason, which command every individual devoutly to worship God in holiness, because we belong to Him and must return to Him, since from Him we came, bind also the civil community by a like law. For, men living together in society are under the power of God no less than individuals are, and society, no less than individuals, owes gratitude to God who gave it being and maintains it and whose ever-bounteous goodness enriches it with countless blessings. Since, then, no one is allowed to be remiss in the service due to God, and since the chief duty of all men is to cling to religion in both its reaching and practice-not such religion as they may have a preference for, but the religion which God enjoins, and which certain and most clear marks show to be the only one true religion -it is a public crime to act as though there were no God. So, too, is it a sin for the State not to have care for religion as a something beyond its scope, or as of no practical benefit; or out of many forms of religion to adopt that one which chimes in with the fancy; for we are bound absolutely to worship God in that way which He has shown to be His will. All who rule, therefore, would hold in honour the holy name of

---

[3] Rom. 13:1.
[4] Rom. 13:2.

God, and one of their chief duties must be to favour religion, to protect it, to shield it under the credit and sanction of the laws, and neither to organize nor enact any measure that may compromise its safety. This is the bounden duty of rulers to the people over whom they rule. For one and all are we destined by our birth and adoption to enjoy, when this frail and fleeting life is ended, a supreme and final good in heaven, and to the attainment of this every endeavour should be directed. Since, then, upon this depends the full and perfect happiness of mankind, the securing of this end should be of all imaginable interests the most urgent. Hence, civil society, established for the common welfare, should not only safeguard the well-being of the community, but have also at heart the interests of its individual members, in such mode as not in any way to hinder, but in every manner to render as easy as may be, the possession of that highest and unchangeable good for which all should seek. Wherefore, for this purpose, care must especially be taken to preserve unharmed and unimpeded the religion whereof the practice is the link connecting man with God.

7. Now, it cannot be difficult to find out which is the true religion, if only it be sought with an earnest and unbiased mind; for proofs are abundant and striking. We have, for example, the fulfilment of prophecies, miracles in great numbers, the rapid spread of the faith in the midst of enemies and in face of overwhelming obstacles, the witness of the martyrs, and the like. From all these it is evident that the only true religion is the one established by Jesus Christ Himself, and which He committed to His Church to protect and to propagate.

8. For the only-begotten Son of God established on earth a society which is called the Church, and to it He handed over the exalted and divine office which He had received from His Father, to be continued through the ages to come. "As the Father hath sent Me, I also send you."[5] "Behold I am with you all

---

[5] John 20:21.

days, even to the consummation of the world."[6] Consequently, as Jesus Christ came into the world that men "might have life and have it more abundantly,"[7] so also has the Church for its aim and end the eternal salvation of souls, and hence it is so constituted as to open wide its arms to all mankind, unhampered by any limit of either time or place. "Preach ye the Gospel to every creature."[8]

9. Over this mighty multitude God has Himself set rulers with power to govern, and He has willed that one should be the head of all, and the chief and unerring teacher of truth, to whom He has given "the keys of the kingdom of heaven."[9] "Feed My lambs, feed My sheep."[10] "I have prayed for thee that thy faith fail not."[11]

10. This society is made up of men, just as civil society is, and yet is supernatural and spiritual, on account of the end for which it was founded, and of the means by which it aims at attaining that end. Hence, it is distinguished and differs from civil society, and, what is of highest moment, it is a society chartered as of right divine, perfect in its nature and in its title, to possess in itself and by itself, through the will and loving kindness of its Founder, all needful provision for its maintenance and action. And just as the end at which the Church aims is by far the noblest of ends, so is its authority the most exalted of all authority, nor can it be looked upon as inferior to the civil power, or in any manner dependent upon it.

11. In very truth, Jesus Christ gave to His Apostles unrestrained authority in regard to things sacred, together with the genuine and most true power of making laws, as also with the twofold right of judging and of punishing, which flow from that power.

---

[6] Matt. 28:20.
[7] John 10:10.
[8] Mark 16:15.
[9] Matt. 16:19.
[10] John 21:16-17.
[11] Luke 22:32.

"All power is given to Me in heaven and on earth: going therefore teach all nations... teaching them to observe all things whatsoever I have commanded you."[12] And in another place: "If he will not hear them, tell the Church."[13] And again: "In readiness to revenge all disobedience."[14] And once more: "That... I may not deal more severely according to the power which the Lord bath given me, unto edification and not unto destruction."[15] Hence, it is the Church, and not the State, that is to be man's guide to heaven. It is to the Church that God has assigned the charge of seeing to, and legislating for, all that concerns religion; of teaching all nations; of spreading the Christian faith as widely as possible; in short, of administering freely and without hindrance, in accordance with her own judgment, all matters that fall within its competence.

12. Now, this authority, perfect in itself, and plainly meant to be unfettered, so long assailed by a philosophy that truckles to the State, the Church, has never ceased to claim for herself and openly to exercise. The Apostles themselves were the first to uphold it, when, being forbidden by the rulers of the synagogue to preach the Gospel, they courageously answered: "We must obey God rather than men."[16] This same authority the holy Fathers of the Church were always careful to maintain by weighty arguments, according as occasion arose, and the Roman Pontiffs have never shrunk from defending it with unbending constancy. Nay, more, princes and all invested with power to rule have themselves approved it, in theory alike and in practice. It cannot be called in question that in the making of treaties, in the transaction of business matters, in the sending and receiving ambassadors, and in the interchange of other kinds of official dealings they have been wont to treat with the Church as with a supreme and legitimate power. And, assuredly, all ought to hold

---

[12] Matt. 28:18-20.
[13] Matt. 18:12.
[14] 2 Cor. 10:6.
[15] 2 Cor. 13:10.
[16] Acts 5:29.

that it was not without a singular disposition of God's providence that this power of the Church was provided with a civil sovereignty as the surest safeguard of her independence.

13. The Almighty, therefore, has given the charge of the human race to two powers, the ecclesiastical and the civil, the one being set over divine, and the other over human, things. Each in its kind is supreme, each has fixed limits within which it is contained, limits which are defined by the nature and special object of the province of each, so that there is, we may say, an orbit traced out within which the action of each is brought into play by its own native right. But, inasmuch as each of these two powers has authority over the same subjects, and as it might come to pass that one and the same thing-related differently, but still remaining one and the same thing-might belong to the jurisdiction and determination of both, therefore God, who foresees all things, and who is the author of these two powers, has marked out the course of each in right correlation to the other. "For the powers that are, are ordained of God."![17] Were this not so, deplorable contentions and conflicts would often arise, and, not infrequently, men, like travellers at the meeting of two roads, would hesitate in anxiety and doubt, not knowing what course to follow. Two powers would be commanding contrary things, and it would be a dereliction of duty to disobey either of the two.

14. But it would be most repugnant to them to think thus of the wisdom and goodness of God. Even in physical things, albeit of a lower order, the Almighty has so combined the forces and springs of nature with tempered action and wondrous harmony that no one of them clashes with any other, and all of them most fitly and aptly work together for the great purpose of the universe. There must, accordingly, exist between these two powers a certain orderly connection, which may be compared to the union of the soul and body in man. The nature and scope of

---

[17] Rom. 13:1.

that connection can be determined only, as We have laid down, by having regard to the nature of each power, and by taking account of the relative excellence and nobleness of their purpose. One of the two has for its proximate and chief object the well-being of this mortal life; the other, the everlasting joys of heaven. Whatever, therefore in things human is of a sacred character, whatever belongs either of its own nature or by reason of the end to which it is referred, to the salvation of souls, or to the worship of God, is subject to the power and judgment of the Church. Whatever is to be ranged under the civil and political order is rightly subject to the civil authority. Jesus Christ has Himself given command that what is Caesar's is to be rendered to Caesar, and that what belongs to God is to be rendered to God.

15. There are, nevertheless, occasions when another method of concord is available for the sake of peace and liberty: We mean when rulers of the State and the Roman Pontiff come to an understanding touching some special matter. At such times the Church gives signal proof of her motherly love by showing the greatest possible kindliness and indulgence.

16. Such, then, as We have briefly pointed out, is the Christian organization of civil society; not rashly or fancifully shaped out, but educed from the highest and truest principles, confirmed by natural reason itself.

17. In such organization of the State there is nothing that can be thought to infringe upon the dignity of rulers, and nothing unbecoming them; nay, so far from degrading the sovereign power in its due rights, it adds to it permanence and luster. Indeed, when more fully pondered, this mutual co-ordination has a perfection in which all other forms of government are lacking, and from which excellent results would flow, were the several component parts to keep their place and duly discharge the office and work appointed respectively for each. And, doubtless, in the constitution of the State such as We have described, divine

and human things are equitably shared; the rights of citizens assured to them, and fenced round by divine, by natural, and by human law; the duties incumbent on each one being wisely marked out, and their fulfilment fittingly insured. In their uncertain and toilsome journey to the everlasting city all see that they have safe guides and helpers on their way, and are conscious that others have charge to protect their persons alike and their possessions, and to obtain or preserve for them everything essential for their present life. Furthermore, domestic society acquires that firmness and solidity so needful to it from the holiness of marriage, one and indissoluble, wherein the rights and duties of husband and wife are controlled with wise justice and equity; due honour is assured to the woman; the authority of the husband is conformed to the pattern afforded by the authority of God; the power of the father is tempered by a due regard for the dignity of the mother and her offspring; and the best possible provision is made for the guardianship, welfare, and education of the children.

18. In political affairs, and all matters civil, the laws aim at securing the common good, and are not framed according to the delusive caprices and opinions of the mass of the people, but by truth and by justice; the ruling powers are invested with a sacredness more than human, and are withheld from deviating from the path of duty, and from overstepping the bounds of rightful authority; and the obedience is not the servitude of man to man, but submission to the will of God, exercising His sovereignty through the medium of men. Now, this being recognized as undeniable, it is felt that the high office of rulers should be held in respect; that public authority should be constantly and faithfully obeyed; that no act of sedition should be committed; and that the civic order of the commonwealth should be maintained as sacred.

19. So, also, as to the duties of each one toward his fellow men, mutual forbearance, kindliness, generosity are placed in the ascendant; the man who is at once a citizen and a Christian is not

drawn aside by conflicting obligations; and, lastly, the abundant benefits with which the Christian religion, of its very nature, endows even the mortal life of man are acquired for the community and civil society. And this to such an extent that it may be said in sober truth: "The condition of the commonwealth depends on the religion with which God is worshipped; and between one and the other there exists an intimate and abiding connection."[18]

20. Admirably, according to his wont, does St. Augustine, in many passages, enlarge upon the nature of these advantages; but nowhere more markedly and to the point than when he addresses the Catholic Church in the following words: "Thou dost teach and train children with much tenderness, young men with much vigour, old men with much gentleness; as the age not of the body alone, but of the mind of each requires. Women thou dost subject to their husbands in chaste and faithful obedience, not for the gratifying of their lust, but for bringing forth children, and for having a share in the family concerns. Thou dost set husbands over their wives, not that they may play false to the weaker sex, but according to the requirements of sincere affection. Thou dost subject children to their parents in a kind of free service, and dost establish parents over their children with a benign rule. . . Thou joinest together, not in society only, but in a sort of brotherhood, citizen with citizen, nation with nation, and the whole race of men, by reminding them of their common parentage. Thou teachest kings to look to the interests of their people, and dost admonish the people to be submissive to their kings. With all care dost thou teach all to whom honour is due, and affection, and reverence, and fear, consolation, and admonition and exhortation, and discipline, and reproach, and punishment. Thou showest that all these are not equally incumbent on all, but that charity is owing to all, and wrongdoing to none."[19] And in another place, blaming the false wisdom of

---

[18] Sacr. Imp. ad Cyrillum Alexand. et Episcopos metrop.; See Labbeus, Collect. Conc., Vol. 3.

[19] De moribus ecclesiae, 1, cap. 30, n. 63 (PL 32, 1336).

certain time-serving philosophers, he observes: "Let those who say that the teaching of Christ is hurtful to the State produce such armies as the maxims of Jesus have enjoined soldiers to bring into being; such governors of provinces; such husbands and wives; such parents and children; such masters and servants; such kings; such judges, and such payers and collectors of tribute, as the Christian teaching instructs them to become, and then let them dare to say that such teaching is hurtful to the State. Nay, rather will they hesitate to own that this discipline, if duly acted up to, is the very mainstay of the commonwealth."[20]

21. There was once a time when States were governed by the philosophy of the Gospel. Then it was that the power and divine virtue of Christian wisdom had diffused itself throughout the laws, institutions, and morals of the people, permeating all ranks and relations of civil society. Then, too, the religion instituted by Jesus Christ, established firmly in befitting dignity, flourished everywhere, by the favour of princes and the legitimate protection of magistrates; and Church and State were happily united in concord and friendly interchange of good offices. The State, constituted in this wise, bore fruits important beyond all expectation, whose remembrance is still, and always will be, in renown, witnessed to as they are by countless proofs which can never be blotted out or ever obscured by any craft of any enemies. Christian Europe has subdued barbarous nations, and changed them from a savage to a civilized condition, from superstition to true worship. It victoriously rolled back the tide of Mohammedan conquest; retained the headship of civilization; stood forth in the front rank as the leader and teacher of all, in every branch of national culture; bestowed on the world the gift of true and many-sided liberty; and most wisely founded very numerous institutions for the solace of human suffering. And if we inquire how it was able to bring about so altered a condition of things, the answer is-beyond all question, in large measure, through religion, under whose auspices so many great

---

[20] Epist. 138 ad Marcellinum, cap. 2, n. 15 (PL 33, 532).

undertakings were set on foot, through whose aid they were brought to completion.

22. A similar state of things would certainly have continued had the agreement of the two powers been lasting. More important results even might have been justly looked for, had obedience waited upon the authority, teaching, and counsels of the Church, and had this submission been specially marked by greater and more unswerving loyalty. For that should be regarded in the light of an ever-changeless law which No of Chartres wrote to Pope Paschal II: "When kingdom and priesthood are at one, in complete accord, the world is well ruled, and the Church flourishes, and brings forth abundant fruit. But when they are at variance, not only smaller interests prosper not, but even things of greatest moment fall into deplorable decay."[21]

23. But that harmful and deplorable passion for innovation which was aroused in the sixteenth century threw first of all into confusion the Christian religion, and next, by natural sequence, invaded the precincts of philosophy, whence it spread amongst all classes of society. From this source, as from a fountain-head, burst forth all those later tenets of unbridled license which, in the midst of the terrible unheavals of the last century, were wildly conceived and boldly proclaimed as the principles and foundation of that new conception of law which was not merely previously unknown, but was at variance on many points with not only the Christian, but even the natural law.

24. Amongst these principles the main one lays down that as all men are alike by race and nature, so in like manner all are equal in the control of their life; that each one is so far his own master as to be in no sense under the rule of any other individual; that each is free to think on every subject just as he may choose, and to do whatever he may like to do; that no man has any right to rule over other men. In a society grounded upon such maxims all

---

[21] Epist. 238, to Pope Paschal II (PL 162, 246B).

government is nothing more nor less than the will of the people, and the people, being under the power of itself alone, is alone its own ruler. It does choose, nevertheless, some to whose charge it may commit itself, but in such wise that it makes over to them not the right so much as the business of governing, to be exercised, however, in its name.

25. The authority of God is passed over in silence, just as if there were no God; or as if He cared nothing for human society; or as if men, whether in their individual capacity or bound together in social relations, owed nothing to God; or as if there could be a government of which the whole origin and power and authority did not reside in God Himself. Thus, as is evident, a State becomes nothing but a multitude which is its own master and ruler. And since the people is declared to contain within itself the spring-head of all rights and of all power, it follows that the State does not consider itself bound by any kind of duty toward God. Moreover, it believes that it is not obliged to make public profession of any religion; or to inquire which of the very many religions is the only one true; or to prefer one religion to all the rest; or to show to any form of religion special favour; but, on the contrary, is bound to grant equal rights to every creed, so that public order may not be disturbed by any particular form of religious belief.

26. And it is a part of this theory that all questions that concern religion are to be referred to private judgment; that every one is to be free to follow whatever religion he prefers, or none at all if he disapprove of all. From this the following consequences logically flow: that the judgment of each one's conscience is independent of all law; that the most unrestrained opinions may be openly expressed as to the practice or omission of divine worship; and that every one has unbounded license to think whatever he chooses and to publish abroad whatever he thinks.

27. Now, when the State rests on foundations like those just named - and for the time being they are greatly in favor - it

readily appears into what and how unrightful a position the Church is driven. For, when the management of public business is in harmony with doctrines of such a kind, the Catholic religion is allowed a standing in civil society equal only, or inferior, to societies alien from it; no regard is paid to the laws of the Church, and she who, by the order and commission of Jesus Christ, has the duty of teaching all nations, finds herself forbidden to take any part in the instruction of the people. With reference to matters that are of twofold jurisdiction, they who administer the civil power lay down the law at their own will, and in matters that appertain to religion defiantly put aside the most sacred decrees of the Church. They claim jurisdiction over the marriages of Catholics, even over the bond as well as the unity and the indissolubility of matrimony. They lay hands on the goods of the clergy, contending that the Church cannot possess property. Lastly, they treat the Church with such arrogance that, rejecting entirely her title to the nature and rights of a perfect society, they hold that she differs in no respect from other societies in the State, and for this reason possesses no right nor any legal power of action, save that which she holds by the concession and favor of the government. If in any State the Church retains her own agreement publicly entered into by the two powers, menforthwith begin to cry out that matters affecting the Church must be separated from those of the State.

28. Their object in uttering this cry is to be able to violate unpunished their plighted faith, and in all things to have unchecked control. And as the Church, unable to abandon her chiefest and most sacred duties, cannot patiently put up with this, and asks that the pledge given to her be fully and scrupulously acted up to, contentions frequently arise between the ecclesiastical and the civil power, of which the issue commonly is that the weaker power yields to the one which is stronger in human resources.

29. Accordingly, it has become the practice and determination under this condition of public polity (now so much admired by

many) either to forbid the action of the Church altogether, or to keep her in check and bondage to the State. Public enactments are in great measure framed with this design. The drawing up of laws, the administration of State affairs, the godless education of youth, the spoliation and suppression of religious orders, the overthrow of the temporal power of the Roman Pontiff, all alike aim to this one end-to paralyse the action of Christian institutions, to cramp to the utmost the freedom of the Catholic Church, and to curtail her ever single prerogative.

30. Now, natural reason itself proves convincingly that such concepts of the government of a State are wholly at variance with the truth. Nature itself bears witness that all power, of every kind, has its origin from God, who is its chief and most august source.

31. The sovereignty of the people, however, and this without any reference to God, is held to reside in the multitude; which is doubtless a doctrine exceedingly well calculated to flatter and to inflame many passions, but which lacks all reasonable proof, and all power of insuring public safety and preserving order. Indeed, from the prevalence of this teaching, things have come to such a pass that may hold as an axiom of civil jurisprudence that seditions may be rightfully fostered. For the opinion prevails that princes are nothing more than delegates chosen to carry out the will of the people; whence it necessarily follows that all things are as changeable as the will of the people, so that risk of public disturbance is ever hanging over our heads. To hold, therefore, that there is no difference in matters of religion between forms that are unlike each other, and even contrary to each other, most clearly leads in the end to the rejection of all religion in both theory and practice. And this is the same thing as atheism, however it may differ from it in name. Men who really believe in the existence of God must, in order to be consistent with themselves and to avoid absurd conclusions, understand that differing modes of divine worship involving dissimilarity and

conflict even on most important points cannot all be equally probable, equally good, and equally acceptable to God.

32. So, too, the liberty of thinking, and of publishing, whatsoever each one likes, without any hindrance, is not in itself an advantage over which society can wisely rejoice. On the contrary, it is the fountain-head and origin of many evils. Liberty is a power perfecting man, and hence should have truth and goodness for its object. But the character of goodness and truth cannot be changed at option. These remain ever one and the same, and are no less unchangeable than nature itself. If the mind assents to false opinions, and the will chooses and follows after what is wrong, neither can attain its native fullness, but both must fall from their native dignity into an abyss of corruption. Whatever, therefore, is opposed to virtue and truth may not rightly be brought temptingly before the eye of man, much less sanctioned by the favor and protection of the law. A well-spent life is the only way to heaven, whither all are bound, and on this account the State is acting against the laws and dictates of nature whenever it permits the license of opinion and of action to lead minds astray from truth and souls away from the practice of virtue. To exclude the Church, founded by God Himself, from life, from laws, from the education of youth, from domestic society is a grave and fatal error. A State from which religion is banished can never be well regulated; and already perhaps more than is desirable is known of the nature and tendency of the so-called civil philosophy of life and morals. The Church of Christ is the true and sole teacher of virtue and guardian of morals. She it is who preserves in their purity the principles from which duties flow, and, by setting forth most urgent reasons for virtuous life, bids us not only to turn away from wicked deeds, but even to curb all movements of the mind that are opposed to reason, even though they be not carried out in action.

33. To wish the Church to be subject to the civil power in the exercise of her duty is a great folly and a sheer injustice. Whenever this is the case, order is disturbed, for things natural

are put above things supernatural; the many benefits which the Church, if free to act, would confer on society are either prevented or at least lessened in number; and a way is prepared for enmities and contentions between the two powers, with how evil result to both the issue of events has taught us only too frequently.

34. Doctrines such as these, which cannot be approved by human reason, and most seriously affect the whole civil order, Our predecessors the Roman Pontiffs (well aware of what their apostolic office required of them) have never allowed to pass uncondemned. Thus, Gregory XVI in his encyclical letter *Mirari Vos*, dated August 15, 1832, inveighed with weighty words against the sophisms which even at his time were being publicly inculcated-namely, that no preference should be shown for any particular form of worship; that it is right for individuals to form their own personal judgments about religion; that each man's conscience is his sole and all-sufficing guide; and that it is lawful for every man to publish his own views, whatever they may be, and even to conspire against the State. On the question of the separation of Church and State the same Pontiff writes as follows: "Nor can We hope for happier results either for religion or for the civil government from the wishes of those who desire that the Church be separated from the State, and the concord between the secular and ecclesiastical authority be dissolved. It is clear that these men, who yearn for a shameless liberty, live in dread of an agreement which has always been fraught with good, and advantageous alike to sacred and civil interests." To the like effect, also, as occasion presented itself, did Pius IX brand publicly many false opinions which were gaining ground, and afterwards ordered them to be condensed in summary form in order that in this sea of error Catholics might have a light which they might safely follow.[22]

---

[22] Pope Pius IX, encyclical Quanta Cura (Dec. 8, 1864): Syllabus. It will suffice to indicate a few of them: Prop. 19. The Church is not a true, perfect, and wholly independent society, possessing in its own unchanging rights conferred upon it by its divine Founder; but it is for the civil power to

35. From these pronouncements of the Popes it is evident that the origin of public power is to be sought for in God Himself, and not in the multitude, and that it is repugnant to reason to allow free scope for sedition. Again, that it is not lawful for the State, any more than for the individual, either to disregard all religious duties or to hold in equal favour different kinds of religion; that the unrestrained freedom of thinking and of openly making known one's thoughts is not inherent in the rights of citizens, and is by no means to be reckoned worthy of favour and support. In like manner it is to be understood that the Church no less than the State itself is a society perfect in its own nature and its own right, and that those who exercise sovereignty ought not so to act as to compel the Church to become subservient or subject to them, or to hamper her liberty in the management of her own affairs, or to despoil her in any way of the other privileges conferred upon her by Jesus Christ. In matters, however, of mixed jurisdiction, it is in the highest degree consonant to nature, as also to the designs of God, that so far from one of the powers separating itself from the other, or still less coming into conflict with it, complete harmony, such as is suited to the end for which each power exists, should be preserved between them.

36. This, then, is the teaching of the Catholic Church concerning the constitution and government of the State. By the words and decrees just cited, if judged dispassionately, no one of the several forms of government is in itself condemned, inasmuch as none of them contains anything contrary to Catholic doctrine, and all of them are capable, if wisely and justly managed, to insure the

---

determine what are the rights of the Church, and the limits within which it may use them. Prop. 29. The State, as the origin and source of all rights, enjoys a right that is unlimited. Prop. 55. The Church must be separated from the Stare and the State from the Church. Prop. 79. It is unsure that the civil liberty of every form of worship, and the full power given to all of openly and publicly manifesting whatsoever opinions and thoughts, lead to the more ready corruption of the minds and morals of the people, and to the spread of the plague of religious indifference.

welfare of the State. Neither is it blameworthy in itself, in any manner, for the people to have a share greater or less, in the government: for at certain times, and under certain laws, such participation may not only be of benefit to the citizens, but may even be of obligation. Nor is there any reason why any one should accuse the Church of being wanting in gentleness of action or largeness of view, or of being opposed to real and lawful liberty. The Church, indeed, deems it unlawful to place the various forms of divine worship on the same footing as the true religion, but does not, on that account, condemn those rulers who, for the sake of securing some great good or of hindering some great evil, allow patiently custom or usage to be a kind of sanction for each kind of religion having its place in the State. And, in fact, the Church is wont to take earnest heed that no one shall be forced to embrace the Catholic faith against his will, for, as St. Augustine wisely reminds us, "Man cannot believe otherwise than of his own will."

37. In the same way the Church cannot approve of that liberty which begets a contempt of the most sacred laws of God, and casts off the obedience due to lawful authority, for this is not liberty so much as license, and is most correctly styled by St. Augustine the "liberty of self ruin," and by the Apostle St. Peter the "cloak of malice."[23] Indeed, since it is opposed to reason, it is a true slavery, "for whosoever committeth sin is the slave of sin."[24] On the other hand, that liberty is truly genuine, and to be sought after, which in regard to the individual does not allow men to be the slaves of error and of passion, the worst of all masters; which, too, in public administration guides the citizens in wisdom and provides for them increased means of well-being; and which, further, protects the State from foreign interference.

38. This honourable liberty, alone worthy of human beings, the Church approves most highly and has never slackened her

---

[23] 1 Peter 2:16.
[24] John 8:34.

endeavour to preserve, strong and unchanged, among nations. And, in truth, whatever in the State is of chief avail for the common welfare; whatever has been usefully established to curb the license of rulers who are opposed to the true interests of the people, or to keep in check the leading authorities from unwarrantably interfering in municipal or family affairs; whatever tends to uphold the honour, manhood, and equal rights of individual citizens-of all these things, as the monuments of past ages bear witness, the Catholic Church has always been the originator, the promoter, or the guardian. Ever, therefore, consistent with herself, while on the one hand she rejects that exorbitant liberty which in individuals and in nations ends in license or in thraldom, on the other hand, she willingly and most gladly welcomes whatever improvements the age brings forth, if these really secure the prosperity of life here below, which is, as it were, a stage in the journey to the life that will know no ending.

39. Therefore, when it is said that the Church is hostile to modern political regimes and that she repudiates the discoveries of modern research, the charge is a ridiculous and groundless calumny. Wild opinions she does repudiate, wicked and seditious projects she does condemn, together with that attitude of mind which points to the beginning of a willful departure from God. But, as all truth must necessarily proceed from God, the Church recognizes in all truth that is reached by research a trace of the divine intelligence. And as all truth in the natural order is powerless to destroy belief in the teachings of revelation, but can do much to confirm it, and as every newly discovered truth may serve to further the knowledge or the praise of God, it follows that whatsoever spreads the range of knowledge will always be willingly and even joyfully welcomed by the Church. She will always encourage and promote, as she does in other branches of knowledge, all study occupied with the investigation of nature. In these pursuits, should the human intellect discover anything not known before, the Church makes no opposition. She never objects to search being made for things that minister to the refinements and comforts of life. So far, indeed, from opposing

these she is now, as she ever has been, hostile alone to indolence and sloth, and earnestly wishes that the talents of men may bear more and more abundant fruit by cultivation and exercise. Moreover, she gives encouragement to every kind of art and handicraft, and through her influence, directing all strivings after progress toward virtue and salvation, she labours to prevent man's intellect and industry from turning him away from God and from heavenly things.

40. All this, though so reasonable and full of counsel, finds little favour nowadays when States not only refuse to conform to the rules of Christian wisdom, but seem even anxious to recede from them further and further on each successive day. Nevertheless, since truth when brought to light is wont, of its own nature, to spread itself far and wide, and gradually take possession of the minds of men, We, moved by the great and holy duty of Our apostolic mission to all nations, speak, as We are bound to do, with freedom. Our eyes are not closed to the spirit of the times. We repudiate not the assured and useful improvements of our age, but devoutly wish affairs of State to take a safer course than they are now taking, and to rest on a more firm foundation without injury to the true freedom of the people; for the best parent and guardian of liberty amongst men is truth. "The truth shall make you free."[25]

41. If in the difficult times in which Our lot is cast, Catholics will give ear to Us, as it behoves them to do, they will readily see what are the duties of each one in matters of opinion as well as action. As regards opinion, whatever the Roman Pontiffs have hitherto taught, or shall hereafter teach, must be held with a firm grasp of mind, and, so often as occasion requires, must be openly professed.

42. Especially with reference to the so-called "liberties" which are so greatly coveted in these days, all must stand by the judgment

---

[25] John 8:32.

of the apostolic see, and have the same mind. Let no man be deceived by the honest outward appearance of these liberties, but let each one reflect whence these have had their origin, and by what efforts they are everywhere upheld and promoted. Experience has made Us well acquainted with their results to the State, since everywhere they have borne fruits which the good and wise bitterly deplore. If there really exist anywhere, or if we in imagination conceive, a State, waging wanton and tyrannical war against Christianity, and if we compare with it the modern form of government just described, this latter may seem the more endurable of the two. Yet, undoubtedly, the principles on which such a government is grounded are, as We have said, of a nature which no one can approve.

43. Secondly, action may relate to private and domestic matters, or to matters public. As to private affairs, the first duty is to conform life and conduct to the gospel precepts, and to refuse to shrink from this duty when Christian virtue demands some sacrifice slightly more difficult to make. All, moreover, are bound to love the Church as their common mother, to obey her laws, promote her honour, defend her rights, and to endeavour to make her respected and loved by those over whom they have authority. It is also of great moment to the public welfare to take a prudent part in the business of municipal administration, and to endeavour above all to introduce effectual measures, so that, as becomes a Christian people, public provision may be made for the instruction of youth in religion and true morality. Upon these things the well-being of every State greatly depends.

44. Furthermore, it is in general fitting and salutary that Catholics should extend their efforts beyond this restricted sphere, and give their attention to national politics. We say "in general" because these Our precepts are addressed to all nations. However, it may in some places be true that, for most urgent and just reasons, it is by no means expedient for Catholics to engage in public affairs or to take an active part in politics. Nevertheless, as We have laid down, to take no share in public matters would

be as wrong as to have no concern for, or to bestow no labour upon, the common good, and the more so because Catholics are admonished, by the very doctrines which they profess, to be upright and faithful in the discharge of duty, while, if they hold aloof, men whose principles offer but small guarantee for the welfare of the State will the more readily seize the reins of government. This would tend also to the injury of the Christian religion, forasmuch as those would come into power who are badly disposed toward the Church, and those who are willing to befriend her would be deprived of all influence.

45. It follows clearly, therefore, that Catholics have just reasons for taking part in the conduct of public affairs. For in so doing they assume not nor should they assume the responsibility of approving what is blameworthy in the actual methods of government, but seek to turn these very methods, so far as is possible, to the genuine and true public good, and to use their best endeavours at the same time to infuse, as it were, into all the veins of the State the healthy sap and blood of Christian wisdom and virtue. The morals and ambitions of the heathens differed widely from those of the Gospel, yet Christians were to be seen living undefiled everywhere in the midst of pagan superstition, and, while always true to themselves, coming to the front boldly wherever an opening was presented. Models of loyalty to their rulers, submissive, so far as was permitted, to the sovereign power, they shed around them on every side a halo of sanctity; they strove to be helpful to their brethren, and to attract others to the wisdom of Jesus Christ, yet were bravely ready to withdraw from public life, nay, even to lay down their life, if they could not without loss of virtue retain honours, dignities, and offices. For this reason, Christian ways and manners speedily found their way not only into private houses but into the camp, the senate, and even into the imperial palaces. "We are but of yesterday," wrote Tertullian, "yet we swarm in all your institutions, we crowd your cities, islands, villages, towns, assemblies, the army itself, your wards and corporations, the palace, the senate, and the law courts."[26] So that the Christian

faith, when once it became lawful to make public profession of the Gospel, appeared in most of the cities of Europe, not like an infant crying in its cradle, but already grown up and full of vigour.

46. In these Our days it is well to revive these examples of Our forefathers. First and foremost, it is the duty of all Catholics worthy of the name and wishful to be known as most loving children of the Church, to reject without swerving whatever is inconsistent with so fair a title; to make use of popular institutions, so far as can honestly be done, for the advancement of truth and righteousness; to strive that liberty of action shall not transgress the bounds marked out by nature and the law of God; to endeavour to bring back all civil society to the pattern and form of Christianity which We have described. It is barely possible to lay down any fixed method by which such purposes are to be attained, because the means adopted must suit places and times widely differing from one another. Nevertheless, above all things, unity of aim must be preserved, and similarity must be sought after in all plans of action. Both these objects will be carried into effect without fail if all will follow the guidance of the apostolic see as their rule of life and obey the bishops whom the Holy Spirit has placed to rule the Church of God.[27] The defense of Catholicism, indeed, necessarily demands that in the profession of doctrines taught by the Church all shall be of one mind and all steadfast in believing; and care must be taken never to connive, in any way, at false opinions, never to withstand them less strenuously than truth allows. In mere matters of opinion it is permissible to discuss things with moderation, with a desire of searching into the truth, without unjust suspicion or angry recriminations.

47. Hence, lest concord be broken by rash charges, let this be understood by all, that the integrity of Catholic faith cannot be

---

[26] Apoplget, 27 (P4 1, 525).

[27] Acts 20:28.

reconciled with opinions verging on naturalism or rationalism, the essence of which is utterly to do away with Christian institutions and to install in society the supremacy of man to the exclusion of God. Further, it is unlawful to follow one line of conduct in private life and another in public, respecting privately the authority of the Church, but publicly rejecting it; for this would amount to joining together good and evil, and to putting man in conflict with himself; whereas he ought always to be consistent, and never in the least point nor in any condition of life to swerve from Christian virtue.

48. But in matters merely political, as, for instance, the best form of government, and this or that system of administration, a difference of opinion is lawful. Those, therefore, whose piety is in other respects known, and whose minds are ready to accept in all obedience the decrees of the apostolic see, cannot in justice be accounted as bad men because they disagree as to subjects We have mentioned; and still graver wrong will be done them, if - as We have more than once perceived with regret - they are accused of violating, or of wavering in, the Catholic faith.

49. Let this be well borne in mind by all who are in the habit of publishing their opinions, and above all by journalists. In the endeavour to secure interests of the highest order there is no room for intestine strife or party rivalries; since all should aim with one mind and purpose to make safe that which is the common object of all - the maintenance of religion and of the State. If, therefore, they have hitherto been dissensions, let them henceforth be gladly buried in oblivion. If rash or injurious acts have been committed, whoever may have been at fault, let mutual charity make amends, and let the past be redeemed by a special submission of all to the apostolic see. In this way Catholics will attain two most excellent results: they will become helpers to the Church in preserving and propagating Christian wisdom, and they will confer the greatest benefit on civil society, the safety of which is exceedingly imperiled by evil teachings and bad passions.

50. This, venerable brethren, is what We have thought it Our duty to expound to all nations of the Catholic world touching the Christian constitution of States and the duties of individual citizens. It behoves Us now with earnest prayer to implore the protection of heaven, beseeching God, who alone can enlighten the minds of men and move their will, to bring about those happy ends for which We yearn and strive, for His greater glory and the general salvation of mankind. As a happy augury of the divine benefits, and in token of Our paternal benevolence, to you, venerable brothers, and to the clergy and to the whole people committed to your charge and vigilance, We grant lovingly in the Lord the apostolic benediction.

Given at St. Peter's in Rome, the first day of November, 1885, the seventh year of Our pontificate.

VII: Libertas

June 20, 1888

ON THE NATURE OF HUMAN LIBERTY

Liberty, the highest of natural endowments, being the portion only of intellectual or rational natures, confers on man this dignity - that he is "in the hand of his counsel"[1] and has power over his actions. But the manner in which such dignity is exercised is of the greatest moment, inasmuch as on the use that is made of liberty the highest good and the greatest evil alike depend. Man, indeed, is free to obey his reason, to seek moral good, and to strive unswervingly after his last end. Yet he is free also to turn aside to all other things; and, in pursuing the empty semblance of good, to disturb rightful order and to fall headlong into the destruction which he has voluntarily chosen. The Redeemer of mankind, Jesus Christ, having restored and exalted the original dignity of nature, vouchsafed special assistance to the will of man; and by the gifts of His grace here, and the promise of heavenly bliss hereafter, He raised it to a nobler state. In like manner, this great gift of nature has ever been, and always will be, deservingly cherished by the Catholic Church, for to her alone has been committed the charge of handing down to all ages the benefits purchased for us by Jesus Christ. Yet there are many who imagine that the Church is hostile to human liberty. Having a false and absurd notion as to what liberty is, either they pervert the very idea of freedom, or they extend it at their pleasure to many things in respect of which man cannot rightly be regarded as free.

2. We have on other occasions, and especially in Our encyclical letter *Immortale Dei*,[2] in treating of the so-called *modern liberties*,

---

[1] Ecclus. 15:14.

distinguished between their good and evil elements; and We have shown that whatsoever is good in those liberties is as ancient as truth itself, and that the Church has always most willingly approved and practiced that good: but whatsoever has been added as new is, to tell the plain truth, of a vitiated kind, the fruit of the disorders of the age, and of an insatiate longing after novelties. Seeing, however, that many cling so obstinately to their own opinion in this matter as to imagine these modern liberties, cankered as they are, to be the greatest glory of our age, and the very basis of civil life, without which no perfect government can be conceived, We feel it a pressing duty, for the sake of the common good, to treat separately of this subject.

3. It is with *moral* liberty, whether in individuals or in communities, that We proceed at once to deal. But, first of all, it will be well to speak briefly of *natural* liberty; for, though it is distinct and separate from moral liberty, natural freedom is the fountainhead from which liberty of whatsoever kind flows, *sua vi suaque sponte*. The unanimous consent and judgment of men, which is the trusty voice of nature, recognizes this natural liberty in those only who are endowed with intelligence or reason; and it is by his use of this that man is rightly regarded as responsible for his actions. For, while other animate creatures follow their senses, seeking good and avoiding evil only by instinct, man has reason to guide him in each and every act of his life. Reason sees that whatever things that are held to be good upon earth may exist or may not, and discerning that none of them are of necessity for us, it leaves the will free to choose what it pleases. But man can judge of this contingency, as We say, only because he has a soul that is simple, spiritual, and intellectual - a soul, therefore, which is not produced by matter, and does not depend on matter for its existence; but which is created immediately by God, and, far surpassing the condition of things material, has a life and action of its own so that, knowing the unchangeable and necessary reasons of what is true and good, it sees that no

---

[2] See nos. 93:37-38.

particular kind of good is necessary to us. When, therefore, it is established that man's soul is immortal and endowed with reason and not bound up with things material, the foundation of natural liberty is at once most firmly laid.

4. As the Catholic Church declares in the strongest terms the simplicity, spirituality, and immortality of the soul, so with unequalled constancy and publicity she ever also asserts its freedom. These truths she has always taught, and has sustained them as a dogma of faith, and whensoever heretics or innovators have attacked the liberty of man, the Church has defended it and protected this noble possession from destruction. History bears witness to the energy with which she met the fury of the Manichaeans and others like them; and the earnestness with which in later years she defended human liberty at the Council of Trent, and against the followers of Jansenius, is known to all. At no time, and in no place, has she held truce with *fatalism*.

5. Liberty, then, as We have said, belongs only to those who have the gift of reason or intelligence. Considered as to its nature, it is the faculty of choosing means fitted for the end proposed, for he is master of his actions who can choose one thing out of many. Now, since everything chosen as a means is viewed as good or useful, and since good, as such, is the proper object of our desire, it follows that freedom of choice is a property of the will, or, rather, is identical with the will in so far as it has in its action the faculty of choice. But the will cannot proceed to act until it is enlightened by the knowledge possessed by the intellect. In other words, the good wished by the will is necessarily good in so far as it is known by the intellect; and this the more, because in all voluntary acts choice is subsequent to a judgment upon the truth of the good presented, declaring to which good preference should be given. No sensible man can doubt that judgment is an act of reason, not of the will. The end, or object, both of the rational will and of its liberty is that good only which is in conformity with reason.

6. Since, however, both these faculties are imperfect, it is possible, as is often seen, that the reason should propose something which is not really good, but which has the appearance of good, and that the will should choose accordingly. For, as the possibility of error, and actual error, are defects of the mind and attest its imperfection, so the pursuit of what has a false appearance of good, though a proof of our freedom, just as a disease is a proof of our vitality, implies defect in human liberty. The will also, simply because of its dependence on the reason, no sooner desires anything contrary thereto than it abuses its freedom of choice and corrupts its very essence. Thus it is that the infinitely perfect God, although supremely free, because of the supremacy of His intellect and of His essential goodness, nevertheless cannot choose evil; neither can the angels and saints, who enjoy the beatific vision. St. Augustine and others urged most admirably against the Pelagians that, if the possibility of deflection from good belonged to the essence or perfection of liberty, then God, Jesus Christ, and the angels and saints, who have not this power, would have no liberty at all, or would have less liberty than man has in his state of pilgrimage and imperfection. This subject is often discussed by the Angelic Doctor in his demonstration that the possibility of sinning is not freedom, but slavery. It will suffice to quote his subtle commentary on the words of our Lord: "Whosoever committeth sin is the slave of sin."[3] "Everything," he says, "is that which belongs to it a naturally. When, therefore, it acts through a power outside itself, it does not act of itself, but through another, that is, as a slave. But man is by nature rational. When, therefore, he acts according to reason, he acts of himself and according to his free will; and this is liberty. Whereas, when he sins, he acts in opposition to reason, is moved by another, and is the victim of foreign misapprehensions. Therefore, 'Whosoever committeth sin is the slave of sin.' "[4] Even the heathen philosophers clearly recognized this truth, especially they who held that the wise man

---

[3] John 8:34.
[4] Thomas Aquinas, On the Gospel of St. John, cap. viii, lect. 4, n. 3 (ed. Vives, Vol. 20 p. 95).

alone is free; and by the term "wise man" was meant, as is well known, the man trained to live in accordance with his nature, that is, in justice and virtue.

7. Such, then, being the condition of human liberty, it necessarily stands in need of light and strength to direct its actions to good and to restrain them from evil. Without this, the freedom of our will would be our ruin. First of all, there must be *law*; that is, a fixed rule of teaching what is to be done and what is to be left undone. This rule cannot affect the lower animals in any true sense, since they act of necessity, following their natural instinct, and cannot of themselves act in any other way. On the other hand, as was said above, he who is free can either act or not act, can do this or do that, as he pleases, because his judgment precedes his choice. And his judgment not only decides what is right or wrong of its own nature, but also what is practically good and therefore to be chosen, and what is practically evil and therefore to be avoided. In other words, the reason prescribes to the will what it should seek after or shun, in order to the eventual attainment of man's last end, for the sake of which all his actions ought to be performed. This ordination of *reason* is called law. In man's free will, therefore, or in the moral necessity of our voluntary acts being in accordance with reason, lies the very root of the necessity of law. Nothing more foolish can be uttered or conceived than the notion that, because man is free by nature, he is therefore exempt from law. Were this the case, it would follow that to become free we must be deprived of reason; whereas the truth is that we are bound to submit to law precisely because we are free by our very nature. For, law is the guide of man's actions; it turns him toward good by its rewards, and deters him from evil by its punishments.

8. Foremost in this office comes the *natural law*, which is written and engraved in the mind of every man; and this is nothing but our reason, commanding us to do right and forbidding sin. Nevertheless, all prescriptions of human reason can have force of law only inasmuch as they are the voice and the interpreters of

some higher power on which our reason and liberty necessarily depend. For, since the force of law consists in the imposing of obligations and the granting of rights, authority is the one and only foundation of all law - the power, that is, of fixing duties and defining rights, as also of assigning the necessary sanctions of reward and chastisement to each and all of its commands. But all this, clearly, cannot be found in man, if, as his own supreme legislator, he is to be the rule of his own actions. It follows, therefore, that the law of nature is the same thing as the *eternal law*, implanted in rational creatures, and inclining them *to their right action and end*; and can be nothing else but the eternal reason of God, the Creator and Ruler of all the world. To this rule of action and restraint of evil God has vouchsafed to give special and most suitable aids for strengthening and ordering the human will. The first and most excellent of these is the power of His divine *grace*, whereby the mind can be enlightened and the will wholesomely invigorated and moved to the constant pursuit of moral good, so that the use of our inborn liberty becomes at once less difficult and less dangerous. Not that the divine assistance hinders in any way the free movement of our will; just the contrary, for grace works inwardly in man and in harmony with his natural inclinations, since it flows from the very Creator of his mind and will, by whom all things are moved in conformity with their nature. As the Angelic Doctor points out, it is because divine grace comes from the Author of nature that it is so admirably adapted to be the safeguard of all natures, and to maintain the character, efficiency, and operations of each.

9. What has been said of the liberty of individuals is no less applicable to them when considered as bound together in civil society. For, what reason and the natural law do for individuals, that *human law*, promulgated for their good, does for the citizens of States. Of the laws enacted by men, some are concerned with what is good or bad by its very nature; and they command men to follow after what is right and to shun what is wrong, adding at the same time a suitable sanction. But such laws by no means derive their origin from civil society, because, just as civil society

did not create human nature, so neither can it be said to be the author of the good which befits human nature, or of the evil which is contrary to it. Laws come before men live together in society, and have their origin in the natural, and consequently in the eternal, law. The precepts, therefore, of the natural law, contained bodily in the laws of men, have not merely the force of human law, but they possess that higher and more august sanction which belongs to the law of nature and the eternal law. And within the sphere of this kind of laws the duty of the civil legislator is, mainly, to keep the community in obedience by the adoption of a common discipline and by putting restraint upon refractory and viciously inclined men, so that, deterred from evil, they may turn to what is good, or at any rate may avoid causing trouble and disturbance to the State. Now, there are other enactments of the civil authority, which do not follow directly, but somewhat remotely, from the natural law, and decide many points which the law of nature treats only in a general and indefinite way. For instance, though nature commands all to contribute to the public peace and prosperity, whatever belongs to the manner, and circumstances, and conditions under which such service is to be rendered must be determined by the wisdom of men and not by nature herself. It is in the constitution of these particular rules of life, suggested by reason and prudence, and put forth by competent authority, that human law, properly so called, consists, binding all citizens to work together for the attainment of the common end proposed to the community, and forbidding them to depart from this end, and, in so far as human law is in conformity with the dictates of nature, leading to what is good, and deterring from evil.

10. From this it is manifest that the eternal law of God is the sole standard and rule of human liberty, not only in each individual man, but also in the community and civil society which men constitute when united. Therefore, the true liberty of human society does not consist in every man doing what he pleases, for this would simply end in turmoil and confusion, and bring on the overthrow of the State; but rather in this, that through the

injunctions of the civil law all may more easily conform to the prescriptions of the eternal law. Likewise, the liberty of those who are in authority does not consist in the power to lay unreasonable and capricious commands upon their subjects, which would equally be criminal and would lead to the ruin of the commonwealth; but the binding force of human laws is in this, that they are to be regarded as applications of the eternal law, and incapable of sanctioning anything which is not contained in the eternal law, as in the principle of all law. Thus, St. Augustine most wisely says: "I think that you can see, at the same time, that there is nothing just and lawful in that temporal law, unless what men have gathered from this eternal law."[5] If, then, by anyone in authority, something be sanctioned out of conformity with the principles of right reason, and consequently hurtful to the commonwealth, such an enactment can have no binding force of law, as being no rule of justice, but certain to lead men away from that good which is the very end of civil society.

11. Therefore, the nature of human liberty, however it be considered, whether in individuals or in society, whether in those who command or in those who obey, supposes the necessity of obedience to some supreme and eternal law, which is no other than the authority of God, commanding good and forbidding evil. And, so far from this most just authority of God over men diminishing, or even destroying their liberty, it protects and perfects it, for the real perfection of all creatures is found in the prosecution and attainment of their respective ends; but the supreme end to which human liberty must aspire is God.

12. These precepts of the truest and highest teaching, made known to us by the light of reason itself, the Church, instructed by the example and doctrine of her divine Author, has ever propagated and asserted; for she has ever made them the measure of her office and of her teaching to the Christian

---

[5] Augustine, De libero arbitrio, lib. I, cap. 6, n. 15 (PL 32, 1229).

nations. As to morals, the laws of the Gospel not only immeasurably surpass the wisdom of the heathen, but are an invitation and an introduction to a state of holiness unknown to the ancients; and, bringing man nearer to God, they make him at once the possessor of a more perfect liberty. Thus, the powerful influence of the Church has ever been manifested in the custody and protection of the civil and political liberty of the people. The enumeration of its merits in this respect does not belong to our present purpose. It is sufficient to recall the fact that slavery, that old reproach of the heathen nations, was mainly abolished by the beneficent efforts of the Church. The impartiality of law and the true brotherhood of man were first asserted by Jesus Christ; and His apostles re-echoed His voice when they declared that in future there was to be neither Jew, nor Gentile, nor barbarian, nor Scythian, but all were brothers in Christ. So powerful, so conspicuous, in this respect is the influence of the Church that experience abundantly testifies how savage customs are no longer possible in any land where she has once set her foot; but that gentleness speedily takes the place of cruelty, and the light of truth quickly dispels the darkness of barbarism. Nor has the Church been less lavish in the benefits she has conferred on civilized nations in every age, either by resisting the tyranny of the wicked, or by protecting the innocent and helpless from injury, or, finally, by using her influence in the support of any form of government which commended itself to the citizens at home, because of its justice, or was feared by their enemies without, because of its power.

13. Moreover, the highest duty is to respect authority, and obediently to submit to just law; and by this the members of a community are effectually protected from the wrong-doing of evil men. Lawful power is from God, "and whosoever resisteth authority resisteth the ordinance of God";[6] wherefore, obedience is greatly ennobled when subjected to an authority which is the most just and supreme of all. But where the power to command

---

[6] Rom. 13:2.

143

is wanting, or where a law is enacted contrary to reason, or to the eternal law, or to some ordinance of God, obedience is unlawful, lest, while obeying man, we become disobedient to God. Thus, an effectual barrier being opposed to tyranny, the authority in the State will not have all its own way, but the interests and rights of all will be safeguarded - the rights of individuals, of domestic society, and of all the members of the commonwealth; all being free to live according to law and right reason; and in this, as We have shown, true liberty really consists.

14. If when men discuss the question of liberty they were careful to grasp its true and legitimate meaning, such as reason and reasoning have just explained, they would never venture to affix such a calumny on the Church as to assert that she is the foe of individual and public liberty. But many there are who follow in the footsteps of ▓▓▓▓▓▓, and adopt as their own his rebellious cry, "I will not serve"; and consequently substitute for true liberty what is sheer and most foolish license. Such, for instance, are the men belonging to that widely spread and powerful organization, who, usurping the name of liberty, style themselves liberals.

15. What *naturalists* or *rationalists* aim at in philosophy, that the supporters of *liberalism*, carrying out the principles laid down by naturalism, are attempting in the domain of morality and politics. The fundamental doctrine of rationalism is the supremacy of the human reason, which, refusing due submission to the divine and eternal reason, proclaims its own independence, and constitutes itself the supreme principle and source and judge of truth. Hence, these followers of liberalism deny the existence of any divine authority to which obedience is due, and proclaim that every man is the law to himself; from which arises that ethical system which they style *independent* morality, and which, under the guise of liberty, exonerates man from any obedience to the commands of God, and substitutes a boundless license. The end of all this it is not difficult to foresee, especially when society is in question. For, when once man is firmly persuaded that he is subject to no one, it follows that the efficient cause of the unity

of civil society is not to be sought in any principle external to man, or superior to him, but simply in the free will of individuals; that the authority in the State comes from the people only; and that, just as every man's individual reason is his only rule of life, so the collective reason of the community should be the supreme guide in the management of all public affairs. Hence the doctrine of the supremacy of the greater number, and that all right and all duty reside in the majority. But, from what has been said, it is clear that all this is in contradiction to reason. To refuse any bond of union between man and civil society, on the one hand, and God the Creator and consequently the supreme Law-giver, on the other, is plainly repugnant to the nature, not only of man, but of all created things; for, of necessity, all effects must in some proper way be connected with their cause; and it belongs to the perfection of every nature to contain itself within that sphere and grade which the order of nature has assigned to it, namely, that the lower should be subject and obedient to the higher.

16. Moreover, besides this, a doctrine of such character is most hurtful both to individuals and to the State. For, once ascribe to human reason the only authority to decide what is true and what is good, and the real distinction between good and evil is destroyed; honor and dishonor differ not in their nature, but in the opinion and judgment of each one; pleasure is the measure of what is lawful; and, given a code of morality which can have little or no power to restrain or quiet the unruly propensities of man, a way is naturally opened to universal corruption. With reference also to public affairs: authority is severed from the true and natural principle whence it derives all its efficacy for the common good; and the law determining what it is right to do and avoid doing is at the mercy of a majority. Now, this is simply a road leading straight to tyranny. The empire of God over man and civil society once repudiated, it follows that religion, as a public institution, can have no claim to exist, and that everything that belongs to religion will be treated with complete indifference. Furthermore, with ambitious designs on sovereignty, tumult and

sedition will be common amongst the people; and when duty and conscience cease to appeal to them, there will be nothing to hold them back but force, which of itself alone is powerless to keep their covetousness in check. Of this we have almost daily evidence in the conflict with *socialists* and members of other seditious societies, who labor unceasingly to bring about revolution. It is for those, then, who are capable of forming a just estimate of things to decide whether such doctrines promote that true liberty which alone is worthy of man, or rather, pervert and destroy it.

17. There are, indeed, some adherents of liberalism who do not subscribe to these opinions, which we have seen to be fearful in their enormity, openly opposed to the truth, and the cause of most terrible evils. Indeed, very many amongst them, compelled by the force of truth, do not hesitate to admit that such liberty is vicious, nay, is simple license, whenever intemperate in its claims, to the neglect of truth and justice; and therefore they would have liberty ruled and directed by right reason, and consequently subject to the natural law and to the divine eternal law. But here they think they may stop, holding that man as a free being is bound by no law of God except such as He makes known to us through our natural reason. In this they are plainly inconsistent. For if - as they must admit, and no one can rightly deny - the will of the Divine Law-giver is to be obeyed, because every man is under the power of God, and tends toward Him as his end, it follows that no one can assign limits to His legislative authority without failing in the obedience which is due. Indeed, if the human mind be so presumptuous as to define the nature and extent of God's rights and its own duties, reverence for the divine law will be apparent rather than real, and arbitrary judgment will prevail over the authority and providence of God. Man must, therefore, take his standard of a loyal and religious life from the eternal law; and from all and every one of those laws which God, in His infinite wisdom and power, has been pleased to enact, and to make known to us by such clear and unmistakable signs as to leave no room for doubt. And the more

so because laws of this kind have the same origin, the same author, as the eternal law, are absolutely in accordance with right reason, and perfect the natural law. These laws it is that embody the government of God, who graciously guides and directs the intellect and the will of man lest these fall into error. Let, then, that continue to remain in a holy and inviolable union which neither can nor should be separated; and in all things-for this is the dictate of right reason itself-let God be dutifully and obediently served.

18. There are others, somewhat more moderate though not more consistent, who affirm that the morality of individuals is to be guided by the divine law, but not the morality of the State, for that in public affairs the commands of God may be passed over, and may be entirely disregarded in the framing of laws. Hence follows the fatal theory of the need of separation between Church and State. But the absurdity of such a position is manifest. Nature herself proclaims the necessity of the State providing means and opportunities whereby the community may be enabled to live properly, that is to say, according to the laws of God. For, since God is the source of all goodness and justice, it is absolutely ridiculous that the State should pay no attention to these laws or render them abortive by contrary enact menu. Besides, those who are in authority owe it to the commonwealth not only to provide for its external well-being and the conveniences of life, but still more to consult the welfare of men's souls in the wisdom of their legislation. But, for the increase of such benefits, nothing more suitable can be conceived than the laws which have God for their author; and, therefore, they who in their government of the State take no account of these laws abuse political power by causing it to deviate from its proper end and from what nature itself prescribes. And, what is still more important, and what We have more than once pointed out, although the civil authority has not the same proximate end as the spiritual, nor proceeds on the same lines, nevertheless in the exercise of their separate powers they must occasionally meet. For their subjects are the same, and

not infrequently they deal with the same objects, though in different ways. Whenever this occurs, since a state of conflict is absurd and manifestly repugnant to the most wise ordinance of God, there must necessarily exist some order or mode of procedure to remove the occasions of difference and contention, and to secure harmony in all things. This harmony has been not inaptly compared to that which exists between the body and the soul for the well-being of both one and the other, the separation of which brings irremediable harm to the body, since it extinguishes its very life.

19. To make this more evident, the growth of liberty ascribed to our age must be considered apart in its various details. And, first, let us examine that liberty in individuals which is so opposed to the virtue of religion, namely, the *liberty of worship*, as it is called. This is based on the principle that every man is free to profess as he may choose any religion or none.

20. But, assuredly, of all the duties which man has to fulfill, that, without doubt, is the chiefest and holiest which commands him to worship God with devotion and piety. This follows of necessity from the truth that we are ever in the power of God, are ever guided by His will and providence, and, having come forth from Him, must return to Him. Add to which, no true virtue can exist without religion, for moral virtue is concerned with those things which lead to God as man's supreme and ultimate good; and therefore religion, which (as St. Thomas says) "performs those actions which are directly and immediately ordained for the divine honor,"[7] rules and tempers all virtues. And if it be asked which of the many conflicting religions it is necessary to adopt, reason and the natural law unhesitatingly tell us to practice that one which God enjoins, and which men can easily recognize by certain exterior notes, whereby Divine Providence has willed that it should be distinguished, because, in a matter of such moment, the most terrible loss would be the

---

[7] Summa theologiae, IIa-IIae, q. lxxxi, a. 6. Answer.

consequence of error. Wherefore, when a liberty such as We have described is offered to man, the power is given him to pervert or abandon with impunity the most sacred of duties, and to exchange the unchangeable good for evil; which, as We have said, is no liberty, but its degradation, and the abject submission of the soul to sin.

21. This kind of liberty, if considered in relation to the State, clearly implies that there is no reason why the State should offer any homage to God, or should desire any public recognition of Him; that no one form of worship is to be preferred to another, but that all stand on an equal footing, no account being taken of the religion of the people, even if they profess the Catholic faith. But, to justify this, it must needs be taken as true that the State has no duties toward God, or that such duties, if they exist, can be abandoned with impunity, both of which assertions are manifestly false. For it cannot be doubted but that, by the will of God, men are united in civil society; whether its component parts be considered; or its form, which implies authority; or the object of its existence; or the abundance of the vast services which it renders to man. God it is who has made man for society, and has placed him in the company of others like himself, so that what was wanting to his nature, and beyond his attainment if left to his own resources, he might obtain by association with others. Wherefore, civil society must acknowledge God as its Founder and Parent, and must obey and reverence His power and authority. Justice therefore forbids, and reason itself forbids, the State to be godless; or to adopt a line of action which would end in godlessness-namely, to treat the various religions (as they call them) alike, and to bestow upon them promiscuously equal rights and privileges. Since, then, the profession of one religion is necessary in the State, that religion must be professed which alone is true, and which can be recognized without difficulty, especially in Catholic States, because the marks of truth are, as it were, engravers upon it. This religion, therefore, the rulers of the State must preserve and protect, if they would provide - as they should do - with

prudence and usefulness for the good of the community. For public authority exists for the welfare of those whom it governs; and, although its proximate end is to lead men to the prosperity found in this life, yet, in so doing, it ought not to diminish, but rather to increase, man's capability of attaining to the supreme good in which his everlasting happiness consists: which never can be attained if religion be disregarded.

22. All this, however, We have explained more fully elsewhere. We now only wish to add the remark that liberty of so false a nature is greatly hurtful to the true liberty of both rulers and their subjects. Religion, of its essence, is wonderfully helpful to the State. For, since it derives the prime origin of all power directly from God Himself, with grave authority it charges rulers to be mindful of their duty, to govern without injustice or severity, to rule their people kindly and with almost paternal charity; it admonishes subjects to be obedient to lawful authority, as to the ministers of God; and it binds them to their rulers, not merely by obedience, but by reverence and affection, forbidding all seditious and venturesome enterprises calculated to disturb public order and tranquillity, and cause greater restrictions to be put upon the liberty of the people. We need not mention how greatly religion conduces to pure morals, and pure morals to liberty. Reason shows, and history confirms the fact, that the higher the morality of States; the greater are the liberty and wealth and power which they enjoy.

23. *We must now consider briefly liberty of speech*, and liberty of the press. It is hardly necessary to say that there can be no such right as this, if it be not used in moderation, and if it pass beyond the bounds and end of all true liberty. For right is a moral power which - as We have before said and must again and again repeat - it is absurd to suppose that nature has accorded indifferently to truth and falsehood, to justice and injustice. Men have a right freely and prudently to propagate throughout the State what things soever are true and honorable, so that as many as possible may possess them; but lying opinions, than which no mental

plague is greater, and vices which corrupt the heart and moral life should be diligently repressed by public authority, lest they insidiously work the ruin of the State. The excesses of an unbridled intellect, which unfailingly end in the oppression of the untutored multitude, are no less rightly controlled by the authority of the law than are the injuries inflicted by violence upon the weak. And this all the more surely, because by far the greater part of the community is either absolutely unable, or able only with great difficulty, to escape from illusions and deceitful subtleties, especially such as flatter the passions. If unbridled license of speech and of writing be granted to all, nothing will remain sacred and inviolate; even the highest and truest mandates of natures, justly held to be the common and noblest heritage of the human race, will not be spared. Thus, truth being gradually obscured by darkness, pernicious and manifold error, as too often happens, will easily prevail. Thus, too, license will gain what liberty loses; for liberty will ever be more free and secure in proportion as license is kept in fuller restraint. In regard, however, to all matter of opinion which God leaves to man's free discussion, full liberty of thought and of speech is naturally within the right of everyone; for such liberty never leads men to suppress the truth, but often to discover it and make it known.

24. A like judgment must be passed upon what is called liberty of teaching. There can be no doubt that truth alone should imbue the minds of men, for in it are found the well-being, the end, and the perfection of every intelligent nature; and therefore nothing but truth should be taught both to the ignorant and to the educated, so as to bring knowledge to those who have it not, and to preserve it in those who possess it. For this reason it is plainly the duty of all who teach to banish error from the mind, and by sure safeguards to close the entry to all false convictions. From this it follows, as is evident, that the liberty of which We have been speaking is greatly opposed to reason, and tends absolutely to pervert men's minds, in as much as it claims for itself the right of teaching whatever it pleases - a liberty which the State cannot grant without failing in its duty. And the more so because the

authority of teachers has great weight with their hearers, who can rarely decide for themselves as to the truth or falsehood of the instruction given to them.

25. Wherefore, this liberty, also, in order that it may deserve the name, must be kept within certain limits, lest the office of teaching be turned with impunity into an instrument of corruption. Now, truth, which should be the only subject matter of those who teach, is of two kinds: natural and supernatural. Of natural truths, such as the principles of nature and whatever is derived from them immediately by our reason, there is a kind of common patrimony in the human race. On this, as on a firm basis, morality, justice, religion, and the very bonds of human society rest: and to allow people to go unharmed who violate or destroy it would be most impious, most foolish, and most inhuman.

26. But with no less religious care must we preserve that great and sacred treasure of the truths which God Himself has taught us. By many and convincing arguments, often used by defenders of Christianity, certain leading truths have been laid down: namely, that some things have been revealed by God; that the only-begotten Son of God was made flesh, to bear witness to the truth; that a perfect society was founded by Him - the Church, namely, of which He is the head, and with which He has promised to abide till the end of the world. To this society He entrusted all the truths which He had taught, in order that it might keep and guard them and with lawful authority explain them; and at the same time He commanded all nations to hear the voice of the Church, as if it were His own, threatening those who would nor hear it with everlasting perdition. Thus, it is manifest that man's best and surest teacher is God, the Source and Principle of all truth; and the only-begotten Son, who is in the bosom of the Father, the Way, the Truth, and the Life, the true Light which enlightens every man, and to whose teaching all must submit: "And they shall all be taught of God."[8]

27. In faith and in the teaching of morality, God Himself made the Church a partaker of His divine authority, and through His heavenly gift she cannot be deceived. She is therefore the greatest and most reliable teacher of mankind, and in her swells an inviolable right to teach them. Sustained by the truth received from her divine Founder, the Church has ever sought to fulfill holily the mission entrusted to her by God; unconquered by the difficulties on all sides surrounding her, she has never ceased to assert her liberty of teaching, and in this way the wretched superstition of paganism being dispelled, the wide world was renewed unto Christian wisdom. Now, reason itself clearly teaches that the truths of divine revelation and those of nature cannot really be opposed to one another, and that whatever is at variance with them must necessarily be false. Therefore, the divine teaching of the Church, so far from being an obstacle to the pursuit of learning and the progress of science, or in any way retarding the advance of civilization, in reality brings to them the sure guidance of shining light. And for the same reason it is of no small advantage for the perfecting of human liberty, since our Saviour Jesus Christ has said that by truth is man made free: "You shall know the truth, and the truth shall make you free."[9] Therefore, there is no reason why genuine liberty should grow indignant, or true science feel aggrieved, at having to bear the just and necessary restraint of laws by which, in the judgment of the Church and of reason itself, human teaching has to be controlled.

28, The Church, indeed - as facts have everywhere proved - looks chiefly and above all to the defense of the Christian faith, while careful at the same time to foster and promote every kind of human learning. For learning is in itself good, and praiseworthy, and desirable; and further, all erudition which is the outgrowth of sound reason, and in conformity with the truth of things, serves not a little to confirm what we believe on the

[8] John 6:45.
[9] John 8:32.

authority of God. The Church, truly, to our great benefit, has carefully preserved the monuments of ancient wisdom; has opened everywhere homes of science, and has urged on intellectual progress by fostering most diligently the arts by which the culture of our age is so much advanced. Lastly, we must not forget that a vast field lies freely open to man's industry and genius, containing all those things which have no necessary connection with Christian faith and morals, or as to which the Church, exercising no authority, leaves the judgment of the learned free and unconstrained.

29. From all this may be understood the nature and character of that liberty which the followers of liberalism so eagerly advocate and proclaim. On the one hand, they demand for themselves and for the State a license which opens the way to every perversity of opinion; and on the other, they hamper the Church in divers ways, restricting her liberty within narrowest limits, although from her teaching not only is there nothing to be feared, but in every respect very much to be gained.

30. Another liberty is widely advocated, namely, *liberty of conscience*. If by this is meant that everyone may, as he chooses, worship God or not, it is sufficiently refuted by the arguments already adduced. But it may also be taken to mean that every man in the State may follow the will of God and, from a consciousness of duty and free from every obstacle, obey His commands. This, indeed, is true liberty, a liberty worthy of the sons of God, which nobly maintains the dignity of man and is stronger than all violence or wrong - a liberty which the Church has always desired and held most dear. This is the kind of liberty the Apostles claimed for themselves with intrepid constancy, which the apologists of Christianity confirmed by their writings, and which the martyrs in vast numbers consecrated by their blood. And deservedly so; for this Christian liberty bears witness to the absolute and most just dominion of God over man, and to the chief and supreme duty of man toward God. It has nothing in common with a seditious and rebellious mind; and in no title

derogates from obedience to public authority; for the right to
command and to require obedience exists only so far as it is in
accordance with the authority of God, and is within the measure
that He has laid down. But when anything is commanded which
is plainly at variance with the will of God, there is a wide
departure from this divinely constituted order, and at the same
time a direct conflict with divine authority; therefore, it is right
not to obey.

31. By the patrons of liberalism, however, who make the State
absolute and omnipotent, and proclaim that man should live
altogether independently of God, the liberty of which We speak,
which goes hand in hand with virtue and religion, is not
admitted; and whatever is done for its preservation is accounted
an injury and an offense against the State. Indeed, if what they
say were really true, there would be no tyranny, no matter how
monstrous, which we should not be bound to endure and submit
to.

32. The Church most earnestly desires that the Christian
teaching, of which We have given an outline, should penetrate
every rank of society in reality and in practice; for it would be of
the greatest efficacy in healing the evils of our day, which are
neither few nor slight, and are the off spring in great part of the
false liberty which is so much extolled, and in which the germs of
safety and glory were supposed to be contained. The hope has
been disappointed by the result. The fruit, instead of being sweet
and wholesome, has proved cankered and bitter. If, then, a
remedy is desired, let it be sought for in a restoration of sound
doctrine, from which alone the preservation of order and, as a
consequence, the defense of true liberty can be confidently
expected.

33. Yet, with the discernment of a true mother, the Church
weighs the great burden of human weakness, and well knows the
course down which the minds and actions of men are in this our
age being borne. For this reason, while not conceding any right

to anything save what is true and honest, she does not forbid public authority to tolerate what is at variance with truth and justice, for the sake of avoiding some greater evil, or of obtaining or preserving some greater good. God Himself in His providence, though infinitely good and powerful, permits evil to exist in the world, partly that greater good may not be impeded, and partly that greater evil may not ensue. In the government of States it is not forbidden to imitate the Ruler of the world; and, as the authority of man is powerless to prevent every evil, it has (as St. Augustine says) to overlook and leave unpunished many things which are punished, and rightly, by Divine Providence.[10] But if, in such circumstances, for the sake of the common good (and this is the only legitimate reason), human law may or even should tolerate evil, it may not and should not approve or desire evil for its own sake; for evil of itself, being a privation of good, is opposed to the common welfare which every legislator is bound to desire and defend to the best of his ability. In this, human law must endeavor to imitate God, who, as St. Thomas teaches, in allowing evil to exist in the world, "neither wills evil to be done, nor wills it not to be done, but wills only to permit it to be done; and this is good."[11] This saying of the Angelic Doctor contains briefly the whole doctrine of the permission of evil.

34. But, to judge aright, we must acknowledge that, the more a State is driven to tolerate evil, the further is it from perfection; and that the tolerance of evil which is dictated by political prudence should be strictly confined to the limits which its justifying cause, the public welfare, requires. Wherefore, if such tolerance would be injurious to the public welfare, and entail greater evils on the State, it would not be lawful; for in such case the motive of good is wanting. And although in the extraordinary condition of these times the Church usually acquiesces in certain modern liberties, not because she prefers them in themselves, but because she judges it expedient to permit them, she would in

---

[10] Augustine, De libero arbitrio, lib. I, cap. 6, n. 14 (PL 32, 1228).
[11] Summa theologiae, Ia, q. xix, a. 9, ad 3m.

happier times exercise her own liberty; and, by persuasion, exhortation, and entreaty would endeavor, as she is bound, to fulfill the duty assigned to her by God of providing for the eternal salvation of mankind. One thing, however, remains always true - that the liberty which is claimed for all to do all things is not, as We have often said, of itself desirable, inasmuch as it is contrary to reason that error and truth should have equal rights.

35. And as to *tolerance*, it is surprising how far removed from the equity and prudence of the Church are those who profess what is called liberalism. For, in allowing that boundless license of which We have spoken, they exceed all limits, and end at last by making no apparent distinction between truth and error, honesty and dishonesty. And because the Church, the pillar and ground of truth, and the unerring teacher of morals, is forced utterly to reprobate and condemn tolerance of such an abandoned and criminal character, they calumniate her as being wanting in patience and gentleness, and thus fail to see that, in so doing, they impute to her as a fault what is in reality a matter for commendation. But, in spite of all this show of tolerance, it very often happens that, while they profess themselves ready to lavish liberty on all in the greatest profusion, they are utterly intolerant toward the Catholic Church, by refusing to allow her the liberty of being herself free.

36. And now to reduce for clearness' sake to its principal heads all that has been set forth with its immediate conclusions, the summing up in this briefly: that man, by a necessity of his nature, is wholly subject to the most faithful and ever-enduring power of God; and that, as a consequence, any liberty, except that which consists in submission to God and in subjection to His will, is unintelligible. To deny the existence of this authority in God, or to refuse to submit to it, means to act, not as a free man, but as one who treasonably abuses his liberty; and in such a disposition of mind the chief and deadly vice of liberalism essentially consists. The form, however, of the sin is manifold; for in more

ways and degrees than one can the will depart from the obedience which is due to God or to those who share the divine power.

37. For, to reject the supreme authority to God, and to cast off all obedience to Him in public matters, or even in private and domestic affairs, is the greatest perversion of liberty and the worst kind of liberalism; and what We have said must be understood to apply to this alone in its fullest sense.

38. Next comes the system of those who admit indeed the duty of submitting to God, the Creator and Ruler of the world, inasmuch as all nature is dependent on His will, but who boldly reject all laws of faith and morals which are above natural reason, but are revealed by the authority of God; or who at least impudently assert that there is no reason why regard should be paid to these laws, at any rate publicly, by the State. How mistaken these men also are, and how inconsistent, we have seen above. From this teaching, as from its source and principle, flows that fatal principle of the separation of Church and State; whereas it is, on the contrary, clear that the two powers, though dissimilar in functions and unequal in degree, ought nevertheless to live in concord, by harmony in their action and the faithful discharge of their respective duties.

39. But this teaching is understood in two ways. Many wish the State to be separated from the Church wholly and entirely, so that with regard to every right of human society, in institutions, customs, and laws, the offices of State, and the education of youth, they would pay no more regard to the Church than if she did not exist; and, at most, would allow the citizens individually to attend to their religion in private if so minded. Against such as these, all the arguments by which We disprove the principle of separation of Church and State are conclusive; with this super-added, that it is absurd the citizen should respect the Church, while the State may hold her in contempt.

40. Others oppose not the existence of the Church, nor indeed could they; yet they despoil her of the nature and rights of a perfect society, and maintain that it does not belong to her to legislate, to judge, or to punish, but only to exhort, to advise, and to rule her subjects in accordance with their own consent and will. By such opinion they pervert the nature of this divine society, and attenuate and narrow its authority, its office of teacher, and its whole efficiency; and at the same time they aggrandize the power of the civil government to such extent as to subject the Church of God to the empire and sway of the State, like any voluntary association of citizens. To refute completely such teaching, the arguments often used by the defenders of Christianity, and set forth by Us, especially in the encyclical letter *Immortale Dei*,[12] are of great avail; for by those arguments it is proved that, by a divine provision, all the rights which essentially belong to a society that is legitimate, supreme, and perfect in all its parts exist in the Church.

41. Lastly, there remain those who, while they do not approve the separation of Church and State, think nevertheless that the Church ought to adapt herself to the times and conform to what is required by the modern system of government. Such an opinion is sound, if it is to be understood of some equitable adjustment consistent with truth and justice; in so far, namely, that the Church, in the hope of some great good, may show herself indulgent, and may conform to the times in so far as her sacred office permits. But it is not so in regard to practices and doctrines which a perversion of morals and a warped judgment have unlawfully introduced. Religion, truth, and justice must ever be maintained; and, as God has intrusted these great and sacred matters to her office as to dissemble in regard to what is false or unjust, or to connive at what is hurtful to religion.

42. From what has been said it follows that it is quite unlawful to demand, to defend, or to grant unconditional freedom of

[12] See no. 93:8-11.

thought, of speech, or writing, or of worship, as if these were so many rights given by nature to man. For, if nature had really granted them, it would be lawful to refuse obedience to God, and there would be no restraint on human liberty. It likewise follows that freedom in these things may be tolerated wherever there is just cause, but only with such moderation as will prevent its degenerating into license and excess. And, where such liberties are in use, men should employ them in doing good, and should estimate them as the Church does; for liberty is to be regarded as legitimate in so far only as it affords greater facility for doing good, but no farther.

43. Whenever there exists, or there is reason to fear, an unjust oppression of the people on the one hand, or a deprivation of the liberty of the Church on the other, it is lawful to seek for such a change of government as will bring about due liberty of action. In such case, an excessive and vicious liberty is not sought, but only some relief, for the common welfare, in order that, while license for evil is allowed by the State, the power of doing good may not be hindered.

44. Again, it is not of itself wrong to prefer a democratic form of government, if only the Catholic doctrine be maintained as to the origin and exercise of power. Of the various forms of government, the Church does not reject any that are fitted to procure the welfare of the subject; she wishes only - and this nature itself requires - that they should be constituted without involving wrong to any one, and especially without violating the rights of the Church.

45. Unless it be otherwise determined, by reason of some exceptional condition of things, it is expedient to take part in the administration of public affairs. And the Church approves of every one devoting his services to the common good, and doing all that he can for the defense, preservation, and prosperity of his country.

46. Neither does the Church condemn those who, if it can be done without violation of justice, wish to make their country independent of any foreign or despotic power. Nor does she blame those who wish to assign to the State the power of self-government, and to its citizens the greatest possible measure of prosperity. The Church has always most faithfully fostered civil liberty, and this was seen especially in Italy, in the municipal prosperity, and wealth, and glory which were obtained at a time when the salutary power of the Church has spread, without opposition, to all parts of the State.

47. These things, venerable brothers, which, under the guidance of faith and reason, in the discharge of Our Apostolic office, We have now delivered to you, We hope, especially by your cooperation with Us, will be useful unto very many. In lowliness of heart We raise Our eyes in supplication to God, and earnestly beseech Him to shed mercifully the light of His wisdom and of His counsel upon men, so that, strengthened by these heavenly gifts, they may in matters of such moment discern what is true, and may afterwards, in public and private at all times and with unshaken constancy, live in accordance with the truth. As a pledge of these heavenly gifts, and in witness of Our good will to you, venerable brothers, and to the clergy and people committed to each of you, We most lovingly grant in the Lord the apostolic benediction.

Given at St. Peter's in Rome, the twentieth day of June, 1888, the tenth year of Our Pontificate.

VIII: Exeunte Iam Anno

December 25, 1888

ON RIGHT ORDERING OF CHRISTIAN LIFE

At the end of the year in which, by a singular mercy of God, We have celebrated the fiftieth anniversary of Our priesthood, We dwell with pleasure upon the past months, and are delighted to recall them to memory. And not without reason; for the occasion, which regarded Us in a personal manner, was of itself neither great nor extraordinary, and yet moved the goodwill of all men to a very great degree, to rejoice with and congratulate Us, so that there was nothing left to be desired.

2. This general joy was most pleasing and gratifying to Us; but what We valued therein most was the agreement of sentiment and the universal testimony to religion which it displayed. For the unanimous consent of well-wishers expressed this fact clearly, that in all places the minds and hearts of all were devoted to the Vicar of Christ, that men looked with confidence to the Apostolic See, in the midst of its misfortunes, as to an ever-springing and pure fount of salvation; and that in every land where the Catholic religion flourishes the Roman Church, mother and mistress of all Churches, is duly reverenced, as it should be, with one mind and heart.

3. For these reasons, through the past months, We have often lifted up our eyes to God in thanksgiving for His most gracious gift of long life, and for the consolations in Our labours which We have mentioned, and at the same time, when needful, We showed our gratitude to those to whom it was due. Now, however, the closing days of the year and of the Jubilee, bid Us renew the recollection of benefits received, and it gives us great pleasure that the whole Church joins with Us in thanksgiving. At

163

the same time We wish by this letter to declare publicly that so many testimonies of devotion and love have gone very far towards lightening Our burden, and the remembrance of them will live always in Our mind.

4. But a holier and higher duty yet remains. For in this devotion and eagerness to show honour to the Roman Pontiff, We acknowledge the power of God Who often is wont to draw and alone can draw great good from matters even of the smallest moment. For God, in His providence, seems to have wished to arouse faith in the midst of wrong thinking men, and to recall the Christian people to the desire of a higher life.

5. We must therefore strive diligently that after beginning well we may also end well, that the counsels of God may be both understood and put in practice. The obedience shown to the Apostolic See will then be full and perfected, if it be joined with Christian virtue, and thus lead to the salvation of souls-the only end to be sought for, which will also abide forever. In the exercise of Our high Apostolic office, bestowed upon Us by the goodness of God, We have many times, as in duty bound, undertaken the defence of truth, and have striven to expound particularly those doctrines which seemed to be most useful to all, in order watchfully and carefully to avoid the dangers of error. But now, as a loving parent, We wish to address all Christians, and in homely words to exhort all to lead a holy life. For beyond the mere name of Christian, beyond the mere profession of faith, Christian virtues are necessary for the Christian, and upon this depends, not only the eternal salvation of their souls, but also the peace and prosperity of the human family and brotherhood.

6. If We look into the kind of life men lead everywhere, it would be impossible to avoid the conclusion that public and private morals differ much from the precepts of the Gospel. Too sadly, alas, do the words of the Apostle St. John apply to our age, *"all that* is *in the world,* is the *concupiscence of the* flesh, *and the concupiscence*

of the eyes and *the pride of life."*[1] For in truth, most men, with little
care whence they come or whither they go, place all their
thoughts and care upon the weak and fleeting goods of this life;
contrary to nature and right reason they willingly give themselves
up to those ways of which their reason tells them they should be
the masters. It is a short step from the desire of luxury to the
striving after the means to obtain it. Hence arises an unbridled
greed for money, which blinds those whom it has led captive,
and in the fulfilment of its passion hurries them madly along,
often without regard for justice or injustice, and not seldom
accompanied by a disgraceful contempt for the poverty of their
neighbour. Thus many who live in the lap of luxury call
themselves brethren of the multitude whom in their heart of
hearts they despise; and in the same way with minds puffed up
by pride, they take no thought to obey any law, or fear any
power. They call self love liberty, and think themselves *"born free
like a wild ass's colt."*[2] Snares and temptation to sin abound; We
know that impious or immoral dramas are exhibited on the stage;
that books and journals are written to jeer at virtue and ennoble
crime; that the very arts, which were intended to give pleasure
and proper recreation, have been made to minister to impurity.
Nor can We look to the future without fear, for new seeds of evil
are sown, and as it were poured into the heart of the rising
generation. As for the public schools, there is no ecclesiastical
authority left in them, and in the years when it is most fitting for
tender minds to be trained carefully in Christian virtue, the
precepts of religion are for the most part unheard. Men more
advanced in age encounter a yet graver peril from evil teaching,
which is of such a kind as to blind the young by misleading
words, instead of filling them with the knowledge of the truth.
Many now-a-days seek to learn by the aid of reason alone, laying
divine faith entirely aside; and, through the removal of its bright
light, they stumble and fail to discern the truth, teaching for
instance, that matter alone exists in the world; that men and
beasts have the same origin and a like nature; there are some,

---

[1] 1 Jn ii, 16.
[2] Job xi, 12.

indeed, who go so far as to doubt the existence of God, the Ruler and Maker of the World, or who err most grievously, like the heathens, as to the nature of God. Hence the very nature and form of virtue, justice, and duty are of necessity destroyed. Thus it is that while they hold up to admiration the high authority of reason, and unduly elevate the subtlety of the human intellect, they fall into the just punishment of pride through ignorance of what is of more importance.

7. When the mind has thus been poisoned, at the same time the moral character becomes deeply and essentially corrupted; and such a state can only be cured with the utmost difficulty in this class of men, because on the one hand wrong opinions vitiate their judgment of what is right, and on the other the light of Christian faith, which is the principle and basis of all justice, is extinguished.

8. In this way We daily see the numerous ills which afflict all classes of men. These poisonous doctrines have utterly corrupted both public and private life; rationalism, materialism, atheism, have begotten socialism, communism, nihilism evil principles which it was not only fitting should have sprung from such parentage but were its necessary offspring. In truth, if the Catholic religion is wilfully rejected, whose divine origin is made clear by such unmistakable signs, what reason is there why every form of religion should not be rejected, not upheld, by such criteria of truth? If the soul is one with the body, and if therefore no hope of a happy eternity remains when the body dies, what reason is there for men to undertake toil and suffering here in subjecting the appetites to right reason? The highest good of man will then lie in enjoying life's pleasures and life's luxuries. And since there is no one who is drawn to virtue by the impulse of his own nature, every man will naturally lay hands on all he can that he may live happily on the spoils of others. Nor is there any power mighty enough to bridle the passions, for it follows that the power of law is broken, and that all authority is loosened, if the belief in an ever-living God, Who commands

what is right and forbids what is wrong is rejected. Hence the bonds of civil society will be utterly shattered when every man is driven by an unappeasable covetousness to a perpetual struggle, some striving to keep their possessions, others to obtain what they desire. This is well-nigh the bent of our age.

9. There is, nevertheless, some consolation for Us even in looking on these evils, and We may lift up Our heart in hope. For God *"created all things that they might be: and He made the nations of the earth for health."*[3] But as all this world cannot be upheld but by His providence and divinity, so also men can only be healed by His power, of Whose goodness they were called from death to life. For Jesus Christ redeemed the human race once by the shedding of His blood, but the power of so great a work and gift is for all ages; *"neither is there salvation in any other."*[4] Hence they who strive by the enforcement of law to extinguish the growing flame of lawless desire, strive indeed for justice; but let them know that they will labor with no result, or next to none, as long as they obstinately reject the power of the gospel and refuse the assistance of the Church. Thus will the evil alone be cured, by changing their ways, and returning back in their public and private life to Jesus Christ and Christianity.

10. Now the whole essence of a Christian life is to reject the corruption of the world and to oppose constantly any indulgence in it; this is taught in the words and deeds, the laws and institutions, the life and death of Jesus Christ, *"the author and finisher of faith."*[5] Hence, however strongly We are deterred by the evil disposition of nature and character, it is our duty to run to the *"fight proposed to us,"*[6] fortified and armed with the same desire and the same arms as He who, *"having joy set before him, endured the cross."*[7] Wherefore let men understand this specially, that it is

---

[3] Wis i, 14.
[4] Acts iv, 12.
[5] Heb xii, 2.
[6] Heb xii, 1.
[7] Heb xii, 2.

most contrary to Christian duty to follow, in worldly fashion, pleasures of every kind, to be afraid of the hardships attending a virtuous life, and to deny nothing to self that soothes and delights the senses. "They that are Christ's, have crucified their flesh, with the vices and concupiscences"[8] so that it follows that they who are not accustomed to suffering, and who hold not ease and pleasure in contempt belong not to Christ. By the infinite goodness of God man lived again to the hope of an immortal life, from which he had been cut off, but he cannot attain to it if he strives not to walk in the very footsteps of Christ and conform his mind to Christ's by the meditation of Christ's example. Therefore this is not a counsel but a duty, and it is the duty, not of those only who desire a more perfect life, but clearly of every man *"always bearing about in our body the mortification of Jesus."*[9] How otherwise could the natural law, commanding man to live virtuously, be kept? For by holy baptism the sin which we contracted at birth is destroyed, but the evil and tortuous roots of sin, which sin has engrafted, and by no means removed. This part of man which is without reason - although it cannot beat those who fight manfully by Christ's grace - nevertheless struggles with reason for supremacy, clouds the whole soul and tyrannically bends the will from virtue with such power that we cannot escape vice or do our duty except by a daily struggle. *"This holy synod teaches that in the baptised there remains concupiscence or an inclination to evil, which, being left to be fought against, cannot hurt those who do not consent to it, and manfully fight against it by the grace of Jesus Christ; for he is not crowned who does not strive lawfully."*[10] There is in this struggle a degree of strength to which only a very perfect virtue, belonging to those who, by putting to flight evil passions, has gained so high a place as to seem almost to live a heavenly life on earth. Granted; grant that few attain such excellence; even the philosophy of the ancients taught that every man should restrain his evil desires, and still more and with greater care those who from daily contact with the world have the greater

---

[8] Gal v, 24.
[9] 2 Cor iv, 10.
[10] Conc. Trid., sess. v, can. 5.

temptations - unless it be foolishly thought that where the danger is greater watchfulness is less needed, or that they who are more grievously ill need fewer medicines.

11. But the toil which is borne in this conflict is compensated by great blessings, beyond and above heavenly and eternal rewards, particularly in this way, that by calming the passions nature is largely restored to its pristine dignity. For man has been born under this law, that the mind should rule the body, that the appetites should be restrained by sound sense and reason; and hence it follows that putting a curb upon our masterful passions is the noblest and greatest freedom. Moreover, in the present state of society it is difficult to see what man could be expected to do without such a disposition. Will he be inclined to do well who has been accustomed to guide his actions by self-love alone? No man can be high-souled, kind, merciful, or restrained, who has not learnt self conquest and a contempt for this world when opposed to virtue. And yet it must be said that it seems to have been pre-determined by the counsel of God that there should be no salvation to men without strife and pain. Truly, though God has given to man pardon for sin, He gave it under the condition that His only begotten Son should pay the due penalty; and although Jesus Christ might have satisfied divine justice in other ways, nevertheless He preferred to satisfy by the utmost suffering and the sacrifice of His life. Thus he has imposed upon His followers this law, signed in His blood, that their life should be an endless strife with the vices of the age. What made the apostles invincible in their mission of teaching truth to the world; what strengthened the martyrs innumerable in their bloody testimony to the Christian faith, but the readiness of their soul to obey fearlessly His laws? And all who have taken heed to live a Christian life and seek virtue have trodden the same path; therefore We must walk in this way if We desire either Our own salvation or that of others. Thus it becomes necessary for every one to guard manfully against the allurements of luxury, and since on every side there is so much ostentation in the enjoyment of wealth, the soul must be fortified against the dangerous snares

of riches lest straining after what are called the good things of life, which cannot satisfy and soon fade away, the soul should lose *"the treasure in heaven which faileth not."* Finally, this is matter of deep grief, that free-thought and evil example have so evil an influence in enervating the soul, that many are now almost ashamed of the name of Christian - a shame which is the sign either of abandoned wickedness or the extreme of cowardice; each detestable and each of the highest injury to man. For what salvation remains for such men, or on what hope can they rely, if they cease to glory in the name of Jesus Christ, if they openly and constantly refuse to mould their lives on the precepts of the gospel? It is the common complaint that the age is barren of brave men. Bring back a Christian code of life, and thereby the minds of men will regain their firmness and constancy. But man's power by itself is not equal to the responsibility of so many duties. As We must ask God for daily bread for the sustenance of the body, so must We pray to Him for strength of soul for its nourishment in virtue. Hence that universal condition and law of life, which We have said is a perpetual battle, brings with it the necessity of prayer to God. For, as is well and wisely said by St. Augustine, pious prayer flies over the world's barriers and calls down the mercy of God from heaven. In order to conquer the emotions of lust, and the snares of the devil, lest we should be led into evil, we are commanded to seek the divine help in the words, *"pray that ye enter not into temptation."*[11] How much more is this necessary, if we wish to labour for the salvation of others? Christ our Lord, the only begotten Son of God, the source of all grace and virtue, first showed by example what he taught in word: *"He passed the whole night in the prayer of God,"*[12] and when nigh to the sacrifice of his life, *"He prayed the longer."*[13]

12. The frailty of nature would be much less fearful, and the moral character would grow weak and enervated with much less ease if that divine precept were not so much disregarded and

---

[11] Mt xxvi, 41.
[12] Lk vi, 12.
[13] Lk xxii, 43.

treated almost with disdain. For God is easily appeased, and desires to aid men, having promised openly to give His grace in abundance to those who ask for it. Nay, He even invites men to ask, and almost insists with most loving words: *"I say unto you, ask and it shall be given you: seek, and you shall find: knock, and it shall be opened to you."*[14] And that we should have no fear in doing this with confidence and familiarity, he softens His words, comparing Himself to a most loving father who desires nothing so much as the love of his children. *"If you then being evil, know how to give good gifts to your children: how much more will your Father who is in heaven, give good things to them that ask Him?"*[15] And this will not seem excessive to one who considers it, if the efficaciousness of prayer seemed so great to St. John Chrysostom that he thought it might be compared with the power of God; for as God created all things by His word, so man by prayer obtains what he wills. For nothing has so great a power as prayer, because in it there are certain qualities with which it pleases God to be moved. For in prayer we separate ourselves from things of earth, and filled with the thought of God alone, we become aware of our human weakness; for the same reason we rest in the embrace of our Father, we seek a refuge in the power of our Creator. We approach the Author of all good, as though we wish Him to gaze upon our weak souls, our failing strength, our poverty; and, full of hope, we implore His aid and guardianship, Who alone can give help to the weak and consolation to the infirm and miserable. With such a condition of mind, thinking but little of ourselves, as is fitting, God is greatly inclined to mercy, for *God resisteth the proud*, but *to the humble he giveth grace.*[16] Let, then, the habit of prayer be sacred to all; let soul and voice join together in prayer, and let our whole daily life agree together, so that, by keeping the laws of God, the course of our days may seem a continual ascent to Him.

---

[14] Lk xi, 9.
[15] Mt vii, 11.
[16] 1 Pet v, 5.

13. The virtue of which we speak, like the others, is produced and nourished by divine faith; for God is the Author of all true blessings that are to be desired for themselves, as we owe to Him our knowledge of His infinite goodness, and our knowledge of the merits of our Redeemer. But, again, nothing is more fitted for the nourishment of divine faith than the pious habit of prayer, and the need of it at this time is seen by its weakness in most, and its absence in many men. For that virtue is especially the source whereby not only private lives may be amended, but also from which a final judgment may be looked for in those matters which in the daily conflict of men do not permit states to live in peace and security. If the multitude is frenzied with a thirst for excessive liberty, if the inhuman lust of the rich never is satisfied, and if to these be added those evils of the same kind to which We have referred fully above, it will be found that nothing can heal them more completely or fully than Christian faith.

14. Here it is fitting We should exhort you whom God has made His helpers by giving the divine power to dispense His Sacraments, to turn to meditation and prayer. If the reformation of private and public morals is needed, it scarcely requires to be said that in both respects the clergy ought to set the highest example. Let them therefore remember that they have been called by Jesus Christ, *"the light of the world, that the soul of the priest should shine like a light illuminating the whole world."*[17] The light of learning, and that in no small degree is needed in the priest, because it is his duty, to fill others with wisdom, to destroy errors, to be a guide to the many in the steep and slippery paths of life. Learning ought to be accompanied by innocence of life, because in the reformation of man example is far better than precept. *"Let your light shine before men, that they may see your good works."*[18] The meaning of the divine word is that the perfection of virtue in priests should be such that they should be like a mirror to the rest of men. "There is nothing which induces others more

---

[17] St. John Chrysost. De Sac. 1, 3, c.l.
[18] Mt v, 16.

effectively to piety and the worship of God, than the life and example of those who have dedicated themselves to the divine ministry: for, since they are separated from the world and placed in a higher sphere, others look on them as though on a mirror, to take examples from them."[19] Therefore if all men must watchfully heed against the allurements of sin, and against seeking too eagerly fleeting pleasures, it is clear how much more faithful and steadfast ought priests to be. The sacredness of their dignity, moreover - as well as the fact that it is not sufficient to restrain their passions-demands in them the habit of stringent self restraint, and also a guard over the powers of the soul, particularly the intellect and will, which hold the supreme place in man. "Thou who hast the mind to leave all (says St. Bernard), remember to reckon thyself among what thou would'st abandon - nay, deny thyself first and before everything." Not before the soul is unshackled and free from every desire, will men have a generous zeal for the salvation of others, without which they cannot properly secure their own everlasting welfare. "There will be one thing only sought (says St. Bernard) by His subjects, one glory, one pleasure - to make ready for the Lord a perfect people. For this they will give everything with much exertion of mind and body, with toil and suffering, with hunger and thirst, with cold and nakedness." The frequent meditation upon the things of heaven wonderfully nourishes and strengthens virtue of this kind, and makes it always fearless of the greatest difficulties for the good of others. Themore pains they take to meditate well, the more clearly will they understand the greatness and holiness of the priestly office. They will understand how sad it is that so many men, redeemed by Jesus Christ, are running headlong to eternal ruin; and by meditation upon God they will be themselves encouraged, and will more effectually excite others to the love of God. Such, then, is the surest method for the salvation of all; and in this men must take heed not to be terrified by difficulties, and not to despair of cure by reason of the long continuance of the evil. The impartial and unchangeable justice

---

[19] Conc. Trid. Sess. xxii, c. 1, de Ref.

of God metes out reward for good deeds and punishment for sin. But since the life of peoples and nations, as such, does not outlast their world, they necessarily receive the rewards due to their deeds on this earth. Indeed it is no new thing that prosperity should come to a wrong-doing state; and this by the just counsel of God, Who from time to time rewards good actions with prosperity, for no people is altogether without merit, and this Augustine considered was the case with the Roman people. The law, nevertheless, is clear that for public prosperity it is to the interest of all that virtue - and justice especially, which is the mother of all virtues - should be practised, "Justice exalteth a nation; but sin maketh nations miserable."[20] It is not Our purpose here to consider how far evil deeds may prosper, not whether empires, when flourishing and managing matters to their own liking, do nevertheless carry about with them, as it were shut up in their bowels, the seed of ruin and wretchedness. We wish this one thing to be understood, of which history has innumerable examples, that injustice is always punished, and with greater severity the longer it has been continued. We are greatly consoled by the words of the Apostle Paul, "For all things are yours; and you are Christ's, and Christ is God's."[21] By the hidden dispensation of divine providence the course of earthly things is so guided that all things that happen to man turn out to the glory of God for the salvation of those who are true disciples of Jesus Christ. Of these the mother and guide, the leader and guardian is the Church; which being united to Christ her spouse in intimate and unchangeable charity is also joined to Him by a common cause of battle and of victory. Hence We are not, and cannot be anxious on account of the Church, but We greatly fear for the salvation of very many, who proudly despise the Church, and by every kind of error rush to ruin; We are concerned for those States which We cannot but see are turned from God and sleeping in the midst of danger in dull security and insensibility. "Nothing is equal to the Church;" [says St. John Chrysostom,] "how many have opposed the Church and have themselves

---

[20] Pr xiv, 34.
[21] I Cor. iii, 22-23.

perished? The Church reaches to the heavens; such is the Church's greatness. She conquers when attacked; when beset by snares she triumphs; she struggles and is not overthrown, she fights and is not conquered." Not only is she not conquered, but she preserves that corrective power over nature, and that effective strength of life that springs from God Himself, and is unchanged by time. And, if by this power she has freed the world grown old in vice and lost in superstition, why should she not again recover it when gone astray? Let strife and suspicion at length cease, let all obstacles be removed, give the possession of all her rights to the Church, whose duty it is to guard and spread abroad the benefits gained by Jesus Christ, then We shall know by experience, where the light of the Gospel is, and what the power of Christ can do.

15. This year, which is now coming to an end, has given, as We have said, many signs of a reviving faith. Would that like the spark it might grow to an ever-increasing flame, which, by burning up the roots of sin, may open a way for the restoration of morals and for salutary counsels. We, indeed, who steer the mystical barque of the Church in such a storm, fix Our mind and heart upon the Divine Pilot Who holds the helm and sits unseen. Thou seest, Lord, how the winds have borne down on every side, how the sea rages and the waves are lashed to fury. Command, we beseech Thee, Who alone canst, the winds and the sea. Give back to man that tranquillity and order-that true peace which the world cannot give. By Thy grace let man be restored to proper order with faith in God, as in duty bound, with justice and love towards our neighbour, with temperance as to ourselves, and with passions controlled by reason. Let Thy kingdom come, let the duty of submitting to Thee and serving Thee be learnt by those who, far from Thee, seek truth and salvation to no purpose. In Thy laws there is justice and fatherly kindness; Thou grantest of Thy own good will the power to keep them. The life of a man on earth is a warfare, but Thou lookest down upon the struggle and helpest man to conquer, Thou raisest him that falls, and crownest him that triumphs.[22]

16. With a mind upheld by these thoughts to cherish a joyful and firm hope, as a pledge of the favours of Heaven and of Our good-will, We most lovingly in the Lord grant to you, Venerable Brethren, and to the clergy and people of the whole Catholic world, the Apostolic blessing.

Given at Rome at St. Peter's, on the birthday of Our Lord Jesus Christ; in the year 1888; the eleventh of Our Pontificate.

---

[22] Cf. S. Aug. in Ps 32.

IX: Sapientiae Christianae

January 10, 1890

ON CHRISTIANS AS CITIZENS

From day to day it becomes more and more evident how needful it is that the principles of Christian wisdom should ever be borne in mind, and that the life, the morals, and the institutions of nations should be wholly conformed to them. For, when these principles have been disregarded, evils so vast have accrued that no right-minded man can face the trials of the time being without grave anxiety or consider the future without alarm. Progress, not inconsiderable indeed, has been made towards securing the well-being of the body and of material things, but the material world, with the possession of wealth, power, and resources, although it may well procure comforts and increase the enjoyment of life, is incapable of satisfying our soul created for higher and more glorious things. To contemplate God, and to tend to Him, is the supreme law of the life of man. For we were created in the divine image and likeness, and are impelled, by our very nature, to the enjoyment of our Creator. But not by bodily motion or effort do we make advance toward God, but through acts of the soul, that is, through knowledge and love. For, indeed, God is the first and supreme truth, and the mind alone feeds on truth. God is perfect holiness and the sovereign good, to which only the will can desire and attain, when virtue is its guide.

2. But what applies to individual men applies equally to society - domestic alike and civil. Nature did not form society in order that man should seek in it his last end, but in order that in it and through it he should find suitable aids whereby to attain to his own perfection. If, then, a political government strives after external advantages only, and the achievement of a cultured and

prosperous life; if, in administering public affairs, it is wont to put God aside, and show no solicitude for the upholding of moral law, it deflects woefully from its right course and from the injunctions of nature; nor should it be accounted as a society or a community of men, but only as the deceitful imitation or appearance of a society.

3. As to what We have called the goods of the soul, which consist chiefly in the practice of the true religion and in the unswerving observance of the Christian precepts, We see them daily losing esteem among men, either by reason of forgetfulness or disregard, in such wise that all that is gained for the well-being of the body seems to be lost for that of the soul. A striking proof of the lessening and weakening of the Christian faith is seen in the insults too often done to the Catholic Church, openly and publicly - insults, indeed, which an age cherishing religion would not have tolerated. For these reasons, an incredible multitude of men is in danger of not achieving salvation; and even nations and empires themselves cannot long remain unharmed, since, when Christian institutions and morality decline, the main foundation of human society goes together with them. Force alone will remain to preserve public tranquillity and order. But force is very feeble when the bulwark of religion has been removed, and, being more apt to beget slavery than obedience, it bears within itself the germs of ever-increasing troubles. The present century has encountered memorable disasters, and it is not certain that some equally terrible are not impending. The very times in which we live are warning us to seek remedies there where alone they are to be found-namely, by re-establishing in the family circle and throughout the whole range of society the doctrines and practices of the Christian religion. In this lies the sole means of freeing us from the ills now weighing us down, of forestalling the dangers now threatening the world. For the accomplishment of this end, venerable brethren, We must bring to bear all the activity and diligence that lie within Our power. Although we have already, under other circumstances, and whenever occasion required, treated of these matters, We deem it expedient in this

letter to define more in detail the duties of the Catholics, inasmuch as these would, if strictly observed, wonderfully contribute to the good of the commonwealth. We have fallen upon times when a violent and well-nigh daily battle is being fought about matters of highest moment, a battle in which it is hard not to be sometimes deceived, not to go astray and, for many, not to lose heart. It behooves us, venerable brethren, to warn, instruct, and exhort each of the faithful with an earnestness befitting the occasion: that none may abandon the way of truth.[1]

4. It cannot be doubted that duties more numerous and of greater moment devolve on Catholics than upon such as are either not sufficiently enlightened in relation to the Catholic faith, or who are entirely unacquainted with its doctrines. Considering that forthwith upon salvation being brought out for mankind, Jesus Christ laid upon His Apostles the injunction to "preach the Gospel to every creature," He imposed, it is evident, upon all men the duty of learning thoroughly and believing what they were taught. This duty is intimately bound up with the gaining of eternal salvation: "He that believeth and is baptized shall be saved; but he that believeth not, shall be condemned."[2] But the man who has embraced the Christian faith, as in duty bound, is by that very fact a subject of the Church as one of the children born of her, and becomes a member of that greatest and holiest body, which it is the special charge of the Roman Pontiff to rule with supreme power, under its invisible head, Jesus Christ.

5. Now, if the natural law enjoins us to love devotedly and to defend the country in which we had birth, and in which we were brought up, so that every good citizen hesitates not to face death for his native land, very much more is it the urgent duty of Christians to be ever quickened by like feelings toward the Church. For the Church is the holy City of the living God, born

---

[1] Tobias 1:2.
[2] Mark 16:16.

of God Himself, and by Him built up and established. Upon this earth, indeed, she accomplishes her pilgrimage, but by instructing and guiding men she summons them to eternal happiness. We are bound, then, to love dearly the country whence we have received the means of enjoyment this mortal life affords, but we have a much more urgent obligation to love, with ardent love, the Church to which we owe the life of the soul, a life that will endure forever. For fitting it is to prefer the good of the soul to the well-being of the body, inasmuch as duties toward God are of a far more hallowed character than those toward men.

6. Moreover, if we would judge aright, the supernatural love for the Church and the natural love of our own country proceed from the same eternal principle, since God Himself is their Author and originating Cause. Consequently, it follows that between the duties they respectively enjoin, neither can come into collision with the other. We can, certainly, and should love ourselves, bear ourselves kindly toward our fellow men, nourish affection for the State and the governing powers; but at the same time we can and must cherish toward the Church a feeling of filial piety, and love God with the deepest love of which we are capable. The order of precedence of these duties is, however, at times, either under stress of public calamities, or through the perverse will of men, inverted. For, instances occur where the State seems to require from men as subjects one thing, and religion, from men as Christians, quite another; and this in reality without any other ground, than that the rulers of the State either hold the sacred power of the Church of no account, or endeavor to subject it to their own will. Hence arises a conflict, and an occasion, through such conflict, of virtue being put to the proof. The two powers are confronted and urge their behests in a contrary sense; to obey both is wholly impossible. No man can serve two masters,[3] for to please the one amounts to contemning the other.

---

[3] Matt. 6:24.

7. As to which should be preferred no one ought to balance for an instant. It is a high crime indeed to withdraw allegiance from God in order to please men, an act of consummate wickedness to break the laws of Jesus Christ, in order to yield obedience to earthly rulers, or, under pretext of keeping the civil law, to ignore the rights of the Church; "we ought to obey God rather than men."[4] This answer, which of old Peter and the other Apostles were used to give the civil authorities who enjoined unrighteous things, we must, in like circumstances, give always and without hesitation. No better citizen is there, whether in time of peace or war, than the Christian who is mindful of his duty; but such a one should be ready to suffer all things, even death itself, rather than abandon the cause of God or of the Church.

8. Hence, they who blame, and call by the name of sedition, this steadfastness of attitude in the choice of duty have not rightly apprehended the force and nature of true law. We are speaking of matters widely known, and which We have before now more than once fully explained. Law is of its very essence a mandate of right reason, proclaimed by a properly constituted authority, for the common good. But true and legitimate authority is void of sanction, unless it proceed from God, the supreme Ruler and Lord of all. The Almighty alone can commit power to a man over his fellow men;[5] nor may that be accounted as right reason which is in disaccord with truth and with divine reason; nor that held to be true good which is repugnant to the supreme and unchangeable good, or that wrests aside and draws away the wills of men from the charity of God.

9. Hallowed, therefore, in the minds of Christians is the very idea of public authority, in which they recognize some likeness and symbol as it were of the Divine Majesty, even when it is exercised by one unworthy. A just and due reverence to the laws

---

[4] Acts 5:29.
[5] Note the extreme importance of this principle; it justifies the doctrine according to which the only conceivable foundation of political authority must be divine in origin.

abides in them, not from force and threats, but from a
consciousness of duty; "for God hath not given us the spirit of
fear."[6]

10. But, if the laws of the State are manifestly at variance with the
divine law, containing enactments hurtful to the Church, or
conveying injunctions adverse to the duties imposed by religion,
or if they violate in the person of the supreme Pontiff the
authority of Jesus Christ, then, truly, to resist becomes a positive
duty, to obey, a crime; a crime, moreover, combined with
misdemeanor against the State itself, inasmuch as every offense
leveled against religion is also a sin against the State. Here anew it
becomes evident how unjust is the reproach of sedition; for the
obedience due to rulers and legislators is not refused, but there is
a deviation from their will in those precepts only which they have
no power to enjoin. Commands that are issued adversely to the
honor due to God, and hence are beyond the scope of justice,
must be looked upon as anything rather than laws. You are fully
aware, venerable brothers, that this is the very contention of the
Apostle St. Paul, who, in writing to Titus, after reminding
Christians that they are "to be subject to princes and powers, and
to obey at a word," at once adds: "And to be ready to every good
work."[7] Thereby he openly declares that, if laws of men contain
injunctions contrary to the eternal law of God, it is right not to
obey them. In like manner, the Prince of the Apostles gave this
courageous and sublime answer to those who would have
deprived him of the liberty of preaching the Gospel: "If it be just
in the sight of God to hear you rather than God, judge ye, for we
cannot but speak the things which we have seen and heard."[8]

11. Wherefore, to love both countries, that of earth below and
that of heaven above, yet in such mode that the love of our
heavenly surpass the love of our earthly home, and that human

[6] 2 Tim. 1:7.
[7] Titus 3:1.
[8] Acts 4:19-20.

laws be never set above the divine law, is the essential duty of Christians, and the fountainhead, so to say, from which all other duties spring. The Redeemer of mankind of Himself has said: "For this was I born, and for this came I into the world, that I should give testimony to the truth."[9] In like manner: "I am come to cast fire upon earth, and what will I but that it be kindled?"[10] In the knowledge of this truth, which constitutes the highest perfection of the mind; in divine charity which, in like manner, completes the will, all Christian life and liberty abide. This noble patrimony of truth and charity entrusted by Jesus Christ to the Church she defends and maintains ever with untiring endeavor and watchfulness.

12. But with what bitterness and in how many guises war has been waged against the Church it would be ill-timed now to urge. From the fact that it has been vouchsafed to human reason to snatch from nature, through the investigations of science, many of her treasured secrets and to apply them befittingly to the divers requirements of life, men have become possessed with so arrogant a sense of their own powers as already to consider themselves able to banish from social life the authority and empire of God. Led away by this delusion, they make over to human nature the dominion of which they think God has been despoiled; from nature, they maintain, we must seek the principle and rule of all truth; from nature, they aver, alone spring, and to it should be referred, all the duties that religious feeling prompts. Hence, they deny all revelation from on high, and all fealty due to the Christian teaching of morals as well as all obedience to the Church, and they go so far as to deny her power of making laws and exercising every other kind of right, even disallowing the Church any place among the civil institutions of the commonweal. These men aspire unjustly, and with their might strive, to gain control over public affairs and lay hands on the rudder of the State, in order that the legislation may the more

---

[9] John 18:37.
[10] Luke 12:49.

easily be adapted to these principles, and the morals of the
people influenced in accordance with them. Whence it comes to
pass that in many countries Catholicism is either openly assailed
or else secretly interfered with, full impunity being granted to the
most pernicious doctrines, while the public profession of
Christian truth is shackled oftentimes with manifold constraints.

13. Under such evil circumstances therefore, each one is bound
in conscience to watch over himself, taking all means possible to
preserve the faith inviolate in the depths of his soul, avoiding all
risks, and arming himself on all occasions, especially against the
various specious sophisms rife among non-believers. In order to
safeguard this virtue of faith in its integrity, We declare it to be
very profitable and consistent with the requirements of the time,
that each one, according to the measure of his capacity and
intelligence, should make a deep study of Christian doctrine, and
imbue his mind with as perfect a knowledge as may be of those
matters that are interwoven with religion and lie within the range
of reason. And as it is necessary that faith should not only abide
untarnished in the soul, but should grow with ever painstaking
increase, the suppliant and humble entreaty of the apostles ought
constantly to be addressed to God: "Increase our faith."[11]

14. But in this same matter, touching Christian faith, there are
other duties whose exact and religious observance, necessary at
all times in the interests of eternal salvation, become more
especially so in these our days. Amid such reckless and
widespread folly of opinion, it is, as We have said, the office of
the Church to undertake the defense of truth and uproot errors
from the mind, and this charge has to be at all times sacredly
observed by her, seeing that the honor of God and the salvation
of men are confided to her keeping. But, when necessity
compels, not those only who are invested with power of rule are
bound to safeguard the integrity of faith, but, as St. Thomas
maintains: "Each one is under obligation to show forth his faith,

---

[11] Luke 17:5.

either to instruct and encourage others of the faithful, or to repel the attacks of unbelievers."[12] To recoil before an enemy, or to keep silence when from all sides such clamors are raised against truth, is the part of a man either devoid of character or who entertains doubt as to the truth of what he professes to believe. In both cases such mode of behaving is base and is insulting to God, and both are incompatible with the salvation of mankind. This kind of conduct is profitable only to the enemies of the faith, for nothing emboldens the wicked so greatly as the lack of courage on the part of the good. Moreover, want of vigor on the part of Christians is so much the more blameworthy, as not seldom little would be needed on their part to bring to naught false charges and refute erroneous opinions, and by always exerting themselves more strenuously they might reckon upon being successful. After all, no one can be prevented from putting forth that strength of soul which is the characteristic of true Christians, and very frequently by such display of courage our enemies lose heart and their designs are thwarted. Christians are, moreover, born for combat, whereof the greater the vehemence, the more assured, God aiding, the triumph: "Have confidence; I have overcome the world."[13] Nor is there any ground for alleging that Jesus Christ, the Guardian and Champion of the Church, needs not in any manner the help of men. Power certainly is not wanting to Him, but in His loving kindness He would assign to us a share in obtaining and applying the fruits of salvation procured through His grace.

15. The chief elements of this duty consist in professing openly and unflinchingly the Catholic doctrine, and in propagating it to the utmost of our power. For, as is often said, with the greatest truth, there is nothing so hurtful to Christian wisdom as that it should not be known, since it possesses, when loyally received, inherent power to drive away error. So soon as Catholic truth is apprehended by a simple and unprejudiced soul, reason yields

---

[12] Summa theologiae, IIa-IIae, qu. iii, art. 2, ad 2m.
[13] John 16:33.

assent. Now, faith, as a virtue, is a great boon of divine grace and goodness; nevertheless, the objects themselves to which faith is to be applied are scarcely known in any other way than through the hearing. "How shall they believe Him of whom they have not heard? and how shall they hear without a preacher? Faith then cometh by hearing, and hearing by the word of Christ."[14] Since, then, faith is necessary for salvation, it follows that the word of Christ must tie preached. The office, indeed, of preaching, that is, of teaching, lies by divine right in the province of the pastors, namely, of the bishops whom "the Holy Spirit has placed to rule the Church of God."[15] It belongs, above all, to the Roman Pontiff, vicar of Jesus Christ, established as head of the universal Church, teacher of all :hat pertains to morals and faith.

16. No one, however, must entertain the notion that private individuals are prevented from taking some active part in this duty of teaching, especially those on whom God has bestowed gifts of mind with the strong wish of rendering themselves useful. These, so often as circumstances demand, may take upon themselves, not, indeed, the office of the pastor, but the task of communicating to others what they have themselves received, becoming, as it were, living echoes of their masters in the faith. Such co-operation on the part of the laity has seemed to the Fathers of the Vatican Council so opportune and fruitful of good that they thought well to invite it. "All faithful Christians, but those chiefly who are in a prominent position, or engaged in teaching, we entreat, by the compassion of Jesus Christ, and enjoin by the authority of the same God and Saviour, that they bring aid to ward off and eliminate these errors from holy Church, and contribute their zealous help in spreading abroad the light of undefiled faith."[16] Let each one, therefore, bear in mind that he both can and should, so far as may be, preach the Catholic faith by the authority of his example, and by open and constant profession of the obligations it imposes. In respect,

---

[14] Rom. 10:14, 17.
[15] Acts 20:28.
[16] Constitution Dei Filius, at end.

consequently, to the duties that bind us to God and the Church, it should be borne earnestly in mind that in propagating Christian truth and warding off errors the zeal of the laity should, as far as possible, be brought actively into play.

17. The faithful would not, however, so completely and advantageously satisfy these duties as is fitting they should were they to enter the field as isolated champions of the faith. Jesus Christ, indeed, has clearly intimated that the hostility and hatred of men, which He first and foremost experienced, would be shown in like degree toward the work founded by Him, so that many would be barred from profiting by the salvation for which all are indebted to His loving kindness. Wherefore, He willed not only to train disciples in His doctrine, but to unite them into one society, and closely conjoin them in one body, "which is the Church,"[17] whereof He would be the head. The life of Jesus Christ pervades, therefore, the entire framework of this body, cherishes and nourishes its every member, uniting each with each, and making all work together to the same end, albeit the action of each be not the same.[18] Hence it follows that not only is the Church a perfect society far excelling every other, but it is enjoined by her Founder that for the salvation of mankind she is to contend "as an army drawn up in battle array."[19] The organization and constitution of Christian society can in no wise be changed, neither can any one of its members live as he may choose, nor elect that mode of fighting which best pleases him. For, in effect, he scatters and gathers not who gathers not with the Church and with Jesus Christ, and all who fight not jointly with him and with the Church are in very truth contending against God.[20]

18. To bring about such a union of minds and uniformity of action - not without reason so greatly feared by the enemies of

---

[17] Col. 1:24.
[18] Cf. Rom. 12:4-5.
[19] Cant. 6:9.
[20] Cf. Luke 11:22.

Catholicism - the main point is that a perfect harmony of opinion should prevail; in which intent we find Paul the Apostle exhorting the Corinthians with earnest zeal and solemn weight of words: "Now I beseech you, brethren, by the name of our Lord Jesus Christ, that you all speak the same thing, and that there be no schisms among you: but that you be perfectly in the same mind, and in the same judgment."[21]

19. The wisdom of this precept is readily apprehended. In truth, thought is the principle of action, and hence there cannot exist agreement of will, or similarity of action, if people all think differently one from the other.

20. In the case of those who profess to take reason as their sole guide, there would hardly be found, if, indeed, there ever could be found, unity of doctrine. Indeed, the art of knowing things as they really are is exceedingly difficult; moreover, the mind of man is by nature feeble and drawn this way and that by a variety of opinions, and not seldom led astray by impressions coming from without; and, furthermore, the influence of the passions oftentimes takes away, or certainly at least diminishes, the capacity for grasping the truth. On this account, in controlling State affairs means are often used to keep those together by force who cannot agree in their way of thinking.

21. It happens far otherwise with Christians; they receive their rule of faith from the Church, by whose authority and under whose guidance they are conscious that they have beyond question attained to truth. Consequently, as the Church is one, because Jesus Christ is one, so throughout the whole Christian world there is, and ought to be, but one doctrine: "One Lord, one faith;"[22] "but having the same spirit of faith,"[23] they possess

---

[21] 1 Cor. 1:10.
[22] Eph. 4:5.
[23] 2 Cor. 4:13.

the saving principle whence proceed spontaneously one and the same will in all, and one and the same tenor of action.

22. Now, as the Apostle Paul urges, this unanimity ought to be perfect. Christian faith reposes not on human but on divine authority, for what God has revealed "we believe not on account of the intrinsic evidence of the truth perceived by the natural light of our reason, but on account of the authority of God revealing, who cannot be deceived nor Himself deceive."[24] It follows as a consequence that whatever things are manifestly revealed by God we must receive with a similar and equal assent. To refuse to believe any one of them is equivalent to rejecting them all, for those at once destroy the very groundwork of faith who deny that God has spoken to men, or who bring into doubt His infinite truth and wisdom. To determine, however, which are the doctrines divinely revealed belongs to the teaching Church, to whom God has entrusted the safekeeping and interpretation of His utterances. But the supreme teacher in the Church is the Roman Pontiff. Union of minds, therefore, requires, together with a perfect accord in the one faith, complete submission and obedience of will to the Church and to the Roman Pontiff, as to God Himself. This obedience should, however, be perfect, because it is enjoined by faith itself, and has this in common with faith, that it cannot be given in shreds; nay, were it not absolute and perfect in every particular, it might wear the name of obedience, but its essence would disappear. Christian usage attaches such value to this perfection of obedience that it has been, and will ever be, accounted the distinguishing mark by which we are able to recognize Catholics. Admirably does the following passage from St. Thomas Aquinas set before us the right view: "The formal object of faith is primary truth, as it is shown forth in the holy Scriptures, and in the teaching of the Church, which proceeds from the fountainhead of truth. It follows, therefore, that he who does not adhere, as to an infallible divine rule, to the teaching of the Church, which

---

[24] Constitution Dei Filius, cap. 3.

proceeds from the primary truth manifested in the holy Scriptures, possesses not the habit of faith; but matters of faith he holds otherwise than true faith. Now, it is evident that he who clings to the doctrines of the Church as to an infallible rule yields his assent to everything the Church teaches; but otherwise, if with reference to what the Church teaches he holds what he likes but does not hold what he does not like, he adheres not to the teaching of the Church as to an infallible rule, but to his own will."[25]

23. "The faith of the whole Church should be one, according to the precept (1 Cor. 1:10): "Let all speak the same thing, and let there be no schisms among you"; and this cannot be observed save on condition that questions which arise touching faith should be determined by him who presides over the whole Church, whose sentence must consequently be accepted without wavering. And hence to the sole authority of the supreme Pontiff does it pertain to publish a new revision of the symbol, as also to decree all other matters that concern the universal Church."[26]

24. In defining the limits of the obedience owed to the pastors of souls, but most of all to the authority of the Roman Pontiff, it must not be supposed that it is only to be yielded in relation to dogmas of which the obstinate denial cannot be disjoined from the crime of heresy. Nay, further, it is not enough sincerely and firmly to assent to doctrines which, though not defined by any solemn pronouncement of the Church, are by her proposed to belief, as divinely revealed, in her common and universal teaching, and which the Vatican Council declared are to be believed "with Catholic and divine faith."[27] But this likewise must be reckoned amongst the duties of Christians, that they allow themselves to be ruled and directed by the authority and leadership of bishops, and, above all, of the apostolic see. And

---

[25] Summa theologiae, IIa-IIae, q. v, art. 3.

[26] Ibid., q. i, arc. 10.

[27] Vatican Council, Constit. de fide catholica, cap. 3, De fide. Cf. H. Denziger, Enchiridion Symbolorium 11 ed., Freiburg i. Br., 1911), p. 476.

how fitting it is that this should be so any one can easily perceive. For the things contained in the divine oracles have reference to God in part, and in part to man, and to whatever is necessary for the attainment of his eternal salvation. Now, both these, that is to say, what we are bound to believe and what we are obliged to do, are laid down, as we have stated, by the Church using her divine right, and in the Church by the supreme Pontiff. Wherefore it belongs to the Pope to judge authoritatively what things the sacred oracles contain, as well as what doctrines are in harmony, and what in disagreement, with them; and also, for the same reason, to show forth what things are to be accepted as right, and what to be rejected as worthless; what it is necessary to do and what to avoid doing, in order to attain eternal salvation. For, otherwise, there would be no sure interpreter of the commands of God, nor would there be any safe guide showing man the way he should live.

25. In addition to what has been laid down, it is necessary to enter more fully into the nature of the Church. She is not an association of Christians brought together by chance, but is a divinely established and admirably constituted society, having for its direct and proximate purpose to lead the world to peace and holiness. And since the Church alone has, through the grace of God, received the means necessary to realize such end, she has her fixed laws, special spheres of action, and a certain method, fixed and conformable to her nature, of governing Christian peoples. But the exercise of such governing power is difficult, and leaves room for numberless conflicts, inasmuch as the Church rules peoples scattered through every portion of the earth, differing in race and customs, who, living under the sway of the laws of their respective countries, owe obedience alike to the civil and religious authorities. The duties enjoined are incumbent on the same persons, as already stated, and between them there exists neither contradiction nor confusion; for some of these duties have relation to the prosperity of the State, others refer to the general good of the Church, and both have as their object to train men to perfection.

26. The tracing out of these rights and duties being thus set forth, it is plainly evident that the governing powers are wholly free to carry out the business of the State; and this not only not against the wish of the Church, but manifestly with her co-operation, inasmuch as she strongly urges to the practice of piety, which implies right feeling towards God, and by that very fact inspires a right-mindedness toward the rulers in the State. The spiritual power, however, has a far loftier purpose, the Church directing her aim to govern the minds of men in the defending of the "kingdom of God, and His justice,"[28] a task she is wholly bent upon accomplishing.

27. No one can, however, without risk to faith, foster any doubt as to the Church alone having been invested with such power of governing souls as to exclude altogether the civil authority. In truth, it was not to Caesar but to Peter that Jesus Christ entrusted the keys of the kingdom of Heaven. From this doctrine touching the relations of politics and religion originate important consequences which we cannot pass over in silence.

28. A notable difference exists between every kind of civil rule and that of the kingdom of Christ. If this latter bear a certain likeness and character to a civil kingdom, it is distinguished from it by its origin, principle, and essence. The Church, therefore, possesses the right to exist and to protect herself by institutions and laws in accordance with her nature. And since she not only is a perfect society in herself, but superior to every other society of human growth, she resolutely refuses, promoted alike by right and by duty, to link herself to any mere party and to subject herself to the fleeting exigencies of politics. On like grounds, the Church, the guardian always of her own right and most observant of that of others, holds that it is not her province to decide which is the best amongst many diverse forms of government and the civil institutions of Christian States, and amid the various kinds of State rule she does not disapprove of

---

[28] Matt. 6:33.

any, provided the respect due to religion and the observance of good morals be upheld. By such standard of conduct should the thoughts and mode of acting of every Catholic be directed.

29. There is no doubt that in the sphere of politics ample matter may exist for legitimate difference of opinion, and that, the single reserve being made of the rights of justice and truth, all may strive to bring into actual working the ideas believed likely to be more conducive than others to the general welfare. But to attempt to involve the Church in party strife, and seek to bring her support to bear against those who take opposite views is only worthy of partisans. Religion should, on the contrary, be accounted by every one as holy and inviolate; nay, in the public order itself of States-which cannot be severed from the laws influencing morals and from religious duties-it is always urgent, and indeed the main preoccupation, to take thought how best to consult the interests of Catholicism. Wherever these appear by reason of the efforts of adversaries to be in danger, all differences of opinion among Catholics should forthwith cease, so that, like thoughts and counsels prevailing, they may hasten to the aid of religion, the general and supreme good, to which all else should be referred. We think it well to treat this matter somewhat more in detail.

30. The Church alike and the State, doubtless, both possess individual sovereignty; hence, in the carrying out of public affairs, neither obeys the other within the limits to which each is restricted by its constitution. It does not hence follow, however, that Church and State are in any manner severed, and still less antagonistic. Nature, in fact, has given us not only physical existence, but moral life likewise. Hence, from the tranquillity of public order, which is the immediate purpose of civil society, man expects to derive his well-being, and still more the sheltering care necessary to his moral life, which consists exclusively in the knowledge and practice of virtue. He wishes, moreover, at the same time, as in duty bound, to find in the Church the aids necessary to his religious perfection, in the knowledge and

practice of the true religion; of that religion which is the queen of virtues, because in binding these to God it completes them all and perfects them. Therefore, they who are engaged in framing constitutions and in enacting laws should bear in mind the moral and religious nature of man, and take care to help him, but in a right and orderly way, to gain perfection, neither enjoining nor forbidding anything save what is reasonably consistent with civil as well as with religious requirements. On this very account, the Church cannot stand by, indifferent as to the import and significance of laws enacted by the State; not insofar, indeed, as they refer to the State, but in so far as, passing beyond their due limits, they trench upon the rights of the Church.

31. From God has the duty been assigned to the Church not only to interpose resistance, if at any time the State rule should run counter to religion, but, further, to make a strong endeavor that the power of the Gospel may pervade the law and institutions of the nations. And inasmuch as the destiny of the State depends mainly on the disposition of those who are at the head of affairs, it follows that the Church cannot give countenance or favor to those whom she knows to be imbued with a spirit of hostility to her; who refuse openly to respect her rights; who make it their aim and purpose to tear asunder the alliance that should, by the very nature of things, connect the interests of religion with those of the State. On the contrary, she is (as she is bound to be) the upholder of those who are themselves imbued with the right way of thinking as to the relations between Church and State, and who strive to make them work in perfect accord for the common good. These precepts contain the abiding principle by which every Catholic should shape his conduct in regard to public life. In short, where the Church does not forbid taking part in public affairs, it is fit and proper to give support to men of acknowledged worth, and who pledge themselves to deserve well in the Catholic cause, and on no account may it be allowed to prefer to them any such individuals as are hostile to religion.

32. Whence it appears how urgent is the duty to maintain perfect union of minds, especially at these our times, when the Christian name is assailed with designs so concerted and subtle. All who have it at heart to attach themselves earnestly to the Church, which is "the pillar and ground of the truth,"[29] will easily steer clear of masters who are "lying and promising them liberty, when they themselves are slaves of corruption."[30] Nay, more, having made themselves sharers in the divine virtue which resides in the Church, they will triumph over the craft of their adversaries by wisdom, and over their violence by courage. This is not now the time and place to inquire whether and how far the inertness and internal dissensions of Catholics have contributed to the present condition of things; but it is certain at least that the perverse-minded would exhibit less boldness, and would not have brought about such an accumulation of ills, if the faith "which worketh by charity"[31] had been generally more energetic and lively in the souls of men, and had there not been so universal a drifting away from the divinely established rule of morality throughout Christianity. May at least the lessons afforded by the memory of the past have the good result of leading to a wiser mode of acting in the future.

33. As to those who mean to take part in public affairs, they should avoid with the very utmost care two criminal excesses: so-called prudence and false courage. Some there are, indeed, who maintain that it is not opportune boldly to attack evil - doing in its might and when in the ascendant, lest, as they say, opposition should exasperate minds already hostile. These make it a matter of guesswork as to whether they are for the Church or against her, since on the one hand they give themselves out as professing the Catholic faith, and yet wish that the Church should allow certain opinions, at variance with her teaching, to be spread abroad with impunity. They moan over the loss of faith and the perversion of morals, yet trouble themselves not to bring any

---

[29] 1 Tim. 3:15.
[30] 2 Peter 2:1, 19.
[31] Gal. 5:6.

remedy; nay, not seldom, even add to the intensity of the
mischief through too much forbearance or harmful dissembling.
These same individuals would not have any one entertain a doubt
as to their good will towards the holy see; yet they have always a
something by way of reproach against the supreme Pontiff.

34. The prudence of men of this cast is of ;hat kind which is
termed by the Apostle Paul 'wisdom of the flesh" and "death" of
the soul, "because it is not subject to the law of God, neither can
it be."[32] Nothing is less calculated to emend such ills than
prudence of this kind. For he enemies of the Church have for
their object-and they hesitate not to proclaim it, and many
among them boast of it - to destroy outright, if possible, the
Catholic religion, which alone the true religion. With such a
purpose in and they shrink from nothing, for they are fully
conscious that the more faint - hearted those who withstand
them become, the more easy will it be to work out their wicked
will. Therefore, they who cherish the "prudence of the flesh" and
who pretend to be unaware that every Christian ought to be a
valiant soldier of Christ; they who would faro obtain the rewards
owing to conquerors, while they are leading the lives of cowards,
untouched in the fight, are so far from thwarting the onward
march of the evil - disposed that, on the contrary, they even help
it forward.

35. On the other hand, not a few, impelled by a false zeal, or -
what is more blameworthy still - affecting sentiments which their
conduct belies, take upon themselves to act a part which does
not belong to them. They would faire see the Church's mode of
action influenced by their ideas and their judgment to such an
extent that everything done otherwise they take ill or accept with
repugnance. Some, yet again, expend their energies in fruitless
contention, being worthy of blame equally with the former. To
act in such manner is nor to follow lawful authority but to
forestall it, and, unauthorized, assume the duties of the spiritual

---

[32] Cf. Rom. 8:6-7.

rulers, to the great detriment of the order which God established in His Church to be observed forever, and which He does not permit to be violated with impunity by any one, whoever he may be.

36. Honor, then, to those who shrink not from entering the arena as often as need calls, believing and being convinced that the violence of injustice will be brought to an end and finally give way to the sanctity of right and religion! They truly seem invested with the dignity of time honored virtue, since they are struggling to defend religion, and chiefly against the faction banded together to attack Christianity with extreme daring and without tiring, and to pursue with incessant hostility the sovereign Pontiff, fallen into their power. But men of this high character maintain without wavering the love of obedience, nor are they wont to undertake anything upon their own authority. Now, since a like resolve to obey, combined with constancy and sturdy courage, is needful, so that whatever trials the pressure of events may bring about, they may be "deficient in nothing,"[33] We greatly desire to fix deep in the minds of each one that which Paul calls the "wisdom of the spirit,[34] for in controlling human actions this wisdom follows the excellent rule of moderation, with the happy result that no one either timidly despairs through lack of courage or presumes overmuch from want to prudence. There is, however, a difference between the political prudence that relates to the general good and that which concerns the good of individuals. This latter is shown forth in the case of private persons who obey the prompting of right reason in the direction of their own conduct; while the former is the characteristic of those who are set over others, and chiefly of rulers of the State, whose duty it is to exercise the power of command, so that the political prudence of private individuals would seem to consist wholly in carrying out faithfully the orders issued by lawful authority.[35]

---

[33] James 1:4.
[34] Rom. 8:6.
[35] "Prudence proceeds from reason, and to reason it specially pertains

37. The like disposition and the same order should prevail in the Christian society by so much the more that the political prudence of the Pontiff embraces diverse and multiform things, for it is his charge not only to rule the Church, but generally so to regulate the actions of Christian citizens that these may be in apt conformity to their hope of gaining eternal salvation. Whence it is clear that, in addition to the complete accordance of thought and deed, the faithful should follow the practical political wisdom of the ecclesiastical authority. Now, the administration of Christian affairs immediately under the Roman Pontiff appertains to the bishops, who, although they attain not to the summit of pontifical power, are nevertheless truly princes in the ecclesiastical hierarchy; and as each one of them administers a particular church, they are "as master-workers... in the spiritual edifice,"[36] and they have members of the clergy to share their duties and carry out their decisions. Every one has to regulate his mode of conduct according to this constitution of the Church, which it is not in the power of any man to change. Consequently, just as in the exercise of their episcopal authority the bishops ought to be united with the apostolic see so should the members of the clergy and the laity live in close union with their bishops. Among the prelates, indeed, one or other there may be affording scope to criticism either in regard to personal conduct or in reference to opinions by him entertained about points of

---

to guide and govern. Whence it follows that, in so much as any one takes part in the control and government of affairs, in so far ought he to be gifted with reason and prudence. But it is evident that the subject, so far as subject, and the servant ought neither to control nor govern, but rather to be controlled and governed. Prudence, then, is not the special virtue of the servant, so far as servant, nor of the subject, so far as subject. But because any man, on account of his character of a reasonable being, may have some share in the government on account of the rational choice which he exercises, it is fitting that in such proportion he should possess the virtue of prudence. Whence it manifestly results that prudence exists in the ruler as the art of building exists in the architect, whereas prudence exists in the subject as the art of building exists in the hand of the workman employed in the construction." Summa theologiae, IIa-IIae, q. xlvii, art. 12, Answer. St. Thomas Aquinas refers to Aristotle, Ethic. Nic., Bk. VI, 8, 1141b 21-29.

[36] Thomas Aquinas Quaest Quodl., 1, G. 7, art. 2, Answer.

Sapientiae Christianae

doctrine; but no private person may arrogate to himself the office of judge which Christ our Lord has bestowed on that one alone whom He placed in charge of His lambs and of His sheep. Let every one bear in mind that most wise teaching of Gregory the Great: "Subjects should be admonished not rashly to judge their prelates, even if they chance to see them acting in a blameworthy manner, lest, justly reproving what is wrong, they be led by pride into greater wrong. They are to be warned against the danger of setting themselves up in audacious opposition to the superiors whose shortcomings they may notice. Should, therefore, the superiors really have committed grievous sins, their inferiors, penetrated with the fear of God, ought not to refuse them respectful submission. The actions of superiors should not be smitten by the sword of the word, even when they are rightly judged to have deserved censure."[37]

38. However, all endeavors will avail but little unless our life be regulated conformably with the discipline of the Christian virtues. Let us call to mind what holy Scripture records concerning the Jewish nation: "As long as they sinned not in the sight of their God, it was well with them: for their God hateth iniquity. And even . . . when they had revolted from the way that God had given them to walk therein, they were destroyed in battles by many nations."[38] Now, the nation of the Jews bore an inchoate semblance to the Christian people, and the vicissitudes of their history in olden times have often foreshadowed the truth that was to come, saving that God in His goodness has enriched and loaded us with far greater benefits, and on this account the sins of Christians are much greater, and bear the stamp of more shameful and criminal ingratitude.

39. The Church, it is certain, at no time and in no particular is deserted by God; hence, there is no reason why she should be alarmed at the wickedness of men; but in the case of nations

---

[37] Regina pastorales, Part 3, cap. 4 (PL 77, 55).
[38] Judith 5:21-22.

199

falling away from Christian virtue there is not a like ground of assurance, "for sin maketh nations miserable."[39] If every bygone age has experienced the force of this truth, wherefore should not our own? There are, in truth, very many signs which proclaim that just punishments are already menacing, and the condition of modern States tends to confirm this belief, since we perceive many of them in sad plight from intestine disorders, and not one entirely exempt. But, should those leagued together in wickedness hurry onward in the road they have boldly chosen, should they increase in influence and power in proportion as they make headway in their evil purposes and crafty schemes, there will be ground to fear lest the very foundations nature has laid for States to rest upon be utterly destroyed. Nor can such misgivings be removed by any mere human effort, especially as a vast number of men, having rejected the Christian faith, are on that account justly incurring the penalty of their pride, since blinded by their passions they search in vain for truth, laying hold on the false for the true, and thinking themselves wise when they call "evil good, and good evil," and "put darkness in the place of light, and light in the place of darkness."[40] It is therefore necessary that God come to the rescue, and that, mindful of His mercy, He turn an eye of compassion on human society.

40. Hence, We renew the urgent entreaty We have already made, to redouble zeal and perseverance, when addressing humble supplications to our merciful God, so that the virtues whereby a Christian life is perfected may be reawakened. It is, however, urgent before all, that charity, which is the main foundation of the Christian life, and apart from which the other virtues exist not or remain barren, should be quickened and maintained. Therefore is it that the Apostle Paul, after having exhorted the Colossians to flee all vice and cultivate all virtue, adds: "Above all things, have charity, which is the bond of perfection."[41] Yea, truly, charity is the bond of perfection, for it binds intimately to

[39] Prov. 14:34.
[40] Isa. 5:20.
[41] Col. 3:14.

God those whom it has embraced and with loving tenderness, causes them to draw their life from God, to act with God, to refer all to God. Howbeit, the love of God should not be severed from the love of our neighbour, since men have a share in the infinite goodness of God and bear in themselves the impress of His image and likeness. "This commandment we have from God, that he who loveth God, love also his brother."[42] "If any man say I love God, and he hateth his brother, he is a liar."[43] And this commandment concerning charity its divine proclaimer styled new, not in the sense that a previous law, or even nature itself, had not enjoined that men should love one another, but because the Christian precept of loving each other in that manner was truly new, and quite unheard of in the memory of man. For, that love with which Jesus Christ is beloved by His Father and with which He Himself loves men, He obtained for His disciples and followers that they might be of one heart and of one mind in Him by charity, as He Himself and His Father are one by their nature.

41. No one is unaware how deeply and from the very beginning the import of that precept has been implanted in the breast of Christians, and what abundant fruits of concord, mutual benevolence, piety, patience, and fortitude it has produced. Why, then, should we not devote ourselves to imitate the examples set by our fathers? The very times in which we live should afford sufficient motives for the practice of charity. Since impious men are bent on giving fresh impulse to their hatred against Jesus Christ, Christians should be quickened anew in piety; and charity, which is the inspirer of lofty deeds, should be imbued with new life. Let dissensions therefore, if there be any, wholly cease; let those strifes which waste the strength of those engaged in the fight, without any advantage resulting to religion, be scattered to the winds; let all minds be united in faith and all hearts in charity,

---

[42] 1 John 4:21.
[43] 1 John 4:20.

so that, as it behooves, life may be spent in the practice of the love of God and the love of men.

42. This is a suitable moment for us to exhort especially heads of families to govern their households according to these precepts, and to be solicitous without failing for the right training of their children. The family may be regarded as the cradle of civil society, and it is in great measure within the circle of family life that the destiny of the States is fostered. Whence it is that they who would break away from Christian discipline are working to corrupt family life, and to destroy it utterly, root and branch. From such an unholy purpose they allow not themselves to be turned aside by the reflection that it cannot, even in any degree, be carried out without inflicting cruel outrage on the parents. These hold from nature their right of training the children to whom they have given birth, with the obligation super-added of shaping and directing the education of their little ones to the end for which God vouch - safed the privilege of transmitting the gift of life. It is, then, incumbent on parents to strain every nerve to ward off such an outrage, and to strive manfully to have and to hold exclusive authority to direct the education of their offspring, as is fitting, in a Christian manner, and first and foremost to keep them away from schools where there is risk of their drinking in the poison of impiety. Where the right education of youth is concerned, no amount of trouble or labor can be undertaken, how great soever, but that even greater still may not be called for. In this regard, indeed, there are to be found in many countries Catholics worthy of general admiration, who incur considerable outlay and bestow much zeal in founding schools for the education of youth. It is highly desirable that such noble example may be generously followed, where time and circumstances demand, yet all should be intimately persuaded that the minds of children are most influenced by the training they receive at home. If in their early years they find within the walls of their homes the rule of an upright life and the discipline of Christian virtues, the future welfare of society will in great measure be guaranteed.

43. And now We seem to have touched upon those matters which Catholics ought chiefly nowadays to follow, or mainly to avoid. It rests with you, venerable brothers, to take measures that Our voice may reach everywhere, and that one and all may understand how urgent it is to reduce to practice the teachings set forth in this Our letter. The observance of these duties cannot be troublesome or onerous, for the yoke of Jesus Christ is sweet, and His burden is light. If anything, however, appear too difficult of accomplishment, you will afford aid by the authority of your example, so that each one of the faithful may make more strenuous endeavor, and display a soul unconquered by difficulties. Bring it home to their minds, as We have Ourselves oftentimes conveyed the warning, that matters of the highest moment and worthy of all honor are at stake, for the safeguarding of which every most toilsome effort should be readily endured; and that a sublime reward is in store for the labors of a Christian life. On the other hand, to refrain from doing battle for Jesus Christ amounts to fighting against Him; He Himself assures us "He will deny before His Father in heaven those who shall have refused to confess Him on earth."[44] As for Ourselves and you all, never assuredly, so long as life lasts, shall We allow Our authority, Our counsels, and Our solicitude to be in any wise lacking in the conflict. Nor is it to be doubted but that especial aid of the great God will be vouchsafed, so long as the struggle endures, to the flock alike and to the pastors. Sustained by this confidence, as a pledge of heavenly gifts, and of Our loving kindness in the Lord to you, venerable brothers, to your clergy and to all your people, We accord the apostolic benediction.

Given at St. Peter's in Rome, the tenth day of January, 1890, the twelfth year of Our pontificate.

---

[44] Luke 9:26.

X: Rerum Novarum

May 15, 1891

ON THE RIGHTS AND DUTIES OF CAPITAL AND LABOR

That the spirit of revolutionary change, which has long been disturbing the nations of the world, should have passed beyond the sphere of politics and made its influence felt in the cognate sphere of practical economics is not surprising. The elements of the conflict now raging are unmistakable, in the vast expansion of industrial pursuits and the marvellous discoveries of science; in the changed relations between masters and workmen; in the enormous fortunes of some few individuals, and the utter poverty of the masses; the increased self reliance and closer mutual combination of the working classes; as also, finally, in the prevailing moral degeneracy. The momentous gravity of the state of things now obtaining fills every mind with painful apprehension; wise men are discussing it; practical men are proposing schemes; popular meetings, legislatures, and rulers of nations are all busied with it - actually there is no question which has taken deeper hold on the public mind.

2. Therefore, venerable brethren, as on former occasions when it seemed opportune to refute false teaching, We have addressed you in the interests of the Church and of the common weal, and have issued letters bearing on political power, human liberty, the Christian constitution of the State, and like matters, so have We thought it expedient now to speak on the condition of the working classes.[1] It is a subject on which We have already

---

[1] The title sometimes given to this encyclical, On the Condiction of the Working Classes, is therefore perfectly justified. A few lines after this sentence, the Pope gives a more comprehensive definition of the subject of Rerum novarum. We are using it as a title.

touched more than once, incidentally. But in the present letter, the responsibility of the apostolic office urges Us to treat the question of set purpose and in detail, in order that no misapprehension may exist as to the principles which truth and justice dictate for its settlement. The discussion is not easy, nor is it void of danger. It is no easy matter to define the relative rights and mutual duties of the rich and of the poor, of capital and of labor. And the danger lies in this, that crafty agitators are intent on making use of these differences of opinion to pervert men's judgments and to stir up the people to revolt.

3. In any case we clearly see, and on this there is general agreement, that some opportune remedy must be found quickly for the misery and wretchedness pressing so unjustly on the majority of the working class: for the ancient workingmen's guilds were abolished in the last century, and no other protective organization took their place. Public institutions and the laws set aside the ancient religion. Hence, by degrees it has come to pass that working men have been surrendered, isolated and helpless, to the hardheartedness of employers and the greed of unchecked competition. The mischief has been increased by rapacious usury, which, although more than once condemned by the Church, is nevertheless, under a different guise, but with like injustice, still practiced by covetous and grasping men. To this must be added that the hiring of labor and the conduct of trade are concentrated in the hands of comparatively few; so that a small number of very rich men have been able to lay upon the teeming masses of the laboring poor a yoke little better than that of slavery itself.

4. To remedy these wrongs the socialists, working on the poor man's envy of the rich, are striving to do away with private property, and contend that individual possessions should become the common property of all, to be administered by the State or by municipal bodies. They hold that by thus transferring property from private individuals to the community, the present mischievous state of things will be set to rights, inasmuch as each

citizen will then get his fair share of whatever there is to enjoy. But their contentions are so clearly powerless to end the controversy that were they carried into effect the working man himself would be among the first to suffer. They are, moreover, emphatically unjust, for they would rob the lawful possessor, distort the functions of the State, and create utter confusion in the community.

5. It is surely undeniable that, when a man engages in remunerative labor, the impelling reason and motive of his work is to obtain property, and thereafter to hold it as his very own. If one man hires out to another his strength or skill, he does so for the purpose of receiving in return what is necessary for the satisfaction of his needs; he therefore expressly intends to acquire a right full and real, not only to the remuneration, but also to the disposal of such remuneration, just as he pleases. Thus, if he lives sparingly, saves money, and, for greater security, invests his savings in land, the land, in such case, is only his wages under another form; and, consequently, a working man's little estate thus purchased should be as completely at his full disposal as are the wages he receives for his labor. But it is precisely in such power of disposal that ownership obtains, whether the property consist of land or chattels. Socialists, therefore, by endeavoring to transfer the possessions of individuals to the community at large, strike at the interests of every wage-earner, since they would deprive him of the liberty of disposing of his wages, and thereby of all hope and possibility of increasing his resources and of bettering his condition in life.

6. What is of far greater moment, however, is the fact that the remedy they propose is manifestly against justice. For, every man has by nature the right to possess property as his own. This is one of the chief points of distinction between man and the animal creation, for the brute has no power of self direction, but is governed by two main instincts, which keep his powers on the alert, impel him to develop them in a fitting manner, and stimulate and determine him to action without any power of

choice. One of these instincts is self preservation, the other the propagation of the species. Both can attain their purpose by means of things which lie within range; beyond their verge the brute creation cannot go, for they are moved to action by their senses only, and in the special direction which these suggest. But with man it is wholly different. He possesses, on the one hand, the full perfection of the animal being, and hence enjoys at least as much as the rest of the animal kind, the fruition of things material. But animal nature, however perfect, is far from representing the human being in its completeness, and is in truth but humanity's humble handmaid, made to serve and to obey. It is the mind, or reason, which is the predominant element in us who are human creatures; it is this which renders a human being human, and distinguishes him essentially from the brute. And on this very account - that man alone among the animal creation is endowed with reason - it must be within his right to possess things not merely for temporary and momentary use, as other living things do, but to have and to hold them in stable and permanent possession; he must have not only things that perish in the use, but those also which, though they have been reduced into use, continue for further use in after time.

7. This becomes still more clearly evident if man's nature be considered a little more deeply. For man, fathoming by his faculty of reason matters without number, linking the future with the present, and being master of his own acts, guides his ways under the eternal law and the power of God, whose providence governs all things. Wherefore, it is in his power to exercise his choice not only as to matters that regard his present welfare, but also about those which he deems may be for his advantage in time yet to come. Hence, man not only should possess the fruits of the earth, but also the very soil, inasmuch as from the produce of the earth he has to lay by provision for the future. Man's needs do not die out, but forever recur; although satisfied today, they demand fresh supplies for tomorrow. Nature accordingly must have given to man a source that is stable and remaining always with him, from which he might look to draw continual

supplies. And this stable condition of things he finds solely in the earth and its fruits. There is no need to bring in the State. Man precedes the State, and possesses, prior to the formation of any State, the right of providing for the substance of his body.

8. The fact that God has given the earth for the use and enjoyment of the whole human race can in no way be a bar to the owning of private property. For God has granted the earth to mankind in general, not in the sense that all without distinction can deal with it as they like, but rather that no part of it was assigned to any one in particular, and that the limits of private possession have been left to be fixed by man's own industry, and by the laws of individual races. Moreover, the earth, even though apportioned among private owners, ceases not thereby to minister to the needs of all, inasmuch as there is not one who does not sustain life from what the land produces. Those who do not possess the soil contribute their labor; hence, it may truly be said that all human subsistence is derived either from labor on one's own land, or from some toil, some calling, which is paid for either in the produce of the land itself, or in that which is exchanged for what the land brings forth.

9. Here, again, we have further proof that private ownership is in accordance with the law of nature. Truly, that which is required for the preservation of life, and for life's well-being, is produced in great abundance from the soil, but not until man has brought it into cultivation and expended upon it his solicitude and skill. Now, when man thus turns the activity of his mind and the strength of his body toward procuring the fruits of nature, by such act he makes his own that portion of nature's field which he cultivates - that portion on which he leaves, as it were, the impress of his personality; and it cannot but be just that he should possess that portion as his very own, and have a right to hold it without any one being justified in violating that right.

10. So strong and convincing are these arguments that it seems amazing that some should now be setting up anew certain

obsolete opinions in opposition to what is here laid down. They assert that it is right for private persons to have the use of the soil and its various fruits, but that it is unjust for any one to possess outright either the land on which he has built or the estate which he has brought under cultivation. But those who deny these rights do not perceive that they are defrauding man of what his own labor has produced. For the soil which is tilled and cultivated with toil and skill utterly changes its condition; it was wild before, now it is fruitful; was barren, but now brings forth in abundance. That which has thus altered and improved the land becomes so truly part of itself as to be in great measure indistinguishable and inseparable from it. Is it just that the fruit of a man's own sweat and labor should be possessed and enjoyed by any one else? As effects follow their cause, so is it just and right that the results of labor should belong to those who have bestowed their labor.

11. With reason, then, the common opinion of mankind, little affected by the few dissentients who have contended for the opposite view, has found in the careful study of nature, and in the laws of nature, the foundations of the division of property, and the practice of all ages has consecrated the principle of private ownership, as being pre-eminently in conformity with human nature, and as conducing in the most unmistakable manner to the peace and tranquillity of human existence. The same principle is confirmed and enforced by the civil laws-laws which, so long as they are just, derive from the law of nature their binding force. The authority of the divine law adds its sanction, forbidding us in severest terms even to covet that which is another's: "Thou shalt not covet thy neighbour's wife; nor his house, nor his field, nor his man-servant, nor his maid-servant, nor his ox, nor his ass, nor anything that is his."[2]

12. The rights here spoken of, belonging to each individual man, are seen in much stronger light when considered in relation to

---

[2] Deut. 5:21.

man's social and domestic obligations. In choosing a state of life, it is indisputable that all are at full liberty to follow the counsel of Jesus Christ as to observing virginity, or to bind themselves by the marriage tie. No human law can abolish the natural and original right of marriage, nor in any way limit the chief and principal purpose of marriage ordained by God's authority from the beginning: "Increase and multiply."[3] Hence we have the family, the "society" of a man's house - a society very small, one must admit, but none the less a true society, and one older than any State. Consequently, it has rights and duties peculiar to itself which are quite independent of the State.

13. That right to property, therefore, which has been proved to belong naturally to individual persons, must in like wise belong to a man in his capacity of head of a family; nay, that right is all the stronger in proportion as the human person receives a wider extension in the family group. It is a most sacred law of nature that a father should provide food and all necessaries for those whom he has begotten; and, similarly, it is natural that he should wish that his children, who carry on, so to speak, and continue his personality, should be by him provided with all that is needful to enable them to keep themselves decently from want and misery amid the uncertainties of this mortal life. Now, in no other way can a father effect this except by the ownership of productive property, which he can transmit to his children by inheritance. A family, no less than a State, is, as We have said, a true society, governed by an authority peculiar to itself, that is to say, by the authority of the father. Provided, therefore, the limits which are prescribed by the very purposes for which it exists be not transgressed, the family has at least equal rights with the State in the choice and pursuit of the things needful to its preservation and its just liberty. We say, "at least equal rights"; for, inasmuch as the domestic household is antecedent, as well in idea as in fact, to the gathering of men into a community, the family must necessarily have rights and duties which are prior to those of the

---

[3] Gen. 1:28.

community, and founded more immediately in nature. If the citizens, if the families on entering into association and fellowship, were to experience hindrance in a commonwealth instead of help, and were to find their rights attacked instead of being upheld, society would rightly be an object of detestation rather than of desire.

14. The contention, then, that the civil government should at its option intrude into and exercise intimate control over the family and the household is a great and pernicious error. True, if a family finds itself in exceeding distress, utterly deprived of the counsel of friends, and without any prospect of extricating itself, it is right that extreme necessity be met by public aid, since each family is a part of the commonwealth. In like manner, if within the precincts of the household there occur grave disturbance of mutual rights, public authority should intervene to force each party to yield to the other its proper due; for this is not to deprive citizens of their rights, but justly and properly to safeguard and strengthen them. But the rulers of the commonwealth must go no further; here, nature bids them stop. Paternal authority can be neither abolished nor absorbed by the State; for it has the same source as human life itself. "The child belongs to the father," and is, as it were, the continuation of the father's personality; and speaking strictly, the child takes its place in civil society, not of its own right, but in its quality as member of the family in which it is born. And for the very reason that "the child belongs to the father" it is, as St. Thomas Aquinas says, "before it attains the use of free will, under the power and the charge of its parents."[4] The socialists, therefore, in setting aside the parent and setting up a State supervision, act against natural justice, and destroy the structure of the home.

15. And in addition to injustice, it is only too evident what an upset and disturbance there would be in all classes, and to how intolerable and hateful a slavery citizens would be subjected. The

---

[4] Summa theologiae, IIa-IIae, q. x, art. 12, Answer.

door would be thrown open to envy, to mutual invective, and to discord; the sources of wealth themselves would run dry, for no one would have any interest in exerting his talents or his industry; and that ideal equality about which they entertain pleasant dreams would be in reality the levelling down of all to a like condition of misery and degradation. Hence, it is clear that the main tenet of socialism, community of goods, must be utterly rejected, since it only injures those whom it would seem meant to benefit, is directly contrary to the natural rights of mankind, and would introduce confusion and disorder into the commonweal. The first and most fundamental principle, therefore, if one would undertake to alleviate the condition of the masses, must be the inviolability of private property. This being established, we proceed to show where the remedy sought for must be found.

16. We approach the subject with confidence, and in the exercise of the rights which manifestly appertain to Us, for no practical solution of this question will be found apart from the intervention of religion and of the Church. It is We who are the chief guardian of religion and the chief dispenser of what pertains to the Church; and by keeping silence we would seem to neglect the duty incumbent on us. Doubtless, this most serious question demands the attention and the efforts of others besides ourselves - to wit, of the rulers of States, of employers of labor, of the wealthy, aye, of the working classes themselves, for whom We are pleading. But We affirm without hesitation that all the striving of men will be vain if they leave out the Church. It is the Church that insists, on the authority of the Gospel, upon those teachings whereby the conflict can be brought to an end, or rendered, at least, far less bitter; the Church uses her efforts not only to enlighten the mind, but to direct by her precepts the life and conduct of each and all; the Church improves and betters the condition of the working man by means of numerous organizations; does her best to enlist the services of all classes in discussing and endeavoring to further in the most practical way, the interests of the working classes; and considers that for this

purpose recourse should be had, in due measure and degree, to the intervention of the law and of State authority.

17. It must be first of all recognized that the condition of things inherent in human affairs must be borne with, for it is impossible to reduce civil society to one dead level. Socialists may in that intent do their utmost, but all striving against nature is in vain. There naturally exist among mankind manifold differences of the most important kind; people differ in capacity, skill, health, strength; and unequal fortune is a necessary result of unequal condition. Such inequality is far from being disadvantageous either to individuals or to the community. Social and public life can only be maintained by means of various kinds of capacity for business and the playing of many parts; and each man, as a rule, chooses the part which suits his own peculiar domestic condition. As regards bodily labor, even had man never fallen from the state of innocence, he would not have remained wholly idle; but that which would then have been his free choice and his delight became afterwards compulsory, and the painful expiation for his disobedience. "Cursed be the earth in thy work; in thy labor thou shalt eat of it all the days of thy life."[5]

18. In like manner, the other pains and hardships of life will have no end or cessation on earth; for the consequences of sin are bitter and hard to bear, and they must accompany man so long as life lasts. To suffer and to endure, therefore, is the lot of humanity; let them strive as they may, no strength and no artifice will ever succeed in banishing from human life the ills and troubles which beset it. If any there are who pretend differently - who hold out to a hard-pressed people the boon of freedom from pain and trouble, an undisturbed repose, and constant enjoyment - they delude the people and impose upon them, and their lying promises will only one day bring forth evils worse than the present. Nothing is more useful than to look upon the

---

[5] Gen. 3:17.

world as it really is, and at the same time to seek elsewhere, as We have said, for the solace to its troubles.

19. The great mistake made in regard to the matter now under consideration is to take up with the notion that class is naturally hostile to class, and that the wealthy and the working men are intended by nature to live in mutual conflict. So irrational and so false is this view that the direct contrary is the truth. Just as the symmetry of the human frame is the result of the suitable arrangement of the different parts of the body, so in a State is it ordained by nature that these two classes should dwell in harmony and agreement, so as to maintain the balance of the body politic. Each needs the other: capital cannot do without labor, nor labor without capital. Mutual agreement results in the beauty of good order, while perpetual conflict necessarily produces confusion and savage barbarity. Now, in preventing such strife as this, and in uprooting it, the efficacy of Christian institutions is marvellous and manifold. First of all, there is no intermediary more powerful than religion (whereof the Church is the interpreter and guardian) in drawing the rich and the working class together, by reminding each of its duties to the other, and especially of the obligations of justice.

20. Of these duties, the following bind the proletarian and the worker: fully and faithfully to perform the work which has been freely and equitably agreed upon; never to injure the property, nor to outrage the person, of an employer; never to resort to violence in defending their own cause, nor to engage in riot or disorder; and to have nothing to do with men of evil principles, who work upon the people with artful promises of great results, and excite foolish hopes which usually end in useless regrets and grievous loss. The following duties bind the wealthy owner and the employer: not to look upon their work people as their bondsmen, but to respect in every man his dignity as a person ennobled by Christian character. They are reminded that, according to natural reason and Christian philosophy, working for gain is creditable, not shameful, to a man, since it enables him

to earn an honorable livelihood; but to misuse men as though they were things in the pursuit of gain, or to value them solely for their physical powers - that is truly shameful and inhuman. Again justice demands that, in dealing with the working man, religion and the good of his soul must be kept in mind. Hence, the employer is bound to see that the worker has time for his religious duties; that he be not exposed to corrupting influences and dangerous occasions; and that he be not led away to neglect his home and family, or to squander his earnings. Furthermore, the employer must never tax his work people beyond their strength, or employ them in work unsuited to their sex and age. His great and principal duty is to give every one what is just. Doubtless, before deciding whether wages axe fair, many things have to be considered; but wealthy owners and all masters of labor should be mindful of this - that to exercise pressure upon the indigent and the destitute for the sake of gain, and to gather one's profit out of the need of another, is condemned by all laws, human and divine. To defraud any one of wages that are his due is a great crime which cries to the avenging anger of Heaven. "Behold, the hire of the laborers... which by fraud has been kept back by you, crieth; and the cry of them hath entered into the ears of the Lord of Sabaoth."[6] Lastly, the rich must religiously refrain from cutting down the workmen's earnings, whether by force, by fraud, or by usurious dealing; and with all the greater reason because the laboring man is, as a rule, weak and unprotected, and because his slender means should in proportion to their scantiness be accounted sacred. Were these precepts carefully obeyed and followed out, would they not be sufficient of themselves to keep under all strife and all its causes?

21. But the Church, with Jesus Christ as her Master and Guide, aims higher still. She lays down precepts yet more perfect, and tries to bind class to class in friendliness and good feeling. The things of earth cannot be understood or valued aright without taking into consideration the life to come, the life that will know

---

[6] James 5:4.

no death. Exclude the idea of futurity, and forthwith the very notion of what is good and right would perish; nay, the whole scheme of the universe would become a dark and unfathomable mystery. The great truth which we learn from nature herself is also the grand Christian dogma on which religion rests as on its foundation - that, when we have given up this present life, then shall we really begin to live. God has not created us for the perishable and transitory things of earth, but for things heavenly and everlasting; He has given us this world as a place of exile, and not as our abiding place. As for riches and the other things which men call good and desirable, whether we have them in abundance, or are lacking in them-so far as eternal happiness is concerned - it makes no difference; the only important thing is to use them aright. Jesus Christ, when He redeemed us with plentiful redemption, took not away the pains and sorrows which in such large proportion are woven together in the web of our mortal life. He transformed them into motives of virtue and occasions of merit; and no man can hope for eternal reward unless he follow in the blood-stained footprints of his Saviour. "If we suffer with Him, we shall also reign with Him."[7] Christ's labors and sufferings, accepted of His own free will, have marvellously sweetened all suffering and all labor. And not only by His example, but by His grace and by the hope held forth of everlasting recompense, has He made pain and grief more easy to endure; "for that which is at present momentary and light of our tribulation, worketh for us above measure exceedingly an eternal weight of glory."[8]

22. Therefore, those whom fortune favors are warned that riches do not bring freedom from sorrow and are of no avail for eternal happiness, but rather are obstacles;[9] that the rich should tremble at the threatenings of Jesus Christ - threatenings so unwonted in the mouth of our Lord[10] - and that a most strict account must be

---

[7] 2 Tim. 2:12.
[8] 2 Cor. 4:17.
[9] Matt. 19:23-24.
[10] Luke 6:24-25.

given to the Supreme Judge for all we possess. The chief and most excellent rule for the right use of money is one the heathen philosophers hinted at, but which the Church has traced out clearly, and has not only made known to men's minds, but has impressed upon their lives. It rests on the principle that it is one thing to have a right to the possession of money and another to have a right to use money as one wills. Private ownership, as we have seen, is the natural right of man, and to exercise that right, especially as members of society, is not only lawful, but absolutely necessary. "It is lawful," says St. Thomas Aquinas, "for a man to hold private property; and it is also necessary for the carrying on of human existence."[11] But if the question be asked: How must one's possessions be used? - the Church replies without hesitation in the words of the same holy Doctor: "Man should not consider his material possessions as his own, but as common to all, so as to share them without hesitation when others are in need. Whence the Apostle with, 'Command the rich of this world... to offer with no stint, to apportion largely.'"[12] True, no one is commanded to distribute to others that which is required for his own needs and those of his household; nor even to give away what is reasonably required to keep up becomingly his condition in life, "for no one ought to live other than becomingly."[13] But, when what necessity demands has been supplied, and one's standing fairly taken thought for, it becomes a duty to give to the indigent out of what remains over. "Of that which remaineth, give alms."[14] It is a duty, not of justice (save in extreme cases), but of Christian charity - a duty not enforced by human law. But the laws and judgments of men must yield place to the laws and judgments of Christ the true God, who in many ways urges on His followers the practice of almsgiving – "It is more blessed to give than to receive";[15] and who will count a kindness done or refused to the poor as done or refused to

---

[11] Summa theologiae, IIa-IIae, q. lxvi, art. 2, Answer.
[12] Ibid.
[13] Ibid., q. xxxii, a. 6, Answer.
[14] Luke 11:41.
[15] Acts 20:35.

Himself - "As long as you did it to one of My least brethren you did it to Me."[16] To sum up, then, what has been said: Whoever has received from the divine bounty a large share of temporal blessings, whether they be external and material, or gifts of the mind, has received them for the purpose of using them for the perfecting of his own nature, and, at the same time, that he may employ them, as the steward of God's providence, for the benefit of others. "He that hath a talent," said St. Gregory the Great, "let him see that he hide it not; he that hath abundance, let him quicken himself to mercy and generosity; he that hath art and skill, let him do his best to share the use and the utility hereof with his neighbor."[17]

23. As for those who possess not the gifts of fortune, they are taught by the Church that in God's sight poverty is no disgrace, and that there is nothing to be ashamed of in earning their bread by labor. This is enforced by what we see in Christ Himself, who, "whereas He was rich, for our sakes became poor";[18] and who, being the Son of God, and God Himself, chose to seem and to be considered the son of a carpenter - nay, did not disdain to spend a great part of His life as a carpenter Himself. "Is not this the carpenter, the son of Mary?"[19]

24. From contemplation of this divine Model, it is more easy to understand that the true worth and nobility of man lie in his moral qualities, that is, in virtue; that virtue is, moreover, the common inheritance of men, equally within the reach of high and low, rich and poor; and that virtue, and virtue alone, wherever found, will be followed by the rewards of everlasting happiness. Nay, God Himself seems to incline rather to those who suffer misfortune; for Jesus Christ calls the poor "blessed";[20] He lovingly invites those in labor and grief to come to Him for

---

[16] Matt.25:40.
[17] Hom. in Evang., 9, n. 7 (PL 76, 1109B).
[18] 2 Cor. 8:9.
[19] Mark 6:3.
[20] Matt.5:3.

solace;[21] and He displays the tenderest charity toward the lowly and the oppressed. These reflections cannot fail to keep down the pride of the well-to-do, and to give heart to the unfortunate; to move the former to be generous and the latter to be moderate in their desires. Thus, the separation which pride would set up tends to disappear, nor will it be difficult to make rich and poor join hands in friendly concord.

25. But, if Christian precepts prevail, the respective classes will not only be united in the bonds of friendship, but also in those of brotherly love. For they will understand and feel that all men are children of the same common Father, who is God; that all have alike the same last end, which is God Himself, who alone can make either men or angels absolutely and perfectly happy; that each and all are redeemed and made sons of God, by Jesus Christ, "the first-born among many brethren"; that the blessings of nature and the gifts of grace belong to the whole human race in common, and that from none except the unworthy is withheld the inheritance of the kingdom of Heaven. "If sons, heirs also; heirs indeed of God, and co-heirs with Christ."[22] Such is the scheme of duties and of rights which is shown forth to the world by the Gospel. Would it not seem that, were society penetrated with ideas like these, strife must quickly cease?

26. But the Church, not content with pointing out the remedy, also applies it. For the Church does her utmost to teach and to train men, and to educate them and by the intermediary of her bishops and clergy diffuses her salutary teachings far and wide. She strives to influence the mind and the heart so that all may willingly yield themselves to be formed and guided by the commandments of God. It is precisely in this fundamental and momentous matter, on which everything depends that the Church possesses a power peculiarly her own. The instruments which she employs are given to her by Jesus Christ Himself for

---

[21] Matt. 11:28.
[22] Rom. 8:17.

the very purpose of reaching the hearts of men, and drive their efficiency from God. They alone can reach the innermost heart and conscience, and bring men to act from a motive of duty, to control their passions and appetites, to love God and their fellow men with a love that is outstanding and of the highest degree and to break down courageously every barrier which blocks the way to virtue.

27. On this subject we need but recall for one moment the examples recorded in history. Of these facts there cannot be any shadow of doubt: for instance, that civil society was renovated in every part by Christian institutions; that in the strength of that renewal the human race was lifted up to better things-nay, that it was brought back from death to life, and to so excellent a life that nothing more perfect had been known before, or will come to be known in the ages that have yet to be. Of this beneficent transformation Jesus Christ was at once the first cause and the final end; as from Him all came, so to Him was all to be brought back. For, when the human race, by the light of the Gospel message, came to know the grand mystery of the Incarnation of the Word and the redemption of man, at once the life of Jesus Christ, God and Man, pervaded every race and nation, and interpenetrated them with His faith, His precepts, and His laws. And if human society is to be healed now, in no other way can it be healed save by a return to Christian life and Christian institutions. When a society is perishing, the wholesome advice to give to those who would restore it is to call it to the principles from which it sprang; for the purpose and perfection of an association is to aim at and to attain that for which it is formed, and its efforts should be put in motion and inspired by the end and object which originally gave it being. Hence, to fall away from its primal constitution implies disease; to go back to it, recovery. And this may be asserted with utmost truth both of the whole body of the commonwealth and of that class of its citizens-by far the great majority - who get their living by their labor.

28. Neither must it be supposed that the solicitude of the Church is so preoccupied with the spiritual concerns of her children as to neglect their temporal and earthly interests. Her desire is that the poor, for example, should rise above poverty and wretchedness, and better their condition in life; and for this she makes a strong endeavor. By the fact that she calls men to virtue and forms them to its practice she promotes this in no slight degree. Christian morality, when adequately and completely practiced, leads of itself to temporal prosperity, for it merits the blessing of that God who is the source of all blessings; it powerfully restrains the greed of possession and the thirst for pleasure-twin plagues, which too often make a man who is void of self-restraint miserable in the midst of abundance;[23] it makes men supply for the lack of means through economy, teaching them to be content with frugal living, and further, keeping them out of the reach of those vices which devour not small incomes merely, but large fortunes, and dissipate many a goodly inheritance.

29. The Church, moreover, intervenes directly in behalf of the poor, by setting on foot and maintaining many associations which she knows to be efficient for the relief of poverty. Herein, again, she has always succeeded so well as to have even extorted the praise of her enemies. Such was the ardor of brotherly love among the earliest Christians that numbers of those who were in better circumstances despoiled themselves of their possessions in order to relieve their brethren; whence "neither was there any one needy among them."[24] To the order of deacons, instituted in that very intent, was committed by the Apostles the charge of the daily doles; and the Apostle Paul, though burdened with the solicitude of all the churches, hesitated not to undertake laborious journeys in order to carry the alms of the faithful to the poorer Christians. Tertullian calls these contributions, given voluntarily by Christians in their assemblies, deposits of piety, because, to cite his own words, they were employed "in feeding

---

[23] 1 Tim. 6:10.
[24] Acts 4:34.

the needy, in burying them, in support of youths and maidens destitute of means and deprived of their parents, in the care of the aged, and the relief of the shipwrecked."[25]

30. Thus, by degrees, came into existence the patrimony which the Church has guarded with religious care as the inheritance of the poor. Nay, in order to spare them the shame of begging, the Church has provided aid for the needy. The common Mother of rich and poor has aroused everywhere the heroism of charity, and has established congregations of religious and many other useful institutions for help and mercy, so that hardly any kind of suffering could exist which was not afforded relief. At the present day many there are who, like the heathen of old, seek to blame and condemn the Church for such eminent charity. They would substitute in its stead a system of relief organized by the State. But no human expedients will ever make up for the devotedness and self sacrifice of Christian charity. Charity, as a virtue, pertains to the Church; for virtue it is not, unless it be drawn from the Most Sacred Heart of Jesus Christ; and whosoever turns his back on the Church cannot be near to Christ.

31. It cannot, however, be doubted that to attain the purpose we are treating of, not only the Church, but all human agencies, must concur. All who are concerned in the matter should be of one mind and according to their ability act together. It is with this, as with providence that governs the world; the results of causes do not usually take place save where all the causes cooperate. It is sufficient, therefore, to inquire what part the State should play in the work of remedy and relief.

32. By the State we here understand, not the particular form of government prevailing in this or that nation, but the State as rightly apprehended; that is to say, any government conformable in its institutions to right reason and natural law, and to those

---

[25] Apologia secunda, 39, (Apologeticus, cap. 39; PL1, 533A).

dictates of the divine wisdom which we have expounded in the encyclical *On the Christian Constitution of the State.*[26] The foremost duty, therefore, of the rulers of the State should be to make sure that the laws and institutions, the general character and administration of the commonwealth, shall be such as of themselves to realize public well-being and private prosperity. This is the proper scope of wise statesmanship and is the work of the rulers. Now a State chiefly prospers and thrives through moral rule, well-regulated family life, respect for religion and justice, the moderation and fair imposing of public taxes, the progress of the arts and of trade, the abundant yield of the land - through everything, in fact, which makes the citizens better and happier. Hereby, then, it lies in the power of a ruler to benefit every class in the State, and amongst the rest to promote to the utmost the interests of the poor; and this in virtue of his office, and without being open to suspicion of undue interference - since it is the province of the commonwealth to serve the common good. And the more that is done for the benefit of the working classes by the general laws of the country, the less need will there be to seek for special means to relieve them.

33. There is another and deeper consideration which must not be lost sight of. As regards the State, the interests of all, whether high or low, are equal. The members of the working classes are citizens by nature and by the same right as the rich; they are real parts, living the life which makes up, through the family, the body of the commonwealth; and it need hardly be said that they are in every city very largely in the majority. It would be irrational to neglect one portion of the citizens and favor another, and therefore the public administration must duly and solicitously provide for the welfare and the comfort of the working classes; otherwise, that law of justice will be violated which ordains that each man shall have his due. To cite the wise words of St. Thomas Aquinas: "As the part and the whole are in a certain sense identical, so that which belongs to the whole in a sense

---

[26] See above, pp. 161-184.

belongs to the part."[27] Among the many and grave duties of rulers who would do their best for the people, the first and chief is to act with strict justice - with that justice which is called *distributive* - toward each and every class alike.

34. But although all citizens, without exception, can and ought to contribute to that common good in which individuals share so advantageously to themselves, yet it should not be supposed that all can contribute in the like way and to the same extent. No matter what changes may occur in forms of government, there will ever be differences and inequalities of condition in the State. Society cannot exist or be conceived of without them. Some there must be who devote themselves to the work of the commonwealth, who make the laws or administer justice, or whose advice and authority govern the nation in times of peace, and defend it in war. Such men clearly occupy the foremost place in the State, and should be held in highest estimation, for their work concerns most nearly and effectively the general interests of the community. Those who labor at a trade or calling do not promote the general welfare in such measure as this, but they benefit the nation, if less directly, in a most important manner. We have insisted, it is true, that, since the end of society is to make men better, the chief good that society can possess is virtue. Nevertheless, it is the business of a well-constituted body politic to see to the provision of those material and external helps "the use of which is necessary to virtuous action."[28] Now, for the provision of such commodities, the labor of the working class - the exercise of their skill, and the employment of their strength, in the cultivation of the land, and in the workshops of trade - is especially responsible and quite indispensable. Indeed, their co-operation is in this respect so important that it may be truly said that it is only by the labor of working men that States grow rich. Justice, therefore, demands that the interests of the working classes should be carefully watched over by the

[27] Summa theologiae, IIa-IIae, q. lxi, are. 1, ad 2m.
[28] Thomas Aquinas, On the Governance of Rulers, 1, 15 (Opera omnia, ed. Vives, Vol. 27, p. 356).

administration, so that they who contribute so largely to the advantage of the community may themselves share in the benefits which they create-that being housed, clothed, and bodily fit, they may find their life less hard and more endurable. It follows that whatever shall appear to prove conducive to the well-being of those who work should obtain favorable consideration. There is no fear that solicitude of this kind will be harmful to any interest; on the contrary, it will be to the advantage of all, for it cannot but be good for the commonwealth to shield from misery those on whom it so largely depends for the things that it needs.

35. We have said that the State must not absorb the individual or the family; both should be allowed free and untrammelled action so far as is consistent with the common good and the interest of others. Rulers should, nevertheless, anxiously safeguard the community and all its members; the community, because the conservation thereof is so emphatically the business of the supreme power, that the safety of the commonwealth is not only the first law, but it is a government's whole reason of existence; and the members, because both philosophy and the Gospel concur in laying down that the object of the government of the State should be, not the advantage of the ruler, but the benefit of those over whom he is placed. As the power to rule comes from God, and is, as it were, a participation in His, the highest of all sovereignties, it should be exercised as the power of God is exercised - with a fatherly solicitude which not only guides the whole, but reaches also individuals.

36. Whenever the general interest or any particular class suffers, or is threatened with harm, which can in no other way be met or prevented, the public authority must step in to deal with it. Now, it is to the interest of the community, as well as of the individual, that peace and good order should be maintained; that all things should be carried on in accordance with God's laws and those of nature; that the discipline of family life should be observed and that religion should be obeyed; that a high standard of morality

should prevail, both in public and private life; that justice should be held sacred and that no one should injure another with impunity; that the members of the commonwealth should grow up to man's estate strong and robust, and capable, if need be, of guarding and defending their country. If by a strike of workers or concerted interruption of work there should be imminent danger of disturbance to the public peace; or if circumstances were such as that among the working class the ties of family life were relaxed; if religion were found to suffer through the workers not having time and opportunity afforded them to practice its duties; if in workshops and factories there were danger to morals through the mixing of the sexes or from other harmful occasions of evil; or if employers laid burdens upon their workmen which were unjust, or degraded them with conditions repugnant to their dignity as human beings; finally, if health were endangered by excessive labor, or by work unsuited to sex or age - in such cases, there can be no question but that, within certain limits, it would be right to invoke the aid and authority of the law. The limits must be determined by the nature of the occasion which calls for the law's interference - the principle being that the law must not undertake more, nor proceed further, than is required for the remedy of the evil or the removal of the mischief.

37. Rights must be religiously respected wherever they exist, and it is the duty of the public authority to prevent and to punish injury, and to protect every one in the possession of his own. Still, when there is question of defending the rights of individuals, the poor and badly off have a claim to especial consideration. The richer class have many ways of shielding themselves, and stand less in need of help from the State; whereas the mass of the poor have no resources of their own to fall back upon, and must chiefly depend upon the assistance of the State. And it is for this reason that wage-earners, since they mostly belong in the mass of the needy, should be specially cared for and protected by the government.

38. Here, however, it is expedient to bring under special notice certain matters of moment. First of all, there is the duty of safeguarding private property by legal enactment and protection. Most of all it is essential, where the passion of greed is so strong, to keep the populace within the line of duty; for, if all may justly strive to better their condition, neither justice nor the common good allows any individual to seize upon that which belongs to another, or, under the futile and shallow pretext of equality, to lay violent hands on other people's possessions. Most true it is that by far the larger part of the workers prefer to better themselves by honest labor rather than by doing any wrong to others. But there are not a few who are imbued with evil principles and eager for revolutionary change, whose main purpose is to stir up disorder and incite their fellows to acts of violence. The authority of the law should intervene to put restraint upon such firebrands, to save the working classes from being led astray by their maneuvers, and to protect lawful owners from spoliation.

39. When work people have recourse to a strike and become voluntarily idle, it is frequently because the hours of labor are too long, or the work too hard, or because they consider their wages insufficient. The grave inconvenience of this not uncommon occurrence should be obviated by public remedial measures; for such paralysing of labor not only affects the masters and their work people alike, but is extremely injurious to trade and to the general interests of the public; moreover, on such occasions, violence and disorder are generally not far distant, and thus it frequently happens that the public peace is imperiled. The laws should forestall and prevent such troubles from arising; they should lend their influence and authority to the removal in good time of the causes which lead to conflicts between employers and employed.

40. The working man, too, has interests in which he should be protected by the State; and first of all, there are the interests of his soul. Life on earth, however good and desirable in itself, is

not the final purpose for which man is created; it is only the way and the means to that attainment of truth and that love of goodness in which the full life of the soul consists. It is the soul which is made after the image and likeness of God; it is in the soul that the sovereignty resides in virtue whereof man is commanded to rule the creatures below him and to use all the earth and the ocean for his profit and advantage. "Fill the earth and subdue it; and rule over the fishes of the sea, and the fowls of the air, and all living creatures that move upon the earth."[29] In this respect all men are equal; there is here no difference between rich and poor, master and servant, ruler and ruled, "for the same is Lord over all."[30] No man may with impunity outrage that human dignity which God Himself treats with great reverence, nor stand in the way of that higher life which is the preparation of the eternal life of heaven. Nay, more; no man has in this matter power over himself. To consent to any treatment which is calculated to defeat the end and purpose of his being is beyond his right; he cannot give up his soul to servitude, for it is not man's own rights which are here in question, but the rights of God, the most sacred and inviolable of rights.

41. From this follows the obligation of the cessation from work and labor on Sundays and certain holy days. The rest from labor is not to be understood as mere giving way to idleness; much less must it be an occasion for spending money and for vicious indulgence, as many would have it to be; but it should be rest from labor, hallowed by religion. Rest (combined with religious observances) disposes man to forget for a while the business of his everyday life, to turn his thoughts to things heavenly, and to the worship which he so strictly owes to the eternal Godhead. It is this, above all, which is the reason arid motive of Sunday rest; a rest sanctioned by God's great law of the Ancient Covenant- "Remember thou keep holy the Sabbath day,"[31] and taught to the world by His own mysterious "rest" after the creation of man:

[29] Gen.1:28.
[30] Rom. 10:12.
[31] Exod.20:8.

"He rested on the seventh day from all His work which He had done."[32]

42. If we turn not to things external and material, the first thing of all to secure is to save unfortunate working people from the cruelty of men of greed, who use human beings as mere instruments for money-making. It is neither just nor human so to grind men down with excessive labor as to stupefy their minds and wear out their bodies. Man's powers, like his general nature, are limited, and beyond these limits he cannot go. His strength is developed and increased by use and exercise, but only on condition of due intermission and proper rest. Daily labor, therefore, should be so regulated as not to be protracted over longer hours than strength admits. How many and how long the intervals of rest should be must depend on the nature of the work, on circumstances of time and place, and on the health and strength of the workman. Those who work in mines and quarries, and extract coal, stone and metals from the bowels of the earth, should have shorter hours in proportion as their labor is more severe and trying to health. Then, again, the season of the year should be taken into account; for not unfrequently a kind of labor is easy at one time which at another is intolerable or exceedingly difficult. Finally, work which is quite suitable for a strong man cannot rightly be required from a woman or a child. And, in regard to children, great care should be taken not to place them in workshops and factories until their bodies and minds are sufficiently developed. For, just as very rough weather destroys the buds of spring, so does too early an experience of life's hard toil blight the young promise of a child's faculties, and render any true education impossible. Women, again, are not suited for certain occupations; a woman is by nature fitted for home-work, and it is that which is best adapted at once to preserve her modesty and to promote the good bringing up of children and the well-being of the family. As a general principle it may be laid down that a workman ought to have leisure and rest

---

[32] Gen. 2:2.

proportionate to the wear and tear of his strength, for waste of strength must be repaired by cessation from hard work.

In all agreements between masters and work people there is always the condition expressed or understood that there should be allowed proper rest for soul and body. To agree in any other sense would be against what is right and just; for it can never be just or right to require on the one side, or to promise on the other, the giving up of those duties which a man owes to his God and to himself.

43. We now approach a subject of great importance, and one in respect of which, if extremes are to be avoided, right notions are absolutely necessary. Wages, as we are told, are regulated by free consent, and therefore the employer, when he pays what was agreed upon, has done his part and seemingly is not called upon to do anything beyond. The only way, it is said, in which injustice might occur would be if the master refused to pay the whole of the wages, or if the workman should not complete the work undertaken; in such cases the public authority should intervene, to see that each obtains his due, but not under any other circumstances.

44. To this kind of argument a fair-minded man will not easily or entirely assent; it is not complete, for there are important considerations which it leaves out of account altogether. To labor is to exert oneself for the sake of procuring what is necessary for the various purposes of life, and chief of all for self preservation. "In the sweat of thy face thou shalt eat bread."[33] Hence, a man's labor necessarily bears two notes or characters. First of all, it is personal, inasmuch as the force which acts is bound up with the personality and is the exclusive property of him who acts, and, further, was given to him for his advantage. Secondly, man's labor is *necessary;* for without the result of labor a man cannot live, and self-preservation is a law of nature, which it

---

[33] Gen. 3:19.

is wrong to disobey. Now, were we to consider labor merely in so far as it is personal, doubtless it would be within the workman's right to accept any rate of wages whatsoever; for in the same way as he is free to work or not, so is he free to accept a small wage or even none at all. But our conclusion must be very different if, together with the personal element in a man's work, we consider the fact that work is also necessary for him to live: these two aspects of his work are separable in thought, but not in reality. The preservation of life is the bounden duty of one and all, and to be wanting therein is a crime. It necessarily follows that each one has a natural right to procure what is required in order to live, and the poor can procure that in no other way than by what they can earn through their work.

45. Let the working man and the employer make free agreements, and in particular let them agree freely as to the wages; nevertheless, there underlies a dictate of natural justice more imperious and ancient than any bargain between man and man, namely, that wages ought not to be insufficient to support a frugal and well-behaved wage-earner. If through necessity or fear of a worse evil the workman accept harder conditions because an employer or contractor will afford him no better, he is made the victim of force and injustice. In these and similar questions, however - such as, for example, the hours of labor in different trades, the sanitary precautions to be observed in factories and workshops, etc. - in order to supersede undue interference on the part of the State, especially as circumstances, times, and localities differ so widely, it is advisable that recourse be had to societies or boards such as We shall mention presently, or to some other mode of safeguarding the interests of the wage-earners; the State being appealed to, should circumstances require, for its sanction and protection.

46. If a workman's wages be sufficient to enable him comfortably to support himself, his wife, and his children, he will find it easy, if he be a sensible man, to practice thrift, and he will not fail, by cutting down expenses, to put by some little savings and thus

secure a modest source of income. Nature itself would urge him to this. We have seen that this great labor question cannot be solved save by assuming as a principle that private ownership must be held sacred and inviolable. The law, therefore, should favor ownership, and its policy should be to induce as many as possible of the people to become owners.

47. Many excellent results will follow from this; and, first of all, property will certainly become more equitably divided. For, the result of civil change and revolution has been to divide cities into two classes separated by a wide chasm. On the one side there is the party which holds power because it holds wealth; which has in its grasp the whole of labor and trade; which manipulates for its own benefit and its own purposes all the sources of supply, and which is not without influence even in the administration of the commonwealth. On the other side there is the needy and powerless multitude, sick and sore in spirit and ever ready for disturbance. If working people can be encouraged to look forward to obtaining a share in the land, the consequence will be that the gulf between vast wealth and sheer poverty will be bridged over, and the respective classes will be brought nearer to one another. A further consequence will result in the great abundance of the fruits of the earth. Men always work harder and more readily when they work on that which belongs to them; nay, they learn to love the very soil that yields in response to the labor of their hands, not only food to eat, but an abundance of good things for themselves and those that are dear to them. That such a spirit of willing labor would add to the produce of the earth and to the wealth of the community is self evident. And a third advantage would spring from this: men would cling to the country in which they were born, for no one would exchange his country for a foreign land if his own afforded him the means of living a decent and happy life. These three important benefits, however, can be reckoned on only provided that a man's means be not drained and exhausted by excessive taxation. The right to possess private property is derived from nature, not from man; and the State has the right to control its use in the interests of the

public good alone, but by no means to absorb it altogether. The State would therefore be unjust and cruel if under the name of taxation it were to deprive the private owner of more than is fair.

48. In the last place, employers and workmen may of themselves effect much, in the matter We are treating, by means of such associations and organizations as afford opportune aid to those who are in distress, and which draw the two classes more closely together. Among these may be enumerated societies for mutual help; various benevolent foundations established by private persons to provide for the workman, and for his widow or his orphans, in case of sudden calamity, in sickness, and in the event of death; and institutions for the welfare of boys and girls, young people, and those more advanced in years.

49. The most important of all are workingmen's unions, for these virtually include all the rest. History attests what excellent results were brought about by the artificers' guilds of olden times. They were the means of affording not only many advantages to the workmen, but in no small degree of promoting the advancement of art, as numerous monuments remain to bear witness. Such unions should be suited to the requirements of this our age - an age of wider education, of different habits, and of far more numerous requirements in daily life. It is gratifying to know that there are actually in existence not a few associations of this nature, consisting either of workmen alone, or of workmen and employers together, but it were greatly to be desired that they should become more numerous and more efficient. We have spoken of them more than once, yet it will be well to explain here how notably they are needed, to show that they exist of their own right, and what should be their organization and their mode of action.

50. The consciousness of his own weakness urges man to call in aid from without. We read in the pages of holy Writ: "It is better that two should be together than one; for they have the advantage of their society. If one fall he shall be supported by the

other. Woe to him that is alone, for when he falleth he hath none to lift him up."[34] And further: "A brother that is helped by his brother is like a strong city."[35] It is this natural impulse which binds men together in civil society; and it is likewise this which leads them to join together in associations which are, it is true, lesser and not independent societies, but, nevertheless, real societies.

51. These lesser societies and the larger society differ in many respects, because their immediate purpose and aim are different. Civil society exists for the common good, and hence is concerned with the interests of all in general, albeit with individual interests also in their due place and degree. It is therefore called a public society, because by its agency, as St. Thomas of Aquinas says, "Men establish relations in common with one another in the setting up of a commonwealth."[36] But societies which are formed in the bosom of the commonwealth are styled *private*, and rightly so, since their immediate purpose is the private advantage of the associates. "Now, a private society," says St. Thomas again, "is one which is formed for the purpose of carrying out private objects; as when two or three enter into partnership with the view of trading in common."[37] Private societies, then, although they exist within the body politic, and are severally part of the commonwealth, cannot nevertheless be absolutely, and as such, prohibited by public authority. For, to enter into a "society" of this kind is the natural right of man; and the State has for its office to protect natural rights, not to destroy them; and, if it forbid its citizens to form associations, it contradicts the very principle of its own existence, for both they and it exist in virtue of the like principle, namely, the natural tendency of man to dwell in society.

---

[34] Eccle.4:9-10.
[35] Prov.18:19.
[36] Contra impugnantes Dei cultum et religionem, Part 2, ch. 8 (Opera omnia, ed. Vives, Vol. 29, p. 16).
[37] Ibid.

52. There are occasions, doubtless, when it is fitting that the law should intervene to prevent certain associations, as when men join together for purposes which are evidently bad, unlawful, or dangerous to the State. In such cases, public authority may justly forbid the formation of such associations, and may dissolve them if they already exist. But every precaution should be taken not to violate the rights of individuals and not to impose unreasonable regulations under pretense of public benefit. For laws only bind when they are in accordance with right reason, and, hence, with the eternal law of God.[38]

53. And here we are reminded of the confraternities, societies, and religious orders which have arisen by the Church's authority and the piety of Christian men. The annals of every nation down to our own days bear witness to what they have accomplished for the human race. It is indisputable that on grounds of reason alone such associations, being perfectly blameless in their objects, possess the sanction of the law of nature. In their religious aspect they claim rightly to be responsible to the Church alone. The rulers of the State accordingly have no rights over them, nor can they claim any share in their control; on the contrary, it is the duty of the State to respect and cherish them, and, if need be, to defend them from attack. It is notorious that a very different course has been followed, more especially in our own times. In many places the State authorities have laid violent hands on these communities, and committed manifold injustice against them; it has placed them under control of the civil law, taken away their rights as corporate bodies, and despoiled them of their property, in such property the Church had her rights, each member of the body had his or her rights, and there were also the rights of those who had founded or endowed these communities for a definite purpose, and, furthermore, of those for whose benefit and

---

[38] "Human law is law only by virtue of its accordance with right reason; and thus it is manifest that it flows from the eternal law. And in so far as it deviates from right reason it is called an unjust law; in such case it is no law at all, but rather a species of violence." Thomas Aquinas, Summa theologiae, Ia-IIae, q. xciii, art. 3, ad 2m.

assistance they had their being. Therefore We cannot refrain from complaining of such spoliation as unjust and fraught with evil results; and with all the more reason do We complain because, at the very time when the law proclaims that association is free to all, We see that Catholic societies, however peaceful and useful, are hampered in every way, whereas the utmost liberty is conceded to individuals whose purposes are at once hurtful to religion and dangerous to the commonwealth.

54. Associations of every kind, and especially those of working men, are now far more common than heretofore. As regards many of these there is no need at present to inquire whence they spring, what are their objects, or what the means they imply. Now, there is a good deal of evidence in favor of the opinion that many of these societies are in the hands of secret leaders, and are managed on principles ill - according with Christianity and the public well-being; and that they do their utmost to get within their grasp the whole field of labor, and force working men either to join them or to starve. Under these circumstances Christian working men must do one of two things: either join associations in which their religion will be exposed to peril, or form associations among themselves and unite their forces so as to shake off courageously the yoke of so unrighteous and intolerable an oppression. No one who does not wish to expose man's chief good to extreme risk will for a moment hesitate to say that the second alternative should by all means be adopted.

55. Those Catholics are worthy of all praise-and they are not a few-who, understanding what the times require, have striven, by various undertakings and endeavors, to better the condition of the working class by rightful means. They have taken up the cause of the working man, and have spared no efforts to better the condition both of families and individuals; to infuse a spirit of equity into the mutual relations of employers and employed; to keep before the eyes of both classes the precepts of duty and the laws of the Gospel - that Gospel which, by inculcating self restraint, keeps men within the bounds of moderation, and tends

to establish harmony among the divergent interests and the various classes which compose the body politic. It is with such ends in view that we see men of eminence, meeting together for discussion, for the promotion of concerted action, and for practical work. Others, again, strive to unite working men of various grades into associations, help them with their advice and means, and enable them to obtain fitting and profitable employment. The bishops, on their part, bestow their ready good will and support; and with their approval and guidance many members of the clergy, both secular and regular, labor assiduously in behalf of the spiritual interest of the members of such associations. And there are not wanting Catholics blessed with affluence, who have, as it were, cast in their lot with the wage-earners, and who have spent large sums in founding and widely spreading benefit and insurance societies, by means of which the working man may without difficulty acquire through his labor not only many present advantages, but also the certainty of honorable support in days to come. How greatly such manifold and earnest activity has benefited the community at large is too well known to require Us to dwell upon it. We find therein grounds for most cheering hope in the future, provided always that the associations We have described continue to grow and spread, and are well and wisely administered. The State should watch over these societies of citizens banded together in accordance with their rights, but it should not thrust itself into their peculiar concerns and their organization, for things move and live by the spirit inspiring them, and may be killed by the rough grasp of a hand from without.

56. In order that an association may be carried on with unity of purpose and harmony of action, its administration and government should be firm and wise. All such societies, being free to exist, have the further right to adopt such rules and organization as may best conduce to the attainment of their respective objects. We do not judge it possible to enter into minute particulars touching the subject of organization; this must depend on national character, on practice and experience, on the

nature and aim of the work to be done, on the scope of the various trades and employments, and on other circumstances of fact and of time - all of which should be carefully considered.

57. To sum up, then, We may lay it down as a general and lasting law that working men's associations should be so organized and governed as to furnish the best and most suitable means for attaining what is aimed at, that is to say, for helping each individual member to better his condition to the utmost in body, soul, and property. It is clear that they must pay special and chief attention to the duties of religion and morality, and that social betterment should have this chiefly in view; otherwise they would lose wholly their special character, and end by becoming little better than those societies which take no account whatever of religion. What advantage can it be to a working man to obtain by means of a society material well-being, if he endangers his soul for lack of spiritual food? "What doth it profit a man, if he gain the whole world and suffer the loss of his soul?"[39] This, as our Lord teaches, is the mark or character that distinguishes the Christian from the heathen. "After all these things do the heathen seek . . . Seek ye first the Kingdom of God and His justice: and all these things shall be added unto you."[40] Let our associations, then, look first and before all things to God; let religious instruction have therein the foremost place, each one being carefully taught what is his duty to God, what he has to believe, what to hope for, and how he is to work out his salvation; and let all be warned and strengthened with special care against wrong principles and false teaching. Let the working man be urged and led to the worship of God, to the earnest practice of religion, and, among other things, to the keeping holy of Sundays and holy days. Let him learn to reverence and love holy Church, the common Mother of us all; and hence to obey the precepts of the Church, and to frequent the sacraments, since

---

[39] Matt. 16:26.
[40] Matt. 6:32-33.

they are the means ordained by God for obtaining forgiveness of sin and fox leading a holy life.

58. The foundations of the organization being thus laid in religion, We next proceed to make clear the relations of the members one to another, in order that they may live together in concord and go forward prosperously and with good results. The offices and charges of the society should be apportioned for the good of the society itself, and in such mode that difference in degree or standing should not interfere with unanimity and good-will. It is most important that office bearers be appointed with due prudence and discretion, and each one's charge carefully mapped out, in order that no members may suffer harm. The common funds must be administered with strict honesty, in such a way that a member may receive assistance in proportion to his necessities. The rights and duties of the employers, as compared with the rights and duties of the employed, ought to be the subject of careful consideration. Should it happen that either a master or a workman believes himself injured, nothing would be more desirable than that a committee should be appointed, composed of reliable and capable members of the association, whose duty would be, conformably with the rules of the association, to settle the dispute. Among the several purposes of a society, one should be to try to arrange for a continuous supply of work at all times and seasons; as well as to create a fund out of which the members may be effectually helped in their needs, not only in the cases of accident, but also in sickness, old age, and distress.

59. Such rules and regulations, if willingly obeyed by all, will sufficiently ensure the well being of the less well-to-do; whilst such mutual associations among Catholics are certain to be productive in no small degree of prosperity to the State. Is it not rash to conjecture the future from the past. Age gives way to age, but the events of one century are wonderfully like those of another, for they are directed by the providence of God, who overrules the course of history in accordance with His purposes

in creating the race of man. We are told that it was cast as a reproach on the Christians in the early ages of the Church that the greater number among them had to live by begging or by labor. Yet, destitute though they were of wealth and influence, they ended by winning over to their side the favor of the rich and the good-will of the powerful. They showed themselves industrious, hard-working, assiduous, and peaceful, ruled by justice, and, above all, bound together in brotherly love. In presence of such mode of life and such example, prejudice gave way, the tongue of malevolence was silenced, and the lying legends of ancient superstition little by little yielded to Christian truth.

60. At the time being, the condition of the working classes is the pressing question of the hour, and nothing can be of higher interest to all classes of the State than that it should be rightly and reasonably settled. But it will be easy for Christian working men to solve it aright if they will form associations, choose wise guides, and follow on the path which with so much advantage to themselves and the common weal was trodden by their fathers before them. Prejudice, it is true, is mighty, and so is the greed of money; but if the sense of what is just and rightful be not deliberately stifled, their fellow citizens are sure to be won over to a kindly feeling towards men whom they see to be in earnest as regards their work and who prefer so unmistakably right dealing to mere lucre, and the sacredness of duty to every other consideration.

61. And further great advantage would result from the state of things We are describing; there would exist so much more ground for hope, and likelihood, even, of recalling to a sense of their duty those working men who have either given up their faith altogether, or whose lives are at variance with its precepts. Such men feel in most cases that they have been fooled by empty promises and deceived by false pretexts. They cannot but perceive that their grasping employers too often treat them with great inhumanity and hardly care for them outside the profit their

labor brings; and if they belong to any union, it is probably one
in which there exists, instead of charity and love, that intestine
strife which ever accompanies poverty when unresigned and
unsustained by religion. Broken in spirit and worn down in body,
how many of them would gladly free themselves from such
galling bondage! But human respect, or the dread of starvation,
makes them tremble to take the step. To such as these Catholic
associations are of incalculable service, by helping them out of
their difficulties, inviting them to companionship and receiving
the returning wanderers to a haven where they may securely find
repose.

62. We have now laid before you, venerable brethren, both who
are the persons and what are the means whereby this most
arduous question must be solved. Every one should put his hand
to the work which falls to his share, and that at once and
straightway, lest the evil which is already so great become
through delay absolutely beyond remedy. Those who rule the
commonwealths should avail themselves of the laws and
institutions of the country; masters and wealthy owners must be
mindful of their duty; the working class, whose interests are at
stake, should make every lawful and proper effort; and since
religion alone, as We said at the beginning, can avail to destroy
the evil at its root, all men should rest persuaded that main thing
needful is to re-establish Christian morals, apart from which all
the plans and devices of the wisest will prove of little avail.

63. In regard to the Church, her cooperation will never be found
lacking, be the time or the occasion what it may; and she will
intervene with all the greater effect in proportion as her liberty of
action is the more unfettered. Let this be carefully taken to heart
by those whose office it is to safeguard the public welfare. Every
minister of holy religion must bring to the struggle the full energy
of his mind and all his power of endurance. Moved by your
authority, venerable brethren, and quickened by your example,
they should never cease to urge upon men of every class, upon
the high-placed as well as the lowly, the Gospel doctrines of

Christian life; by every means in their power they must strive to secure the good of the people; and above all must earnestly cherish in themselves, and try to arouse in others, charity, the mistress and the queen of virtues. For, the happy results we all long for must be chiefly brought about by the plenteous outpouring of charity; of that true Christian charity which is the fulfilling of the whole Gospel law, which is always ready to sacrifice itself for others' sake, and is man's surest antidote against worldly pride and immoderate love of self; that charity whose office is described and whose Godlike features are outlined by the Apostle St. Paul in these words: "Charity is patient, is kind, . . . seeketh not her own, . . . suffereth all things, . . . endureth all things."[41]

64. On each of you, venerable brethren, and on your clergy and people, as an earnest of God's mercy and a mark of Our affection, we lovingly in the Lord bestow the apostolic benediction.

Given at St. Peter's in Rome, the fifteenth day of May, 1891, the fourteenth year of Our pontificate.

---

[41] 1 Cor. 13:4-7.

XI: Providentissimus Deus

November 18, 1893

ON THE STUDY OF HOLY SCRIPTURE

The God of all Providence, Who in the adorable designs of His
love at first elevated the human race to the participation of the
Divine nature, and afterwards delivered it from universal guilt
and ruin, restoring it to its primitive dignity, has in consequence
bestowed upon man a splendid gift and safeguard - making
known to him, by supernatural means, the hidden mysteries of
His Divinity, His wisdom and His mercy. For although in Divine
revelation there are contained some things which are not beyond
the reach of unassisted reason, and which are made the objects
of such revelation in order "that all may come to know them
with facility, certainty, and safety from error, yet not on this
account can supernatural Revelation be said to be absolutely
necessary; it is only necessary because God has ordinated man to
a supernatural end."[1] This supernatural revelation, according to
the belief of the universal Church, is contained both in unwritten
Tradition, and in written Books, which aretherefore called sacred
and canonical because, "being written under the inspiration of
the Holy Ghost, they have God for their author and as such have
been delivered to the Church."[2] This belief has been perpetually
held and professed by the Church in regard to the Books of both
Testaments; and there are well-known documents of the gravest
kind, coming down to us from the earliest times, which proclaim
that God, Who spoke first by the Prophets, then by His own
mouth, and lastly by the Apostles, composed also the Canonical
Scriptures,[3] and that these are His own oracles and words[4] - a

---

[1] Conc. Vac. *sess*. iii. *cap*. ii. *de revel.*
[2] *Ibid.*
[3] S. Aug. *de civ. dei* xi., 3.
[4] S. Clem. Rom. I ad. Cor. 45; S. Polycarp. ad Phil. 7; S. Iren. *c haer.*

Letter, written by our heavenly Father, and transmitted by the sacred writers to the human race in its pilgrimage so far from its heavenly country.[5] If, then, such and so great is the excellence and the dignity of the Scriptures, that God Himself has composed them, and that they treat of God's marvellous mysteries, counsels and works, it follows that the branch of sacred Theology which is concerned with the defence and elucidation of these divine Books must be excellent and useful in the highest degree.

2. Now We, who by the help of God, and not without fruit, have by frequent Letters and exhortation endeavoured to promote other branches of study which seemed capable of advancing the glory of God and contributing to the salvation of souls, have for a long time cherished the desire to give an impulse to the noble science of Holy Scripture, and to impart to Scripture study a direction suitable to the needs of the present day. The solicitude of the Apostolic office naturally urges, and even compels us, not only to desire that this grand source of Catholic revelation should be made safely and abundantly accessible to the flock of Jesus Christ, but also not to suffer any attempt to defile or corrupt it, either on the part of those who impiously and openly assail the Scriptures, or of those who are led astray into fallacious and imprudent novelties. We are not ignorant, indeed, Venerable Brethren, that there are not a few Catholics, men of talent and learning, who do devote themselves with ardour to the defence of the sacred writings and to making them better known and understood. But whilst giving to these the commendation they deserve, We cannot but earnestly exhort others also, from whose skill and piety and learning we have a right to expect good results, to give themselves to the same most praiseworthy work. It is Our wish and fervent desire to see an increase in the number of the approved and persevering labourers in the cause of Holy Scripture; and more especially that those whom Divine Grace

---

ii. 28, 2.

[5] S. Chrys. *in Gen. hom.* 2, 2; S. Aug. *in Ps.* xxx., *serm.*, 2, I; S. Greg. M. ad Theod. *ep.* iv., 31.

has called to Holy Orders, should, day-by-day, as their state demands, display greater diligence and industry in reading, meditating, and explaining it.

Holy Scripture Most Profitable To Doctrine and Morality

3. Among the reasons for which the Holy Scripture is so worthy of commendation - in addition to its own excellence and to the homage which we owe to God's Word - the chief of all is, the innumerable benefits of which it is the source; according to the infallible testimony of the Holy Ghost Himself, who says: "All Scripture, inspired of God, is profitable to teach, to reprove, to correct, to instruct in justice, that the man of God may be perfect, furnished to every good work."[6] That such was the purpose of God in giving the Scripture of men is shown by the example of Christ our Lord and of His Apostles. For He Himself Who "obtained authority by miracles, merited belief by authority, and by belief drew to Himself the multitude"[7] was accustomed in the exercise of His Divine Mission, to appeal to the Scriptures. He uses them at times to prove that He is sent by God, and is God Himself. From them He cites instructions for His disciples and confirmation of His doctrine. He vindicates them from the calumnies of objectors; he quotes them against Sadducees and Pharisees, and retorts from them upon Satan himself when he dares to tempt Him. At the close of His life His utterances are from Holy Scripture, and it is the Scripture that He expounds to His disciples after His resurrection, until He ascends to the glory of His Father. Faithful to His precepts, the Apostles, although He Himself granted "signs and wonders to be done by their hands"[8] nevertheless used with the greatest effect the sacred writings, in order to persuade the nations everywhere of the wisdom of Christianity, to conquer the obstinacy of the Jews, and to suppress the outbreak of heresy. This is plainly seen in

---

[6] 2 Tim. iii., 16-17.

[7] S. Aug. *de util. cred.* xiv. 32.

[8] Act xiv., 3.

their discourses, especially in those of St. Peter: these were often little less than a series of citations from the Old Testament supporting in the strongest manner the new dispensation. We find the same thing in the Gospels of St. Matthew and St. John and in the Catholic Epistles; and most remarkably of all in the words of him who "boasts that he learned the law at the feet of Gamaliel, in order that, being armed with spiritual weapons, he might afterwards say with confidence, 'The arms of our warfare are not carnal but mighty unto God.' "[9] Let all, therefore, especially the novices of the ecclesiastical army, understand how deeply the sacred Books should be esteemed, and with what eagerness and reverence they should approach this great arsenal of heavenly arms. For those whose duty it is to handle Catholic doctrine before the learned or the unlearned will nowhere find more ample matter or more abundant exhortation, whether on the subject of God, the supreme Good and the all-perfect Being, or of the works which display His Glory and His love. Nowhere is there anything more full or more express on the subject of the Saviour of the world than is to be found in the whole range of the Bible. As St. Jerome says, "To be ignorant of the Scripture is not to know Christ."[10] In its pages His Image stands out, living and breathing; diffusing everywhere around consolation in trouble, encouragement to virtue and attraction to the love of God. And as to the Church, her institutions, her nature, her office, and her gifts, we find in Holy Scripture so many references and so many ready and convincing arguments, that as St. Jerome again most truly says: "A man who is well grounded in the testimonies of the Scripture is the bulwark of the Church."[11] And if we come to morality and discipline, an apostolic man finds in the sacred writings abundant and excellent assistance; most holy precepts, gentle and strong exhortation, splendid examples of every virtue, and finally the promise of eternal reward and the threat of eternal punishment, uttered in terms of solemn import, in God's name and in God's own words.

---

[9] St. Hieron. *de stud. Script. ad. Paulin.* ep. liii. 3.
[10] *In Isiam Prol.*
[11] *In Isaiam* liv., 12.

4. And it is this peculiar and singular power of Holy Scripture, arising from the inspiration of the Holy Ghost, which gives authority to the sacred orator, fills him with apostolic liberty of speech, and communicates force and power to his eloquence. For those who infuse into their efforts the spirit and strength of the Word of God, speak "not in word only but in power also, and in the Holy Ghost, and in much fulness."[12] Hence those preachers are foolish and improvident who, in speaking of religion and proclaiming the things of God, use no words but those of human science and human prudence, trusting to their own reasonings rather than to those of God. Their discourses may be brilliant and fine, but they must be feeble and they must be cold, for they are without the fire of the utterance of God[13] and they must fall far short of that mighty power which the speech of God possesses: "for the Word of God is living and effectual, and more piercing than any two-edged sword; and reaching unto the division of the soul and the spirit."[14] But, indeed, all those who have a right to speak are agreed that there is in the Holy Scripture an eloquence that is wonderfully varied and rich, and worthy of great themes. This St. Augustine thoroughly understood and has abundantly set forth.[15] This also is confirmed by the best preachers of all ages, who have gratefully acknowledged that they owed their repute chiefly to the assiduous use of the Bible, and to devout meditation on its pages.

5. The Holy Fathers well knew all this by practical experience, and they never cease to extol the sacred Scripture and its fruits. In innumerable passages of their writings we find them applying to it such phrases as "an inexhaustible treasury of heavenly doctrine,"[16] or "an overflowing fountain of salvation,"[17] or

---

[12] 1 Thess. i., 5.
[13] Jerem. xxiii., 29.
[14] Hebr. iv., 12.
[15] *De doctr. Chr.* iv., 6, 7.
[16] S. Chrys. in *Gen. Hom.* xxi., 2; Hom. lx., 3; S. Aug. *de Disc. Christ.*, ii.

putting it before us as fertile pastures and beautiful gardens in which the flock of the Lord is marvellously refreshed and delighted.[18] Let us listen to the words of St. Jerome, in his Epistle to Nepotian: "Often read the divine Scriptures; yea, let holy reading be always in thy hand; study that which thou thyself must preach. . . Let the speech of the priest be ever seasoned with Scriptural reading."[19] St. Gregory the Great, than whom no one has more admirably described the pastoral office, writes in the same sense: "Those," he says, "who are zealous in the work of preaching must never cease the study of the written word of God."[20] St. Augustine, however, warns us that "vainly does the preacher utter the Word of God exteriorly unless he listens to it interiorly;"[21] and St. Gregory instructs sacred orators "first to find in Holy Scripture the knowledge of themselves, and then to carry it to others, lest in reproving others they forget themselves."[22] Admonitions such as these had, indeed, been uttered long before by the Apostolic voice which had learnt its lesson from Christ Himself, Who "began to do and teach." It was not to Timothy alone, but to the whole order of the clergy, that the command was addressed: "Take heed to thyself and to doctrine; be earnest in them. For in doing this thou shah both save thyself and them that hear thee."[23] For the saving and for the perfection of ourselves and of others there is at hand the very best of help in the Holy Scriptures, as the Book of Psalms, among others, so constantly insists; but those only will find it who bring to this divine reading not only docility and attention, but also piety and an innocent life. For the Sacred Scripture is not like other books. Dictated by the Holy Ghost, it contains things of the deepest importance, which in many instances are most difficult and obscure. To understand and explain such

---

[17] S. Athan. *ep. fest.* xxxix.

[18] S. Aug. serm. xxvi., 24; S. Ambr. *in Ps.* cxviii., *serm.* xix, 2.

[19] S. Hier. *de vita cleric.* ad Nepot.

[20] S. Greg. M., *Regul. past.* ii., II (al. 22); Moral. xviii., 26 (a1.14).

[21] S. Aug. *serm.* clxxix., I.

[22] S. Greg. M. *Regul. past.*, iii., 24 (*al.* 48).

[23] 1 Tim. iv., 16.

things there is always required the "coming"[24] of the same Holy Spirit; that is to say, His light and His grace; and these, as the Royal Psalmist so frequently insists, are to be sought by humble prayer and guarded by holiness of life.

What the Bible Owes to the Catholic Church

6. It is in this that the watchful care of the Church shines forth conspicuously. By admirable laws and regulations, she has always shown herself solicitous that "the celestial treasure of the Sacred Books, so bountifully bestowed upon man by the Holy Spirit, should not lie neglected."[25] She has prescribed that a considerable portion of them shall be read and piously reflected upon by all her ministers in the daily office of the sacred psalmody. She has ordered that in Cathedral Churches, in monasteries, and in other convents in which study can conveniently be pursued, they shall be expounded and interpreted by capable men; and she has strictly commanded that her children shall be fed with the saving words of the Gospel at least on Sundays and solemn feasts.[26] Moreover, it is owing to the wisdom and exertions of the Church that there has always been continued from century to century that cultivation of Holy Scripture which has been so remarkable and has borne such ample fruit.

7. And here, in order to strengthen Our teaching and Our exhortations, it is well to recall how, from the beginning of Christianity, all who have been renowned for holiness of life and sacred learning have given their deep and constant attention to Holy Scripture. If we consider the immediate disciples of the Apostles, St. Clement of Rome, St. Ignatius of Antioch, St. Polycarp - or the apologists, such as St. Justin and St. Irenaeus, we find that in their letters and their books, whether in defence

---

[24] S. Hier. in *Mic.* i., 10.
[25] Conc. Trid. *sess.* v. *decret. de reform*, I.
[26] *Ibid.* 1-2.

of the Catholic Faith or in its commendation, they draw faith, strength, and unction from the Word of God. When there arose, in various Sees, Catechetical and Theological schools, of which the most celebrated were those of Alexandria and of Antioch, there was little taught in those schools but what was contained in the reading, the interpretation and the defence of the divine written word. From them came forth numbers of Fathers and writers whose laborious studies and admirable writings have justly merited for the three following centuries the appellation of the golden age of biblical exegesis. In the Eastern Church, the greatest name of all is Origen - a man remarkable alike for penetration of genius and for persevering labour; from whose numerous works and his great *Hexapla* almost all have drawn that came after him. Others who have widened the field of this science may also be named, as especially eminent; thus, Alexandria could boast of St. Clement and St. Cyril; Palestine, of Eusebius and the other St. Cyril; Cappadocia, of St. Basil the Great and the two St. Gregories of Nazianzus and Nyssa; Antioch, of St. John Chrysostom, in whom the science of Scripture was rivalled by the splendour of his eloquence. In the Western Church there were many names as great: Tertullian, St. Cyprian, St. Hilary, St. Ambrose, St. Leo the Great, St. Gregory the Great; most famous of all, St. Augustine and St. Jerome, of whom the former was so marvellously acute in penetrating the sense of God's Word and so fertile in the use that he made of it for the promotion of the Catholic truth, and the latter has received from the Church, by reason of his pre-eminent knowledge of Scripture and his labours in promoting its use, the name of the "great Doctor."[27] From this period down to the eleventh century, although Biblical studies did not flourish with the same vigour and the same fruitfulness as before, yet they did flourish, and principally by the instrumentality of the clergy. It was their care and solicitude that selected the best and most useful things that the ancients had left, arranged them in order, and published them with additions of their own - as did S.

---

[27] See the *Collect on his feast*, September 30.

Isidore of Seville, Venerable Bede, and Alcuin, among the most prominent; it was they who illustrated the sacred pages with "glosses" or short commentaries, as we see in Walafrid Strabo and St. Anselm of Laon, or expended fresh labour in securing their integrity, as did St. Peter Damian and Blessed Lanfranc. In the twelfth century many took up with great success the allegorical exposition of Scripture. In this kind, St. Bernard is pre-eminent; and his writings, it may be said, are Scripture all through. With the age of the scholastics came fresh and welcome progress in the study of the Bible. That the scholastics were solicitous about the genuineness of the Latin version is evident from the *Correctoria Biblica*, or lists of emendations, which they have left. But they expended their labours and industry chiefly on interpretation and explanation. To them we owe the accurate and clear distinction, such as had not been given before, of the various senses of the sacred words; the assignment of the value of each "sense" in theology; the division of books into parts, and the summaries of the various parts; the investigation of the objects of the writers; the demonstration of the connection of sentence with sentence, and clause with clause; all of which is calculated to throw much light on the more obscure passages of the sacred volume. The valuable work of the scholastics in Holy Scripture is seen in their theological treatises and in their Scripture commentaries; and in this respect the greatest name among them all is St. Thomas of Aquin.

8. When our predecessor, Clement V., established chairs of Oriental literature in the Roman College and in the principal Universities of Europe, Catholics began to make more accurate investigation on the original text of the Bible, as well as on the Latin version. The revival amongst us of Greek learning, and, much more, the happy invention of the art of printing, gave a strong impetus to Biblical studies. In a brief space of time, innumerable editions, especially of the Vulgate, poured from the press and were diffused throughout the Catholic world; so honoured and loved was Holy Scripture during that very period against which the enemies of the Church direct their calumnies.

Nor must we forget how many learned men there were, chiefly
among the religious orders, who did excellent work for the Bible
between the Council of Vienne and that of Trent; men who, by
the employment of modern means and appliances, and by the
tribute of their own genius and learning, not only added to the
rich stores of ancient times, but prepared the way for the
succeeding century, the century which followed the Council of
Trent, when it almost seemed that the great age of the Fathers
had returned. For it is well known, and We recall it with pleasure,
that Our predecessors from Pius IV to Clement VIII caused to
be prepared the celebrated editions of the Vulgate and the
Septuagint, which, having been published by the command and
authority of Sixtus V and of the same Clement, are now in
common use. At this time, moreover, were carefully brought out
various other ancient versions of the Bible, and the Polyglots of
Antwerp and of Paris, most important for the investigation of
the true meaning of the text; nor is there any one Book of either
Testament which did not find more than one expositor, nor any
grave question which did not profitably exercise the ability of
many inquirers, among whom there are not a few - more
especially of those who made most use of the Fathers - who have
acquired great reputation. From that time downwards the labour
and solicitude of Catholics has never been wanting; for, as time
went on, eminent scholars have carried on Biblical study with
success, and have defended Holy Scripture against rationalism
with the same weapons of philology and kindred sciences with
which it had been attacked. The calm and fair consideration of
what has been said will clearly show that the Church has never
failed in taking due measures to bring the Scriptures within reach
of her children, and that she has ever held fast and exercised
profitably that guardianship conferred upon her by Almighty
God for the protection and glory of His Holy Word; so that she
has never required, nor does she now require, any stimulation
from without.

How to Study Holy Scripture

9. We must now, Venerable Brethren, as our purpose demands, impart to you such counsels as seem best suited for carrying on successfully the study of Biblical science.

10. But first it must be clearly understood whom we have to oppose and contend against, and what are their tactics and their arms. In earlier times the contest was chiefly with those who, relying on private judgment and repudiating the divine traditions and teaching office of the Church, held the Scriptures to be the one source of revelation and the final appeal in matters of Faith. Now, we have to meet the Rationalists, true children and inheritors of the older heretics, who, trusting in their turn to their own way of thinking, have rejected even the scraps and remnants of Christian belief which had been handed down to them. They deny that there is any such thing as revelation or inspiration, or Holy Scripture at all; they see, instead, only the forgeries and the falsehoods of men; they set down the Scripture narratives as stupid fables and lying stories: the prophecies and the oracles of God are to them either predictions made up after the event or forecasts formed by the light of nature; the miracles and the wonders of God's power are not what they are said to be, but the startling effects of natural law, or else mere tricks and myths; and the Apostolic Gospels and writings are not the work of the Apostles at all. These detestable errors, whereby they think they destroy the truth of the divine Books, are obtruded on the world as the peremptory pronouncements of a certain newly-invented "free science;" a science, however, which is so far from final that they are perpetually modifying and supplementing it. And there are some of them who, notwithstanding their impious opinions and utterances about God, and Christ, the Gospels and the rest of Holy Scripture, would faro be considered both theologians and Christians and men of the Gospel, and who attempt to disguise by such honourable names their rashness and their pride. To them we must add not a few professors of other sciences who approve their views and give them assistance, and are urged to attack the Bible by a similar intolerance of revelation. And it is deplorable to see these attacks growing every

day more numerous and more severe. It is sometimes men of learning and judgment who are assailed; but these have little difficulty in defending themselves from evil consequences. The efforts and the arts of the enemy are chiefly directed against the more ignorant masses of the people. They diffuse their deadly poison by means of books, pamphlets, and newspapers; they spread it by addresses and by conversation; they are found everywhere; and they are in possession of numerous schools, taken by violence from the Church, in which, by ridicule and scurrilous jesting, they pervert the credulous and unformed minds of the young to the contempt of Holy Scripture. Should not these things, Venerable Brethren, stir up and set on fire the heart of every Pastor, so that to this "knowledge, falsely so called,"[28] may be opposed the ancient and true science which the Church, through the Apostles, has received from Christ, and that Holy Scripture may find the champions that are needed in so momentous a battle?

11. Let our first care, then be to see that in Seminaries and Academical institutions the study of Holy Scripture be placed on such a footing as its own importance and the circumstances of the time demand. With this view, the first thing which requires attention is the wise choice of Professors. Teachers of Sacred Scripture are not to be appointed at hap-hazard out of the crowd; but they must be men whose character and fitness are proved by their love of, and their long familiarity with, the Bible, and by suitable learning and study.

12. It is a matter of equal importance to provide in time for a continuous succession of such teachers; and it will be well, wherever this can be done, to select young men of good promise who have successfully accomplished their theological course, and to set them apart exclusively for Holy Scripture, affording them facilities for full and complete studies. Professors thus chosen and thus prepared may enter with confidence on the task that is

---

[28] 1 Tim. vi., 20.

appointed for them; and that they may carry out their work well and profitably, let them take heed to the instructions We now proceed to give.

13. At the commencement of a course of Holy Scripture let the Professor strive earnestly to form the judgment of the young beginners so as to train them equally to defend the sacred writings and to penetrate their meaning. This is the object of the treatise which is called "Introduction." Here the student is taught how to prove the integrity and authority of the Bible, how to investigate and ascertain its true sense, and how to meet and refute objections. It is needless to insist upon the importance of making these preliminary studies in an orderly and thorough fashion, with the accompaniment and assistance of Theology; for the whole subsequent course must rest on the foundation thus laid and make use of the light thus acquired. Next, the teacher will turn his earnest attention to that more fruitful division of Scripture science which has to do with Interpretation; wherein is imparted the method of using the word of God for the advantage of religion and piety. We recognize without hesitation that neither the extent of the matter nor the time at disposal allows each single Book of the Bible to be separately gone through. But the teaching should result in a definite and ascertained method of interpretation-and therefore the Professor should equally avoid the mistake of giving a mere taste of every Book, and of dwelling at too great length on a part of one Book. If most schools cannot do what is done in the large institutions- that is, take the students through the whole of one or two Books continuously and with a certain development-yet at least those parts which are selected should be treated with suitable fulness; in such a way that the students may learn from the sample that is thus put before them to love and use the remainder of the sacred Book during the whole of their lives. The Professor, following the tradition of antiquity, will make use of the Vulgate as his text; for the Council of Trent decreed that "in public lectures, disputations, preaching, and exposition,"[29] the Vulgate is the

"authentic" version; and this is the existing custom of the Church. At the same time, the other versions which Christian antiquity has approved, should not be neglected, more especially the more ancient MSS. For although the meaning of the Hebrew and Greek is substantially rendered by the Vulgate, nevertheless wherever there may be ambiguity or want of clearness, the "examination of older tongues,"[30] to quote St. Augustine, will be useful and advantageous. But in this matter we need hardly say that the greatest prudence is required, for the "office of a commentator," as St. Jerome says, "is to set forth not what he himself would prefer, but what his author says."[31] The question of "readings" having been, when necessary, carefully discussed, the next thing is to investigate and expound the meaning. And the first counsel to be given is this: That the more our adversaries contend to the contrary, so much the more solicitously should we adhere to the received and approved canons of interpretation. Hence, whilst weighing the meanings of words, the connection of ideas, the parallelism of passages, and the like, we should by all means make use of such illustrations as can be drawn from apposite erudition of an external sort; but this should be done with caution, so as not to bestow on questions of this kind more labour and time than are spent on the Sacred Books themselves, and not to overload the minds of the students with a mass of information that will be rather a hindrance than a help.

Holy Scripture and Theology; Interpretation; the Fathers

14. The Professor may now safely pass on to the use of Scripture in matters of Theology. On this head it must be observed that in addition to the usual reasons which make ancient writings more or less difficult to understand, there are some which are peculiar to the Bible. For the language of the Bible is employed to

---

[29] *Sess.* iv., *decr. de edit. et usu sacr. libror.*
[30] *De doctr. chr.* iii., 4.
[31] *Ad Pammachium.*

express, under the inspiration of the Holy Ghost, many things which are beyond the power and scope of the reason of man - that is to say, divine mysteries and all that is related to them. There is sometimes in such passages a fullness and a hidden depth of meaning which the letter hardly expresses and which the laws of interpretation hardly warrant. Moreover, the literal sense itself frequently admits other senses, adapted to illustrate dogma or to confirm morality. Wherefore it must be recognized that the sacred writings are wrapt in a certain religious obscurity, and that no one can enter into their interior without a guide;[32] God so disposing, as the Holy Fathers commonly teach, in order that men may investigate them with greater ardour and earnestness, and that what is attained with difficulty may sink more deeply into the mind and heart; and, most of all, that they may understand that God has delivered the Holy Scriptures to the Church, and that in reading and making use of His Word, they must follow the Church as their guide and their teacher. St. Irenaeus long since laid down, that where the *charismata* of God were, there the truth was to be learnt, and that Holy Scripture was safely interpreted by those who had the Apostolic succession.[33] His teaching, and that of other Holy Fathers, is taken up by the Council of the Vatican, which, in renewing the decree of Trent declares its "mind" to be this - that "in things of faith and morals, belonging to the building up of Christian doctrine, that is to be considered the true sense of Holy Scripture which has been held and is held by our Holy Mother the Church, whose place it is to judge of the true sense and interpretation of the Scriptures; and therefore that it is permitted to no one to interpret Holy Scripture against such sense or also against the unanimous agreement of the Fathers."[34] By this most wise decree the Church by no means prevents or restrains the pursuit of Biblical science, but rather protects it from error, and largely assists its real progress. A wide field is still left open to the

---

[32] S. Hier. ad Paulin. *de studio Script. ep*. liii., 4.

[33] *C. haer*. iv., 26, 5.

[34] *Sess*. iii., cap. ii., de revel.; cf. Conc. Trid, *sess*. iv. *decret de edit. et usu sacr. libror.*

private student, in which his hermeneutical skill may display itself with signal effect and to the advantage of the Church. On the one hand, in those passages of Holy Scripture which have not as yet received a certain and definitive interpretation, such labours may, in the benignant providence of God, prepare for and bring to maturity the judgment of the Church; on the other, in passages already defined, the private student may do work equally valuable, either by setting them forth more clearly to the flock and more skilfully to scholars, or by defending them more powerfully from hostile attack. Wherefore the first and dearest object of the Catholic commentator should be to interpret those passages which have received an authentic interpretation either from the sacred writers themselves, under the inspiration of the Holy Ghost (as in many places of the New Testament), or from the Church, under the assistance of the same Holy Spirit, whether by her solemn judgment or her ordinary and universal *magisterium*[35] - to interpret these passages in that identical sense, and to prove, by all the resources of science, that sound hermeneutical laws admit of no other interpretation. In the other passages, the analogy of faith should be followed, and Catholic doctrine, as authoritatively proposed by the Church, should be held as the supreme law; for, seeing that the same God is the author both of the Sacred Books and of the doctrine committed to the Church, it is clearly impossible that any teaching can by legitimate means be extracted from the former, which shall in any respect be at variance with the latter. Hence it follows that all interpretation is foolish and false which either makes the sacred writers disagree one with another, or is opposed to the doctrine of the Church. The Professor of Holy Scripture, therefore, amongst other recommendations, must be well acquainted with the whole circle of Theology and deeply read in the commentaries of the Holy Fathers and Doctors, and other interpreters of mark.[36] This is inculcated by St. Jerome, and still more frequently by St. Augustine, who thus justly complains: "If there is no branch of teaching, however humble and easy to

---

[35] Conc. Vat. *sess.* iii., cap. ii., *de fide.*
[36] *Ibid.* 6, 7.

learn, which does not require a master, what can be a greater sign of rashness and pride than to refuse to study the Books of the divine mysteries by the help of those who have interpreted them?"[37] The other Fathers have said the same, and have confirmed it by their example, for they "endeavoured to acquire the understanding of the Holy Scriptures not by their own lights and ideas, but from the writings and authority of the ancients, who in their turn, as we know, received the rule of interpretation in direct line from the Apostles."[38] The Holy Fathers "to whom, after the Apostles, the Church owes its growth - who have planted, watered, built, governed, and cherished it,"[39] the Holy Fathers, We say, are of supreme authority, whenever they all interpret in one and the same manner any text of the Bible, as pertaining to the doctrine of faith or morals; for their unanimity clearly evinces that such interpretation has come down from the Apostles as a matter of Catholic faith. The opinion of the Fathers is also of very great weight when they treat of these matters in their capacity of doctors, unofficially; not only because they excel in their knowledge of revealed doctrine and in their acquaintance with many things which are useful in understanding the apostolic Books, but because they are men of eminent sanctity and of ardent zeal for the truth, on whom God has bestowed a more ample measure of His light. Wherefore the expositor should make it his duty to follow their footsteps with all reverence, and to use their labours with intelligent appreciation.

15. But he must not on that account consider that it is forbidden, when just cause exists, to push inquiry and exposition beyond what the Fathers have done; provided he carefully observes the rule so wisely laid down by St. Augustine-not to depart from the literal and obvious sense, except only where reason makes it untenable or necessity requires;[40] a rule to which it is the more necessary to adhere strictly in these times, when the thirst for

---

[37] Ad Honorat. *de util. cred.* xvii., 35.
[38] Rufinus *Hist eccl.* ii., 9.
[39] S. Aug. c. Julian. ii, 10, 37.
[40] *De Gen. ad litt.* I, viii., c. 7, 13.

novelty and unrestrained freedom of thought make the danger of error most real and proximate. Neither should those passages be neglected which the Fathers have understood in an allegorical or figurative sense, more especially when such interpretation is justified by the literal, and when it rests on the authority of many. For this method of interpretation has been received by the Church from the Apostles, and has been approved by her own practice, as the holy Liturgy attests; although it is true that the holy Fathers did not thereby pretend directly to demonstrate dogmas of faith, but used it as a means of promoting virtue and piety, such as, by their own experience, they knew to be most valuable. The authority of other Catholic interpreters is not so great; but the study of Scripture has always continued to advance in the Church, and, therefore, these commentaries also have their own honourable place, and are serviceable in many ways for the refutation of assailants and the explanation of difficulties. But it is most unbecoming to pass by, in ignorance or contempt, the excellent work which Catholics have left in abundance, and to have recourse to the works of non-Catholics - and to seek in them, to the detriment of sound doctrine and often to the peril of faith, the explanation of passages on which Catholics long ago have successfully employed their talent and their labour. For although the studies of non-Catholics, used with prudence, may sometimes be of use to the Catholic student, he should, nevertheless, bear well in mind-as the Fathers also teach in numerous passages[41] - that the sense of Holy Scripture can nowhere be found incorrupt outside of the Church, and cannot be expected to be found in writers who, being without the true faith, only gnaw the bark of the Sacred Scripture, and never attain its pith.

16. Most desirable is it, and most essential, that the whole teaching of Theology should be pervaded and animated by the use of the divine Word of God. This is what the Fathers and the

---

[41] Cfr. Clem. Alex. *Strom.* vii., 16; Orig. *de princ.* iv., 8; *in Levit. hom.* 4, 8; Tertull. *de praescr.* 15, *seqq.*; S. Hilar. Pict. *in Matth.* 13, I.

greatest theologians of all ages have desired and reduced to practice. It was chiefly out of the Sacred Writings that they endeavoured to proclaim and establish the Articles of Faith and the truths therewith connected, and it was in them, together with divine Tradition, that they found the refutation of heretical error, and the reasonableness, the true meaning, and the mutual relation of the truths of Catholicism. Nor will any one wonder at this who considers that the Sacred Books hold such an eminent position among the sources of revelation that without their assiduous study and use, Theology cannot be placed on its true footing, or treated as its dignity demands. For although it is right and proper that students in academies and schools should be chiefly exercised in acquiring a scientific knowledge of dogma, by means of reasoning from the Articles of Faith to their consequences, according to the rules of approved and sound philosophy - nevertheless the judicious and instructed theologian will by no means pass by that method of doctrinal demonstration which draws its proof from the authority of the Bible; "for (Theology) does not receive her first principles from any other science, but immediately from God by revelation. And, therefore, she does not receive of other sciences as from a superior, but uses them as her inferiors or handmaids."[42] It is this view of doctrinal teaching which is laid down and recommended by the prince of theologians, St. Thomas Aquinas;[43] who, moreover, shows - such being the essential character of Christian Theology - how she can defend her own principles against attack: "If the adversary," he says, "do but grant any portion of the divine revelation, we have an argument against him; thus, against a heretic we can employ Scripture authority, and against those who deny one article, we can use another. But if our opponent reject divine revelation entirely, there is then no way left to prove the Article of Faith by reasoning; we can only solve the difficulties which are raised against them."[44] Care must be taken, then, that beginners approach the study of the Bible well prepared and

[42] S. Greg. M. *Moral* xx., 9 (al. II).
[43] *Summ. theol.* p. i., q. i., a. 5 ad 2.
[44] *Ibid.* a. 8.

furnished; otherwise, just hopes will be frustrated, or, perchance, what is worse, they will unthinkingly risk the danger of error, falling an easy prey to the sophisms and laboured erudition of the Rationalists. The best preparation will be a conscientious application to philosophy and theology under the guidance of St. Thomas Aquinas, and a thorough training therein - as We ourselves have elsewhere pointed out and directed. By this means, both in Biblical studies and in that part of Theology which is called positive, they will pursue the right path and make satisfactory progress.

The Authority of Holy Scripture; Modern Criticism; Physical Science

17. To prove, to expound, to illustrate Catholic Doctrine by the legitimate and skilful interpretation of the Bible, is much; but there is a second part of the subject of equal importance and equal difficulty - the maintenance in the strongest possible way of its full authority. This cannot be done completely or satisfactorily except by means of the living and proper *magisterium* of the Church. The Church, "by reason of her wonderful propagation, her distinguished sanctity and inexhaustible fecundity in good, her Catholic unity, and her unshaken stability, is herself a great and perpetual motive of credibility, and an unassailable testimony to her own Divine mission."[45] But since the divine and infallible *magisterium* of the Church rests also on the authority of Holy Scripture, the first thing to be done is to vindicate the trustworthiness of the sacred records at least as human documents, from which can be clearly proved, as from primitive and authentic testimony, the Divinity and the mission of Christ our Lord, the institution of a hierarchical Church and the primacy of Peter and his successors. It is most desirable, therefore, that there should be numerous members of the clergy well prepared to enter upon a contest of this nature, and to repulse hostile assaults, chiefly trusting in that armour of God recommended by the Apostle,[46] but also not unaccustomed to

---

[45] Conc. Vat. sess. iii., c. iii. *de fide*.

modern methods of attack. This is beautifully alluded to by St. John Chrysostom, when describing the duties of priests: "We must use every endeavour that the 'Word of God may dwell in us abundantly'[47] and not merely for one kind of fight must we be prepared-for the contest is many-sided and the enemy is of every sort; and they do not all use the same weapons nor make their onset in the same way. Wherefore it is needful that the man who has to contend against all should be acquainted with the engines and the arts of all-that he should be at once archer and slinger, commandant and officer, general and private soldier, foot-soldier and horseman, skilled in sea-fight and in siege; for unless he knows every trick and turn of war, the devil is well able, if only a single door be left open, to get in his fierce bands and carry off the sheep."[48] The sophisms of the enemy and his manifold arts of attack we have already touched upon. Let us now say a word of advice on the means of defence. The first means is the study of the Oriental languages and of the art of criticism. These two acquirements are in these days held in high estimation, and therefore the clergy, by making themselves more or less fully acquainted with them as time and place may demand, will the better be able to discharge their office with becoming credit; for they must make themselves "all to all,"[49] always "ready to satisfy every one that asketh them a reason for the hope that is in them."[50] Hence it is most proper that Professors of Sacred Scripture and theologians should master those tongues in which the sacred Books were originally written; and it would be well that Church students also should cultivate them, more especially those who aspire to academic degrees. And endeavours should be made to establish in all academic institutions - as has already been laudably done in many - chairs of the other ancient languages, especially the Semitic, and of subjects connected therewith, for the benefit principally of those who are intended

---

[46] Eph. vi., 13, *seqq*.
[47] Cfr., *Coloss*. iii., 16.
[48] *De sacerdotio* iv., 4.
[49] I Cor. ix., 22.
[50] I Peter iii., 15.

to profess sacred literature. These latter, with a similar object in view, should make themselves well and thoroughly acquainted with the art of true criticism. There has arisen, to the great detriment of religion, an inept method, dignified by the name of the "higher criticism," which pretends to judge of the origin, integrity and authority of each Book from internal indications alone. It is clear, on the other hand, that in historical questions, such as the origin and the handing down of writings, the witness of history is of primary importance, and that historical investigation should be made with the utmost care; and that in this matter internal evidence is seldom of great value, except as confirmation. To look upon it in any other light will be to open the door to many evil consequences. It will make the enemies of religion much more bold and confident in attacking and mangling the Sacred Books; and this vaunted "higher criticism" will resolve itself into the reflection of the bias and the prejudice of the critics. It will not throw on the Scripture the light which is sought, or prove of any advantage to doctrine; it will only give rise to disagreement and dissension, those sure notes of error, which the critics in question so plentifully exhibit in their own persons; and seeing that most of them are tainted with false philosophy and rationalism, it must lead to the elimination from the sacred writings of all prophecy and miracle, and of everything else that is outside the natural order.

18. In the second place, we have to contend against those who, making an evil use of physical science, minutely scrutinize the Sacred Book in order to detect the writers in a mistake, and to take occasion to vilify its contents. Attacks of this kind, bearing as they do on matters of sensible experience, are peculiarly dangerous to the masses, and also to the young who are beginning their literary studies; for the young, if they lose their reverence for the Holy Scripture on one or more points, are easily led to give up believing in it altogether. It need not be pointed out how the nature of science, just as it is so admirably adapted to show forth the glory of the Great Creator, provided it be taught as it should be, so if it be perversely imparted to the

youthful intelligence, it may prove most fatal in destroying the principles of true philosophy and in the corruption of morality. Hence to the Professor of Sacred Scripture a knowledge of natural science will be of very great assistance in detecting such attacks on the Sacred Books, and in refuting them. There can never, indeed, be any real discrepancy between the theologian and the physicist, as long as each confines himself within his own lines, and both are careful, as St. Augustine warns us, "not to make rash assertions, or to assert what is not known as known."[51] If dissension should arise between them, here is the rule also laid down by St. Augustine, for the theologian: "Whatever they can really demonstrate to be true of physical nature, we must show to be capable of reconciliation with our Scriptures; and whatever they assert in their treatises which is contrary to these Scriptures of ours, that is to Catholic faith, we must either prove it as well as we can to be entirely false, or at all events we must, without the smallest hesitation, believe it to be so."[52] To understand how just is the rule here formulated we must remember, first, that the sacred writers, or to speak more accurately, the Holy Ghost "Who spoke by them, did not intend to teach men these things (that is to say, the essential nature of the things of the visible universe), things in no way profitable unto salvation."[53] Hence they did not seek to penetrate the secrets of nature, but rather described and dealt with things in more or less figurative language, or in terms which were commonly used at the time, and which in many instances are in daily use at this day, even by the most eminent men of science. Ordinary speech primarily and properly describes what comes under the senses; and somewhat in the same way the sacred writers-as the Angelic Doctor also reminds us - `went by what sensibly appeared,"[54] or put down what God, speaking to men, signified, in the way men could understand and were accustomed to.

---

[51] *In Gen. op. imperf.* ix., 30.
[52] *De Gen. ad litt.* i. 21, 41.
[53] S. Aug. *ib*. ii., 9, 20.
[54] *Summa theol.* p. I, q. lxx., a. I, ad 3.

19. The unshrinking defence of the Holy Scripture, however, does not require that we should equally uphold all the opinions which each of the Fathers or the more recent interpreters have put forth in explaining it; for it may be that, in commenting on passages where physical matters occur, they have sometimes expressed the ideas of their own times, and thus made statements which in these days have been abandoned as incorrect. Hence, in their interpretations, we must carefully note what they lay down as belonging to faith, or as intimately connected with faith-what they are unanimous in. For "in those things which do not come under the obligation of faith, the Saints were at liberty to hold divergent opinions, just as we ourselves are,"[55] according to the saying of St. Thomas. And in another place he says most admirably: "When philosophers are agreed upon a point, and it is not contrary to our faith, it is safer, in my opinion, neither to lay down such a point as a dogma of faith, even though it is perhaps so presented by the philosophers, nor to reject it as against faith, lest we thus give to the wise of this world an occasion of despising our faith."[56] The Catholic interpreter, although he should show that those facts of natural science which investigators affirm to be now quite certain are not contrary to the Scripture rightly explained, must nevertheless always bear in mind, that much which has been held and proved as certain has afterwards been called in question and rejected. And if writers on physics travel outside the boundaries of their own branch, and carry their erroneous teaching into the domain of philosophy, let them be handed over to philosophers for

Inspiration Incompatible with Error

20. The principles here laid down will apply cognate sciences, and especially to History. It is a lamentable fact that there are many who with great labour carry out and publish investigations on the monuments of antiquity, the manners and institutions of

---

[55] *In Sent.* ii., Dist. q. i., a. 3.
[56] *Opusc.* x.

nations and other illustrative subjects, and whose chief purpose in all this is too often to find mistakes in the sacred writings and so to shake and weaken their authority. Some of these writers display not only extreme hostility, but the greatest unfairness; in their eyes a profane book or ancient document is accepted without hesitation, whilst the Scripture, if they only find in it a suspicion of error, is set down with the slightest possible discussion as quite untrustworthy. It is true, no doubt, that copyists have made mistakes in the text of the Bible; this question, when it arises, should be carefully considered on its merits, and the fact not too easily admitted, but only in those passages where the proof is clear. It may also happen that the sense of a passage remains ambiguous, and in this case good hermeneutical methods will greatly assist in clearing up the obscurity. But it is absolutely wrong and forbidden, either to narrow inspiration to certain parts only of Holy Scripture, or to admit that the sacred writer has erred. For the system of those who, in order to rid themselves of these difficulties, do not hesitate to concede that divine inspiration regards the things of faith and morals, and nothing beyond, because (as they wrongly think) in a question of the truth or falsehood of a passage, we should consider not so much what God has said as the reason and purpose which He had in mind in saying it-this system cannot be tolerated. For all the books which the Church receives as sacred and canonical, are written wholly and entirely, with all their parts, at the dictation of the Holy Ghost; and so far is it from being possible that any error can co-exist with inspiration, that inspiration not only is essentially incompatible with error, but excludes and rejects it as absolutely and necessarily as it is impossible that God Himself, the supreme Truth, can utter that which is not true. This is the ancient and unchanging faith of the Church, solemnly defined in the Councils of Florence and of Trent, and finally confirmed and more expressly formulated by the Council of the Vatican. These are the words of the last: "The Books of the Old and New Testament, whole and entire, with all their parts, as enumerated in the decree of the same Council (Trent) and in the ancient Latin Vulgate, are to be received as sacred and canonical. And the Church holds them as sacred and canonical, not because, having been composed by human industry, they were afterwards approved by her authority; nor only because they contain revelation without error; but because, having been written under the inspiration of the Holy Ghost, they have God for their author."[57] Hence, because the Holy Ghost employed men as His instruments, we cannot therefore say that it was these inspired instruments who, perchance, have fallen into error, and not the primary author. For, by supernatural power, He so moved and impelled them to write-He was so present to them-that the things which He ordered, and those only, they, first, rightly understood, then willed faithfully to write down, and finally expressed in apt words and with infallible truth. Otherwise, it could not be said that He was the Author of the entire Scripture. Such has always been the persuasion of the Fathers. "Therefore," says St. Augustine, "since they wrote the things which He showed and uttered to them, it cannot be pretended that He is not the writer; for His members executed what their Head dictated."[58] And St. Gregory the Great thus pronounces: "Most superfluous it is to inquire who wrote these things-we loyally believe the Holy Ghost to be the Author of the book. He wrote it Who dictated it for writing; He wrote it Who inspired its execution. "[59]

21. It follows that those who maintain that an error is possible in any genuine passage of the sacred writings, either pervert the Catholic notion of inspiration, or make God the author of such error. And so emphatically were all the Fathers and Doctors agreed that the divine writings, as left by the hagiographers, are free from all error, that they laboured earnestly, with no less skill than reverence, to reconcile with each other those numerous passages which seem at variance - the very passages which in great measure have been taken up by the "higher criticism;" for they were unanimous in laying it down, that those writings, in

---

[57] *Sess.* iii., c. ii., *de Rev.*
[58] *De consensu Evangel.* 1. I, c. 35.
[59] *Praef.* in Job, n. 2.

their entirety and in all their parts were equally from the *afflatus* of Almighty God, and that God, speaking by the sacred writers, could not set down anything but what was true. The words of St. Augustine to St. Jerome may sum up what they taught: "On my part I confess to your charity that it is only to those Books of Scripture which are now called canonical that I have learned to pay such honour and reverence as to believe most firmly that none of their writers has fallen into any error. And if in these Books I meet anything which seems contrary to truth, I shall not hesitate to conclude either that the text is faulty, or that the translator has not expressed the meaning of the passage, or that I myself do not understand."[60]

22. But to undertake fully and perfectly, and with all the weapons of the best science, the defence of the Holy Bible is far more than can be looked for from the exertions of commentators and theologians alone. It is an enterprise in which we have a right to expect the co-operation of all those Catholics who have acquired reputation in any branch of learning whatever. As in the past, so at the present time, the Church is never without the graceful support of her accomplished children; may their services to the Faith grow and increase! For there is nothing which We believe to be more needful than that truth should find defenders more powerful and more numerous than the enemies it has to face; nor is there anything which is better calculated to impress the masses with respect for truth than to see it boldly proclaimed by learned and distinguished men. Moreover, the bitter tongues of objectors will be silenced, or at least they will not dare to insist so shamelessly that faith is the enemy of science, when they see that scientific men of eminence in their profession show towards faith the most marked honour and respect. Seeing, then, that those can do so much for the advantage of religion on whom the goodness of Almighty God has bestowed, together with the grace of the faith, great natural talent, let such men, in this bitter conflict of which the Holy Scripture is the object, select each of

---

[60] Ep. lxxxii., i. *et crebrius alibi.*

them the branch of study most suitable to his circumstances, and endeavour to excel therein, and thus be prepared to repulse with credit and distinction the assaults on the Word of God. And it is Our pleasing duty to give deserved praise to a work which certain Catholics have taken up-that is to say, the formation of societies and the contribution of considerable sums of money, for the purpose of supplying studious and learned men with every kind of help and assistance in carrying out complete studies. Truly an excellent fashion of investing money, and well-suited to the times in which we live! The less hope of public patronage there is for Catholic study, the more ready and the more abundant should be the liberality of private persons-those to whom God has given riches thus willingly making use of their means to safeguard the treasure of His revealed doctrine.

Summary

23. In order that all these endeavours and exertions may really prove advantageous to the cause of the Bible, let scholars keep steadfastly to the principles which We have in this Letter laid down. Let them loyally hold that God, the Creator and Ruler of all things, is also the Author of the Scriptures - and that therefore nothing can be proved either by physical science or archaeology which can really contradict the Scriptures. If, then, apparent contradiction be met with, every effort should be made to remove it. Judicious theologians and commentators should be consulted as to what is the true or most probable meaning of the passage in discussion, and the hostile arguments should be carefully weighed. Even if the difficulty is after all not cleared up and the discrepancy seems to remain, the contest must not be abandoned; truth cannot contradict truth, and we may be sure that some mistake has been made either in the interpretation of the sacred words, or in the polemical discussion itself; and if no such mistake can be detected, we must then suspend judgment for the time being. There have been objections without number perseveringly directed against the Scripture for many a long year, which have been proved to be futile and are now never heard of;

and not unfrequently interpretations have been placed on certain passages of Scripture (not belonging to the rule of faith or morals) which have been rectified by more careful investigations. As time goes on, mistaken views die and disappear; but "truth remaineth and groweth stronger for ever and ever."[61] Wherefore, as no one should be so presumptuous as to think that he understands the whole of the Scripture, in which St. Augustine himself confessed that there was more that he did not know, than that he knew,[62] so, if he should come upon anything that seems incapable of solution, he must take to heart the cautious rule of the same holy Doctor: "It is better even to be oppressed by unknown but useful signs, than to interpret them uselessly and thus to throw off the yoke only to be caught in the trap of error."[63]

24. Such, Venerable Brethren, are the admonitions and the instructions which, by the help of God, We have thought it well, at the present moment, to offer to you on the study of Holy Scripture. It will now be your province to see that what we have said be observed and put in practice with all due reverence and exactness; that so, we may prove our gratitude to God for the communication to man of the Words of his Wisdom, and that all the good results so much to be desired may be realized, especially as they affect the training of the students of the Church, which is our own great solicitude and the Church's hope. Exert yourselves with willing alacrity, and use your authority and your persuasion in order that these studies may be held in just regard and may flourish, in Seminaries and in the educational Institutions which are under your jurisdiction. Let them flourish in completeness and in happy success, under the direction of the Church, in accordance with the salutary teaching and example of the Holy Fathers and the laudable traditions of antiquity; and, as time goes on, let them be widened and extended as the interests and glory of truth may require - the interest of that Catholic Truth which

[61] 3 Esdr. iv., 38.
[62] ad Ianuar. *ep.* lv., 21.
[63] *De doctr. chr.* iii., 9, 18.

comes from above, the never-failing source of man's salvation. Finally, We admonish with paternal love all students and ministers of the Church always to approach the Sacred Writings with reverence and piety; for it is impossible to attain to the profitable understanding thereof unless the arrogance of "earthly" science be laid aside, and there be excited in the heart the holy desire for that wisdom "which is from above." In this way the intelligence which is once admitted to these sacred studies, and thereby illuminated and strengthened, will acquire a marvellous facility in detecting and avoiding the fallacies of human science, and in gathering and using for eternal salvation all that is valuable and precious; whilst at the same time the heart will grow warm, and will strive with ardent longing to advance in virtue and in divine love. "Blessed are they who examine His testimonies; they shall seek Him with their whole heart."[64]

25. And now, filled with hope in the divine assistance, and trusting to your pastoral solicitude - as a pledge of heavenly grace and a sign of Out special goodwill - to you all, and to the Clergy and the whole flock entrusted to you, We lovingly impart in Our Lord the Apostolic Benediction.

Given at St. Peter's, at Rome, the 18th day of November, 1893, the eighteenth year of Our Pontificate.

---

[64] Ps. xviii., 2.

XII: Satis Cognitum

June 29, 1896

ON THE UNITY OF THE CHURCH

It is sufficiently well known unto you that no small share of Our thoughts and of Our care is devoted to Our endeavour to bring back to the *fold*, placed under the guardianship of Jesus Christ, the Chief Pastor of souls, sheep that have strayed. Bent upon this, We have thought it most conducive to this salutary end and purpose to describe the exemplar and, as it were, the lineaments of the Church. Amongst these the most worthy of Our chief consideration is *Unity*. This the Divine Author impressed on it as a lasting sign of truth and of unconquerable strength. The essential beauty and comeliness of the Church ought greatly to influence the minds of those who consider it. Nor is it improbable that ignorance may be dispelled by the consideration; that false ideas and prejudices may be dissipated from the minds chiefly of those who find themselves in error without fault of theirs; and that even a love for the Church may be stirred up in the souls of men, like unto that charity wherewith Christ loved and united himself to that spouse redeemed by His precious blood. "Christ loved the Church, and delivered Himself up for it"[1]

If those about to come back to their most loving Mother (not yet fully known, or culpably abandoned) should perceive that their return involves, not indeed the shedding of their blood (at which price nevertheless the Church was bought by Jesus Christ), but some lesser trouble and labour, let them clearly understand that this burden has been laid on them not by the will of man but by the will and command of God. They may thus, by the help of heavenly grace, realize and feel the truth of the divine saying, "My yoke is sweet and my burden light."[2]

---

[1] Eph. 5:25.

275

Wherefore, having put all Our hope in the "Father of lights,"
from whom "cometh every best gift and every perfect gift"[3] -
from Him, namely, who alone "gives the increase"[4] - We
earnestly pray that He will graciously grant Us the power of
bringing conviction home to the minds of men.

Human Co-operation

2. Although God can do by His own power all that is effected by
created natures, nevertheless in the counsels of His loving
Providence He has preferred to help men by the instrumentality
of men. And, as in the natural order He does not usually give full
perfection except by means of man's work and action, so also He
makes use of human aid for that which lies beyond the limits of
nature, that is to say, for the sanctification and salvation of souls.
But it is obvious that nothing can be communicated amongst
men save by means of external things which the senses can
perceive. For this reason the Son of God assumed human
nature-"who being in the form of God.... emptied himself, taking
the form of a servant, being made in the likeness of man"[5] -and
thus living on earth He taught his doctrine and gave His laws,
conversing with men.

The Church Always Visible

3. And, since it was necessary that His divine mission should be
perpetuated to the end of rime, He took to Himself Disciples,
trained by himself, and made them partakers of His own
authority. And, when He had invoked upon them from Heaven
the *Spirit of Truth*, He bade them go through the whole world and
faithfully preach to all nations, what He had taught and what He
had commanded, so that by the profession of His doctrine, and

---

[2] Matt. 6:30.
[3] Ep. James 1:17.
[4] 1 Cor. 3:6.
[5] Philipp. 2:6-7.

the observance of His laws, the human race might attain to holiness on earth and never-ending happiness in Heaven. In this wise, and on this principle, the Church was begotten. If we consider the chief end of His Church and the proximate efficient causes of salvation, it is undoubtedly *spiritual*; but in regard to those who constitute it, and to the things which lead to these spiritual gifts, it is *external* and necessarily visible. The Apostles received a mission to teach by visible and audible signs, and they discharged their mission only by words and acts which certainly appealed to the senses. So that their voices falling upon the ears of those who heard them begot faith in souls-"Faith cometh by hearing, and hearing by the words of Christ."[6] And faith itself - that is assent given to the first and supreme truth - though residing essentially in the intellect, must be manifested by outward profession-"For with the heart we believe unto justice, but with the mouth confession is made unto salvation."[7] In the same way in man, nothing is more internal than heavenly grace which begets sanctity, but the ordinary and chief means of obtaining grace are external: that is to say, the sacraments which are administered by men specially chosen for that purpose, by means of certain ordinances.

Jesus Christ commanded His Apostles and their successors to the end of time to teach and rule the nations. He ordered the nations to accept their teaching and obey their authority. But his correlation of rights and duties in the Christian commonwealth not only could not have been made permanent, but could not even have been initiated except through the senses, which are of all things the messengers and interpreters.

For this reason the Church is so often called in Holy Writ a *body*, and even the body of Christ - "Now you are the body of Christ"[8] -and precisely because it is a body is the Church visible: and

---

[6] Rom. 10:17.
[7] Rom. 10:10.
[8] 1 Cor. 12:27.

because it is the body of Christ is it living and energizing, because by the infusion of His power Christ guards and sustains it, just as the vine gives nourishment and renders fruitful the branches united to it. And as in animals the vital principle is unseen and invisible, and is evidenced and manifested by the movements and action of the members, so the principle of supernatural life in the Church is clearly shown in that which is done by it.

From this it follows that those who arbitrarily conjure up and picture to themselves a hidden and invisible Church are in grievous and pernicious error: as also are those who regard the Church as a human institution which claims a certain obedience in discipline and external duties, but which is without the perennial communication of the gifts of divine grace, and without all that which testifies by constant and undoubted signs to the existence of that life which is drawn from God. It is assuredly as impossible that the Church of Jesus Christ can be the one or the other, as that man should be a body alone or a soul alone. The connection and union of both elements is as absolutely necessary to the true Church as the intimate union of the soul and body is to human nature. The Church is not something dead: it is the body of Christ endowed with supernatural life. As Christ, the Head and Exemplar, is not wholly in His visible human nature, which Photinians and Nestorians assert, nor wholly in the invisible divine nature, as the Monophysites hold, but is one, from and in both natures, visible and invisible; so the mystical body of Christ is the true Church, only because its visible parts draw life and power from the supernatural gifts and other things whence spring their very nature and essence. But since the Church is *such* by divine will and constitution, *such* it must uniformly remain to the end of time. If it did nor, then it would not have been founded as perpetual, and the end set before it would have been limited to some certain place and to some certain period of time; both of which are contrary to the truth. The union consequently of visible and invisible elements because it harmonizes with the natural order and by God's will belongs to the very essence of the Church, must necessarily remain so long as the Church itself shall endure. Wherefore Chrysostom writes: "Secede not from the Church: for nothing is stronger than the Church. Thy hope is the Church; thy salvation is the Church; thy refuge is the Church. It is higher than the heavens and wider than the earth. It never grows old, but is ever full of vigour. Wherefore Holy Writ pointing to its strength and stability calls it a mountain."[9]

Also Augustine says: "Unbelievers think that the Christian religion will last for a certain period in the world and will then disappear. But it will remain as long as the sun - as long as the sun rises and sets: that is, as long as the ages of time shall roll, the Church of God - the true body of Christ on earth - will not disappear."[10] And in another place: "The Church will totter if its foundation shakes; but how can Christ be moved?...Christ remaining immovable, it (the Church), shall never be shaken. Where are they that say that the Church has disappeared from the world, when it cannot even be shaken?"[11]

He who seeks the truth must be guided by these fundamental principles. That is to say, that Christ the Lord instituted and formed the Church: wherefore when we are asked what its nature is, the main thing is to see what Christ wished and what in fact He did. Judged by such a criterion it is the unity of the Church which must be principally considered; and of this, for the general good, it has seemed useful to speak in this Encyclical.

How Christ Made His Church

4. It is so evident from the clear and frequent testimonies of Holy Writ that the true Church of Jesus Christ is *one*, that no Christian can dare to deny it. But in judging and determining the

---

[9] Hom. De capto Eutropio, n. 6.
[10] In Psalm. lxx., n. 8.
[11] Enarratio in Psalm. ciii., sermo ii., n. 5

nature of this unity many have erred in various ways. Not the foundation of the Church alone, but its whole constitution, belongs to the class of things effected by Christ's free choice. For this reason the entire case must be judged by what was actually done. We must consequently investigate not how the Church may possibly be one, but how He, who founded it, willed that it should be one.

But when we consider what was actually done we find that Jesus Christ did not, in point of fact, institute a Church to embrace several communities similar in nature, but in themselves distinct, and lacking those bonds which render the Church unique and indivisible after that manner in which in the symbol of our faith we profess: "I believe in one Church."

"The Church in respect of its unity belongs to the category of things indivisible by nature, though heretics try to divide it into many parts...We say, therefore, that the Catholic Church is unique in its essence, in its doctrine, in its origin, and in its excellence...Furthermore, the eminence of the Church arises from its unity, as the principle of its constitution - a unity surpassing all else, and having nothing like unto it or equal to it."[12] For this reason Christ, speaking of the mystical edifice, mentions only one Church, which he calls *His own-"I will build my church;" any other Church except this one, since it has not been founded by Christ, cannot be the true Church. This becomes even more evident when the purpose of the Divine Founder is considered. For what did Christ, the Lord, ask? What did He wish in regard to the Church founded, or about to be founded? This: to transmit to it the same mission and the same mandate which He had received from the Father, that they should be perpetuated. This He clearly resolved to do: this He actually did. "As the Father hath sent me, I also send you."[13] "Ad thou hast sent Me into the world I also have sent them into the world."[14]*

---

[12] S. Clemens Alexandrinus, Stronmatum lib. viii., c. 17.
[13] John 20:21.
[14] John 17:18.

But the mission of Christ is to save that which had perished: that is to say, not some nations or peoples, but the whole human race, without distinction of time or place. "The Son of Man came that the world might be saved by Him."[15] "For there is no other name under Heaven given to men whereby we must be saved."[16] The Church, therefore, is bound to communicate without stint to all men, and to transmit through all ages, the salvation effected by Jesus Christ, and the blessings flowing there from. Wherefore, by the will of its Founder, it is necessary that this Church should be one in all lands and at all times. To justify the existence of more than one Church it would be necessary to go outside this world, and to create a new and unheard-of race of men.

That the one Church should embrace all men everywhere and at all times was seen and foretold by Isaiah, when looking into the future he saw the appearance of a mountain conspicuous by its all surpassing altitude, which set forth the image of "The House of the Lord" - that is, of the Church, "And in the last days the mountain of the House of the Lord shall be prepared on the top of the mountains."[17]

But this mountain which towers over all other mountains is *one*; and the House of the Lord to which *all nations* shall come to seek the rule of living is also one. "And all nations shall flow into it. And many people shall go, and say: Come, and let us go up to the mountain of the Lord, and to the House of the God of Jacob, and He will teach us His ways, and we will walk in His paths."[18]

Explaining this passage, Optatus of Milevis says: "It is written in the prophet Isaiah: 'from Sion the law shall go forth and the word of the Lord from Jerusalem.' For it is not on Mount Sion

---

[15] John 3:17.
[16] Acts 4:12.
[17] Isa. 2:2.
[18] Ibid., 2:2-3.

that Isaiah sees the valley, but on the holy mountain, that is, the Church, which has raised itself conspicuously throughout the entire Roman world under the whole heavens....The Church is, therefore, the spiritual Sion in which Christ has been constituted King by God the Father, and which exists throughout the entire earth, on which there is but one Catholic Church."[19] And Augustine says: "What can be so manifest as a mountain, or so well known? There are, it is true, mountains which are unknown because they are situated in some remote part of the earth...But this mountain is not unknown; for it has filled the whole face of the world, and about this it is said that it is prepared on the summit of the mountains."[20]

Christ the Head of the Church

5. Furthermore, the Son of God decreed that the Church should be His mystical body, with which He should be united as the Head, after the manner of the human body which He assumed, to which the natural head is physiologically united. As He took to Himself a mortal body, which He gave to suffering and death in order to pay the price of man's redemption, so also He has one mystical body in which and through which He renders men partakers of holiness and of eternal salvation. God "hath made Him (Christ) head over all the Church, which is His body."[21] Scattered and separated members cannot possibly cohere with the head so as to make one body. But St. Paul says: "All members of the body, whereas they are many, yet are one body, so also is Christ."[22] Wherefore this mystical body, he declares, is "compacted and fitly joined together. The head, Christ: from whom the whole body, being compacted and fitly jointed together, by what every joint supplieth according to the operation in the measure of every part."[23] And so dispersed

---

[19] De Schism. Donatist., lib. iii., n. 2.
[20] In Ep. Joan., tract i., n. 13.
[21] Eph. 1:22-23.
[22] 1 Cor. 12:12.
[23] Eph. 4:15-16.

members, separated one from the other, cannot be united with one and the same head. "There is one God, and one Christ; and His Church is one and the faith is one; and one the people, joined together in the solid unity of the body in the bond of concord. This unity cannot be broken, nor the one body divided by the separation of its constituent parts."[24] And to set forth more clearly the unity of the Church, he makes use of the illustration of a living body, the members of which cannot possibly live unless united to the head and drawing from it their vital force. Separated from the head they must of necessity die. "The Church," he says, "cannot be divided into parts by the separation and cutting asunder of its members. What is cut away from the mother cannot live or breathe apart."[25] What similarity is there between a dead and a living body? "For no man ever hated his own flesh, but nourisheth and cherisheth it, as also Christ doth the Church: because we are members of His body, of His flesh, and of His bones."[26]

Another head like to Christ must be invented - that is, another Christ - if besides the one Church, which is His body, men wish to set up another. "See what you must beware of - see what you must avoid - see what you must dread. It happens that, as in the human body, some member may be cut off - a hand, a finger, a foot. Does the soul follow the amputated member? As long as it was in the body, it lived; separated, it forfeits its life. So the Christian is a Catholic as long as he lives in the body: cut off from it he becomes a heretic - the life of the spirit follows not the amputated member."[27]

The Church of Christ, therefore, is one and the same for ever; those who leave it depart from the will and command of Christ, the Lord - leaving the path of salvation they enter on that of perdition. "Whosoever is separated from the Church is united to

---

[24] S. Cyprianus, De Cath. Eccl. Unitate, n. 23.
[25] Ibid.
[26] Eph. 5:29-30.
[27] S. Augustinus, Sermo cclxvii., n. 4.

an adulteress. He has cut himself off from the promises of the Church, and he who leaves the Church of Christ cannot arrive at the rewards of Christ....He who observes not this unity observes not the law of God, holds not the faith of the Father and the Son, clings not to life and salvation."[28]

Unity in Faith

6. But He, indeed, Who made this one Church, also gave it *unity*, that is, He made it such that all who are to belong to it must be united by the closest bonds, so as to form one society, one kingdom, one body - "one body and one spirit as you are called in one hope of your calling."[29] Jesus Christ, when His death was nigh at hand, declared His will in this matter, and solemnly offered it up, thus addressing His Father: "Not for them only do I pray, but for them also who through their word shall believe in Me...that they also may be one in Us...that they may be made perfect in one."[30] Yea, He commanded that this unity should be so closely knit and so perfect amongst His followers that it might, in some measure, shadow forth the union between Himself and His Father: "I pray that they all may be one as Thou Father in Me and I in Thee."[31]

Agreement and union of minds is the necessary foundation of this perfect concord amongst men, from which concurrence of wills and similarity of action are the natural results. Wherefore, in His divine wisdom, He ordained in His Church *Unity of Faith*; a virtue which is the first of those bonds which unite man to God, and whence we receive the name of the *faithful* - "one Lord, one faith, one baptism."[32] That is, as there is one Lord and one baptism, so should all Christians, without exception, have but one faith. And so the Apostle St. Paul not merely begs, but

---

[28] S. Cyprianus, De Cath. Eccl. Unitate, n. 6.
[29] Eph. 4:4.
[30] John 17:20-21, 23.
[31] Ibid. 21.
[32] Eph. 4:5.

entreats and implores Christians to be all of the same mind, and to avoid difference of opinions: "I beseech you, brethren, by the name of our Lord Jesus Christ, that you all speak the same thing, and that there be no schisms amongst you, and that you be perfect in the same mind and in the same judgment."[33] Such passages certainly need no interpreter; they speak clearly enough for themselves. Besides, all who profess Christianity allow that there can be but one faith. It is of the greatest importance and indeed of absolute necessity, as to which many are deceived, that the nature and character of this unity should be recognized. And, as We have already stated, this is not to be ascertained by conjecture, but by the certain knowledge of what was done; that is by seeking for and ascertaining what kind of unity in faith has been commanded by Jesus Christ.

The Kind of Unity in Faith Commanded by Christ

7. The heavenly doctrine of Christ, although for the most part committed to writing by divine inspiration, could not unite the minds of men if left to the human intellect alone. It would, for this very reason, be subject to various and contradictory interpretations. This is so, not only because of the nature of the doctrine itself and of the mysteries it involves, but also because of the divergencies of the human mind and of the disturbing element of conflicting passions. From a variety of interpretations a variety of beliefs is necessarily begotten; hence come controversies, dissensions and wranglings such as have arisen in the past, even in the first ages of the Church. Irenaeus writes of heretics as follows: "Admitting the sacred Scriptures they distort the interpretations."[34] And Augustine: "Heresies have arisen, and certain perverse views ensnaring souls and precipitating them into the abyss only when the Scriptures, good in themselves, are not properly understood."[35] Besides Holy Writ it was absolutely

---

[33] 1 Cor. 1:10.
[34] Lib. iii., cap. 12, n. 12.
[35] In Evang. Joan., tract xviii., cap. 5, n. I.

necessary to insure this union of men's minds - to effect and preserve unity of ideas - that there should be another principle. This the wisdom of God requires: for He could not have willed that the faith should be one if He did not provide means sufficient for the preservation of this unity; and this Holy Writ clearly sets forth as We shall presently point out. Assuredly the infinite power of God is not bound by anything, all things obey it as so many passive instruments. In regard to this external principle, therefore, we must inquire which one of all the means in His power Christ did actually adopt. For this purpose it is necessary to recall in thought the institution of Christianity.

The Magisterium (or Teaching Authority) of the Church to be Perpetual

8. We are mindful only of what is witnessed to by Holy Writ and what is otherwise well known. Christ proves His own divinity and the divine origin of His mission by miracles; He teaches the multitudes heavenly doctrine by word of mouth; and He absolutely commands that the assent of faith should be given to His teaching, promising eternal rewards to those who believe and eternal punishment to those who do not. "If I do not the works of my Father, believe Me not."[36] "If I had not done among them the works than no other man had done, they would not have sin."[37] "But if I do (the works) though you will not believe Me, believe the works."[38] Whatsoever He commands, He commands by the same authority. He requires the assent of the mind to all truths without exception. It was thus the duty of all who heard Jesus Christ, if they wished for eternal salvation, not merely to accept His doctrine as a whole, but to assent with their entire mind to all and every point of it, since it is unlawful to withhold faith from God even in regard to one single point.

[36] John 10:37.
[37] Ibid. 15:24.
[38] Ibid. 10:38.

When about to ascend into heaven He sends His Apostles in virtue of the same power by which He had been sent from the Father; and he charges them to spread abroad and propagate His teaching. "All power is given to Me in Heaven and in earth. Going therefore teach all nations....teaching them to observe all things whatsoever I have commanded you."[39] So that those obeying the Apostles might be saved, and those disobeying should perish. "He that believeth and is baptized shall be saved, but he that believed not shall be condemned."[40] But since it is obviously most in harmony with God's providence that no one should have confided to him a great and important mission unless he were furnished with the means of properly carrying it out, for this reason Christ promised that He would send the Spirit of Truth to His Disciples to remain with them for ever. "But if I go I will send Him (the Paraclete) to you....But when He, the Spirit of Truth is come, He will teach you all truth."[41] "And I will ask the Father, and He shall give you another Paraclete, that he may abide with you for ever, the Spirit of 'Truth."[42] "He shall give testimony of Me, and you shall give testimony."[43] Hence He commands that the teaching of the Apostles should be religiously accepted and piously kept as if it were His own - "He who hears you hears Me, he who despises you despises Me."[44] Wherefore the Apostles are ambassadors of Christ as He is the ambassador of the Father. "As the Father sent Me so also I send you."[45] Hence as the Apostles and Disciples were bound to obey Christ, so also those whom the Apostles taught were, by God's command, bound to obey them. And, therefore, it was no more allowable to repudiate one iota of the Apostles' teaching than it was to reject any point of the doctrine of Christ Himself.

---

[39] Matt. 28:18-20.
[40] Mark 16:16.
[41] John 16:7-13.
[42] Ibid. 14:16-17.
[43] Ibid. 15:26-27.
[44] Luke 10:16.
[45] John 20:21.

Truly the voice of the Apostles, when the Holy Ghost had come down upon them, resounded throughout the world. Wherever they went they proclaimed themselves the ambassadors of Christ Himself. "By whom (Jesus Christ) we have received grace and Apostleship for obedience to the faith in all nations for His name."[46] And God makes known their divine mission by numerous miracles. "But they going forth preached everywhere: the Lord working withal, and confirming the word with signs that followed."[47] But what is this word? That which comprehends all things, that which they had learnt from their Master; because they openly and publicly declare that they cannot help speaking of what they had seen and heard.

But, as we have already said, the Apostolic mission was not destined to die with the Apostles themselves, or to come to an end in the course of time, since it was intended for the people at large and instituted for the salvation of the human race. For Christ commanded His Apostles to preach the "Gospel to every creature, to carry His name to nations and kings, and to be witnesses to him to the ends of the earth." He further promised to assist them in the fulfilment of their high mission, and that, not for a few years or centuries only, but for all time - "even to the consummation of the world." Upon which St. Jerome says: "He who promises to remain with His Disciples to the end of the world declares that they will be for ever victorious, and that He will never depart from those who believe in Him."[48] But how could all this be realized in the Apostles alone, placed as they were under the universal law of dissolution by death? It was consequently provided by God that the Magisterium instituted by Jesus Christ should not end with the life of the Apostles, but that it should be perpetuated. We see it in truth propagated, and, as it were, delivered from hand to hand. For the Apostles consecrated bishops, and each one appointed those who were to succeed them immediately "in the ministry of the word."

---

[46] Rom. 1:5.
[47] Mark 16:20.
[48] In Matt., lib. iv., cap. 28, v. 20.

Nay more: they likewise required their successors to choose fitting men, to endow them with like authority, and to confide to them the office and mission of teaching. "Thou, therefore, my son, be strong in the grace which is in Christ Jesus: and the things which thou hast heard of me by many witnesses, the same command to faithful men, who shall be fit to teach others also."[49] Wherefore, as Christ was sent by God and the Apostles by Christ, so the Bishops and those who succeeded them were sent by the Apostles. "The Apostles were appointed by Christ to preach the Gospel to us. Jesus Christ was sent by God. Christ is therefore from God, and the Apostles from Christ, and both according to the will of God....Preaching therefore the word through the countries and cities, when they had proved in the Spirit the first-fruits of their teaching they appointed bishops and deacons for the faithful....They appointed them and then ordained them, so that when they themselves had passed away other tried men should carry on their ministry."[50] On the one hand, therefore, it is necessary that the mission of teaching whatever Christ had taught should remain perpetual and immutable, and on the other that the duty of accepting and professing all their doctrine should likewise be perpetual and immutable. "Our Lord Jesus Christ, when in His Gospel He testifies that those who not are with Him are His enemies, does not designate any special form of heresy, but declares that all heretics who are not with Him and do not gather with Him, scatter His flock and are His adversaries: He that is not with Me is against Me, and he that gathereth not with Me scattereth."[51]

Every Revealed Truth, without Exception, Must be Accepted

9. The Church, founded on these principles and mindful of her office, has done nothing with greater zeal and endeavour than she has displayed in guarding the integrity of the faith. Hence she

[49] 2 Tim. 2:1-2.
[50] S. Clemens Rom. Epist.I ad Corinth. capp. 42, 44.
[51] S. Cyprianus, Ep. lxix., ad Magnum, n. I.

regarded as rebels and expelled from the ranks of her children all who held beliefs on any point of doctrine different from her own. The Arians, the Montanists, the Novatians, the Quartodecimans, the Eutychians, did not certainly reject all Catholic doctrine: they abandoned only a tertian portion of it. Still who does not know that they were declared heretics and banished from the bosom of the Church? In like manner were condemned all authors of heretical tenets who followed them in subsequent ages. "There can be nothing more dangerous than those heretics who admit nearly the whole cycle of doctrine, and yet by one word, as with a drop of poison, infect the real and simple faith taught by our Lord and handed down by Apostolic tradition."[52]

The practice of the Church has always been the same, as is shown by the unanimous teaching of the Fathers, who were wont to hold as outside Catholic communion, and alien to the Church, whoever would recede in the least degree from any point of doctrine proposed by her authoritative Magisterium. Epiphanius, Augustine, Theodoret, drew up a long list of the heresies of their times. St. Augustine notes that other heresies may spring up, to a single one of which, should any one give his assent, he is by the very fact cut off from Catholic unity. "No one who merely disbelieves in all (these heresies) can for that reason regard himself as a Catholic or call himself one. For there may be or may arise some other heresies, which are not set out in this work of ours, and, if any one holds to one single one of these he is not a Catholic."[53]

The need of this divinely instituted means for the preservation of unity, about which we speak is urged by St. Paul in his epistle to the Ephesians. In this he first admonishes them to preserve with every care concord of minds: "Solicitous to keep the unity of the Spirit in the bond of peace."[54] And as souls cannot be perfectly

---

[52] Auctor Tract. de Fide Orthodoxa contra Arianos.
[53] S. Augustinus, De Haeresibus, n. 88.

united in charity unless minds agree in faith, he wishes all to hold
the same faith: "One Lord, one faith," and this so perfectly *one* as
to prevent all danger of error: "that henceforth we be no more
children, tossed to and fro, and carried about with every wind of
doctrine by the wickedness of men, by cunning craftiness, by
which they lie in wait to deceive"[55]: and this he teaches is to be
observed, not for a time only-"but until we all meet in the unity
of faith...unto the measure of the age of the fulness of Christ."[56]
But, in what has Christ placed the primary principle, and the
means of preserving this unity? In that-"He gave some Apostles-
and other some pastors and doctors, for the perfecting of the
saints, for the work of the ministry, for the edifying of the body
of Christ."[57]

Wherefore, from the very earliest times the fathers and doctors
of the Church have been accustomed to follow and, with one
accord to defend this rule. Origen writes: "As often as the
heretics allege the possession of the canonical scriptures, to
which all Christians give unanimous assent, they seem to say:
`Behold the word of truth is in the houses.' But we should
believe them not and abandon not the primary and ecclesiastical
tradition. We should believe not otherwise than has been handed
down by the tradition of the Church of God."[58] Irenaeus too
says: "The doctrine of the Apostles is the true faith...which is
known to us through the Episcopal succession...which has
reached even unto our age by the very fact that the Scriptures
have been zealously guarded and fully interpreted."[59] And
Tertullian: "It is therefore clear that all doctrine which agrees
with that of the Apostolic churches - the matrices and original
centres of the faith, must be looked upon as the truth, holding
without hesitation that the Church received it from the Apostles,

---

[54] Eph. 4:3, et seq.
[55] Eph. 4:14.
[56] Eph. 4:13
[57] Eph. 4:11-12.
[58] Vetus Interpretatio Commentariorum in Matt. n. 46.
[59] Contra Haereses, lib. iv., cap. 33, n. 8.

the Apostles from Christ and Christ from God....We are in communion with the Apostolic churches, and by the very fact that they agree amongst themselves we have a testimony of the truth."[60] And so Hilary: "Christ teaching from the ship signifies that those who are outside the Church can never grasp the divine teaching; for the ship typifies the Church where the word of life is deposited and preached. Those who are outside are like sterile and worthless sand: they cannot comprehend."[61] Rufinus praises Gregory of Nazianzum and Basil because "they studied the text of Holy Scripture alone, and took the interpretation of its meaning not from their own inner consciousness, but from the writings and on the authority of the ancients, who in their turn, as it is clear, took their rule for understanding the meaning from the Apostolic succession."[62]

Wherefore, as appears from what has been said, Christ instituted in the Church a *living, authoritative* and *permanent Magisterium*, which by His own power He strengthened, by the Spirit of truth He taught, and by miracles confirmed. He willed and ordered, under the gravest penalties, that its teachings should be received as if they were His own. As often, therefore, as it is declared on the authority of this teaching that this or that is contained in the deposit of divine revelation, it must be believed by every one as true. If it could in any way be false, an evident contradiction follows; for then God Himself would be the author of error in man. "Lord, if we be in error, we are being deceived by Thee."[63] In this wise, all cause for doubting being removed, can it be lawful for anyone to reject any one of those truths without by the very fact falling into heresy?-without separating himself from the Church?-without repudiating in one sweeping act the whole of Christian teaching? For such is the nature of faith that nothing can be more absurd than to accept some things and reject others. Faith, as the Church teaches, is "that supernatural virtue by

---

[60] De Praescrip., cap. xxxi.
[61] Comment. in Matt. xiii., n. I.
[62] Hist. Eccl., lib. ii., cap. 9.
[63] Richardus de S. Victore, De Trin., lib. i., cap. 2.

which, through the help of God and through the assistance of
His grace, we believe what he has revealed to be true, not on
account of the intrinsic truth perceived by the natural light of
reason, but because of the authority of God Himself, the
Revealer, who can neither deceive nor be deceived."[64] If then it
be certain that anything is revealed by God, and this is not
believed, then nothing whatever is believed by divine Faith: for
what the Apostle St. James judges to be the effect of a moral
deliquency, the same is to be said of an erroneous opinion in the
matter of faith. "Whosoever shall offend in one point, is become
guilty of all."[65] Nay, it applies with greater force to an erroneous
opinion. For it can be said with less truth that every law is
violated by one who commits a single sin, since it may be that he
only virtually despises the majesty of God the Legislator. But he
who dissents even in one point from divinely revealed truth
absolutely rejects all faith, since he thereby refuses to honour
God as the supreme truth and the *formal motive of faith*. "In many
things they are with me, in a few things not with me; but in those
few things in which they are not with me the many things in
which they are will not profit them."[66] And this indeed most
deservedly; for they, who take from Christian doctrine what they
please, lean on their own judgments, not on faith; and not
"bringing into captivity every understanding unto the obedience
of Christ,"[67] they more truly obey themselves than God. "You,
who believe what you like, believe yourselves rather than the
gospel."[68]

For this reason the Fathers of the Vatican Council laid down
nothing new, but followed divine revelation and the
acknowledged and invariable teaching of the Church as to the
very nature of faith, when they decreed as follows: "All those
things are to be believed by divine and Catholic faith which are

---

[64] Conc. Vat., Sess. iii., cap. 3.
[65] James 2:10.
[66] S. Augustinus in Psal. liv., n. 19.
[67] 2 Cor. 10:5.
[68] S. Augustinus, lib. xvii., Contra Faustum Manichaeum, cap. 3.

contained in the written or unwritten word of God, and which are proposed by the Church as divinely revealed, either by a solemn definition or in the exercise of its ordinary and universal Magisterium."[69] Hence, as it is clear that God absolutely willed that there should be unity in His Church, and as it is evident what kind of unity He willed, and by means of what principle He ordained that this unity should be maintained, we may address the following words of St. Augustine to all who have not deliberately closed their minds to the truth: "When we see the great help of God, such manifest progress and such abundant fruit, shall we hesitate to take refuge in the bosom of that Church, which, as is evident to all, possesses the supreme authority of the Apostolic See through the Episcopal succession? In vain do heretics rage round it; they are condemned partly by the judgment of the people themselves, partly by the weight of councils, partly by the splendid evidence of miracles. To refuse to the Church the primacy is most impious and above measure arrogant. And if all learning, no matter how easy and common it may be, in order to be fully understood requires a teacher and master, what can be greater evidence of pride and rashness than to be unwilling to learn about the books of the divine mysteries from the proper interpreter, and to wish to condemn them unknown?"[70]

It is then undoubtedly the office of the church to guard Christian doctrine and to propagate it in its integrity and purity. But this is not all: the object for which the Church has been instituted is not wholly attained by the performance of this duty. For, since Jesus Christ delivered Himself up for the salvation of the human race, and to this end directed all His teaching and commands, so He ordered the Church to strive, by the truth of its doctrine, to sanctify and to save mankind. But faith alone cannot compass so great, excellent, and important an end. There must needs be also the fitting and devout worship of God, which is to be found

---

[69] Sess. iii., cap. 3.
[70] De Unitate Credendi, cap. xvii., n. 35.

chiefly in the divine Sacrifice and in the dispensation of the Sacraments, as well as salutary laws and discipline. All these must be found in the Church, since it continues the mission of the Saviour for ever. The Church alone offers to the human race that religion-that state of absolute perfection - which He wished, as it were, to be *incorporated* in it. And it alone supplies those means of salvation which accord with the ordinary counsels of Providence.

The Church a Divine Society

10. But as this heavenly doctrine was never left to the arbitrary judgment of private individuals, but, in the beginning delivered by Jesus Christ, was afterwards committed by Him exclusively to the Magisterium already named, so the power of performing and administering the divine mysteries, together with the authority of ruling and governing, was not bestowed by God on all Christians indiscriminately, but on certain chosen persons. For to the Apostles and their legitimate successors alone these words have reference: "Going into the whole world preach the Gospel." "Baptizing them." "Do this in commemoration of Me." "Whose sins you shall forgive they are forgiven them." And in like manner He ordered the Apostles only and those who should lawfully succeed them to *feed* - that is to govern with authority - all Christian souls. Whence it also follows that it is necessarily the duty of Christians to be subject and to obey. And these duties of the Apostolic office are, in general, all included in the words of St. Paul: "Let a man so account of us as of the ministers of Christ, and the dispensers of the mysteries of God."[71]

Wherefore Jesus Christ bade all men, present and future, follow Him as their leader and Saviour; and this, not merely as individuals, but as forming a society, organized and united in mind. In this way a duly constituted society should exist, formed out of the divided multitude of peoples, one in faith, one in end, one in the participation of the means adapted to the attainment

---

[71] 1 Cor. 4:1.

of the end, and one as subject to one and the same authority. To this end He established in the Church all principles which necessarily tend to make organized human societies, and through which they attain the perfection proper to each. That is, in it (the Church), all who wished to be the sons of God by adoption might attain to the perfection demanded by their high calling, and might obtain salvation. The Church, therefore, as we have said, is man's guide to whatever pertains to Heaven. This is the office appointed unto it by God: that it may watch over and may order all that concerns religion, and may, without let or hindrance, exercise, according to its judgment, its charge over Christianity. Wherefore they who pretend that the Church has any wish to interfere in Civil matters, or to infringe upon the rights of the State, know it not, or wickedly calumniate it.

God indeed even made the Church a society far more perfect than any other. For the end for which the Church exists is as much higher than the end of other societies as divine grace is above nature, as immortal blessings are above the transitory things on the earth. Therefore the Church is a society *divine* in its origin, *supernatural* in its end and in means proximately adapted to the attainment of that end; but it is a *human* community inasmuch as it is composed of men. For this reason we find it called in Holy Writ by names indicating a perfect society. It is spoken of as *the House of God, the city placed upon the mountain* to which all nations must come. But it is also the *fold* presided over by one Shepherd, and into which all Christ's sheep must betake themselves. Yea, it is called *the kingdom which God has raised up* and which *will stand for ever*. Finally it is the *body of Christ* - that is, of course, His *mystical* body, but a body living and duly organized and composed of many members; members indeed which have not all the same functions, but which, united one to the other, are kept bound together by the guidance and authority of the head.

Indeed no true and perfect human society can be conceived which is not governed by some supreme authority. Christ

therefore must have given to His Church a supreme authority to
which all Christians must render obedience. For this reason, as
the unity of the faith is of necessity required for the unity of the
church, inasmuch as it is the *body of the faithful*, so also for this
same unity, inasmuch as the Church is a divinely constituted
society, unity of government, which effects and involves *unity of
communion*, is necessary *jure divino*. "The unity of the Church is
manifested in the mutual connection or communication of its
members, and likewise in the relation of all the members of the
Church to one head."[72]

From this it is easy to see that men can fall away from the unity
of the Church by schism, as well as by heresy. "We think that this
difference exists between heresy and schism" (writes St. Jerome):
"heresy has no perfect dogmatic teaching, whereas schism,
through some Episcopal dissent, also separates from the
Church."[73] In which judgment St. John Chrysostom concurs: "I
say and protest (he writes) that it is as wrong to divide the
Church as to fall into heresy."[74] Wherefore as no heresy can ever
be justifiable, so in like manner there can be no justification for
schism. "There is nothing more grievous than the sacrilege of
schism....there can be no just necessity for destroying the unity of
the Church."[75]

The Supreme Authority Founded by Christ

11. The nature of this supreme authority, which all Christians are
bound to obey, can be ascertained only by finding out what was
the evident and positive will of Christ. Certainly Christ is a King
for ever; and though invisible, He continues unto the end of time
to govern and guard His church from Heaven. But since He
willed that His kingdom should be visible He was obliged, when

[72] St. Thomas, 2a 2ae, 9, xxxix., a. I.
[73] S. Hieronymus, Comment. in Epist. ad Titum, cap. iii., v. 10-11.
[74] Hom. xi., in Epist. ad Ephes., n. 5.
[75] S. Augustinus, Contra Epistolam Parmeniani, lib. ii., cap. ii., n. 25.

He ascended into Heaven, to designate a vice-gerent on earth. "Should anyone say that Christ is the one head and the one shepherd, the one spouse of the one Church, he does not give an adequate reply. It is clear, indeed, that Christ is the author of grace in the Sacraments of the Church; it is Christ Himself who baptizes; it is He who forgives sins; it is He who is the true priest who bath offered Himself upon the altar of the cross, and it is by His power that His body is daily consecrated upon the altar; and still, because He was not to be visibly present to all the faithful, He made choice of ministers through whom the aforesaid Sacraments should be dispensed to the faithful as said above" (cap. 74). "For the same reason, therefore, because He was about to withdraw His visible presence from the Church, it was necessary that He should appoint someone in His place, to have the charge of the Universal Church. Hence before His Ascension He said to Peter: 'Feed my sheep.' "[76]

Jesus Christ, therefore, appointed Peter to be that head of the Church; and He also determined that the authority instituted in perpetuity for the salvation of all should be inherited by His successors, in whom the same permanent authority of Peter himself should continue. And so He made that remarkable promise to Peter and to no one else: "Thou are Peter, and upon this rock I will build my church."[77] "To Peter the Lord spoke: to one, therefore, that He might establish unity upon one."[78] "Without any prelude He mentions St. Peter's name and that of his father (Blessed art thou Simon, son of John) and He does not wish Him to be called any more Simon; claiming him for Himself according to His divine authority He aptly names him Peter, from petra the rock, since upon him He was about to found His Church."[79]

The Universal Jurisdiction of St. Peter

---

[76] St. Thomas, Contra Gentiles, lib. iv., cap. 76.
[77] Matt. 16:18.
[78] S. Pacianus ad Sempronium, Ep. iii., n. 11.
[79] S. Cyrillus Alexandrinus, In Evang. Joan., lib. ii., in cap. i., v. 42

12. From this text it is clear that by the will and command of God the Church rests upon St. Peter, just as a building rests on its foundation. Now the proper nature of a foundation is to be a principle of cohesion for the various parts of the building. It must be the necessary condition of stability and strength. Remove it and the whole building falls. It is consequently the office of St. Peter to support the Church, and to guard it in all its strength and indestructible unity. How could he fulfill this office without the power of commanding, forbidding, and judging, which is properly called *jurisdiction*? It is only by this power of jurisdiction that nations and commonwealths are held together. A primacy of honour and the shadowy right of giving advice and admonition, which is called *direction*, could never secure to any society of men unity or strength. The words - *and the gates of Hell shall not prevail against it* - proclaim and establish the authority of which we speak. "What is the *it*?" (writes Origen). "Is it the rock upon which Christ builds the Church or the Church? The expression indeed is ambiguous, as if the rock and the Church were one and the same. I indeed think that this is so, and that neither against the rock upon which Christ builds His Church nor against the Church shall the gates of Hell prevail."[80] The meaning of this divine utterance is, that, notwithstanding the wiles and intrigues which they bring to bear against the Church, it can never be that the church committed to the care of Peter shall succumb or in any wise fail. "For the Church, as the edifice of Christ who has wisely built 'His house upon a rock,' cannot be conquered by the gates of Hell, which may prevail over any man who shall be off the rock and outside the Church, but shall be powerless against it."[81] Therefore God confided His Church to Peter so that he might safely guard it with his unconquerable power. He invested him, therefore, with the needful authority; since the right to rule is absolutely required by him who has to guard human society really and effectively. This, furthermore, Christ gave: "To thee will I give the keys of the kingdom of Heaven." And He is clearly still speaking of the Church, which a

---

[80] Origenes, Comment. in Matt., tom. xii., n. ii.
[81] Ibid.

short time before He had called *His own*, and which He declared He wished to build on Peter as a foundation. The Church is typified not only as an *edifice* but as a *Kingdom*, and every one knows that the keys constitute the usual sign of governing authority. Wherefore when Christ promised to give to Peter the keys of the Kingdom of Heaven, he promised to give him power and authority over the Church. "The Son committed to Peter the office of spreading the knowledge of His Father and Himself over the whole world. He who increased the Church in all the earth, and proclaimed it to be stronger than the heavens, gave to a mortal man all power in Heaven when He handed him the Keys."[82] In this same sense He says: "Whatsoever thou shall bind upon earth it shall be bound also in Heaven, and whatsoever thou shalt loose on earth it shall be loosed also in Heaven." This metaphorical expression of binding and loosing indicates the power of making laws, of judging and of punishing; and the power is said to be of such amplitude and force that God will ratify whatever is decreed by it. Thus it is supreme and absolutely independent, so that, having no other power on earth as its superior, it embraces the whole Church and all things committed to the Church.

The promise is carried out when Christ the Lord after His Resurrection, having thrice asked Peter whether he loved Him more than the rest, lays on him the injunction: "Feed my lambs - feed my sheep." That is He confides to him, without exception, all those who were to belong to His fold. "The Lord does not hesitate. He interrogates, not to learn but to teach. When He was about to ascend into Heaven He left us, as it were, a vice-gerent of His love....and so because Peter alone of all others professes his love he is preferred to all-that being the most perfect he should govern the more perfect."[83]

---

[82] S. Johannes Chrysostomus, Hom. liv., in Matt. v., 2.

[83] S. Ambrosius, Exposit. in Evang. secundum Lucam, lib. x., nn. 175-176.

These, then, are the duties of a shepherd: to place himself as leader at the head of his flock, to provide proper food for it, to ward off dangers, to guard against insidious foes, to defend it against violence: in a word to rule and govern it. Since therefore Peter has been placed as shepherd of the Christian flock he has received the power of governing all men for whose salvation Jesus Christ shed His blood. "Why has He shed His blood? To buy the sheep which He handed over to Peter and his successors."[84]

And since all Christians must be closely united in the communion of one immutable faith, Christ the Lord, in virtue of His prayers, obtained for Peter that in the fulfilment of his office he should never fall away from the faith. "But I have asked for thee that thy faith fail not,"[85] and He furthermore commanded him to impart light and strength to his brethren as often as the need should arise: "Confirm thy brethren."[86] He willed then that he whom He had designated as the foundation of the Church should be the defence of its faith. "Could not Christ who confided to him the Kingdom by His own authority have strengthened the faith of one whom He designated a rock to show the foundation of the Church?"[87] For this reason Jesus Christ willed that Peter should participate in certain names, signs of great things which properly belong to Himself alone: in order that identity of titles should show identity of power. So He who is Himself "the chief corner-stone in whom all the building being framed together, groweth up in a holy temple in the Lord,"[88] placed Peter as it were a stone to support the Church. "When he heard `thou art a rock,' he was ennobled by the announcement. Although he is a rock, not as Christ is a rock, but as Peter is a rock. For Christ is by His very being an immovable rock; Peter only through this rock. Christ imparts His gifts, and is not

---

[84] S. Joannes Chrysostomus, De Sacerdotio, lib. ii.
[85] Luke 22:32
[86] Ibid.
[87] S. Ambrosius, De Fide, lib. iv., n. 56.
[88] Eph. 2:21.

exhausted...He is a priest, and makes priests. He is a rock, and constitutes a rock."[89] He who is the King of His Church, "Who bath the key of David, who openeth and no man shutteth, who shutteth and no man openeth,"[90] having delivered *the keys* to Peter declared him Prince of the Christian commonwealth. So, too, He, the Great Shepherd, who calls Himself "the Good Shepherd," constitued Peter the pastor "of His lambs and sheep. Feed My lambs, feed My Sheep." Wherefore Chrysostom says: "He was preeminent among the Apostles: He was the mouthpiece of the Apostles and the head of the Apostolic College...at the same time showing him that henceforth he ought to have confidence, and as it were blotting out his denial, He commits to him the government of his brethren...He saith to him: 'If thou lovest Me, be over my brethren.' " Finally He who confirms in "every good work and word"[91] commands Peter "to confirm his brethren."

Rightly, therefore, does St. Leo the Great say: "From the whole world Peter alone is chosen to take the lead in calling all nations, to be the head of all the Apostles and of all the Fathers of the Church. So that, although in the people of God there are many priests and many pastors Peter should by right rule all of those over whom Christ Himself is the chief ruler."[92] And so St. Gregory the great, writing to the Emperor Maurice Augustus, says: "It is evident to all who know the gospel that the charge of the whole Church was committed to St. Peter, the Apostle and Prince of all the Apostles, by the word of the Lord....Behold! he hath received the keys of the heavenly kingdom-the power of binding and loosing is conferred upon him: the care of the whole government of the Church is confided to him."[93]

The Roman Pontiffs Possess Supreme Power in the Church Jure Divino

---

[89] Hom. de Poenitentia, n. 4 in Appendice opp. S. Basilii.
[90] Apoc. 3:7.
[91] 2 Thess. 2:16.
[92] Sermo iv., cap. 2.
[93] Epist. lib. v., Epist. xx.

13. It was necessary that a government of this kind, since it belongs to the constitution and formation of the Church, as its principal element - that is as the principle of unity and the foundation of lasting stability - should in no wise come to an end with St. Peter, but should pass to his successors from one to another. "There remains, therefore, the ordinance of truth, and St. Peter, persevering in the strength of the rock which he had received, hath not abandoned the government of the Church which had been confided to him."[94] For this reason the Pontiffs who succeed Peter in the Roman Episcopate receive the supreme power in the church, *jure divino*. "We define" (declare the Fathers of the Council of Florence) "that the Holy and Apostolic See and the Roman Pontiff hold the primacy of the Church throughout the whole world: and that the same Roman Pontiff is the successor of St. Peter, the Prince of the Apostles, and the true Vicar of Christ, the head of the whole Church, and the father and teacher of all Christians; and that full power was given to him, in Blessed Peter, by our Lord Jesus Christ to feed, to rule, and to govern the universal Church, as is also contained in the acts of ecumenical councils and in the sacred canons."[95] Similarly the Fourth Council of Lateran declares: "The Roman Church, as the mother and mistress of all the faithful, by the will of Christ obtains primacy of jurisdiction over all other Churches." These declarations were preceded by the consent of antiquity which ever acknowledged, without the slightest doubt or hesitation, the Bishops of Rome, and revered them, as the legitimate successors of St. Peter.

Who is unaware of the many and evident testimonies of the holy Fathers which exist to this effect? Most remarkable is that of St. Irenaeus who, referring to the Roman Church, says: "With this Church, on account of its preeminent authority, it is necessary that every Church should be in concord"[96]; and St. Cyprian also says of the Roman Church, that "it is the root and mother of the

---

[94] S. Leo M. sermo iii., cap. 3.
[95] Conc. Florentinum.
[96] Contra Haereses, lib. iii., cap. 3, n. 2.

Catholic Church, the chair of Peter, and the *principal Church* whence sacerdotal unity has its source."[97] He calls it *the chair of Peter* because it is occupied by the successor of Peter: he calls it the principal Church, on account of the primacy conferred on Peter himself and his legitimate successors; and *the source of unity*, because the Roman Church is the efficient cause of unity in the Christian commonwealth. For this reason Jerome addresses Damasus thus: "My words are spoken to the successor of the Fisherman, to the disciple of the Cross....I communicate with none save your Blessedness, that is with the chair of Peter. For this I know is the rock on which the Church is built."[98] Union with the Roman See of Peter is to him always the public criterion of a Catholic. "I acknowledge everyone who is united with the See of Peter."[99] And for a like reason St. Augustine publicly attests that, "the primacy of the Apostolic chair always existed in the Roman Church"[100]; and he denies that anyone who dissents from the Roman faith can be a Catholic. "You are not to be looked upon as holding the true Catholic faith if you do not teach that the faith of Rome is to be held" (Sermo cxx., n. 13). So, too, St. Cyprian: "To be in communion with Cornelius is to be in communion with the Catholic Church" (Ep. lv., n. 1). In the same way Maximus the Abbot teaches that obedience to the Roman Pontiff is the proof of the true faith and of legitimate communion. Therefore if a man does not want to be, or to be called, a heretic, let him not strive to please this or that man...but let him hasten before all things to be in communion with the Roman See. If he be in communion with it, he should be acknowledged by all and everywhere as faithful and orthodox. He speaks in vain who tries to persuade me of the orthodoxy of those who, like himself, refuse obedience to his Holiness the Pope of the most holy Church of Rome: that is to the Apostolic See." The reason and motive of this he explains to be that "the Apostolic See has received and hath government, authority, and

---

[97] Ep. xlviii., ad Cornelium, n. 3. and Ep. liac., ad eundem, n. 14.

[98] Ep. xv., ad Damasum, n. 2.

[99] Ep. xvi., ad Damasum, n. 2.

[100] Ep. xliii., n. 7.

power of binding and loosing from the Incarnate Word Himself; and, according to all holy synods, sacred canons and decrees, in all things and through all things, in respect of all the holy churches of God throughout the whole world, since the Word in Heaven who rules the Heavenly powers binds and loosens there."[101]

Wherefore what was acknowledged and observed as Christian faith, not by one nation only nor in one age, but by the East and by the West, and through all ages, this Philip, the priest, the Pontifical legate at the Council of Ephesus, no voice being raised in dissent, recalls: "No one can doubt, yea, it is known unto all ages, that St. Peter, the Prince of the Apostles, the pillar of the faith and the ground of the Catholic Church, received the keys of the Kingdom from Our Lord Jesus Christ. That is: the power of forgiving and retaining sins was given to him who, up to the present time, lives and exercises judgment in the persons of his successors."[102] The pronouncement of the Council of Chalcedon on the same matter is present to the minds of all: "Peter has spoken through Leo,"[103] to which the voice of the Third Council of Constantinople responds as an echo: "The chief Prince of the Apostles was fighting on our side: for we have had as our ally his follower and the successor to his see: and the paper and the ink were seen, and Peter spoke through Agatho."[104]

In the formula of Catholic faith drawn up and proposed by Hormisdas, which was subscribed at the beginning of the sixth century in the great Eighth Council by the Emperor Justinian, by Epiphanius, John and Menna, the Patriarchs, this same is declared with great weight and solemnity. "For the pronouncement of Our Lord Jesus Christ saying: '*Thou art Peter, and upon this rock I will build my Church*,' cannot be passed over. What is said is proved by the result, because Catholic faith has

---

[101] Defloratio ex Epistola ad Petrum illustrem.
[102] Actio iii.
[103] Actio ii.
[104] Actio xviii.

always been preserved without stain in the Apostolic See."[105] We have no wish to quote every available declaration; but it is well to recall the formula of faith which Michael Paleologus professed in the Second Council of Lyons: "The same holy Roman Church possesses the sovereign and plenary primacy and authority over the whole Catholic Church, which, truly and humbly, it acknowledges to have received together with the plenitude of power from the Lord Himself, in the person of St. Peter, the Prince or Head of the Apostles, of whom the Roman Pontiff is the successor. And as it is bound to defend the truth of faith beyond all others, so also if any question should arise concerning the faith it must be determined by its judgment."[106]

Bishops Belong to the Essential Constitution of the Church

14. But if the authority of Peter and his successors is plenary and supreme, it is not to be regarded as the sole authority. For He who made Peter the foundation of the Church also "chose, twelve, whom He called apostles"[107]; and just as it is necessary that the authority of Peter should be perpetuated in the Roman Pontiff, so, by the fact that the bishops succeed the Apostles, they inherit their ordinary power, and thus the episcopal order necessarily belongs to the essential constitution of the Church. Although they do not receive plenary, or universal, or supreme authority, they are not to be looked as vicars of the Roman Pontiffs; because they exercise a power really their own, and are most truly called the *ordinary* pastors of the peoples over whom they rule.

But since the successor of Peter is one, and those of the Apostles are many, it is necessary to examine into the relations which exist between him and them according to the divine constitution of the Church. Above all things the need of union between the

---

[105] Post Epistolam, xxvi., ad omnes Episc. Hispan., n. 4.
[106] Actio iv.
[107] Luke 6:13.

bishops and the successors of Peter is clear and undeniable. This bond once broken, Christians would be separated and scattered, and would in no wise form one body and one flock. "The safety of the Church depends on the dignity of the chief priest, to whom if an extraordinary and supreme power is not given, there are as many schisms to be expected in the Church as there are priests."[108] It is necessary, therefore, to bear this in mind, viz., that nothing was conferred on the apostles apart from Peter, but that several things were conferred upon Peter apart from the Apostles. St. John Chrysostom in explaining the words of Christ asks: "Why, passing over the others, does He speak to Peter about these things?" And he replies unhesitatingly and at once, "Because he was pre-eminent among the Apostles, the mouthpiece of the Disciples, and the head of the college."[109] He alone was designated as the foundation of the Church. To him He gave the power of binding and *loosing*; to him alone was given the power of *feeding*. On the other hand, whatever authority and office the Apostles received, they received in conjunction with Peter. "If the divine benignity willed anything to be in common between him and the other princes, whatever He did not deny to the others He gave only through him. So that whereas Peter alone received many things, He conferred nothing on any of the rest without Peter participating in it."[110]

Bishops Separated from Peter and His Successors Lose All Jurisdiction

15. From this it must be clearly understood that Bishops are deprived of the right and power of ruling, if they deliberately secede from Peter and his successors; because, by this secession, they are separated from the foundation on which the whole edifice must rest. They are therefore outside the *edifice* itself; and for this very reason they are separated from the *fold*, whose leader

---

[108] S. Hieronymus, Dialog, contra Luciferianos, n. 9.
[109] Hom. lxxxviii. in Joan., n. I.
[110] S. Leo M. sermo iv., cap. 2.

is the Chief Pastor; they are exiled from the *Kingdom*, the keys of which were given by Christ to Peter alone.

These things enable us to see the heavenly ideal, and the divine exemplar, of the constitution of the Christian commonwealth, namely: When the Divine founder decreed that the Church should be one in faith, in government, and in communion, He chose Peter and his successors as the principle and centre, as it were, of this unity. Wherefore St. Cyprian says: "The following is a short and easy proof of the faith. The Lord saith to Peter: 'I say to thee thou art Peter'; on him alone He buildeth His Church; and although after His Resurrection He gives a similar power to all the Apostles and says: 'As the Father hath sent me,' etc., still in order to make the necessary unity clear, by His own authority He laid down the source of that unity as beginning from one."[111] And Optatus of Milevis says: "You cannot deny that you know that in the city of Rome the Episcopal chair was first conferred on Peter. In this Peter, the head of all the Apostles (hence his name Cephas), has sat; in which chair alone unity was to be preserved for all, lest any of the other apostles should claim anything as exclusively his own. So much so, that he who would place another chair against that one chair, would be a schismatic and a sinner."[112] Hence the teaching of Cyprian, that heresy and schism arise and are begotten from the fact that due obedience is refused to the supreme authority. "Heresies and schisms have no other origin than that obedience is refused to the priest of God, and that men lose sight of the fact that there is one judge in the place of Christ in this world."[113] No one, therefore, unless in communion with Peter can share in his authority, since it is absurd to imagine that he who is outside can command in the Church. Wherefore Optatus of Milevis blamed the Donatists for this reason: "Against which ages (of hell) we read that Peter received the saving keys, that is to say, our prince, to whom it was said by Christ: 'To thee will I give the keys of the Kingdom

---

[111] De Unit. Eccl., n. 4.
[112] De Schism. Donat., lib. ii.
[113] Epist. xii. ad Cornelium, n. 5.

of Heaven, and the gates of Hell shall not conquer them.'
Whence is it therefore that you strive to obtain for yourselves the
keys of the Kingdom of Heaven-you who fight against the chair
of Peter?"[114]

But the Epsicopal order is rightly judged to be in communion
with Peter, as Christ commanded, if it be subject to and obeys
Peter; otherwise it necessarily becomes a lawless and disorderly
crowd. It is not sufficient for the due preservation of the unity of
the faith that the head should merely have been charged with the
office of superintendent, or should have been invested solely
with a power of direction. But it is absolutely necessary that he
should have received real and sovereign authority which the
whole community is bound to obey. What had the Son of God in
view when he promised the keys of the Kingdom of Heaven to
Peter *alone*? *Biblical usage* and the unanimous teaching of the
Fathers clearly show that supreme authority is designated in the
passage by the word *keys*. Nor is it lawful to interpret in a
different sense what was given to Peter alone, and what was
given to the other Apostles conjointly with him. If the power of
binding, loosening, and feeding confers upon each and every one
of the Bishops the successors of the Apostles a real authority to
rule the people committed to him, certainly the same power must
have the same effect in his case to whom the duty of feeding the
lambs and sheep has been assigned by God. "Christ constituted
[Peter] not only pastor, but pastor of pastors; Peter therefore
feeds the lambs and feeds the sheep, feeds the children and feeds
the mothers, governs the subjects and rules the prelates, because
the lambs and the sheep form the whole of the Church."[115]
Hence those remarkable expressions of the ancients concerning
St. Peter, which most clearly set forth the fact that he was placed
in the highest degree of dignity and authority. They frequently
call him "the Prince of the College of the Disciples; the Prince of
the holy Apostles; the leader of that choir; the mouthpiece of all

---

[114] Lib. ii., n. 4-5.
[115] S. Brunonis Episcopi Signiensis Comment. in Joan., part iii., cap.
21, n. 55.

the Apostles; the head of that family; the ruler of the whole world; the first of the Apostles; the safeguard of the Church." In this sense St. Bernard writes as follows to Pope Eugenius: "Who art thou? The great priest - the high priest. Thou art the Prince of Bishops and the heir of the Apostles…Thou art he to whom the keys were given. There are, it is true, other gatekeepers of heaven and to pastors of flocks, but thou are so much the more glorious as thou hast inherited a different and more glorious name than all the rest. They have flocks consigned to them, one to each; to thee all the flocks are confided as one flock to one shepherd, and not alone the sheep, but the shepherds. You ask how I prove this? From the words of the Lord. To which - I do not say - of the Bishops, but even of the Apostles have all the sheep been so absolutely and unreservedly committed? If thou lovest me, Peter, feed my sheep. Which sheep? Of this or that country, or kingdom? My sheep, He says: to whom therefore is it not evident that he does not designate some, but all? We can make no exception where no distinction is made."[116]

But it is opposed to the truth, and in evident contradiction with the divine constitution of the Church, to hold that while each Bishop is *individually* bound to obey the authority of the Roman Pontiffs, taken *collectively* the Bishops are not so bound. For it is the nature and object of a foundation to support the unity of the whole edifice and to give stability to it, rather than to *each component part*; and in the present case this is much more applicable, since Christ the Lord wished that by the strength and solidity of the foundation the gates of hell should be prevented from prevailing against the Church. All are agreed that the divine promise must be understood of the Church as a whole, and not of any certain portions of it. These can indeed be overcome by the assaults of the powers of hell, as in point of fact has befallen some of them. Moreover, he who is set over the whole flock must have authority, not only over the sheep dispersed throughout the Church, but also when they are assembled

---

[116] De Consideratione, lib. ii., cap. 8.

together. Do the sheep when they are all assembled together rule and guide the shepherd? Do the successors of the Apostles assembled together constitute the foundation on which the successor of St. Peter rests in order to derive therefrom strength and stability? Surely jurisdiction and authority belong to him in whose power have been placed the keys of the Kingdom taken collectively. And as the Bishops, each in his own district, command with real power not only individuals but the whole community, so the Roman pontiffs, whose jurisdiction extends to the whole Christian commonwealth, must have all its parts, even taken collectively, subject and obedient to their authority. Christ the Lord, as we have quite sufficiently shown, made Peter and his successors His *vicars*, to exercise for ever in the Church the power which He exercised during His mortal life. Can the Apostolic College be said to have been above its master in authority?

This power over the Episcopal College to which we refer, and which is clearly set forth in Holy Writ, has ever been acknowledged and attested by the Church, as is clear from the teaching of General Councils. "We read that the Roman Pontiff has pronounced judgments on the prelates of all the churches; we do not read that anybody has pronounced sentence on him."[117] The reason for which is stated thus: "there is no authority greater than that of the Apostolic See,"[118] wherefore Gelasius on the decrees of Councils says: "That which the First See has not approved of cannot stand; but what it has thought well to decree has been received by the whole Church."[119] It has ever been unquestionably the office of the Roman Pontiffs to ratify or to reject the decrees of Councils. Leo the great rescinded the acts of the Conciliabulum of Ephesus. Damasus rejected those of Rimini, and Hadrian I. those of Constantinople. The 28th Canon of the Council of Chalcedon, by the very fact that it lacks the

---

[117] Hadrianus ii., in Allocutione iii., ad Synodum Romanum an. 869, Cf. Actionem vii., Conc. Constantinopolitani iv.

[118] Nicholaus in Epist. lxxxvi. ad Michael. Imperat.

[119] Epist. xxvi., ad Episcopos Dardaniae, n. 5.

assent and approval of the Apostolic See, is admitted by all to be worthless. Rightly, therefore, has Leo X. laid down in the 5th council of Lateran "that the Roman Pontiff alone, as having authority over all Councils, has full jurisdiction and power to summon, to transfer, to dissolve Councils, as is clear, not only from the testimony of Holy Writ, from the teaching of the Fathers and of the Roman Pontiffs, and from the decrees of the sacred canons, but from the teaching of the very Councils themselves." Indeed, Holy Writ attests that the keys of the Kingdom of Heaven were given to Peter alone, and that the power of binding and loosening was granted to the Apostles and to Peter; but there is nothing to show that the Apostles received supreme power *without Peter*, and *against Peter*. Such power they certainly did not receive from Jesus Christ. Wherefore, in the decree of the Vatican Council as to the nature and authority of the primacy of the Roman Pontiff, no newly conceived opinion is set forth, but the venerable and constant belief of every age.[120]

Nor does it beget any confusion in the administration that Christians are bound to obey a twofold authority. We are prohibited in the first place by Divine Wisdom from entertaining any such thought, since this form of government was constituted by the counsel of God Himself. In the second place we must note that the due order of things and their mutual relations are disturbed if there be a twofold magistracy of the same rank set over a people, neither of which is amenable to the other. But the authority of the Roman Pontiff is supreme, universal, independent; that of the bishops limited, and dependent. "It is not congruous that two superiors with equal authority should be placed over the same flock; but that two, one of whom is higher than the other, should be placed over the same people is not incongruous. Thus the parish priest, the bishop, and the Pope, are placed immediately over the same people."[121] So the Roman Pontiffs, mindful of their duty, wish above all things, that the

---

[120] Sess. iv., cap. 3.
[121] St. Thomas in iv Sent, dist. xvii., a. 4, ad q. 4, ad 3.

divine constitution of the Church should be preserved.
Therefore, as they defend with all necessary care and vigilance
their own authority, so they have always laboured, and will
continue to labour, that the authority of the bishops may be
upheld. Yea, they look up whatever honour or obedience is given
to the bishops as paid to themselves. "My honour is the honour
of the Universal Church. My honour is the strength and stability
of my brethren. Then am I honoured when due honour is given
to everyone."[122]

Appeal to Sheep Not of the Fold

16. In what has been said we have faithfully described the
exemplar and form of the Church as divinely constituted. We
have treated at length of its unity: we have explained sufficiently
its nature, and pointed out the way in which the Divine Founder
of the Church willed that it should be preserved. There is no
reason to doubt that all those, who by Divine Grace and mercy
have had the happiness to have been born, as it were, in the
bosom of the Catholic Church, and to have lived in it, will listen
to Our Apostolic Voice: "My sheep hear my voice,"[123] and that
they will derive from Our words fuller instruction and a more
perfect disposition to keep united with their respective pastors,
and through them with the Supreme Pastor, so that they may
remain more securely within the one fold, and may derive
therefrom a greater abundance of salutary fruit. But We, who,
notwithstanding our unfitness for this great dignity and office,
govern by virtue of the authority conferred on us by Jesus Christ,
as we "look on Jesus, the author and finisher of our faith"[124] feel
Our heart fired by His charity. What Christ has said of Himself
We may truly repeat of Ourselves: "Other sheep I have that are
not of this fold: them also I must bring and they shall hear my
voice."[125] Let all those, therefore, who detest the wide-spread

---

[122] S. Gregorius M. Epistolarum, lib viii., ep. xxx., ad Eulogium.
[123] John 10:27.
[124] Heb. 12:2.
[125] John 10:16.

irreligion of our times, and acknowledge and confess Jesus Christ to be the Son of God and the Saviour of the human race, but who have wandered away from the Spouse, listen to Our voice. Let them not refuse to obey Our paternal charity. Those who acknowledge Christ must acknowledge Him wholly and entirely. "The Head and the body are Christ wholly and entirely. The Head is the only-begotten son of God, the body is His Church; the bridegroom and the bride, two in one flesh. All who dissent from the Scriptures concerning Christ, although they may be found in all places in which the Church is found, are not in the Church; and again all those who agree with the Scriptures concerning the Head, and do not communicate in the unity of the Church, are not in the Church."[126]

And with the same yearning Our soul goes out to those whom the foul breath of irreligion has not entirely corrupted, and who at least seek to have the true God, the Creator of Heaven and earth, as their Father. Let such as these take counsel with themselves, and realize that they can in no wise be counted among the children of God, unless they take Christ Jesus as their Brother, and at the same time the Church as their mother. We lovingly address to all the words of St. Augustine: "Let us love the Lord our God; let us love His Church; the Lord as our Father, the Church as our Mother. Let no one say, I go indeed to idols, I consult fortune-tellers and soothsayers; but I leave not the Church of God: I am a Catholic. Clinging to thy Mother, thou offendest thy Father. Another, too, says: 'Far be it from me; I do not consult fortune - telling, I seek not soothsaying, I seek not profane divinations, I go not to the worship of devils, I serve not stones: but I am on the side of Donatus.' What doth it profit thee not to offend the Father, who avenges an offence against the Mother? What doth it profit to confess the Lord, to honour God, to preach Him, to acknowledge His Son, and to confess that He sits on the right hand of the Father, if you blaspheme

---

[126] S. Augustinus, Contra Donatistas Epistola, sive De Unit. Eccl., cap. iv., n. 7.

His Church?...If you had a beneficent friend, whom you honoured daily - and even once calumniated his spouse, would you ever enter his house? Hold fast, therefore, O dearly beloved, hold fast altogether God as your Father, and the Church as your Mother."[127]

Above all things, trusting in the mercy of God, who is able to move the hearts of men and to incline them as and when He pleases, We most earnestly commend to His loving kindness all those of whom We have spoken. As a pledge of Divine grace, and as a token of Our affection, We lovingly impart to you, in the Lord, Venerable Brethren, to your clergy and people, Our Apostolic Blessing.

Given at St. Peter's, Rome, the 29th day of June, in the year 1896, and the nineteenth of our Pontificate.

---

[127] Enarratio in Psal. lxxxviii., sermo ii., n. 14.

XII: Divinum Illud Munus

May 9, 1897

ON THE HOLY SPIRIT

That divine office which Jesus Christ received from His Father for the welfare of mankind, and most perfectly fulfilled, had for its final object to put men in possession of the eternal life of glory, and proximately during the course of ages to secure to them the life of divine grace, which is destined eventually to blossom into the life of heaven. Wherefore, our Saviour never ceases to invite, with infinite affection, all men, of every race and tongue, into the bosom of His Church: "Come ye all to Me," "I am the Life," "I am the Good Shepherd." Nevertheless, according to His inscrutable counsels, He did not will to entirely complete and finish this office Himself on earth, but as He had received it from the Father, so He transmitted it for its completion to the Holy Ghost. It is consoling to recall those assurances which Christ gave to the body of His disciples a little before He left the earth: "It is expedient to you that I go: for if I go not, the Paraclete will not come to you: but if I go, I will send Him to you."[1] In these words He gave as the chief reason of His departure and His return to the Father, the advantage which would most certainly accrue to His followers from the coming of the Holy Ghost, and, at the same time, He made it clear that the Holy Ghost is equally sent by-and therefore proceeds from-Himself and the Father; that He would complete, in His office of Intercessor, Consoler, and Teacher, the work which Christ Himself had begun in His mortal life. For, in the redemption of the world, the completion of the work was by Divine Providence reserved to the manifold power of that Spirit, who, in the creation, "adorned the heavens,"[2] and "filled the whole world."[3]

---

[1] 1 John 16:7.
[2] Job 26:13.

The Leonine Encyclicals

The Two Principal Aims of Our Pontificate

2. Now We have earnestly striven, by the help of His grace, to follow the example of Christ, Our Saviour, the Prince of Pastors, and the Bishop of our Souls, by diligently carrying on His office, entrusted by Him to the Apostles and chiefly to Peter, "whose dignity faileth not, even in his unworthy successor."[4] In pursuance of this object We have endeavoured to direct all that We have attempted and persistently carried out during a long pontificate towards two chief ends: in the first place, towards the restoration, both in rulers and peoples, of the principles of the Christian life in civil and domestic society, since there is no true life for men except from Christ; and, secondly, to promote the reunion of those who have fallen away from the Catholic Church either by heresy or by schism, since it is most undoubtedly the will of Christ that all should be united in one flock under one Shepherd. But now that We are looking forward to the approach of the closing days of Our life, Our soul is deeply moved to dedicate to the Holy Ghost, who is the life-giving Love, all the work We have done during Our pontificate, that He may bring it to maturity and fruitfulness. In order the better and more fully to carry out this Our intention, We have resolved to address you at the approaching sacred season of Pentecost concerning the indwelling and miraculous power of the Holy Ghost; and the extent and efficiency of His action, both in the whole body of the Church and in the individual souls of its members, through the glorious abundance of His divine graces. We earnestly desire that, as a result, faith may be aroused in your minds concerning the mystery of the adorable Trinity, and especially that piety may increase and be inflamed towards the Holy Ghost, to whom especially all of us owe the grace of following the paths of truth and virtue; for, as St. Basil said, "Who denieth that the dispensations concerning man, which have been made by the great God and our Saviour, Jesus Christ, according to the

---

[3] Wisdom 1:7.
[4] St. Leo the Great, Sermon ii., On the Anniversary of his Election.

goodness of God, have been fulfilled through the grace of the Spirit?"[5]

The Catholic Doctrine of the Blessed Trinity

3. Before We enter upon this subject, it will be both desirable and useful to say a few words about the Mystery of the Blessed Trinity. This dogma is called by the doctors of the Church "the substance of the New Testament," that is to say, the greatest of all mysteries, since it is the fountain and origin of them all. In order to know and contemplate this mystery, the angels were created in Heaven and men upon earth. In order to teach more fully this mystery, which was but foreshadowed in the Old Testament, God Himself came down from the angels unto men: "No man bath seen God at any time; the only begotten Son, who is in the bosom of the Father, He bath declared Him."[6] Whosoever then writes or speaks of the Trinity must keep before His eyes the prudent warning of the Angelic Doctor: "When we speak of the Trinity, we must do so with caution and modesty, for, as St. Augustine saith, nowhere else are more dangerous errors made, or is research more difficult, or discovery more fruitful."[7] The danger that arises is lest the Divine Persons be confounded one with the other in faith or worship, or lest the one Nature in them be separated: for "This is the Catholic Faith, that we should adore one God in Trinity and Trinity in Unity." Therefore Our predecessor Innocent XII, absolutely refused the petition of those who desired a special festival in honour of God the Father. For, although the separate mysteries connected with the Incarnate Word are celebrated on certain fixed days, yet there is no special feast on which the Word is honoured according to His Divine Nature alone. And even the Feast of Pentecost was instituted in the earliest times, not simply to honour the Holy Ghost in Himself, but to commemorate His coming, or His

---

[5] Of the Holy Ghost, c. xvi., v. 39.

[6] John 1:18.

[7] Summ. Th. la., q. xxxi. De Trin. 1 L, c. 3.

external mission. And all this has been wisely ordained, lest from distinguishing the Persons men should be led to distinguish the Divine Essence. Moreover the Church, in order to preserve in her children the purity of faith, instituted the Feast of the Most Holy Trinity, which John XXII. afterwards extended to the Universal Church. He also permitted altars and churches to be dedicated to the Blessed Trinity, and, with the divine approval, sanctioned the Order for the Ransom of Captives, which is specially devoted to the Blessed Trinity and bears Its name. Many facts confirm its truths. The worship paid to the saints and angels, to the Mother of God, and to Christ Himself, finally redounds to the honour of the Blessed Trinity. In prayers addressed to one Person, there is also mention of the others; in the litanies after the individual Persons have been separately invoked, a common invocation of all is added: all psalms and hymns conclude with the doxology to the Father, Son, and Holy Ghost; blessings, sacred rites, and sacraments are either accompanied or concluded by the invocation of the Blessed Trinity. This was already foreshadowed by the Apostle in those words: "For of Him, and by Him, and in Him, are all things: to Him be glory for ever,"[8] thereby signifying both the Trinity of Persons and the Unity of Nature: for as this is one and the same in each of the Persons, so to each is equally owing supreme glory, as to one and the same God. St. Augustine commenting upon this testimony writes: "The words of the Apostle, of Him, and by Him, and in Him are not to be taken indiscriminately; of Him refers to the Father, by Him to the Son, in Him to the Holy Ghost."[9] The Church is accustomed most fittingly to attribute to the Father those works of the Divinity in which power excels, to the Son those in which wisdom excels, and those in which love excels to the Holy Ghost. Not that all perfections and external operations are not common to the Divine Persons; for "the operations of the Trinity are indivisible, even as the essence of the Trinity is indivisible"[10]; because as the three Divine Persons

---

[8] Rom. 11:36.
[9] De Trin. 1. vi., c. 10; 1. i., c. 6.
[10] St. Aug., De Trin., I. 1, cc. 4-5.

"are inseparable, so do they act inseparably."[11] But by a certain comparison, and a kind of affinity between the operations and the properties of the Persons, these operations are attributed or, as it is said, "appropriated" to One Person rather than to the others. "Just as we make use of the traces of similarity or likeness which we find in creatures for the manifestation of the Divine Persons, so do we use Their essential attributes; and this manifestation of the Persons by Their essential attributes is called appropriation."[12] In this manner the Father, who is "the principle of the whole God-head"[13] is also the efficient cause of all things, of the Incarnation of the Word, and the sanctification of souls; "of Him are all things": of Him, referring to the Father. But the Son, the Word, the Image of God is also the exemplar cause, whence all creatures borrow their form and beauty, their order and harmony. He is for us the Way, the Truth, and the Life; the Reconciles of man with God. "By Him are all things": by Him, referring to the Son. The Holy Ghost is the ultimate cause of all things, since, as the will and all other things finally rest in their end, so He, who is the Divine Goodness and the Mutual Love of the Father and Son, completes and perfects, by His strong yet gentle power, the secret work of man's eternal salvation. "In Him are all things": in Him, referring to the Holy Ghost.

The Holy Ghost and the Incarnation

4. Having thus paid the due tribute of faith and worship owing to the Blessed Trinity, and which ought to be more and more inculcated upon the Christian people, we now turn to the exposition of the power of the Holy Ghost. And, first of all, we must look to Christ, the Founder of the Church and the Redeemer of our race. Among the external operations of God, the highest of all is the mystery of the Incarnation of the Word, in which the splendour of the divine perfections shines forth so

---

[11] St. Aug., i6.
[12] St. Th. Ia., q. 39, xxxix., a. 7.
[13] St. Aug. De Trin. 1 iv., c. 20.

brightly that nothing more sublime can even be imagined, nothing else could have been more salutary to the human race. Now this work, although belonging to the whole Trinity, is still appropriated especially to the Holy Ghost, so that the Gospels thus speak of the Blessed Virgin: "She was found with child of the Holy Ghost," and "that which is conceived in her is of the Holy Ghost."[14] And this is rightly attributed to Him who is the love of the Father and the Son, since this "great mystery of piety"[15] proceeds from the infinite love of God towards man, as St. John tells us: "God so loved the world as to give His only begotten Son."[16] Moreover, human nature was thereby elevated to a personal union with the Word; and this dignity is given, not on account of any merits, but entirely and absolutely through grace, and therefore, as it were, through the special gift of the Holy Ghost. On this point St. Augustine writes: "This manner in which Christ was born of the Holy Ghost, indicates to us the grace of God, by which humanity, with no antecedent merits, at the first moment of its existence, was united with the Word of God, by so intimate a personal union, that He, who was the Son of Man, was also the Son of God, and He who was the Son of God was also the Son of Man."[17] By the operation of the Holy Spirit, not only was the conception of Christ accomplished, but also the sanctification of His soul, which, in Holy Scripture, is called His "anointing."[18] Wherefore all His actions were "performed in the Holy Ghost,"[19] and especially the sacrifice of Himself: "Christ, through the Holy Ghost, offered Himself without spot to God."[20] Considering this, no one can be surprised that all the gifts of the Holy Ghost inundated the soul of Christ. In Him resided the absolute fullness of grace, in the greatest and most efficacious manner possible; in Him were all

---

[14] Matt. 1:18,20.
[15] 1 Tim. 3:16.
[16] John 3:16.
[17] Enchir., c. xl. St. Th., 3a., q. xxxii., a. 1.
[18] Acts 10:38.
[19] St. Basil de Sp. S., c. xvi.
[20] Heb. 9:14.

the treasures of wisdom and knowledge, *graces gratis datae*, virtues, and all other gifts foretold in the prophecies of Isaias,[21] and also signified in that miraculous dove which appeared at the Jordan, when Christ, by His baptism, consecrated its waters for a new sacrament. On this the words of St. Augustine may appropriately be quoted: "It would be absurd to say that Christ received the Holy Ghost when He was already thirty years of age, for He came to His baptism without sin, and therefore not without the Holy Ghost. At this time, then (that is, at His baptism), He was pleased to prefigure His Church, in which those especially who are baptized receive the Holy Ghost."[22] Therefore, by the conspicuous apparition of the Holy Ghost over Christ and by His invisible power in His soul, the twofold mission of the Spirit is foreshadowed, namely, His outward and visible mission in the Church, and His secret indwelling in the souls of the just.

The Holy Ghost and the Church

5. The Church which, already conceived, came forth from the side of the second Adam in His sleep on the Cross, first showed herself before the eyes of men on the great day of Pentecost. On that day the Holy Ghost began to manifest His gifts in the mystic body of Christ, by that miraculous outpouring already foreseen by the prophet Joel,[23] for the Paraclete "sat upon the apostles as though new spiritual crowns were placed upon their heads in tongues of fire."[24] Then the apostles "descended from the mountain," as St. John Chrysostom writes, "not bearing in their hands tables of stone like Moses, but carrying the Spirit in their mind, and pouring forth the treasure and the fountain of doctrines and graces."[25] Thus was fully accomplished that last promise of Christ to His apostles of sending the Holy Ghost, who was to complete and, as it were, to seal the deposit of

---

[21] Isa. 4:1; 11:23.
[22] De. Trin. 1., xv., c. 26.
[23] Joel 2:28-29.
[24] S. Cyril Hier. Catech. 17.
[25] In Matt. Hom. L, 2 Cor. iii., 3.

doctrine committed to them under His inspiration. "I have yet many things to say to you, but you cannot bear them now; but when He, the Spirit of Truth, shall come, He will teach you all truth."[26] For He who is the Spirit of Truth, inasmuch as He proceedeth both from the Father, who is the eternally True, and from the Son, who is the substantial Truth, receiveth from each both His essence and the fullness of all truth. This truth He communicates to His Church, guarding her by His all powerful help from ever falling into error, and aiding her to foster daily more and more the germs of divine doctrine and to make them fruitful for the welfare of the peoples. And since the welfare of the peoples, for which the Church was established, absolutely requires that this office should be continued for all time, the Holy Ghost perpetually supplies life and strength to preserve and increase the Church. "I will ask the Father, and He will give you another Paraclete, that He may abide with you for ever, the Spirit of Truth."[27]

6. By Him the bishops are constituted, and by their ministry are multiplied not only the children, but also the fathers-that is to say, the priests-to rule and feed the Church by that Blood wherewith Christ has redeemed Her. "The Holy Ghost hath placed you bishops to rule the Church of God, which He bath purchased with His own Blood."[28] And both bishops and priests, by the miraculous gift of the Spirit, have the power of absolving sins, according to those words of Christ to the Apostles: "Receive ye the Holy Ghost; whose sins you shall forgive they are forgiven them, and whose you shall retain they are retained."[29] That the Church is a divine institution is most clearly proved by the splendour and glory of those gifts and graces with which she is adorned, and whose author and giver is the Holy Ghost. Let it suffice to state that, as Christ is the Head of the Church, so is the Holy Ghost her soul. "What the soul is in our body, that is the

---

[26] John 16:12-13.
[27] John 14:16-17.
[28] Acts 20:28.
[29] John 20:23, 22.

Holy Ghost in Christ's body, the Church."[30] This being so, no further and fuller "manifestation and revelation of the Divine Spirit" may be imagined or expected; for that which now takes place in the Church is the most perfect possible, and will last until that day when the Church herself, having passed through her militant career, shall be taken up into the joy of the saints triumphing in heaven.

The Holy Ghost in the Souls of the Just

7. The manner and extent of the action of the Holy Ghost in individual souls is no less wonderful, although somewhat more difficult to understand, inasmuch as it is entirely invisible. This outpouring of the Spirit is so abundant, that Christ Himself, from whose gift it proceeds, compares it to an overflowing river, according to those words of St. John: "He that believeth in Me, as the Scripture saith, out of his midst shall flow rivers of living water"; to which testimony the Evangelist adds the explanation: "Now this He said of the Spirit which they should receive who believed in Him."[31] It is indeed true that in those of the just who lived before Christ, the Holy Ghost resided by grace, as we read in the Scriptures concerning the prophets, Zachary, John the Baptist, Simeon, and Anna; so that on Pentecost the Holy Ghost did not communicate Himself in such a way "as then for the first time to begin to dwell in the saints, but by pouring Himself forth more abundantly; crowning, not beginning His gifts; not commencing a new work, but giving more abundantly."[32] But if they also were numbered among the children of God, they were in a state like that of servants, for "as long as the heir is a child he differeth nothing from a servant, but is under tutors and governors."[33] Moreover, not only was their justice derived from the merits of Christ who was to come, but the communication of the Holy Ghost after Christ was much more abundant, just as the

---

[30] St. Aug., Serm. 187, de Temp.
[31] John 7:38, 39.
[32] St. Leo the Great, Hom. iii., de Pentec.
[33] Gal. 4:1, 2.

325

price surpasses in value the earnest and the reality excels the image. Wherefore St. John declares: "As yet the Spirit was not given, because Jesus was not yet glorified."[34] So soon, therefore, as Christ, "ascending on high," entered into possession of the glory of His Kingdom which He had won with so much labour, He munificently opened out the treasures of the Holy Ghost: "He gave gifts to men."[35] For "that giving or sending forth of the Holy Ghost after Christ's glorification was to be such as had never been before; not that there had been none before, but it had not been of the same kind."[36]

8. Human nature is by necessity the servant of God: "The creature is a servant; we are the servants of God by nature."[37] On account, however, of original sin, our whole nature had fallen into such guilt and dishonour that we had become enemies to God. "We were by nature the children of wrath."[38] There was no power which could raise us and deliver us from this ruin and eternal destruction. But God, the Creator of mankind and infinitely merciful, did this through His only begotten Son, by whose benefit it was brought about that man was restored so that rank and dignity whence he had fallen, and was adorned with still more abundant graces. No one can express the greatness of this work of divine grace in the souls of men. Wherefore, both in Holy Scripture and in the writings of the fathers, men are styled regenerated, new creatures, partakers of the Divine Nature, children of God, god-like, and similar epithets. Now these great blessings are justly attributed as especially belonging to the Holy Ghost. He is "the Spirit of adoption of sons, whereby we cry: Abba, Father." He fills our hearts with the sweetness of paternal love: "The Spirit Himself giveth testimony to our spirit that we are the sons of God."[39]

---

[34] John 7:39.
[35] Eph. 4:8.
[36] St. Aug., De Trin., 1. iv. c. 20.
[37] St. Cyr. Alex., Thesaur. l. v., c. 5.
[38] Eph. 2:3.
[39] Rom. 8:15-16.

This truth accords with the similitude observed by the Angelic Doctor between both operations of the Holy Ghost; for through Him "Christ was conceived in holiness to be by nature the Son of God," and "others are sanctified to be the sons of God by adoption."[40] This spiritual generation proceeds from love in a much more noble manner than the natural: namely, from the untreated Love.

9. The beginnings of this regeneration and renovation of man are by Baptism. In this sacrament, when the unclean spirit has been expelled from the soul, the Holy Ghost enters in and makes it like to Himself. "That which is born of the Spirit, is spirit."[41] The same Spirit gives Himself more abundantly in Confirmation, strengthening and confirming Christian life; from which proceeded the victory of the martyrs and the triumph of the virgins over temptations and corruptions. We have said that the Holy Ghost gives Himself: "the charity of God is poured out into our hearts by the Holy Ghost who is given to us."[42] For He not only brings to us His divine gifts, but is the Author of them and is Himself the supreme Gift, who, proceeding from the mutual love of the Father and the Son, is justly believed to be and is called "Gift of God most High." To show the nature and efficacy of this gift it is well to recall the explanation given by the doctors of the Church of the words of Holy Scripture. They say that God is present and exists in all things, "by His power, in so far as all things are subject to His power; by His presence, inasmuch as all things are naked and open to His eyes; by His essence, inasmuch as he is present to all as the cause of their being."[43] But God is in man, not only as in inanimate things, but because he is more fully known and loved by him, since even by nature we spontaneously love, desire, and seek after the good. Moreover, God by grace resides in the just soul as in a temple, in a most intimate and peculiar manner. From this proceeds that

[40] St. Th. 3a, q. xxxii., a. I.
[41] John 3:6.
[42] Rom. 5:5.
[43] St. Th. Ia, q. viii., a. 3.

union of affection by which the soul adheres most closely to God, more so than the friend is united to his most loving and beloved friend, and enjoys God in all fulness and sweetness. Now this wonderful union, which is properly called "indwelling," differing only in degree or state from that with which God beatifies the saints in heaven, although it is most certainly produced by the presence of the whole Blessed Trinity-"We will come to Him and make our abode with Him,"[44] nevertheless is attributed in a peculiar manner to the Holy Ghost. For, whilst traces of divine power and wisdom appear even in the wicked man, charity, which, as it were, is the special mark of the Holy Ghost, is shared in only by the just. In harmony with this, the same Spirit is called Holy, for He, the first and supreme Love, moves souls and leads them to sanctity, which ultimately consists in the love of God. Wherefore the apostle when calling us to the temple of God, does not expressly mention the Father or the Son, or the Holy Ghost: "Know ye not that your members are the temple of the Holy Ghost, who is in you, whom you have from God?"[45] The fullness of divine gifts is in many ways a consequence of the indwelling of the Holy Ghost in the souls of the just. For, as St. Thomas teaches, "when the Holy Ghost proceedeth as love, He proceedeth in the character of the first gift; whence Augustine with that, through the gift which is the Holy Ghost, many other special gifts are distributed among the members of Christ."[46] Among these gifts are those secret warnings and invitations, which from time to time are excited in our minds and hearts by the inspiration of the Holy Ghost. Without these there is no beginning of a good life, no progress, no arriving at eternal salvation. And since these words and admonitions are uttered in the soul in an exceedingly secret manner, they are sometimes aptly compared in Holy Writ to the breathing of a coming breeze, and the Angelic Doctor likens them to the movements of the heart which are wholly hidden in the living body. "Thy heart has a certain hidden power, and

---

[44] John 14:23.
[45] 1 Cor. 6:19.
[46] Summ. Th., la. q. xxxviii., a. 2. St. Aug. de Trin., xv., c. 19.

therefore the Holy Ghost, who invisibly vivifies and unites the Church, is compared to the heart."[47] More than this, the just man, that is to say he who lives the life of divine grace, and acts by the fitting virtues as by means of faculties, has need of those seven gifts which are properly attributed to the Holy Ghost. By means of them the soul is furnished and strengthened so as to obey more easily and promptly His voice and impulse. Wherefore these gifts are of such efficacy that they lead the just man to the highest degree of sanctity; and of such excellence that they continue to exist even in heaven, though in a more perfect way. By means of these gifts the soul is excited and encouraged to seek after and attain the evangelical beatitudes, which, like the flowers that come forth in the spring time, are the signs and harbingers of eternal beatitude. Lastly there are those blessed fruits, enumerated by the Apostle,[48] which the Spirit, even in this mortal life, produces and shows forth in the just; fruits filled with all sweetness and joy, inasmuch as they proceed from the Spirit, "who is in the Trinity the sweetness of both Father and Son, filling all creatures with infinite fullness and profusion."[49] The Divine Spirit, proceeding from the Father and the Word in the eternal light of sanctity, Himself both Love and Gift, after having manifested Himself through the veils of figures in the Old Testament, poured forth all his fullness upon Christ and upon His mystic Body, the Church; and called back by his presence and grace men who were going away in wickedness and corruption with such salutary effect that, being no longer of the earth earthy, they relished and desired quite other things, becoming of heaven heavenly.

On Devotion to the Holy Ghost

10. These sublime truths, which so clearly show forth the infinite goodness of the Holy Ghost towards us, certainly demand that

---

[47] Summ. Th. 3a, q. vii., a. I, ad 3.
[48] Gal. 5:22.
[49] St. Aug. de Trin. 1. vi., c. 9.

we should direct towards Him the highest homage of our love and devotion. Christians may do this most effectually if they will daily strive to know Him, to love Him, and to implore Him more earnestly; for which reason may this Our exhortation, flowing spontaneously from a paternal heart, reach their ears. Perchance there are still to be found among them, even nowadays, some, who if asked, as were those of old by St. Paul the Apostle, whether they have received the Holy Ghost, might answer in like manner: "We have not so much as heard whether there be a Holy Ghost."[50] At least there are certainly many who are very deficient in their religious practices, but their faith is involved in much darkness. Wherefore all preachers and those having care of souls should remember that it is their duty to instruct their people more diligently and more fully about the Holy Ghost- avoiding, however, difficult and subtle controversies, and eschewing the dangerous folly of those who rashly endeavour to pry into divine mysteries. What should be chiefly dwelt upon and clearly explained is the multitude and greatness of the benefits which have been bestowed, and are constantly bestowed, upon us by this Divine Giver, so that errors and ignorance concerning matters of such moment may be entirely dispelled, as unworthy of "the children of light." We urge this, not only because it affects a mystery by which we are directly guided to eternal life, and which must therefore be firmly believed; but also because the more clearly and fully the good is known the more earnestly it is loved. Now we owe to the Holy Ghost, as we mentioned in the second place, love, because He is God: "Thou shalt love the Lord thy God with thy whole heart, and with thy whole soul, and with thy whole strength."[51] He is also to be loved because He is the substantial, eternal, primal Love, and nothing is more lovable than love. And this all the more because He has overwhelmed us with the greatest benefits, which both testify to the benevolence of the Giver and claim the gratitude of the receiver. This love has a twofold and most conspicuous utility. In the first place it will excite us to acquire daily a clearer knowledge about the Holy

---

[50] Acts 19:2.
[51] Deut. 6:5.

Ghost; for, as the Angelic Doctor says, "the lover is not content with the superficial knowledge of the beloved, but striveth to inquire intimately into all that appertains to the beloved, and thus to penetrate into the interior; as is said of the Holy Ghost, Who is the Love of God, that He searcheth even the profound things of God."[52] In the second place it will obtain for us a still more abundant supply of heavenly gifts; for whilst a narrow heart contracteth the hand of the giver, a grateful and mindful heart causeth it to expand. Yet we must strive that this love should be of such a nature as not to consist merely in dry speculations or external observances, but rather to run forward towards action, and especially to fly from sin, which is in a more special manner offensive to the Holy Spirit. For whatever we are, that we are by the divine goodness; and this goodness is specially attributed to the Holy Ghost. The sinner offends this his Benefactor, abusing His gifts; and taking advantage of His goodness becomes more hardened in sin day by day. Again, since He is the Spirit of Truth, whosoever faileth by weakness or ignorance may perhaps have some excuse before Almighty God; but he who resists the truth through malice and turns away from it, sins most grievously against the Holy Ghost. In our days this sin has become so frequent that those dark times seem to have come which were foretold by St. Paul, in which men, blinded by the just judgment of God, should take falsehood for truth, and should believe in "the prince of this world," who is a liar and the father thereof, as a teacher of truth: "God shall send them the operation of error, to believe lying."[53] In the last times some shall depart from the faith, giving heed to spirits of error and the doctrines of devils."[54] But since the Holy Ghost, as We have said, dwells in us as in His temple, We must repeat the warning of the Apostle: "Grieve not the Holy Spirit of God, whereby you are sealed."[55] Nor is it enough to fly from sin; every Christian ought to shine with the splendour of virtue so as to be pleasing to so great and so

---

[52] 1 Cor. ii., 10; Summ. Theol., Ia. 2ae., q. 28, a. 2.
[53] 2 Thess. 2:10.
[54] 1 Tim. 4:1.
[55] Eph. 4:30.

beneficent a guest; and first of all with chastity and holiness, for chaste and holy things befit the temple. Hence the words of the Apostle: "Know you not that you are the temple of God, and that the Spirit of God dwelleth in you? But if any man violate the temple of God, him shall God destroy. For the temple of God is holy, which you are"[56]: a terrible, indeed, but a just warning.

11. Lastly, we ought to pray to and invoke the Holy Spirit, for each one of us greatly needs His protection and His help. The more a man is deficient in wisdom, weak in strength, borne down with trouble, prone to sin, so ought he the more to fly to Him who is the never-ceasing fount of light, strength, consolation, and holiness. And chiefly that first requisite of man, the forgiveness of sins, must be sought for from Him: "It is the special character of the Holy Ghost that He is the Gift of the Father and the Son. Now the remission of all sins is given by the Holy Ghost as by the Gift of God."[57] Concerning this Spirit the words of the Liturgy are very explicit: "For He is the remission of all sins."[58] How He should be invoked is clearly taught by the Church, who addresses Him in humble supplication, calling upon Him by the sweetest names: "Come, Father of the poor! Come, Giver of gifts! Come, Light of our hearts! O, best of Consolers, sweet Guest of the soul, our refreshment!"[59] She earnestly implores Him to wash, heal, water our minds and hearts, and to give to us who trust in Him "the merit of virtue, the acquirement of salvation, and joy everlasting." Nor can it be in any way doubted that He will listen to such prayer, since we read the words written by His own inspiration: "The Spirit Himself asketh for us with unspeakable groanings."[60] Lastly, we ought confidently and continually to beg of Him to illuminate us daily more and more with His light and inflame us with His charity: for, thus inspired with faith and love, we may press

---

[56] 1 Cor. 3:16-17.
[57] Summ. Th. 3a, q. iii., a. 8, ad 3m.
[58] Roman Missal, Tuesday after Pentecost.
[59] Hymn, Veni Sancte Spiritus.
[60] Rom. 8:26.

onward earnestly towards our eternal reward, since He "is the pledge of our inheritance."[61]

12. Such, Venerable Brethren, are the teachings and exhortations which We have seen good to utter, in order to stimulate devotion to the Holy Ghost. We have no doubt that, chiefly by means of your zeal and earnestness, they will bear abundant fruit among Christian peoples. We Ourselves shall never in the future fail to labour towards so important an end; and it is even Our intention, in whatever ways may appear suitable, to further cultivate and extend this admirable work of piety. Meanwhile, as two years ago, in Our Letter *Provida Matris*, We recommended to Catholics special prayers at the Feast of Pentecost, for the Re-union of Christendom, so now We desire to make certain further decrees on the same subject.

An Annual Novena Decreed

13. Wherefore, We decree and command that throughout the whole Catholic Church, this year and in every subsequent year, a Novena shall take place before Whit-Sunday, in all parish churches, and also, if the local Ordinaries think fit, in other churches and oratories. To all who take part in this Novena and duly pray for Our intention, We grant for each day an Indulgence of seven years and seven quarantines; moreover, a Plenary Indulgence on any one of the days of the Novena, or on Whit-Sunday itself, or on any day during the Octave; provided they shall have received the Sacraments of Penance and the Holy Eucharist, and devoutly prayed for Our intention. We will that those who are legitimately prevented from attending the Novena, or who are in places where the devotions cannot, in the judgment of the Ordinary, be conveniently carried out in church, shall equally enjoy the same benefits, provided they make the Novena privately and observe the other conditions. Moreover We are pleased to grant, in perpetuity, from the Treasury of the

---

[61] Eph. 1:14.

Church, that whosoever, daily during the Octave of Pentecost up to Trinity Sunday inclusive, offer again publicly or privately any prayers, according to their devotion, to the Holy Ghost, and satisfy the above conditions, shall a second time gain each of the same Indulgences. All these Indulgences We also permit to be applied to the suffrage of the souls in Purgatory.

14. And now Our mind and heart turn back to those hopes with which We began, and for the accomplishment of which We earnestly pray, and will continue to pray, to the Holy Ghost. Unite, then, Venerable Brethren, your prayers with Ours, and at your exhortation let all Christian peoples add their prayers also, invoking the powerful and ever-acceptable intercession of the Blessed Virgin. You know well the intimate and wonderful relations existing between her and the Holy Ghost, so that she is justly called His Spouse. The intercession of the Blessed Virgin was of great avail both in the mystery of the Incarnation and in the coming of the Holy Ghost upon the Apostles. May she continue to strengthen our prayers with her suffrages, that, in the midst of all the stress and trouble of the nations, those divine prodigies may be happily revived by the Holy Ghost, which were foretold in the words of David: "Send forth Thy Spirit and they shall be created, and Thou shalt renew the face of the earth."[62]

15. As a pledge of Divine favour and a testimony of Our affection, Venerable Brethren, to you, to your Clergy, and people, We gladly impart in the Lord the Apostolic Benediction.

Given at St. Peter's, in Rome, on the 9th day of May, 1897, in the 20th year of Our Pontificate.

---

[62] Ps. 103:30.

XIII: Testem Benevolentiae Nostrae

January 22, 1899

ON AMERICANISM

To Our Beloved Son, James Cardinal Gibbons,
Cardinal Priest of the Title Sancta Maria, Beyond the Tiber, Archbishop of
Baltimore:

Beloved Son, Health and Apostolic Blessing:

We send to you by this letter a renewed expression of that good
will which we have not failed during the course of our pontificate
to manifest frequently to you and to your colleagues in the
episcopate and to the whole American people, availing ourselves
of every opportunity offered us by the progress of your church
or whatever you have done for safeguarding and promoting
Catholic interests. Moreover, we have often considered and
admired the noble gifts of your nation which enable the
American people to be alive to every good work which promotes
the good of humanity and the splendor of civilization. Although
this letter is not intended, as preceding ones, to repeat the words
of praise so often spoken, but rather to call attention to some
things to be avoided and corrected; still because it is conceived in
that same spirit of apostolic charity which has inspired all our
letters, we shall expect that you will take it as another proof of
our love; the more so because it is intended to suppress certain
contentions which have arisen lately among you to the detriment
of the peace of many souls.

It is known to you, beloved son, that the biography of Isaac
Thomas Hecker, especially through the action of those who
under took to translate or interpret it in a foreign language, has
excited not a little controversy, on account of certain opinions
brought forward concerning the way of leading Christian life.

We, therefore, on account of our apostolic office, having to guard the integrity of the faith and the security of the faithful, are desirous of writing to you more at length concerning this whole matter.

The underlying principle of these new opinions is that, in order to more easily attract those who differ from her, the Church should shape her teachings more in accord with the spirit of the age and relax some of her ancient severity and make some concessions to new opinions. Many think that these concessions should be made not only in regard to ways of living, but even in regard to doctrines which belong to the deposit of the faith. They contend that it would be opportune, in order to gain those who differ from us, to omit certain points of her teaching which are of lesser importance, and to tone down the meaning which the Church has always attached to them. It does not need many words, beloved son, to prove the falsity of these ideas if the nature and origin of the doctrine which the Church proposes are recalled to mind. The Vatican Council says concerning this point: "For the doctrine of faith which God has revealed has not been proposed, like a philosophical invention to be perfected by human ingenuity, but has been delivered as a divine deposit to the Spouse of Christ to be faithfully kept and infallibly declared. Hence that meaning of the sacred dogmas is perpetually to be retained which our Holy Mother, the Church, has once declared, nor is that meaning ever to be departed from under the pretense or pretext of a deeper comprehension of them."[1]

We cannot consider as altogether blameless the silence which purposely leads to the omission or neglect of some of the principles of Christian doctrine, for all the principles come from the same Author and Master, "the Only Begotten Son, Who is in the bosom of the Father."[2] They are adapted to all times and all nations, as is clearly seen from the words of our Lord to His

---

[1] Constitutio de Fide Catholica, Chapter iv.
[2] John 1:18.

apostles: "Going, therefore, teach all nations; teaching them to observe all things whatsoever I have commanded you, and behold, I am with you all days, even to the end of the world."[3] Concerning this point the Vatican Council says: "All those things are to be believed with divine and catholic faith which are contained in the Word of God, written or handed down, and which the Church, either by a solemn judgment or by her ordinary and universal magisterium, proposes for belief as having been divinely revealed."[4]

Let it be far from anyone's mind to suppress for any reason any doctrine that has been handed down. Such a policy would tend rather to separate Catholics from the Church than to bring in those who differ. There is nothing closer to our heart than to have those who are separated from the fold of Christ return to it, but in no other way than the way pointed out by Christ.

The rule of life laid down for Catholics is not of such a nature that it cannot accommodate itself to the exigencies of various times and places.[5] The Church has, guided by her Divine Master, a kind and merciful spirit, for which reason from the very beginning she has been what St. Paul said of himself: "I became all things to all men that I might save all."

History proves clearly that the Apostolic See, to which has been entrusted the mission not only of teaching but of governing the whole Church, has continued "in one and the same doctrine, one and the same sense, and one and the same judgment."[6]

But in regard to ways of living she has been accustomed to so yield that, the divine principle of morals being kept intact, she

---

[3] Matt. 28:19.
[4] Const. de fide, Chapter iii.
[5] VOL. XXIV-13.
[6] Const. de fide, Chapter iv.

has never neglected to accommodate herself to the character and genius of the nations which she embraces.

Who can doubt that she will act in this same spirit again if the salvation of souls requires it? In this matter the Church must be the judge, not private men who are often deceived by the appearance of right. In this, all who wish to escape the blame of our predecessor, Pius the Sixth, must concur. He condemned as injurious to the Church and the spirit of God who guides her the doctrine contained in proposition lxxviii of the Synod of Pistoia, "that the discipline made and approved by the Church should be submitted to examination, as if the Church could frame a code of laws useless or heavier than human liberty can bear."

But, beloved son, in this present matter of which we are speaking, there is even a greater danger and a more manifest opposition to Catholic doctrine and discipline in that opinion of the lovers of novelty, according to which they hold such liberty should be allowed in the Church, that her supervision and watchfulness being in some sense lessened, allowance be granted the faithful, each one to follow out more freely the leading of his own mind and the trend of his own proper activity. They are of opinion that such liberty has its counterpart in the newly given civil freedom which is now the right and the foundation of almost every secular state.

In the apostolic letters concerning the constitution of states, addressed by us to the bishops of the whole Church, we discussed this point at length; and there set forth the difference existing between the Church, which is a divine society, and all other social human organizations which depend simply on free will and choice of men.

It is well, then, to particularly direct attention to the opinion which serves as the argument in behalf of this greater liberty sought for and recommended to Catholics.

It is alleged that now the Vatican decree concerning the infallible teaching authority of the Roman Pontiff having been proclaimed that nothing further on that score can give any solicitude, and accordingly, since that has been safeguarded and put beyond question a wider and freer field both for thought and action lies open to each one. But such reasoning is evidently faulty, since, if we are to come to any conclusion from the infallible teaching authority of the Church, it should rather be that no one should wish to depart from it, and moreover that the minds of all being leavened and directed thereby, greater security from private error would be enjoyed by all. And further, those who avail themselves of such a way of reasoning seem to depart seriously from the over-ruling wisdom of the Most High—which wisdom, since it was pleased to set forth by most solemn decision the authority and supreme teaching rights of this Apostolic See—willed that decision precisely in order to safeguard the minds of the Church's children from the dangers of these present times.

These dangers, viz., the confounding of license with liberty, the passion for discussing and pouring contempt upon any possible subject, the assumed right to hold whatever opinions one pleases upon any subject and to set them forth in print to the world, have so wrapped minds in darkness that there is now a greater need of the Church's teaching office than ever before, lest people become unmindful both of conscience and of duty.

We, indeed, have no thought of rejecting everything that modern industry and study has produced; so far from it that we welcome to the patrimony of truth and to an ever-widening scope of public well-being whatsoever helps toward the progress of learning and virtue. Yet all this, to be of any solid benefit, nay, to have a real existence and growth, can only be on the condition of recognizing the wisdom and authority of the Church.

Coming now to speak of the conclusions which have been deduced from the above opinions, and for them, we readily believe there was no thought of wrong or guile, yet the things

themselves certainly merit some degree of suspicion. First, all
external guidance is set aside for those souls who are striving
after Christian perfection as being superfluous or indeed, not
useful in any sense—the contention being that the Holy Spirit
pours richer and more abundant graces than formerly upon the
souls of the faithful, so that without human intervention He
teaches and guides them by some hidden instinct of His own.
Yet it is the sign of no small over-confidence to desire to
measure and determine the mode of the Divine communication
to mankind, since it wholly depends upon His own good
pleasure, and He is a most generous dispenser 'of his own gifts.
"The Spirit breatheth whereso He listeth."[7]

"And to each one of us grace is given according to the measure
of the giving of Christ."[8]

And shall any one who recalls the history of the apostles, the
faith of the nascent church, the trials and deaths of the martyrs—
and, above all, those olden times, so fruitful in saints—dare to
measure our age with these, or affirm that they received less of
the divine outpouring from the Spirit of Holiness? Not to dwell
upon this point, there is no one who calls in question the truth
that the Holy Spirit does work by a secret descent into the souls
of the just and that He stirs them alike by warnings and impulses,
since unless this were the case all outward defense and authority
would be unavailing. "For if any persuades himself that he can
give assent to saving, that is, to gospel truth when proclaimed,
without any illumination of the Holy Spirit, who give's unto all
sweetness both to assent and to hold, such an one is deceived by
a heretical spirit."[9]

Moreover, as experience shows, these monitions and impulses of
the Holy Spirit are for the most part felt through the medium of

---

[7] John 3:8.
[8] Eph. 4:7.
[9] From the Second Council of Orange, Canon 7.

the aid and light of an external teaching authority. To quote St. Augustine. "He (the Holy Spirit) co-operates to the fruit gathered from the good trees, since He externally waters and cultivates them by the outward ministry of men, and yet of Himself bestows the inward increase."[10] This, indeed, belongs to the ordinary law of God's loving providence that as He has decreed that men for the most part shall be saved by the ministry also of men, so has He wished that those whom He calls to the higher planes of holiness should be led thereto by men; hence St. Chrysostom declares we are taught of God through the instrumentality of men.[11] Of this a striking example is given us in the very first days of the Church.

For though Saul, intent upon blood and slaughter, had heard the voice of our Lord Himself and had asked, "What dost Thou wish me to do?" yet he was bidden to enter Damascus and search for Ananias. Acts ix: "Enter the city and it shall be there told to thee what thou must do."

Nor can we leave out of consideration the truth that those who are striving after perfection, since by that fact they walk in no beaten or well-known path, are the most liable to stray, and hence have greater need than others of a teacher and guide. Such guidance has ever obtained in the Church; it has been the universal teaching of those who throughout the ages have been eminent for wisdom and sanctity—and hence to reject it would be to commit one's self to a belief at once rash and dangerous.

A thorough consideration of this point, in the supposition that no exterior guide is granted such souls, will make us see the difficulty of locating or determining the direction and application of that more abundant influx of the Holy Spirit so greatly extolled by innovators To practice virtue there is absolute need of the assistance of the Holy Spirit, yet we find those who are

---

[10] De Gratia Christi, Chapter xix.
[11] Homily I in Inscrib. Altar.

fond of novelty giving an unwarranted importance to the natural virtues, as though they better responded to the customs and necessities of the times and that having these as his outfit man becomes more ready to act and more strenuous in action. It is not easy to understand how persons possessed of Christian wisdom can either prefer natural to supernatural virtues or attribute to them a greater efficacy and fruitfulness. Can it be that nature conjoined with grace is weaker than when left to herself?

Can it be that those men illustrious for sanctity, whom the Church distinguishes and openly pays homage to, were deficient, came short in the order of nature and its endowments, because they excelled in Christian strength? And although it be allowed at times to wonder at acts worthy of admiration which are the outcome of natural virtue—is there anyone at all endowed simply with an outfit of natural virtue? Is there any one not tried by mental anxiety, and this in no light degree? Yet ever to master such, as also to preserve in its entirety the law of the natural order, requires an assistance from on high These single notable acts to which we have alluded will frequently upon a closer investigation be found to exhibit the appearance rather than the reality of virtue. Grant that it is virtue, unless we would "run in vain" and be unmindful of that eternal bliss which a good God in his mercy has destined for us, of what avail are natural virtues unless seconded by the gift of divine grace? Hence St. Augustine well says: "Wonderful is the strength, and swift the course, but outside the true path." For as the nature of man, owing to the primal fault, is inclined to evil and dishonor, yet by the help of grace is raised up, is borne along with a new greatness and strength, so, too, virtue, which is not the product of nature alone, but of grace also, is made fruitful unto everlasting life and takes on a more strong and abiding character.

This over-esteem of natural virtue finds a method of expression in assuming to divide all virtues in active and passive, and it is alleged that whereas passive virtues found better place in past times, our age is to be characterized by the active. That such a division and distinction cannot be maintained is patent—for there is not, nor can there be, merely passive virtue. "Virtue," says St. Thomas Aquinas, "designates the perfection of some faculty, but end of such faculty is an act, and an act of virtue is naught else than the good use of free will," acting, that is to say, under the grace of God if the act be one of supernatural virtue.

He alone could wish that some Christian virtues be adapted to certain times and different ones for other times who is unmindful of the apostle's words: "That those whom He foreknew, He predestined to be made conformable to the image of His Son."[12] Christ is the teacher and the exemplar of all sanctity, and to His standard must all those conform who wish for eternal life. Nor does Christ know any change as the ages pass, "for He is yesterday and today and the same forever."[13] To the men of all ages was the precept given: "Learn of Me, because I am meek and humble of heart."[14]

To every age has He been made manifest to us as obedient even unto death; in every age the apostle's dictum has its force: "Those who are Christ's have crucified their flesh with its vices and concupiscences." Would to God that more nowadays practiced these virtues in the degree of the saints of past times, who in humility, obedience and self-restraint were powerful "in word and in deed" —to the great advantage not only of religion, but of the state and the public welfare.

From this disregard of the angelical virtues, erroneously styled passive, the step was a short one to a contempt of the religious life which has in some degree taken hold of minds. That such a value is generally held by the upholders of new views, we infer from certain statements concerning the vows which religious orders take. They say vows are alien to the spirit of our times, in

---

[12] Rom. 8:29.
[13] Heb. 13:8.
[14] Matt. 11:29.

that they limit the bounds of human liberty; that they are more suitable to weak than to strong minds; that so far from making for human perfection and the good of human organization, they are hurtful to both; but that this is as false as possible from the practice and the doctrine of the Church is clear, since she has always given the very highest approval to the religious method of life; nor without good cause, for those who under the divine call have freely embraced that state of life did not content themselves with the observance of precepts, but, going forward to the evangelical counsels, showed themselves ready and valiant soldiers of Christ. Shall we judge this to be a characteristic of weak minds, or shall we say that it is useless or hurtful to a more perfect state of life?

Those who so bind themselves by the vows of religion, far from having suffered a loss of liberty, enjoy that fuller and freer kind, that liberty, namely, by which Christ hath made us free. And this further view of theirs, namely, that the religious life is either entirely useless or of little service to the Church, besides being injurious to the religious orders cannot be the opinion of anyone who has read the annals of the Church. Did not your country, the United States, derive the beginnings both of faith and of culture from the children of these religious families? to one of whom but very lately, a thing greatly to your praise, you have decreed that a statue be publicly erected. And even at the present time wherever the religious families are found, how speedy and yet how fruitful a harvest of good works do they not bring forth! How very many leave home and seek strange lands to impart the truth of the gospel and to widen the bounds of civilization; and this they do with the greatest cheerfulness amid manifold dangers! Out of their number not less, indeed, than from the rest of the clergy, the Christian world finds the preachers of God's word, the directors of conscience, the teachers of youth and the Church itself the examples of all sanctity.

Nor should any difference of praise be made between those who follow the active state of life and those others who, charmed with solitude, give themselves to prayer and bodily mortification. And how much, indeed, of good report these have merited, and do merit, is known surely to all who do not forget that the "continual prayer of the just man" avails to placate and to bring down the blessings of heaven when to such prayers bodily mortification is added.

But if there be those who prefer to form one body without the obligation of the vows let them pursue such a course. It is not new in the Church, nor in any wise censurable. Let them be careful, however, not to set forth such a state above that of religious orders. But rather, since mankind are more disposed at the present time to indulge themselves in pleasures, let those be held in greater esteem "who having left all things have followed Christ."

Finally, not to delay too long, it is stated that the way and method hitherto in use among Catholics for bringing back those who have fallen away from the Church should be left aside and another one chosen, in which matter it will suffice to note that it is not the part of prudence to neglect that which antiquity in its long experience has approved and which is also taught by apostolic authority. The scriptures teach us that it is the duty of all to be solicitous for the salvation of one's neighbor, according to the power and position of each. The faithful do this by religiously discharging the duties of their state of life, by the uprightness of their conduct, by their works of Christian charity and by earnest and continuous prayer to God. On the other hand, those who belong to the clergy should do this by an enlightened fulfillment of their preaching ministry, by the pomp and splendor of ceremonies especially by setting forth that sound form of doctrine which Saint Paul inculcated upon Titus and Timothy. But if, among the different ways of preaching the word of God that one sometimes seems to be preferable, which directed to non-Catholics, not in churches, but in some suitable place, in such wise that controversy is not sought, but friendly conference, such a method is certainly without fault. But let those who undertake such ministry be set apart by the authority of the bishops and let them be men whose science and virtue has been previously ascertained. For we think that there are many in your country who are separated from Catholic truth more by ignorance than by ill-will, who might perchance more easily be drawn to the one fold of Christ if this truth be set forth to them in a friendly and familiar way.

From the foregoing it is manifest, beloved son, that we are not able to give approval to those views which, in their collective sense, are called by some "Americanism." But if by this name are to be understood certain endowments of mind which belong to the American people, just as other characteristics belong to various other nations, and if, moreover, by it is designated your political condition and the laws and customs by which you are governed, there is no reason to take exception to the name. But if this is to be so understood that the doctrines which have been adverted to above are not only indicated, but exalted, there can be no manner of doubt that our venerable brethren, the bishops of America, would be the first to repudiate and condemn it as being most injurious to themselves and to their country. For it would give rise to the suspicion that there are among you some who conceive and would have the Church in America to be different from what it is in the rest of the world.

But the true church is one, as by unity of doctrine, so by unity of government, and she is catholic also. Since God has placed the center and foundation of unity in the chair of Blessed Peter, she is rightly called the Roman Church, for "where Peter is, there is the church." Wherefore, if anybody wishes to be considered a real Catholic, he ought to be able to say from his heart the selfsame words which Jerome addressed to Pope Damasus: "I, acknowledging no other leader than Christ, am bound in fellowship with Your Holiness; that is, with the chair of Peter. I know that the church was built upon him as its rock, and that whosoever gathereth not with you, scattereth."

We having thought it fitting, beloved son, in view of your high office, that this letter should be addressed specially to you. It will also be our care to see that copies are sent to the bishops of the United States, testifying again that love by which we embrace your whole country, a country which in past times has done so much for the cause of religion, and which will by the Divine assistance continue to do still greater things. To you, and to all the faithful of America, we grant most lovingly, as a pledge of Divine assistance, our apostolic benediction.

Given at Rome, from St. Peter's, the 22nd day of January, 1899, and the thirty-first of our pontificate.

XIV: Graves de Communi Re

January 18, 1901

ON CHRISTIAN DEMOCRACY

The grave discussions on economical questions which for same time past have disturbed the peace of several countries of the world are growing in frequency and intensity to such a degree that the minds of thoughtful men are filled, and rightly so, with worry and alarm. These discussions take their rise in the bad philosophical and ethical teaching which is now widespread among the people. The changes, also, which the mechanical inventions of the age have introduced, the rapidity of communication between places, and the devices of every kind for diminishing labor and increasing gain, all add bitterness to the strife; and, lastly, matters have been brought to such a pass by the struggle between capital and labor, fomented as it is by professional agitators, that the countries where these disturbances most frequently occur find themselves confronted with ruin and disaster.

2. At the very beginning of Our pontificate We clearly pointed out what the peril was which confronted society on this head, and We deemed it Our duty to warn Catholics, in unmistakable language,[1] how great the error was which was lurking in the utterances of socialism, and how great the danger was that threatened not only their temporal possessions, but also their morality and religion. That was the purpose of Our encyclical letter *Quod Apostolici Muneris* which We published on the 28th of December in the year 1878; but, as these dangers day by day threatened still greater disaster, both to individuals and the commonwealth, We strove with all the more energy to avert

---

[1] See above, Quod Apostolici Muneris, no. 79: Rerum novarum, no. 115.

them. This was the object of Our encyclical *Rerum Novarum* of the 15th of May, 1891, in which we dwelt at length on the rights and duties which both classes of society - those namely, who control capital, and those who contribute labor - are bound in relation to each other; and at the same time, We made it evident that the remedies which are most useful to protect the cause of religion, and to terminate the contest between the different classes of society, were to be found in the precepts of the Gospel.

3. Nor, with God's grace, were Our hopes entirely frustrated. Even those who are not Catholics, moved by the power of truth, avowed that the Church must be credited with a watchful care over all classes of society, and especially those whom fortune had least favored. Catholics, of course, profited abundantly by these letters, for they not only received encouragement and strength for the excellent undertakings in which they were engaged, but also obtained the light which they needed in order to study this order of problems with great sureness and success. Hence it happened that the differences of opinion which prevailed among them were either removed or lessened. In the order of action, much has been done in favor of the proletariat, especially in those places where poverty was at its worst. Many new institutions were set on foot, those which were already established were increased, and all reaped the benefit of a greater stability. Such are, for instance, the popular bureaus which supply information to the uneducated; the rural banks which make loans to small farmers; the societies for mutual help or relief; the unions of working men and other associations or institutions of the same kind. Thus, under the auspices of the Church, a measure of united action among Catholics was secured, as well as some planning in the setting up of agencies for the protection of the masses which, in fact, are as often oppressed by guile and exploitation of their necessities as by their own indigence and toil.

4. This work of popular aid had, at first, no name of its own. The name of Christian Socialism, with its derivatives, which was adopted by some was very properly allowed to fall into disuse. Afterwards, some asked to have it called the popular Christian Movement. In the countries most concerned with this matter, there are some who are known as Social Christians. Elsewhere, the movement is described as Christian Democracy and its partisans as Christian Democrats, in opposition to what the socialists call Social Democracy. Not much exception is taken to the first of these two names, i.e., Social Christians, but many excellent men find the term Christian Democracy objectionable. They hold it to be very ambiguous and for this reason open to two objections. It seems by implication covertly to favor popular government and to disparage other methods of political administration. Secondly, it appears to belittle religion by restricting its scope to the care of the poor, as if the other sections of society were not of its concern. More than that, under the shadow of its name there might easily lurk a design to attack all legitimate power, either civil or sacred. Wherefore, since this discussion is now so widespread, and so bitter, the consciousness of duty warns Us to put a check on this controversy and to define what Catholics are to think on this matter. We also propose to describe how the movement may extend its scope and be made more useful to the commonwealth.

5. What Social Democracy is and what Christian Democracy ought to be, assuredly no one can doubt. The first, with due consideration to the greater or less intemperance of its utterance, is carried to such an excess by many as to maintain that there is really nothing existing above the natural order of things, and that the acquirement and enjoyment of corporal and external goods constitute man's happiness. It aims at putting all government in the hands of the masses, reducing all ranks to the same level, abolishing all distinction of class, and finally introducing community of goods. Hence, the right to own private property is to be abrogated, and whatever property a man possesses, or whatever means of livelihood he has, is to be common to all.

6. As against this, Christian Democracy, by the fact that it is Christian, is built, and necessarily so, on the basic principles of divine faith, and it must provide better conditions for the masses, with the ulterior object of promoting the perfection of souls made for things eternal. Hence, for Christian Democracy, justice is sacred; it must maintain that the right of acquiring and possessing property cannot be impugned, and it must safeguard the various distinctions and degrees which are indispensable in every well-ordered commonwealth. Finally, it must endeavor to preserve in every human society the form and the character which God ever impresses on it. It is clear, therefore, that there in nothing in common between Social and Christian Democracy. They differ from each other as much as the sect of socialism differs from the profession of Christianity.

7. Moreover, it would be a crime to distort this name of Christian Democracy to politics, for, although democracy, both in its philological and philosophical significations, implies popular government, yet in its present application it must be employed without any political significance, so as to mean nothing else than this beneficent Christian action in behalf of the people. For, the laws of nature and of the Gospel, which by right are superior to all human contingencies, are necessarily independent of all particular forms of civil government, while at the same time they are in harmony with everything that is not repugnant to morality and justice. They are, therefore, and they must remain absolutely free from the passions and the vicissitudes of parties, so that, under whatever political constitution, the citizens may and ought to abide by those laws which command them to love God above all things, and their neighbors as themselves. This has always been the policy of the Church. The Roman Pontiffs acted upon this principle, whenever they dealt with different countries, no matter what might be the character of their governments. Hence, the mind and the action of Catholics devoted to promoting the welfare of the working classes can never be actuated with the purpose of favoring and introducing one government in place of another.

8. In the same manner, we must remove from Christian Democracy another possible subject of reproach, namely, that while looking after the advantage of the working people it should seem to overlook the upper classes of society, for they also are of the greatest use in preserving and perfecting the commonwealth. The Christian law of charity, which has just been mentioned, will prevent us from so doing. For it embraces all men, irrespective of ranks, as members of one and the same family, children of the same most beneficent Father, redeemed by the same Saviour, and called to the same eternal heritage. Hence the doctrine of the Apostle, who warns us that "We are one body and one spirit called to the one hope in our vocation; one Lord, one faith and one baptism; one God and the Father of all who is above all, and through all, and in us all."[2] Wherefore, on account of the union established by nature between the common people and the other classes of society, and which Christian brotherhood makes still closer, whatever diligence we devote to assisting the people will certainly profit also the other classes, the more so since, as will be thereafter shown, their co-operation is proper and necessary for the success of this undertaking.

9. Let there be no question of fostering under this name of Christian Democracy any intention of diminishing the spirit of obedience, or of withdrawing people from their lawful rulers. Both the natural and the Christian law command us to revere those who in their various grades are shown above us in the State, and to submit ourselves to their just commands. It is quite in keeping with our dignity as men and Christians to obey, not only exteriorly, but from the heart, as the Apostle expresses it, "for conscience' sake," when he commands us to keep our soul subject to the higher powers.[3] It is abhorrent to the profession of Christianity that any one should feel unwilling to be subject and obedient to those who rule in the Church, and first of all to the bishops whom (without prejudice to the universal power of the

---

[2] Eph.4:4-6.
[3] Rom. 13:1, 5.

Roman Pontiff) "the Holy Spirit has placed to rule the Church of God which Christ has purchased by His Blood."[4] He who thinks or acts otherwise is guilty of ignoring the grave precept of the Apostle who bids us to obey our rulers and to be subject to them, for they watch as having to give an account of our souls.[5] Let the faithful everywhere implant these principles deep in their souls, and put them in practice in their daily life, and let the ministers of the Gospel meditate them profoundly, and incessantly labor, not merely by exhortation but especially by example, to teach them to others.

10. We have recalled these principles, which on other occasions We had already elucidated, in the hope that all dispute about the name of Christian Democracy will cease and that all suspicion of any danger coming from what the name signifies will be put at rest. And with reason do We hope so; for, neglecting the opinions of certain men whose views on the nature and efficacy of this kind of Christian Democracy are not free from exaggeration and from error, let no one condemn that zeal which, in accordance with the natural and divine laws, aims to make the condition of those who toil more tolerable; to enable them to obtain, little by little, those means by which they may provide for the future; to help them to practice in public and in private the duties which morality and religion inculcate; to aid them to feel that they are not animals but men, not heathens but Christians, and so to enable them to strive more zealously and more eagerly for the one thing which is necessary; viz., that ultimate good for which we are born into this world. This is the intention; this is the work of those who wish that the people should be animated by Christian sentiments and should be protected from the contamination of socialism which threatens them.

---

[4] Acts 20:28.
[5] Heb. 13:17.

11. We have designedly made mention here of virtue and religion. For, it is the opinion of some, and the error is already very common, that the social question is merely an economic one, whereas in point of fact it is, above all, a moral and religious matter, and for that reason must be settled by the principles of morality and according to the dictates of religion. For, even though wages are doubled and the hours of labor are shortened and food is cheapened, yet, if the working man hearkens to the doctrines that are taught on this subject, as he is prone to do, and is prompted by the examples set before him to throw off respect for God and to enter upon a life of immorality, his labors and his gain will avail him naught.

12. Trial and experience have made it abundantly clear that many a workman lives in cramped and miserable quarters, in spite of his shorter hours and larger wages, simply because he has cast aside the restraints of morality and religion. Take away the instinct which Christian wisdom has planted and nurtured in men's hearts, take away foresight, temperance, frugality, patience, and other rightful, natural habits, no matter how much he may strive, he will never achieve prosperity. That is the reason why We have incessantly exhorted Catholics to enter these associations for bettering the condition of the laboring classes, and to organize other undertakings with the same object in view; but We have likewise warned them that all this should be done under the auspices of religion, with its help and under its guidance.

13. The zeal of Catholics on behalf of the masses is especially praiseworthy because it is engaged in the very same field in which, under the benign inspiration of the Church the active industry of charity has always labored, adapting itself in all cases to the varying exigencies of the times. For the law of mutual charity perfects, as it were, the law of justice, not merely by giving each man his due and in not impeding him in the exercise of his rights, but also by befriending him, "not with the word alone, or the lips, but in deed and in truth";[6] being mindful of

355

what Christ so lovingly said to His own: "A new commandment I give unto you, that you love one another, as I have loved you, that you love also one another. By this shall all men know that you are My disciples, if you have love one for the other."[7] This zeal in coming to the rescue of our fellow men should, of course, be solicitous, first for the eternal good of souls, but it must not neglect what is good and helpful for this life.

14. We should remember what Christ said to the disciple of the Baptist who asked him: "Art thou he that art to come or look we for another?"[8] He invoked, as proof of the mission given to Him among men, His exercise of charity, quoting for them the text of Isaias: "The blind see, the lame walk, the lepers are cleansed, the deaf hear, the dead rise again, the poor have the Gospel preached to them."[9] And speaking also of the last judgment and of the rewards and punishments He will assign, He declared that He would take special account of the charity men exercised toward each other. And in that discourse there is one thing that especially excites our surprise, viz., that Christ omits those works of mercy which comfort the soul and referring only to those which comfort the body, He regards them as being done to Himself: "For I was hungry and you gave Me to eat; I was thirsty and you gave Me to drink; I was a stranger and you took Me in; naked and you covered Me; sick and you visited Me; I was in prison and you came to Me."[10]

15. To the teachings which enjoin the twofold charity of spiritual and corporal works Christ adds His own example, so that no one may fail to recognize the importance which He attaches to it. In the present instance we recall the sweet words that came from His paternal heart: "I have pity on the multitude,"[11] as well as the

---

[6] 1 John 3:18.
[7] John 13:34-35.
[8] Matt. 11:3.
[9] Matt. 11:4-5.
[10] Matt.25:35-36.
[11] Mark 8:2.

desire He had to assist them even if it were necessary to invoke His miraculous power. Of His tender compassion we have the proclamation made in holy Writ, viz., that "He went about doing good and healing all that were oppressed by the devil."[12] This law of charity which He imposed upon His Apostles, they in the most holy and zealous way put into practice; and after them those who embraced Christianity originated that wonderful variety of institutions for alleviating all the miseries by which mankind is afflicted. And these institutions carried on and continually increased their powers of relief and were the especial glories of Christianity and of the civilization of which it was the source, so that right-minded men never fail to admire those foundations, aware as they are of the proneness of men to concern themselves about their own and neglect the needs of others.

16. Nor are we to eliminate from the list of good works the giving of money for charity, in pursuance of what Christ has said: "But yet that which remaineth, give alms."[13] Against this, the socialist cries out and demands its abolition as injurious to the native dignity of man. But, if it is done in the manner which the Scripture enjoins,[14] and in conformity with the true Christian spirit, it neither connotes pride in the giver nor inflicts shame upon the one who receives. Far from being dishonorable for man, it draws closer the bonds of human society of augmenting the force of the obligation of the duties which men are under with regard to each other. No one is so rich that he does not need another's help; no one so poor as not to be useful in some way to his fellow man; and the disposition to ask assistance from others with confidence and to grant it with kindness is part of our very nature. Thus, justice and charity are so linked with each other, under the equable and sweet law of Christ, as to form an admirable cohesive power in human society and to lead all of its

---

[12] Acts 10:38.
[13] Luke 11:41.
[14] Matt. 6:2-4.

members to exercise a sort of providence in looking after their own and in seeking the common good as well.

17. As regards not merely the temporary aid given to the laboring classes, but the establishment of permanent institutions in their behalf, it is most commendable for charity to undertake them. It will thus see that more certain and more reliable means of assistance will be afforded to the necessitous. That kind of help is especially worthy of recognition which forms the minds of mechanics and laborers to thrift and foresight, so that in course of time they may be able, in part at least, to look out for themselves. To aim at that is not only to dignify the duty of the rich toward the poor, but to elevate the poor themselves, for, while it urges them to work in order to improve their condition, it preserves them meantime from danger, it refrains immoderation in their desires, and acts as a spur in the practice of virtue. Since, therefore, this is of such great avail and so much in keeping with the spirit of the times, it is a worthy object for the charity of righteous men to undertake with prudence and zeal.

18. Let it be understood, therefore, that this devotion of Catholics to comfort and elevate the mass of the people is in keeping with the spirit of the Church and is most conformable to the examples which the Church has always held up for imitation. It matters very little whether it goes under the name of the Popular Christian Movement or Christian Democracy, if the instructions that have been given by Us be fully carried out with fitting obedience. But it is of the greatest importance that Catholics should be one in mind, will, and action in a matter of such great moment. And it is also of importance that the influence of these undertakings should be extended by the multiplication of men and means devoted to the same object.

19. Especially must there be appeals to the kindly assistance of those whose rank, wealth, and intellectual as well as spiritual culture give them a certain standing in the community. If their

help is not extended, scarcely anything can be done which will help in promoting the well-being of the people. Assuredly, the more earnestly many of those who are prominent citizens conspire effectively to attain that object, the quicker and surer will the end be reached. We would, however, have them understand that they are not at all free to look after or neglect those who happen to be beneath them, but that it is a strict duty which binds them. For, no one lives only for his personal advantage in a community; he lives for the common good as well, so that, when others cannot contribute their share for the general good, those who can do so are obliged to make up the deficiency. The very extent of the benefits they have received increases the burden of their responsibility, and a stricter account will have to be rendered to God who bestowed those blessings upon them. What should also urge all to the fulfillment of their duty in this regard is the widespread disaster which will eventually fall upon all classes of society if his assistance does not arrive in time; and therefore is it that he who neglects the cause of the distressed masses is disregarding his own interest as well as that of the community.

20. If this action, which is social in the Christian sense of the term develops and grows in accordance with its own nature, there will be no danger, as is feared, that those other institutions, which the piety of our ancestors have established and which are now flourishing, will decline or be absorbed by new foundations. Both of them spring from the same root of charity and religion, and not only do not conflict with each other, but can easily be made to coalesce and combine so perfectly as to provide, all the better by the pooling of their beneficent efforts, for the needs of the masses and for the daily increasing perils to which they are exposed.

21. The condition of things at present proclaims, and proclaims vehemently, that there is need for a union of brave minds with all the resources they can command. The harvest of misery is before our eyes, and the dreadful projects of the most disastrous

national upheavals are threatening us from the growing power of the socialistic movement. They have insidiously worked their way into the very heart of the community, and in the darkness of their secret gatherings, and in the open light of day, in their writings and their harangues, they are urging the masses onward to sedition; they fling aside religious discipline; they scorn duties; they clamor only for rights; they are working incessantly on the multitudes of the needy which daily grow greater, and which, because of their poverty are easily deluded and led into error. It is equally the concern of the State and of religion, and all good men should deem it a sacred duty to preserve and guard both in the honor which is their due.

22. That this most desirable agreement of wills should be maintained, it is essential that all refrain from giving any cause of dissension which hurt and divide minds. Hence, in newspapers and in speeches to the people, let them avoid subtle and practically useless questions which are neither easy to solve nor easy to understand except by minds of unusual ability and after the most serious study. It is quite natural for people to hesitate on doubtful subjects, and that different men should hold different opinions, but those who sincerely seek after truth will preserve equanimity, modesty, and courtesy in matters of dispute. They will not let differences of opinion deteriorate into conflicts of wills. Besides, to whatever opinion a man's judgment may incline, if the matter is yet open to discussion, let him keep it, provided he be always disposed to listen with religious obedience to what the Holy See may decide on the question.

23. The action of Catholics, of whatever description it may be, will work with greater effect if all of the various associations, while preserving their individual rights, move together under one primary and directive force. In Italy, We desire that this directive force should emanate from the Institute of Catholic Congresses and Reunions so often praised by Us, to which Our predecessor and We Ourselves have committed the charge of controlling the common action of Catholics under the authority and direction of

the bishops of the country. So let it be for other nations, in case there be any leading organization of this description to which this matter has been legitimately entrusted.

24. Now, in all questions of this sort where the interests of the Church and the Christian people are so closely allied, it is evident what they who are in the sacred ministry should do, and it is clear how industrious they should be in inculcating right doctrine and in teaching the duties of prudence and charity. To go out and move among the people, to exert a healthy influence on them by adapting themselves to the present condition of things, is what more than once in addressing the clergy We have advised. More frequently, also, in writing to the bishops and other dignitaries of the Church, and especially of late,[15] We have lauded this affectionate solicitude for the people and declared it to be the special duty of both the secular and regular clergy. But in the fulfillment of this obligation let there be the greatest caution and prudence exerted, and let it be done after the fashion of the saints. Francis, who was poor and humble, Vincent of Paul, the father of the afflicted classes, and very many others whom the Church keeps ever in her memory were wont to lavish their care upon the people, but in such wise as not to be engrossed overmuch or to be unmindful of themselves or to let it prevent them from laboring with the same assiduity in the perfection of their own soul and the cultivation of virtue.

25. There remains one thing upon which We desire to insist very strongly, in which not only the ministers of the Gospel, but also

---

[15] Letter to the Minister General of the Minorites, November 25, 1898. In this letter, the Pope recalled the instructions given in Aeterni Patris concerning the way to be followed in higher studies; the doctrine of Thomas Aquinas should be followed by all the religious who wish truly to philosophize (qui vere philosophari volunt); paramount importance of the study of holy Scripture; how to preach the word of God; forceful exhortation addressed to the Franciscans to go out of their monasteries and, following the example of St. Francis, devote themselves to the salvation of the masses; importance of the Third Order of St. Francis with regard to this work.

all those who are devoting themselves to the cause of the people, can with very little difficulty bring about a most commendable result. That is to inculcate in the minds of the people, in a brotherly way and whenever the opportunity presents itself, the following principles; viz.: to keep aloof on all occasions from seditious acts and seditious men; to hold inviolate the rights of others; to show a proper respect to superiors; to willingly perform the work in which they are employed; not to grow weary of the restraint of family life which in many ways is so advantageous; to keep to their religious practices above all, and in their hardships and trials to have recourse to the Church for consolation. In the furtherance of all this, it is of great help to propose the splendid example of the Holy Family of Nazareth, and to advise the invocation of its protection, and it also helps to remind the people of the examples of sanctity which have shone in the midst of poverty, and to hold up before them the reward that awaits them in the better life to come.

26. Finally, We recur again to what We have already declared and We insist upon it most solemnly; viz., that whatever projects individuals or associations form in this matter should be formed under episcopal authority. Let them not be led astray by an excessive zeal in the cause of charity. If it leads them to be wanting in proper submission, it is not a sincere zeal; it will not have any useful result and cannot be acceptable to God. God delights in the souls of those who put aside their own designs and obey the rulers of His Church as if they were obeying Him; He assists them even when they attempt difficult things and benignly leads them to their desired end. Let them show, also, examples of virtue, so as to prove that a Christian is a hater of idleness and self indulgence, that he stands firm and unconquered in the midst of adversity. Examples of that kind have a power of moving people to dispositions of soul that make for salvation, and have all the greater force as the condition of those who give them is higher in the social scale.

27. We exhort you, venerable brethren, to provide for all this, as the necessities of men and of places may require, according to your prudence and your zeal, meeting as usual in council to combine with each other in your plans for the furtherance of these projects. Let your solicitude watch and let your authority be effective in controlling, compelling, and also in preventing, lest any one under the pretext of good should cause the vigor of sacred discipline to be relaxed or the order which Christ has established in His Church to be disturbed. Thus, by the rightful, harmonious and ever-increasing labor of all Catholics, let it become more and more evident that the tranquillity of order and the true prosperity flourish especially among those peoples whom the Church controls and influences; and that she holds it as her sacred duty to admonish every one of what the law of God enjoins, to unite the rich and the poor in the bonds of fraternal charity, and to lift up and strengthen men's souls in the times when adversity presses heavily upon them.

28. Let Our commands and Our wishes be confirmed by the words so full of apostolic charity which the blessed Paul addressed to the Romans: "I beseech you therefore brethren, be reformed in the newness of your mind; he that giveth, with simplicity; he that ruleth, with carefulness; he that showeth mercy, with cheerfulness. Let love be without dissimulation. Hating that which is evil; cleaving to that which is good; loving one another with the charity of brotherhood; with honor preventing one another; in carefulness, not slothful; rejoicing in hope; patient in tribulation; instant in prayer. Communicating to the necessities of the saints. Pursuing hospitality. Rejoice with them that rejoice; weep with them that weep; being of one mind to one another; to no man rendering evil for evil; providing good things not only in the sight of God but also in the sight,[16] of men.

---

[16] Rom. 12:1, 2, 8-13, 15-17.

29. As a pledge of these benefits receive the apostolic benediction which, venerable brethren, We grant most lovingly in the Lord to you and your clergy and people.

Given at St. Peter's in Rome, the eighteenth day of January, 1901, the thirteenth year of Our pontificate.

XV: Mirae Caritatis

May 28, 1902

ON THE HOLY EUCHARIST

To examine into the nature and to promote the effects of those manifestations of His wondrous love which, like rays of light, stream forth from Jesus Christ - this, as befits Our sacred office, has ever been, and this, with His help, to the last breath of Our life will ever be Our earnest aim and endeavour. For, whereas Our lot has been cast in an age that is bitterly hostile to justice and truth, we have not failed, as you have been reminded by the Apostolic letter which we recently addressed to you, to do what in us lay, by Our instructions and admonitions, and by such practical measures as seemed best suited for their purpose, to dissipate the contagion of error in its many shapes, and to strengthen the sinews of the Christian life. Among these efforts of Ours there are two in particular, of recent memory, closely related to each other, from the recollection whereof we gather some fruit of comfort, the more seasonable by reason of the many causes of sorrow that weigh us down. One of these is the occasion on which We directed, as a thing most desirable, that the entire human race should be consecrated by a special act to the Sacred Heart of Christ our Redeemer; the other that on which We so urgently exhorted all those who bear the name Christian to cling loyally to Him Who, by divine ordinance, is "the Way, the Truth, and the Life," not for individuals alone bur for every rightly constituted society. And now that same apostolic charity, ever watchful over the vicissitudes of the Church, moves and in a manner compels Us to add one thing more, in order to fill up the measure of what We have already conceived and carried out. This is, to commend to all Christians, more earnestly than heretofore, the all - holy Eucharist, forasmuch as it is a divine gift proceeding from the very Heart of the Redeemer, Who "with desire desireth" this singular mode of union with men, a gift most admirably adapted to be the means whereby the salutary fruits of His redemption may be distributed. Indeed We have not failed in the past, more than once, to use Our authority and to exercise Our zeal in this behalf. It gives Us much pleasure to recall to mind that We have officially approved, and enriched with canonical privileges, not a few institutions and confraternities having for their object the perpetual adoration of the Sacred Host; that We have encouraged the holding of Eucharistic Congresses, the results of which have been as profitable as the attendance at them has been numerous and distinguished; that We have designated as the heavenly patron of these and similar undertakings St. Paschal Baylon, whose devotion to the mystery of the Eucharist was so extraordinary.

2. Accordingly, Venerable Brethren, it has seemed good to Us to address you on certain points connected with this same mystery, for the defence and honour of which the solicitude of the Church has been so constantly engaged, for which Martyrs have given their lives, which has afforded to men of the highest genius a theme to be illustrated by their learning, their eloquence, their skill in all the arts; and this We will do in order to render more clearly evident and more widely known those special characteristics by virtue of which it is so singularly adapted to the needs of these our times. It was towards the close of His mortal life that Christ our Lord left this memorial of His measureless love for men, this powerful means of support "for the life of the world."[1] And precisely for this reason, We, being so soon to depart from this life, can wish for nothing better than that it may be granted to us to stir up and foster in the hearts of all men the dispositions of mindful gratitude and due devotion towards this wondrous Sacrament, wherein most especially lie, as We hold, the hope and the efficient cause of salvation and of that peace which all men so anxiously seek.

---

[1] John 6:52.

3. Some there are, no doubt, who will express their surprise that for the manifold troubles and grievous afflictions by which our age is harassed We should have determined to seek for remedies and redress in this quarter rather than elsewhere, and in some, perchance, Our words will excite a certain peevish disgust. But this is only the natural result of pride; for when this vice has taken possession of the heart, it is inevitable that Christian faith, which demands a most willing docility, should languish, and that a murky darkness in regard of divine truths should close in upon the mind; so that in the case of many these words should be made good: "Whatever things they know not, they blaspheme."[2] We, however, so far from being hereby turned aside from the design which We have taken in hand, are on the contrary determined all the more zealously and diligently to hold up the light for the guidance of the well disposed, and, with the help of the united prayers of the faithful, earnestly to implore forgiveness for those who speak evil of holy things.

The Source of Life

4. To know with an entire faith what is the excellence of the Most Holy Eucharist is in truth to know what that work is which, in the might of His mercy, God, made man, carried out on behalf of the human race. For as a right faith teaches us to acknowledge and to worship Christ as the sovereign cause of our salvation, since He by His wisdom, His laws, His ordinances, His example, and by the shedding of His blood, made all things new; so the same faith likewise teaches us to acknowledge Him and to worship Him as really present in the Eucharist, as verily abiding through all time in the midst of men, in order that as their Master, their Good Shepherd, their most acceptable Advocate with the Father, He may impart to them of His own inexhaustible abundance the benefits of that redemption which He has accomplished. Now if any one will seriously consider the benefits which flow from the Eucharist he will understand that

---

[2] Jude 1:10.

conspicuous and chief among them all is that in which the rest, without exception, are included; in a word it is for men the source of life, of that life which best deserves the name. "The bread which I will give is my flesh, for the life of the world."[3] In more than one way, as We have elsewhere declared, is Christ "the life." He Himself declared that the reason of His advent among men was this, that He might bring them the assured fulness of a more than merely human life. "I am come that they may have life, and may have it more abundantly."[4] Everyone is aware that no sooner had "the goodness and kindness of God our Saviour appeared,"[5] than there at once burst forth a certain creative force which issued in a new order of things and pused through all the veins of society, civil and domestic. Hence arose new relations between man and man; new rights and new duties, public and private; henceforth a new direction was given to government, to education, to the arts; and most important of all, man's thoughts and energies were turned towards religious truth and the pursuit of holiness. Thus was life communicated to man, a life truly heavenly and divine. And thus we are to account for those expressions which so often occur in Holy Writ, "the tree of life," "the word of life," "the book of life," "the crown of life," and particularly "the bread of life."

5. But now, since this life of which We are speaking bears a definite resemblance to the natural life of man, as the one draws its nourishment and strength from food, so also the other must have its own food whereby it may be sustained and augmented. And here it will be opportune to recall to mind on what occasion and in what manner Christ moved and prepared the hearts of men for the worthy and due reception of the living bread which He was about to give them. No sooner had the rumour spread of the miracle which He had wrought on the shores of the lake of Tiberias, when with the multiplied loaves He fed the multitude, than many forthwith flocked to Him in the hope that they, too,

---

[3] John 6:52.
[4] John 10:10.
[5] Tit. 3:4.

perchance, might be the recipients of like favour. And, just as He had taken occasion from the water which she had drawn from the well to stir up in the Samaritan woman a thirst for that "water which springeth up unto life everlasting,"[6] so now Jesus availed Himself of this opportunity to excite in the minds of the multitude a keen hunger for the bread "which endureth unto life everlasting."[7] Or, as He was careful to explain to them, was the bread which He promised the same as that heavenly manna which had been given to their fathers during their wanderings in the desert, or again the same as that which, to their amazement, they had recently received from Him; but He was Himself that bread: "I," said He, "am the bread of life."[8] And He urges this still further upon them all both by invitation and by precept: "if any man shall eat of this bread, he shall live for ever; and the bread which I will give is my flesh, for the life of the world."[9] And in these other words He brings home to them the gravity of the precept: "Amen, Amen, I say to you, unless you shall eat the flesh of the Son of Man and drink His blood, you shall not have life in you."[10] Away then with the widespread but most mischievous error of those who give it as their opinion that the reception of the Eucharist is in a manner reserved for those narrow-minded persons (as they are deemed) who rid themselves of the cares of the world in order to find rest in some kind of professedly religious life. For this gift, than which nothing can be more excellent or more conducive to salvation, is offered to all those, whatever their office or dignity may be, who wish - as every one ought to wish - to foster in themselves that life of divine grace whose goal is the attainment of the life of blessedness with God.

6. Indeed it is greatly to be desired that those men would rightly esteem and would make due provision for life everlasting, whose

---

[6] John 4:14.
[7] John 6:27.
[8] John 6:48.
[9] John 6:52.
[10] John 6:54.

industry or talents or rank have put it in their power to shape the course of human events. But alas! we see with sorrow that such men too often proudly flatter themselves that they have conferred upon this world as it were a fresh lease of life and prosperity, inasmuch as by their own energetic action they are urging it on to the race for wealth, to a struggle for the possession of commodities which minister to the love of comfort and display. And yet, whithersoever we turn, we see that human society, if it be estranged from God, instead of enjoying that peace in its possessions for which it had sought, is shaken and tossed like one who is in the agony and heat of fever; for while it anxiously strives for prosperity, and trusts to it alone, it is pursuing an object that ever escapes it, clinging to one that ever eludes the grasp. For as men and states alike necessarily have their being from God, so they can do nothing good except in God through Jesus Christ, through whom every best and choicest gift has ever proceeded and proceeds. But the source and chief of all these gifts is the venerable Eucharist, which not only nourishes and sustains that life the desire whereof demands our most strenuous efforts, but also enhances beyond measure that dignity of man of which in these days we hear so much. For what can be more honourable or a more worthy object of desire than to be made, as far as possible, sharers and partakers in the divine nature? Now this is precisely what Christ does for us in the Eucharist, wherein, after having raised man by the operation of His grace to a supernatural state, he yet more closely associates and unites him with Himself. For there is this difference between the food of the body and that of the soul, that whereas the former is changed into our substance, the latter changes us into its own; so that St. Augustine makes Christ Himself say: "You shall not change Me into yourself as you do the food of your body, but you shall be changed into Me."[11]

The Mystery of Faith

---

[11] Confessions 1. vii., c. x.

7. Moreover, in this most admirable Sacrament, which is the chief means whereby men are engrafted on the divine nature, men also find the most efficacious help towards progress in every kind of virtue. And first of all in faith. In all ages faith has been attacked; for although it elevates the human mind by bestowing on it the knowledge of the highest truths, yet because, while it makes known the existence of divine mysteries, it yet leaves in obscurity the mode of their being, it is therefore thought to degrade the intellect. But whereas in past times particular articles of faith have been made by turns the object of attack; the seat of war has since been enlarged and extended, until it has come to this, that men deny altogether that there is anything above and beyond nature. Now nothing can be better adapted to promote a renewal of the strength and fervour of faith in the human mind than the mystery of the Eucharist, the "mystery of faith," as it has been most appropriately called. For in this one mystery the entire supernatural order, with all its wealth and variety of wonders, is in a manner summed up and contained: "He hath made a remembrance of His wonderful works, a merciful and gracious Lord; He bath given food to them that fear Him."[12] For whereas God has subordinated the whole supernatural order to the Incarnation of His Word, in virtue whereof salvation has been restored to the human race, according to those words of the Apostle; "He bath purposed...to re-establish all things in Christ, that are in heaven and on earth, in Him,"[13] the Eucharist, according to the testimony of the holy Fathers, should be regarded as in a manner a continuation and extension of the Incarnation. For in and by it the substance of the incarnate Word is united with individual men, and the supreme Sacrifice offered on Calvary is in a wondrous manner renewed, as was signified beforehand by Malachi in the words: "In every place there is sacrifice, and there is offered to My name a pure oblation."[14] And this miracle, itself the very greatest of its kind, is accompanied by innumerable other miracles; for here all

---

[12] Ps. 110:4-5.
[13] Eph. 1:9-10.
[14] Mal. 1:2.

the laws of nature are suspended; the whole substance of the bread and wine are changed into the Body and the Blood; the species of bread and wine are sustained by the divine power without the support of any underlying substance; the Body of Christ is present in many places at the same time, that is to say, wherever the Sacrament is consecrated. And in order that human reason may the more willingly pay its homage to this great mystery, there have not been wanting, as an aid to faith, certain prodigies wrought in His honour, both in ancient times and in our own, of which in more than one place there exist public and notable records and memorials. It is plain that by this Sacrament faith is fed, in it the mind finds its nourishment, the objections of rationalists are brought to naught, and abundant light is thrown on the supernatural order.

8. But that decay of faith in divine things of which We have spoken is the effect not only of pride, but also of moral corruption. For if it is true that a strict morality improves the quickness of man's intellectual powers, and if on the other hand, as the maxims of pagan philosophy and the admonitions of divine wisdom combine to teach us, the keenness of the mind is blunted by bodily pleasures, how much more, in the region of revealed truths, do these same pleasures obscure the light of faith, or even, by the just judgment of God, entirely extinguish it. For these pleasures at the present day an insatiable appetite rages, infecting all classes as with an infectious disease, even from tender years. Yet even for so terrible an evil there is a remedy close at hand in the divine Eucharist. For in the first place it puts a check on lust by increasing charity, according to the words of St. Augustine, who says, speaking of charity, "As it grows, lust diminishes; when it reaches perfection, lust is no more."[15] Moreover the most chaste flesh of Jesus keeps down the rebellion of our flesh, as St. Cyril of Alexandria taught, "For Christ abiding in us lulls to sleep the law of the flesh which rages in our members."[16] Then too the special and most pleasant fruit

---

[15] De diversis quaestionibus, lxxxiii., q. 36.

of the Eucharist is that which is signified in the words of the prophet: "What is the good thing of Him," that is, of Christ, "and what is His beautiful thing, but the corn of the elect and the wine that engendereth virgins,"[17] producing, in other words, that flower and fruitage of a strong and constant purpose of virginity which, even in an age enervated by luxury, is daily multiplied and spread abroad in the Catholic Church, with those advantages to religion and to human society, wherever it is found, which are plain to see.

9. To this it must be added that by this same Sacrament our hope of everlasting blessedness, based on our trust in the divine assistance, is wonderfully strengthened. For the edge of that longing for happiness which is so deeply rooted in the hearts of all men from their birth is whetted even more and more by the experience of the deceitfulness of earthly goods, by the unjust violence of wicked men, and by all those other afflictions to which mind and body are subject. Now the venerable Sacrament of the Eucharist is both the source and the pledge of blessedness and of glory, and this, not for the soul alone, but for the body also. For it enriches the soul with an abundance of heavenly blessings, and fills it with a sweet joy which far surpasses man's hope and expectations; it sustains him in adversity, strengthens him in the spiritual combat, preserves him for life everlasting, and as a special provision for the journey accompanies him thither. And in the frail and perishable body that divine Host, which is the immortal Body of Christ, implants a principle of resurrection, a seed of immortality, which one day must germinate. That to this source man's soul and body will be indebted for both these boons has been the constant teaching of the Church, which has dutifully reaffirmed the affirmation of Christ: "He that eateth my flesh and drinketh my blood bath everlasting life; and I will raise him up at the last day."[18]

---

[16] Lib. iv., c. ii., in Joan., vi., 57
[17] Zach. 9:17.
[18] John 6:55.

10. In connection with this matter it is of importance to consider that in the Eucharist, seeing that it was instituted by Christ as "a perpetual memorial of His Passion,"[19] is proclaimed to the Christian the necessity of a salutary self-chastisement. For Jesus said to those first priests of His: "Do this in memory of Me"[20]; that is to say, do this for the commemoration of My pains, My sorrows, My grievous afflictions, My death upon the Cross. Wherefore this Sacrament is at the same time a Sacrifice, seasonable throughout the entire period of our penance; and it is likewise a standing exhortation to all manner of toil, and a solemn and severe rebuke to those carnal pleasures which some are not ashamed so highly to praise and extol: "As often as ye shall eat this bread, and drink this chalice, ye shall announce the death of the Lord, until He come."[21]

The Bond of Charity

11. Furthermore, if anyone will diligently examine into the causes of the evils of our day, he will find that they arise from this, that as charity towards God has grown cold, the mutual charity of men among themselves has likewise cooled. Men have forgotten that they are children of God and brethren in Jesus Christ; they care for nothing except their own individual interests; the interests and the rights of others they not only make light of, but often attack and invade. Hence frequent disturbances and strifes between class and class: arrogance, oppression, fraud on the part of the more powerful: misery, envy, and turbulence among the poor. These are evils for which it is in vain to seek a remedy in legislation, in threats of penalties to be incurred, or in any other device of merely human prudence. Our chief care and endeavour ought to be, according to the admonitions which We have more than once given at considerable length, to secure the union of classes in a mutual interchange of dutiful services, a union which,

---

[19] Opusc. lvii. Offic. de festo Corporis Christi.
[20] Luke 22:18.
[21] 1 Cor. 11:26.

having its origin in God, shall issue in deeds that reflect the true spirit of Jesus Christ and a genuine charity. This charity Christ brought into the world, with it He would have all hearts on fire. For it alone is capable of affording to soul and body alike, even in this life, a foretaste of blessedness; since it restrains man's inordinate self-love, and puts a check on avarice, which "is the root of all evil."[22] And whereas it is right to uphold all the claims of justice as between the various classes of society, nevertheless it is only with the efficacious aid of charity, which tempers justice, that the "equality" which St. Paul commended,[23] and which is so salutary for human society, can be established and maintained. This then is what Christ intended when he instituted this Venerable Sacrament, namely, by awakening charity towards God to promote mutual charity among men. For the latter, as is plain, is by its very nature rooted in the former, and springs from it by a kind of spontaneous growth. Nor is it possible that there should be any lack of charity among men, or rather it must needs be enkindled and flourish, if men would but ponder well the charity which Christ has shown in this Sacrament. For in it He has not only given a splendid manifestation of His power and wisdom, but "has in a manner poured out the riches of His divine love towards men."[24] Having before our eyes this noble example set us by Christ, Who bestows on us all that He has assuredly we ought to love and help one another to the utmost, being daily more closely united by the strong bond of brotherhood. Add to this that the outward and visible elements of this Sacrament supply a singularly appropriate stimulus to union. On this topic St. Cyprian writes: "In a word the Lord's sacrifice symbolises the oneness of heart, guaranteed by a persevering and inviolable charity, which should prevail among Christians. For when our Lord calls His Body bread, a substance which is kneaded together out of many grains, He indicates that we His people, whom He sustains, are bound together in close union; and when He speaks of His Blood as wine, in which the

---

[22] 1 Tim. 6:10.
[23] 2 Cor. 8:14.
[24] Conc. Trid., Sess. XIIL, De Euch. c. ii.

juice pressed from many clusters of grapes is mingled in one fluid, He likewise indicates that we His flock are by the commingling of a multitude of persons made one."[25] In like manner the angelic Doctor, adopting the sentiments of St. Augustine,[26] writes: "Our Lord has bequeathed to us His Body and Blood under the form of substances in which a multitude of things have been reduced to unity, for one of them, namely bread, consisting as it does of many grains is yet one, and the other, that is to say wine, has its unity of being from the confluent juice of many grapes; and therefore St. Augustine elsewhere says: 'O Sacrament of mercy, O sign of unity, O bond of charity!' "[27] All of which is confirmed by the declaration of the Council of Trent that Christ left the Eucharist in His Church "as a symbol of that unity and charity whereby He would have all Christians mutually joined and united…a symbol of that one body of which He is Himself the head, and to which He would have us, as members attached by the closest bonds of faith, hope, and charity."[28] The same idea had been expressed by St. Paul when he wrote: "For we, being many, are one bread, one body, all we who partake of the one bread."[29] Very beautiful and joyful too is the spectacle of Christian brotherhood and social equality which is afforded when men of all conditions, gentle and simple, rich and poor, learned and unlearned, gather round the holy altar, all sharing alike in this heavenly banquet. And if in the records of the Church it is deservedly reckoned to the special credit of its first ages that "the multitude of the believers had but one heart and one soul,"[30] there can be no shadow of doubt that this immense blessing was due to their frequent meetings at the Divine table; for we find it recorded of them: "They were persevering in the doctrine of the Apostles and in the communion of the breaking of bread."[31]

---

[25] Ep. 96 ad Magnum n. 5 (a1.6).
[26] Tract. xxxvi., in Joan. nn. 13, 17.
[27] Summ. Theol. P. IIL, q. lxxix., a.l.
[28] Conc. Trid., Sess. XIIL, De Euchar., c. ii.
[29] 1 Cor. 10:17.
[30] Acts 4:32.

12. Besides all this, the grace of mutual charity among the living, which derives from the Sacrament of the Eucharist so great an increase of strength, is further extended by virtue of the Sacrifice to all those who are numbered in the Communion of Saints. For the Communion of Saints, as everyone knows, is nothing but the mutual communication of help, expiation, prayers, blessings, among all the faithful, who, whether they have already attained to the heavenly country, or are detained in the purgatorial fire, or are yet exiles here on earth, all enjoy the common franchise of that city whereof Christ is the head, and the constitution is charity. For faith teaches us, that although the venerable Sacrifice may be lawfully offered to God alone, yet it may be celebrated in honour of the saints reigning in heaven with God Who has crowned them, in order that we may gain for ourselves their patronage. And it may also be offered - in accordance with an apostolic tradition - for the purpose of expiating the sins of those of the brethren who, having died in the Lord, have not yet fully paid the penalty of their transgressions.

13. That genuine charity, therefore, which knows how to do and to suffer all things for the salvation and the benefit of all, leaps forth with all the heat and energy of a flame from that most holy Eucharist in which Christ Himself is present and lives, in which He indulges to the utmost. His love towards us, and under the impulse of that divine love ceaselessly renews His Sacrifice. And thus it is not difficult to see whence the arduous labours of apostolic men, and whence those innumerable designs of every kind for the welfare of the human race which have been set on foot among Catholics, derive their origin, their strength, their permanence, their success.

14. These few words on a subject so vast will, we doubt not, prove most helpful to the Christian flock, if you in your zeal, Venerable Brethren, will cause them to be expounded and enforced as time and occasion may serve. But indeed a

[31] Acts 2:42.

Sacrament so great and so rich in all manner of blessings can never be extolled as it deserves by human eloquence, nor adequately venerated by the worship of man. This Sacrament, whether as the theme of devout meditation, or as the object of public adoration, or best of all as a food to be received in the utmost purity of conscience, is to be regarded as the centre towards which the spiritual life of a Christian in all its ambit gravitates; for all other forms of devotion, whatsoever they may be, lead up to it, and in it find their point of rest. In this mystery more than in any other that gracious invitation and still more gracious promise of Christ is realised and finds its daily fulfilment: "Come to me all ye that labour and are heavily burdened, and I will refresh you."[32]

15. In a word this Sacrament is, as it were, the very soul of the Church; and to it the grace of the priesthood is ordered and directed in all its fulness and in each of its successive grades. From the same source the Church draws and has all her strength, all her glory, her every supernatural endowment and adornment, every good thing that is here; wherefore she makes it the chiefest of all her cares to prepare the hearts of the faithful for an intimate union with Christ through the Sacrament of His Body and Blood, and to draw them thereto. And to this end she strives to promote the veneration of the august mystery by surrounding it with holy ceremonies. To this ceaseless and ever watchful care of the Church or Mother, our attention is drawn by that exhortation which was uttered by the holy Council of Trent, and which is so much to the purpose that for the benefit of the Christian people We here reproduce it in its entirety. "The Holy Synod admonishes, exhorts, asks and implores by the tender mercy of our God, that all and each of those who bear the name of Christian should at last unite and find peace in this sign of unity, in this bond of charity, in this symbol of concord; and that, mindful of the great majesty and singular love of Jesus Christ our Lord, Who gave His precious life as the price of our salvation,

---

[32] Matt. 11:28.

and His flesh for our food, they should believe and revere these sacred mysteries of His Body and Blood with such constancy of unwavering faith, with such interior devotion and worshipful piety, that they may be in condition to receive frequently that supersubstantial bread, and that it may be to them the life of their souls and keep their mind in soundness of faith; so that strengthened with its strength they may be enabled after the journey of this sorrowful pilgrimage to reach the heavenly country, there to see and feed upon that bread of angels which here they eat under the sacramental veils."[33]

16. History bears witness that the virtues of the Christian life have flourished best wherever and whenever the frequent reception of the Eucharist has most prevailed. And on the other hand it is no less certain that in days when men have ceased to care for this heavenly bread, and have lost their appetite for it, the practice of Christian religion has gradually lost its force and vigour. And indeed it was a needful measure of precaution against a complete falling away that Innocent III, in the Council of the Lateran, most strictly enjoined that no Christian should abstain from receiving the communion of the Lord's Body at least in the solemn paschal season. But it is clear that this precept was imposed with regret, and only as a last resource; for it has always been the desire of the Church that at every Mass some of the faithful should be present and should communicate. "The holy Synod would wish that in every celebration of the Mass some of the faithful should take part, not only by devoutly assisting thereat, but also by the sacramental reception of the Eucharist, in order that they might more abundantly partake of the fruits of this holy Sacrifice."[34]

The Sacrifice of the Mass

---

[33] Conc. Trid., Sess. XXII, c. vi.
[34] Conc. Trid., Sess. XIII. de Euchar. c. viii.

17. Most abundant, assuredly, are the salutary benefits which are stored up in this most venerable mystery, regarded as a Sacrifice; a Sacrifice which the Church is accordingly wont to offer daily "for the salvation of the whole world." And it is fitting, indeed in this age it is specially important, that by means of the united efforts of the devout, the outward honour and the inward reverence paid to this Sacrifice should be alike increased. Accordingly it is our wish that its manifold excellence may be both more widely known and more attentively considered. There are certain general principles the truth of which can be plainly perceived by the light of reason; for instance, that the dominion of God our Creator and Preserver over all men, whether in their private or in their public life, is supreme and absolute; that our whole being and all that we possess, whether individually or as members of society, comes from the divine bounty; that we on our part are bound to show to God, as our Lord, the highest reverence, and, as He is our greatest benefactor, the deepest gratitude. But how many are there who at the present day acknowledge and discharge these duties with full and exact observance? In no age has the spirit of contumacy and an attitude of defiance towards God been more prevalent than in our own; an age in which that unholy cry of the enemies of Christ: "We will not have this man to rule over us,"[35] makes itself more and more loudly heard, together with the utterance of that wicked purpose: "let us make away with Him"[36]; nor is there any motive by which many are hurried on with more passionate fury, than the desire utterly to banish God not only from the civil government, but from every form of human society. And although men do not everywhere proceed to this extremity of criminal madness, it is a lamentable thing that so many are sunk in oblivion of the divine Majesty and of His favours, and in particular of the salvation wrought for us by Christ. Now a remedy must be found for this wickedness on the one hand, and this sloth on the other, in a general increase among the faithful of fervent devotion towards the Eucharistic Sacrifice, than which

---

[35] Luke 14:14.
[36] Jer. 11:2.

nothing can give greater honour, nothing be more pleasing, to God. For it is a divine Victim which is here immolated; and accordingly through this Victim we offer to the most blessed Trinity all that honour which the infinite dignity of the Godhead demands; infinite in value and infinitely acceptable is the gift which we present to the Father in His only-begotten son; so that for His benefits to us we not only signify our gratitude, but actually make an adequate return.

18. Moreover there is another twofold fruit which we may and must derive from this great Sacrifice. The heart is saddened when it considers what a flood of wickedness, the result - as We have said - of forgetfulness and contempt of the divine Majesty, has inundated the world. It is not too much to say that a great part of the human race seems to be calling down upon itself the anger of heaven; though indeed the crop of evils which has grown up here on earth is already ripening to a just judgment. Here then is a motive whereby the faithful may be stirred to a devout and earnest endeavour to appease God the avenger of sin, and to win from Him the help which is so needful in these calamitous times. And they should see that such blessings are to be sought principally by means of this Sacrifice. For it is only in virtue of the death which Christ suffered that men can satisfy, and that most abundantly, the demands of God's justice, and can obtain the plenteous gifts of His clemency. And Christ has willed that the whole virtue of His death, alike for expiation and impetration, should abide in the Eucharist, which is no mere empty commemoration thereof, but a true and wonderful though bloodless and mystical renewal of it.

19. To conclude, we gladly acknowledge that it has been a cause of no small joy to us that during these last years a renewal of love and devotion towards the Sacrament of the Eucharist has, as it seems, begun to show itself in the hearts of the faithful; a fact which encourages us to hope for better times and a more favourable state of affairs. Many and varied, as we said at the commencement, are the expedients which an inventive piety has

devised; and worthy of special mention are the confraternities instituted either with the object of carrying out the Eucharistic ritual with greater splendour, or for the perpetual adoration of the venerable Sacrament by day and night, or for the purpose of making reparation for the blasphemies and insults of which it is the object. But neither We nor you, Venerable Brethren, can allow ourselves to rest satisfied with what has hitherto been done; for there remain many things which must be further developed or begun anew, to the end that this most divine of gifts this greatest of mysteries, may be better understood and more worthily honoured and revered, even by those who already take their part in the religious services of the Church. Wherefore, works of this kind which have been already set on foot must be ever more zealously promoted; old undertakings must be revived wherever perchance they may have fallen into decay; for instance, Confraternities of the holy Eucharist, intercessory prayers before the blessed Sacrament exposed for the veneration of the faithful, solemn processions, devout visits to God's tabernacle, and other holy and salutary practices of some kind; nothing must be omitted which a prudent piety may suggest as suitable. But the chief aim of our efforts must be that the frequent reception of the Eucharist may be everywhere revived among Catholic peoples. For this is the lesson which is taught us by the example, already referred to, of the primitive Church, by the decrees of Councils, by the authority of the Fathers and of the holy men in all ages. For the soul, like the body, needs frequent nourishment; and the holy Eucharist provides that food which is best adapted to the support of its life. Accordingly all hostile prejudices, those vain fears to which so many yield, and their specious excuses from abstaining from the Eucharist, must be resolutely put aside; for there is question here of a gift than which none other can be more serviceable to the faithful people, either for the redeeming of time from the tyranny of anxious cares concerning perishable things, or for the renewal of the Christian spirit and perseverance therein. To this end the exhortations and example of all those who occupy a prominent position will powerfully contribute, but most especially the resourceful and diligent zeal of the clergy. For priests, to whom Christ our Redeemer entrusted the office of consecrating and dispensing the mystery of His Body and Blood, can assuredly make no better return for the honour which has been conferred upon them, than by promoting with all their might the glory of his Eucharist, and by inviting and drawing the hearts of men to the health-giving springs of this great Sacrament and Sacrifice, seconding hereby the longings of His most Sacred Heart.

20. May God grant that thus, in accordance with Our earnest desire, the excellent fruits of the Eucharist may daily manifest themselves in greater abundance, to the happy increase of faith, hope, and charity, and of ail Christian virtues; and may this turn to the recovery and advantage of the whole body politic; and may the wisdom of God's most provident charity, Who instituted this mystery for all time "for the life of the world," shine forth with an ever brighter sight.

21. Encouraged by such hopes as these, Venerable Brethren, We, as a presage of the divine liberality and as a pledge of our own charity, most lovingly bestow on each of you, and on the clergy and flock committed to the care of each, our Apostolic Benediction.

Given at Rome, at St. Peter's on the 28th day of May, being the Vigil of the Solemnity of Corpus Christi, in the year 1902, of Our Pontificate the five and twentieth.

Made in the USA
Coppell, TX
22 February 2021